The Economics of Leisure and Tourism

John Tribe

Butterworth-Heinemann
Linacre House, Jordan Hill, Oxford OX2 8DP
225 Wildwood Avenue, Woburn, MA 01801-2041
A division of Reed Educational and Professional Publishing Ltd

A member of the Reed Elsevier plc group

OXFORD   AUCKLAND   BOSTON
JOHANNESBURG   MELBOURNE   NEW DELHI

First published 1995
Reprinted 1996, 1997, 1998, 1999

British Library Cataloguing in Publication Data
Tribe, John
   Economics of Leisure and Tourism
   I. Title
   338.4791

ISBN 0 7506 2342 X

Printed and bound in Great Britain by
Martins The Printers Ltd, Berwick upon Tweed

FOR EVERY TITLE THAT WE PUBLISH, BUTTERWORTH-HEINEMANN
WILL PAY FOR BTCV TO PLANT AND CARE FOR A TREE.

The Economics of Leisure and Tourism

Contents

Preface

There is no theory for theory's sake in this book.

Rather a number of key economic themes in leisure and tourism are explored and theory is only used in so far as it illuminates these areas. The key themes are:

- How is the provision of leisure and tourism determined?
- Could it be provided in a different way?
- What are the key opportunities and threats facing leisure and tourism?
- What are the economic impacts of leisure and tourism?
- What are the environmental impacts of leisure and tourism?
- How can economics be used to manage leisure and tourism?

Thus, in contrast to general economics introductory texts, the marginal productivity theory of labour theory is excluded, but pricing of externalities is included on the grounds that the latter is more useful to students of travel and tourism than the former.

The other key features of this text are:

- visual mapping of the content of each chapter
- liberal use of press cuttings to illustrate points
- chapter objectives
- key points summarized
- data response questions
- short answer questions
- integrated case studies

Above all it is hoped that this text will create a lasting interest in the economics of leisure and tourism and generate a spirit of critical enquiry into leisure and tourism issues affecting consumers, producers and hosts.

Finally, students are encouraged to keep this textbook current. Space has been left in key tables for the insertion of recent data, but care needs to be taken to keep to the original sources. Students should also attempt to update case material where possible.

John Tribe

Acknowledgements

The author extends thanks to those organizations which have given permission to reproduce text and data. Articles from *The Independent, Guardian* and *Observer* newspapers as well as the *Travel Trade Gazette* have helped to illustrate many points, as have guidelines from the World Travel and Tourism Environment Research Centre. Statistics have also generously been provided by the British Tourist Authority, Leisure Consultants, Elsevier Publications, the Department of Employment and the World Travel and Tourism Review.

Crown copyright is reproduced with the permission of the Controller of Her Majesty's Stationery Office.

1

Introduction

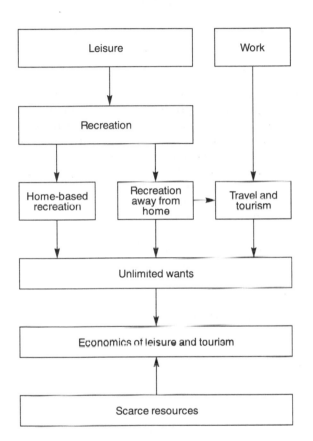

Objectives

- Why is Disneyland Paris called EuroDismal?
- Is passenger forecasting a load of old crystal balls?
- What is the connection between the *Financial Times*, Alton Towers and Thames Television?
- Will the sun, sea and sand of Magaluf degenerate into vomit, violence and vandalism?

This book will help you investigate these issues. The objectives of this chapter are to define and integrate the areas of study of this book. First the scope of leisure and tourism will be discussed, and second the scope and techniques of economics will be outlined. The final part of the chapter explains how the study area of leisure and tourism can be analysed using economic techniques.

By studying this chapter students will be able to:

- understand the scope of leisure and tourism and their interrelationship
- explain the basic economic concerns of scarcity, choice and opportunity costs
- outline the allocation of resources in different economic systems
- explain the methodology of economics
- understand the use of models in economics
- understand the use of economics to analyse issues in leisure and tourism
- access sources of information

Definition and scope of leisure and tourism

Defining leisure and tourism is like defining an orange. We all know an orange when we see one and we can generally distinguish it from a banana without too much difficulty. We could try a definition. 'An orange is a round citrus fruit, of orange colour and with orange taste'. But you can be sure that once a definition has been made, problems arise. Does a definition of an orange using the term 'orange' add to our understanding? If the object I am looking at seems to be an orange but is oval-shaped, is it an orange? Is a satsuma an orange? Questions such as these inevitably arise and are important, particularly where data collection or interpretation is concerned. For example, the number of oranges imported into the UK is a different number according to whether related fruit such as satsumas and clementines are included in the definition. Similar problems occur in using and measuring the term 'unemployment'. In 1994, UK unemployment was around 2.6 million. But are people on training schemes unemployed? Are those fraudulently claiming unemployment benefit unemployed? According to the definition used, unemployment can in fact range from around 1.5 million to around 4 million.

What then is leisure and tourism? A common element in many definitions of leisure is that of free time. Thus working, sleeping and household chores are excluded. However, should we then include people who are sick or recovering from illness? If the definition is extended to include doing things that one wants to do, this problem is avoided, but another arises. What about the parts of people's jobs that they enjoy, or things done to support their employment in their spare time? For example, is a computer programmer's use of computers in non-working time a leisure activity?

Similar questions arise in defining tourism. The common element in definitions of tourism is that of 'temporary visiting'. Questions of scope immediately arise. Are people who are engaged in study overseas tourists? Are people travelling on business tourists?

Aware of the problems involved, some working definitions of travel and tourism are now attempted.

Working definitions

- Leisure = discretionary time

  Discretionary time is the time remaining after working, commuting, sleeping and doing necessary household and personal chores which can be used in a chosen way.

- Recreation = pursuits undertaken in leisure time

Recreational pursuits include home-based activities such as reading and watching television, and those outside the home including sports, theatre, cinema and tourism.

- Tourism = visiting for at least one night for leisure and holiday, business and professional or other tourism purposes.

  Visiting means a temporary movement to destinations outside the normal home and workplace.

- Leisure and tourism sector organizations = organizations producing goods and services for use in leisure time, organizations seeking to influence the use of leisure time and organizations supplying leisure and tourism organizations. Many organizations produce goods and services for leisure and non-leisure use, for example computer manufacturers.

Figure 1.1 shows the relationship between leisure and tourism and the constituent parts are discussed below.

Home-based leisure

This includes:

- listening to music
- watching TV and videos
- listening to the radio
- reading
- DIY
- gardening
- playing games
- exercise
- hobbies

Recreation away from home

This includes:

- sports participation
- watching entertainment

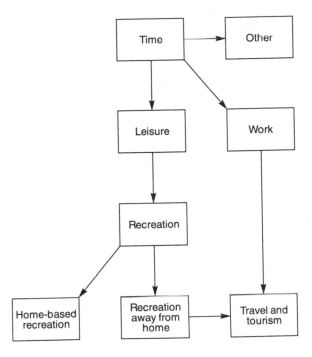

Figure 1.1 Leisure and tourism.

- hobbies
- visiting attractions
- eating and drinking
- betting and gaming

Travel and tourism

This includes:

- travelling to destination
- accommodation at destination
- recreation

Definition, scope and methodology of economics

The nature of economics

Resources and wants

Economics arises from a basic imbalance that is evident throughout the world. On the one side there are resources which can be used to make goods and services. These are classified by economists into land (raw materials), labour and capital (machines). On the other side we have people's wants. The worldwide economic fact of life is that people's wants appear unlimited and exceed the resources available to satisfy these wants. This is true not just for people with low incomes, but for people with high incomes too. Clearly the basic needs of rich people are generally satisfied in terms of food, clothing and shelter, but it is evident that their material wants in terms of cars, property, holidays and recreation are rarely fully satisfied.

Scarcity and choice

The existence of limited resources and unlimited wants gives rise to the basic economic problem of scarcity. The existence of scarcity means that choices have to be made about resource use and allocation. Economics is concerned with the choice questions that arise from scarcity:

- What to produce?
- How to produce it?
- To whom will goods and services be allocated?

Opportunity cost

Since resources can be used in different ways to make different goods and services, and since they are limited in relation to wants, the concept of opportunity cost arises. This can be viewed at different levels.

At the individual level, consumers have limited income. So if they spend their income on a mountain bike, they can consider what else they could have bought with the money, such as 50 CDs. Individuals also have limited time. If an individual decides to work extra overtime, leisure time must be given up.

At a local or national government level the same choices can be analysed. Local councils have limited budgets. If they decide to build a leisure centre, that money could have been used to provide more home help to the elderly. Even if they

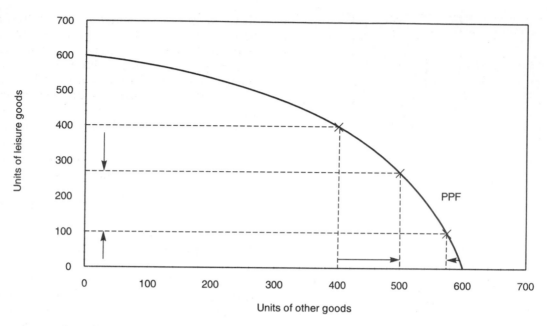

Figure 1.2 Opportunity cost and the production possibility frontier (PPF).

raised local taxes to build the new leisure centre there would be an opportunity cost, since the taxpayers would have to give up something in order to pay the extra taxes. At a national government level, subsidizing the arts means less money available for student grants.

Opportunity cost can be defined as the alternatives or other opportunities that have to be foregone to achieve a particular thing. Figure 1.2 illustrates this concept by use of a production possibility frontier (PPF). It is assumed first that the economy only produces two types of goods (leisure goods, and other goods) and second, that it uses all its resources fully.

Curve PPF plots all the possible combinations of leisure goods and other goods that can be produced in this economy. It is drawn concave to the origin (bowed outwards) since, as more and more resources are concentrated on the production of one commodity, the resources available become less suitable for producing that commodity.

Curve PPF shows that if all resources were geared towards the production of leisure goods, 600 units could be produced with no production of other goods. At the other extreme, 600 units of other goods could be produced with no units of leisure goods. The PPF describes the opportunity cost of increasing production of either of these goods. For example, increasing production of leisure goods from 0 to 100 can only be done by diverting resources from the production of other goods, and production of these falls from 600 to 580 units. Thus the opportunity cost at this point of 100 units of leisure goods is the 20 units of other goods that must be foregone. Similarly, if all resources are being used to produce a combination of 400 units of leisure goods and 400 units of other goods, the opportunity cost of producing an extra 100 units of other goods would be 130 units of leisure goods.

Allocative mechanisms

The existence of scarcity of resources and unlimited wants means that any economy must have a system for determining what, how and for whom goods are produced. The main systems for achieving this are:

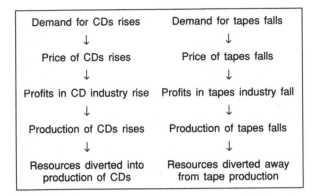

Demand for CDs rises	Demand for tapes falls
↓	↓
Price of CDs rises	Price of tapes falls
↓	↓
Profits in CD industry rise	Profits in tapes industry fall
↓	↓
Production of CDs rises	Production of tapes falls
↓	↓
Resources diverted into production of CDs	Resources diverted away from tape production

Figure 1.3 The price mechanism in action.

- free market economies
- centrally planned economies
- mixed economies

Free market economies work by allowing private ownership of firms. The owners of such firms produce goods and services by purchasing resources. The motive for production is profit and thus firms will tend to produce those goods and services which are in demand. Figure 1.3 shows the market mechanism in action.

Centrally planned economies do not allow the private ownership of firms which instead are state-owned. Production decisions are taken by state planning committees and resources are mobilized accordingly. Consumers generally have some choice of what to buy, but only from the range determined by state planners.

Mixed economies incorporate elements from each system. Private ownership of firms tends to predominate, but production and consumption of goods and services may be influenced by public ownership of some enterprises and by the use of taxes and government spending.

The allocative mechanism has important implications for leisure and tourism. The collapse of communism in the eastern bloc has meant that many economies are now in transition from centrally planned to market systems. Tourism facilities, such as hotels and restaurants, in these countries are having to revolutionize their organizational culture and become more customer-oriented. The economies of Cuba and China are

still nominally centrally planned, but free enterprise is currently flourishing under the economic reforms in China, and a visit to the Great Wall is repaid by privately owned souvenir shops jostling for custom. Exhibit 1.1 illustrates the loosening of central planning restrictions in Cuba.

Exhibit 1.1 Cuba allows limited private enterprise

Cuba took another cautious step towards establishing a mixed economy yesterday when its communist government authorized limited private enterprise in a wide range of trades, crafts and services. The move, announced in a decree signed by President Fidel Castro, lifted a long-standing state monopoly of production, employment and sales. Ordinary Cubans welcomed the decision and predicted the return to city streets of the private vendors who disappeared in the late 1960s when state control was extended to all sectors of the economy.

Taxi drivers, mechanics, plumbers, carpenters, painters, hair dressers, cobblers, cooks, domestics, craftsmen, farm products salesmen and computer programmers are among those who will now be able to run their own businesses.

Cuban finance officials recently visited China and Vietnam. It is said that the latest move may have been influenced by examples of private enterprise alongside a state economy in the two countries.

Source: *Guardian*, 10 September 1993 (adapted).

Equally, the mix of the British mixed economy is of direct importance to leisure and tourism provision. The 'Thatcher revolution', which involved 'rolling back the frontiers of the state', involved privatization of British Airways (BA) and the British Airports Authority (BAA), and also limited the spending powers of local government, thus reducing public provision in arts and leisure. Exhibit 1.2 illustrates the extension of this policy to the privatization of Britain's forests and considers views for and against this process.

Exhibit 1.2 Selling off the family tree

Although the government insists there are no plans 'at present' to privatize the Forestry Commission, with assets of £1.6bn and 6300 employees, forestry unions are in no doubt that their organization has been subjected to 'creeping privatization' since 1981 when the government ordered the commission to begin a programme of 'asset sales'. By July 1992, it had sold 410 000 acres of plantations and prime forests and passed almost £170m to the Treasury. Now with land prices depressed, it has been given a firm target: sell a further 247 000 acres by the end of this decade and aim to raise a further £150m. And that could be just the start.

The commission was established in 1919 to provide a strategic timber reserve after 'the desperate timber shortages of the first world war'. The Countryside Acts of 1967 and 1968 formally recognized the importance of state forests for public recreation. The commission was then given new powers to provide campsites, picnic places and visitor centres. The Ramblers' Association is so concerned by the privatization threat to the commission's 'freedom to roam' policy that its main event this summer will be devoted to preserving access to the forests. Dave Beskine, the association's assistant director, say: 'While the commission has been a model landowner, private landlords often seem hostile to access'.

The radical right has long regarded the commission as a corporate anachronism at odds with the market economy. When the Adam Smith Institute launched a report, *Pining for Profit*, in the late 1980s, it undoubtedly struck a chord in government circles by calculating that the agency had been a drain on the Exchequer for more than 70 years, to the tune of £1bn at today's prices.

Source: *Guardian*, 16 March 1993 (adapted).

The debate surrounding the mix of private versus public provision tends to centre on several key issues. Advocates of the free market argue that the system allows maximum consumer choice or sovereignty. They point to the efficiency of the system as firms compete to cut costs and improve products, the fact that the system does not need wastefully to employ officials to plan and monitor production, and lower taxes under free market systems. Their evidence is the one-way flow of human traffic observed across the Florida Straits from Cuba and past the former Iron Curtain from Eastern Europe in search of the free market.

Critics of the free market argue that choice is

an illusion. Thus, although by day the shops in Oxford Street are full of every conceivable product, by night their doorways are full of homeless people. Only those with purchasing power can exercise choice and purchasing power is unequally distributed in free market economies.

Macroeconomics and microeconomics

Economics is often subdivided into the separate areas of microeconomics and macroeconomics. Microeconomics studies individual consumer and household behaviour as well as the behaviour of firms. It analyses how these interact in particular markets to produce an equilibrium price and quantity sold. Thus microeconomics looks at the price of air travel, the output of running shoes and the choice between leisure and work.

Macroeconomics looks at the economy as a whole. The national economy is composed of all the individual market activities added together. Thus macroeconomics looks at aggregates such as national product and inflation.

Marginal analysis

The concept of 'the margin' is central to much economic analysis. Consumer, producer and social welfare theories are based on the idea that an equilibrium position can be achieved which represents the best possible solution. This position can theoretically be found by comparing the marginal benefit (MB) of doing something with the marginal cost (MC). For example, MC to a firm is the cost of producing one extra unit. MB is the revenue gained from selling one extra unit. Clearly a firm can increase its profit by producing more if MB > MC. It should not expand such that MC > MB, and thus profits are maximized, and the firm is in equilibrium, because it cannot better its position, where MC = MB.

The methodology of economics

Economics is a social science. As such it draws some of its methodology or way of working from other sciences such as physics or chemistry, but also has important differences.

The 'science' of social science

The science part of economics is that it is a discipline that attempts to develop a body of principles. Economic principles attempt to explain the behaviour of households and firms in the economy. It therefore shares some common methods with other sciences.

The first of these is the need to distinguish between positive and normative statements. Positive statements are those which can be tested by an appeal to the facts. They are statements of what is or what will be. 'Swimming cuts cholesterol' is a positive statement. It can be tested, and accepted or refuted. Normative statements are those which are statements of opinion, and therefore cannot be tested by an appeal to the facts. 'There should be a swimming pool in every town' is a normative statement.

Second, economics uses scientific method. The scientific method acts as a filter which determines which theories become part of the established body of principles of economics, and whether existing theories should maintain their place. Figure 1.4 illustrates the scientific testing of theories.

New and existing theories are subject to testing and are accepted, rejected, amended or superseded according to the results of testing. Thus the body of economic principles is, like that of other sciences, organic in the sense that knowledge is being extended and some theories are shown to be no longer valid.

This can be illustrated by considering the shape of the earth. Hundreds of years ago, people were in agreement that the earth was flat. This theory was confirmed by scholars who reasoned that if it was not flat people would fall off it. It was further reasoned that the stars were attached to a canopy above the earth and this fitted observations nicely. This then was the accepted set of principles until the theory no longer tested true. It was developments in geometry and astronomy that first led to serious questioning of the accepted principles and circumnavigation of the earth endorsed such findings. Modern space programmes continue to confirm our current belief in a round earth by providing supporting photographic evidence.

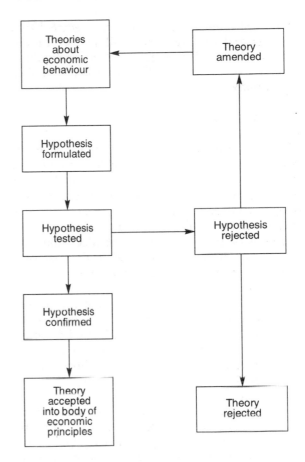

Figure 1.4 Scientific testing of theories.

Academic journals in economics, leisure and tourism provide the arena for testing old and new hypotheses in this field.

The 'social' of social science

The difference between social sciences such as economics, sociology and psychology and natural sciences such as physics and chemistry is that the former study people rather than inanimate objects. This means first that their investigative methods are often different. It is difficult to perform laboratory experiments in economics and often data must be collected from historical records or from surveys. Second it means that economic 'laws' are different from physics laws.

If interest rates increase it can be predicted that the demand for credit will fall but we cannot predict that will be true for every individual. The law of gravity, on the other hand, applies universally.

Economic models

Economic models are built to describe relationships between economic variables and predict the effects of changing these variables. They can be compared to models used elsewhere. For example, civil engineers build models of bridges and subject them to stress in a wind tunnel. The purpose of the model is to predict what will happen in the real world, and in the case of a bridge ensure that the design is safe in extreme conditions.

Models are generally simplified abstractions of the real world. They have two key components. First assumptions are made which build the foundations for the model. For example, the model of firms' behaviour under perfect competition assumes that firms maximize profits, that there are many buyers and sellers, and that the products bought and sold are identical. Second implications or outcomes are predicted by the working of the model. For example, theory predicts that firms operating under conditions of perfect competition will not be able to earn abnormally high profits in the long run. As the channel crossing becomes a more competitive environment, with the opening of the tunnel, the predictions of competition theory can be tested empirically, or in other words by making observations.

The term *ceteris paribus* is often used in economic analysis, meaning all other things remaining unchanged. This is important because in the real world several factors often occur at the same time, some exaggerating a particular effect, and some countering it. So for example it can be said that for most goods an increase in price will lead to a fall in demand *ceteris paribus*. Thus a rise in cinema ticket prices should cause a fall in demand. Clearly if other things are allowed to change this might not happen. For example, if incomes rose significantly this might more than offset the increase in price and we might observe demand for cinema tickets rising whilst prices rise.

The economics of leisure and tourism

The rest of this book uses economic analysis to explore issues in leisure and tourism, approaching the area in the following way:

Part One: Organizations and markets in leisure and tourism

This section analyses the demand for leisure and tourism goods and services and their supply in an attempt to understand the factors that influence which goods and services are supplied and what prices are charged for them.

Chapter 2: Leisure and tourism organizations

- What is the mission of British Airports Authority?
- How was finance raised for the Channel tunnel?
- What was the BSkyB floatation?
- How does the Department of National Heritage influence the leisure and tourism sector?

In order to analyse the supply of leisure and tourism goods and services, the motives, missions and structures of leisure and tourism organizations are scrutinized in this chapter.

Chapter 3: The market for leisure and tourism products

- What is the economic function of ticket touts?
- How do changes in the exchange rate affect the demand for foreign holidays?
- How are squash courts allocated at peak times?

In market economies the 'invisible hand' of the price mechanism performs an essential function.

It signals consumer demands to producers. Producers wishing to maximize their profits will allocate resources into markets where demand and prices are rising and away from markets where demand and prices are falling.

Chapter 4: Choice, elasticity and demand forecasting

- If wages increase, do people demand less leisure time?
- How do consumers choose between Eurostar and BA?
- How can we predict the demand for golf balls for the next 5 years?

This chapter examines how consumers behave in markets to maximize their personal satisfaction, and also considers techniques for forecasting demand.

Chapter 5: Supply and costs

- Why do ski holidays cost more during school holiday periods?
- What are the fixed costs of football?
- Why do students get cheap seats in West End theatres but have to pay full price for ice creams?
- Why do Thomson brochures get best rack space in Lunn Poly?

This chapter investigates production, the use of inputs and the behaviour of firms' costs. It also analyses the motives of mergers and take-overs.

Chapter 6: Price and market strategy in the real world

- How can the person sitting next to you on a flight to New York have paid twice your ticket price?
- Can you haggle at the Hilton?
- The newspaper price war: who wins?

This chapter looks at the classic strategies for increasing profits and market share.

Chapter 7: Market intervention

- Are CD prices a rip-off?
- Should we privatize the BBC?
- Why do we subsidize opera but not rock?

This chapter investigates the problems of the unregulated free market and considers the arguments for intervention.

Part Two: Leisure and tourism organizations and the external environment

Things are changing fast. The operating environment within which organizations work is often characterized by the four Ds:

- difficult
- dangerous
- dynamic
- diverse

The aim of this section is to enable organizations to scan their environments and plan their futures, by using opportunities and threats analysis. Chapters 8–11 investigate different parts of the operating environment and the latter part of Chapter 11 summarizes the issues.

Chapter 8: The competitive environment

- What prompted BA's dirty tricks against Virgin?
- Who will win the battle of the Channel crossing?
- Will the national lottery drain the pools?

Current or potential threats from competitors or new products need to be monitored. This chapter provides a framework for auditing the competitive environment.

Chapter 9: The economic environment

- When will the next recession start?
- Are interest rates going up or down?
- What levels of consumer spending are likely next year?

Chapter 9 analyses how leisure and tourism organizations are affected by changes in the national economy and investigates the trends in key macroeconomic variables.

Chapter 10: The political and sociocultural environment

- What is the green revolution?
- How will the grey revolution affect leisure demand?
- Politics: which party will be celebrating the new year in 2000?

This chapter investigates the political and sociocultural aspects of the organization's operating environment.

Chapter 11: The technological environment and opportunities and threats analysis

- Will leisure disappear into cyberspace?
- Are video cassettes yesterday's technology?
- PC power: opportunity or threat?

Opportunities and threats analysis is often used in marketing and strategic planning. The key issues from the competitive and political, economic, sociocultural and technological (PEST) environments are highlighted as opportunities and threats to enable organizations to plan effective strategies to exploit opportunities and counter threats.

Part Three: Investing in leisure and tourism

This section analyses the trends in and factors affecting investment in the leisure and tourism sector, looking separately at the private sector and the public sector.

Chapter 12: Investment appraisal in the private sector

- Is there a future for a son of Concorde?
- Why did the Disneyland Paris investment forecasters get their sums wrong?

- How accurate have Eurotunnel cash flow projections been?

Profit is the main motive for private sector investment in leisure and tourism capital. This chapter investigates the factors which determine the profitability of investments and considers techniques for appraising investment projects.

Chapter 13: Investment and the public sector

- Why does leisure provision differ so widely between local authorities?
- Can government investment in leisure contribute to urban regeneration?
- Should the BBC have different investment criteria to commercial broadcasters?

This chapter considers how decision-making for investment projects in the public sector differs from practice in the private sector.

Part Four: Leisure and tourism impacts on the national economy

Whilst Chapter 9 investigated the impact of the economy on leisure and tourism organizations, this section looks at this from the other direction and analyses the impacts of the leisure and tourism sector on the economy.

Chapter 14: Leisure and tourism; income, employment and inflation

- Which industry is the world's biggest employer?
- What is the cheapest holiday destination?
- Why are wages in the hospitality sector so low?
- How much of £100 tourist spending in the Hotel Beijing Toronto stays in China?

This chapter attempts to measure the contribution of the leisure and tourism sector to national economies. In 1990, for example, travel and tourism was estimated to employ 118 million people wordwide. Inflation and price indices are also examined in this chapter, with particular emphasis on comparing prices in tourism destinations.

Chapter 15: Leisure and tourism and economic growth

- Can tourism save Castro's Cuba?
- How has China cornered the toy market?
- Why do Japanese play golf overseas, but some locals think this to be a handicap?
- Can the UK's industrial heritage make up for its lost industry?

This chapter reviews the contribution that the leisure and tourism sector can make to the economic growth of national economies. It particularly looks at the potential the sector can contribute to growth strategies in developing countries.

Part Five: International aspects of leisure and tourism

This section considers the impact of leisure and tourism on foreign currency earnings, analyses the effects of exchange rates on leisure and tourism organizations and charts the growth of multinationals.

Chapter 16: Leisure and tourism; the balance of payments and exchange rates

- What can be done to turn around the UK's growing tourism deficit?
- How does Disneyland Paris contribute to the French balance of payments?
- Why is the low pound good for UK leisure but bad for UK tourists?

This chapter examines the contribution of the leisure and tourism sector to countries' balance of payments, and considers how the sector is affected by changes in the exchange rate.

Chapter 17: Multinational organizations

- Why is BA going global?
- Why are British-owned ferries registered in the Bahamas?
- Why are Dunlop tennis balls made in the Philippines?
- Why have the Chinese threatened to ban satellite TV?

This chapter investigates the growth of the multinational enterprise and considers benefits and costs to parent and host economies.

Part Six: Leisure and tourism and environmental issues

This part is divided into two chapters. The first critically evaluates the contribution of leisure and tourism to human well-being. The second chapter suggests how economic analysis can be used to modify leisure and tourism developments to minimize the costs and maximize the benefits to society.

Chapter 18: Environmental impacts of leisure and tourism

- How does aircraft noise add to our gross national product (GNP)?
- Why do we pump raw sewage into the sea?
- How can successful tourism development self-destruct?
- Why has war been declared on mountain bikes?

This chapter looks beyond conventional economic analysis and casts a critical environmental economist's eye over the benefits that are claimed for development of leisure and tourism industries.

Chapter 19: Sustainability and 'green' leisure and tourism

- What are Surfers against Sewage trying to achieve?

- What are the costs and benefits of Terminal 5 construction at London Airport, Heathrow?
- How are Forte's hotels going green, and reducing costs?
- How can we encourage green recreation and green tourism?

This chapter examines the meaning of green leisure and tourism, and considers how economics can help deliver a sustainable future for these industries.

Part Seven: Integrated case studies

Chapter 20: Integrated case studies

- Can Raleigh stay at the top of the mountain bike league?
- What are the economics of booze?
- How can India compete in international tourism?
- What opportunities and threats face the hotel industry?

Real world issues are complex. They are not neatly divided into sections on costs, sections on competition and sections on exchange rates. This chapter contains integrated case studies which provide problems requiring analysis using tools developed throughout the book.

Sources of data

Sources of data for the economics of leisure and tourism can be found in newspapers, journals, magazines, reports and statistical publications as well as company annual reports. Table 1.1 lists the main sources.

Review of key terms

- Leisure = discretionary time.
- Recreation = pursuits undertaken in leisure time.
- Tourism = visiting for at least one night for leisure and holiday, business and professional or other tourism purposes.
- Economic problem = scarcity and choice.
- Leisure and tourism sector organizations = organizations producing goods and services for use in leisure time, and organizations seeking to influence the use of leisure time.
- Opportunity cost = the alternatives or other opportunities that have to be foregone to achieve a particular thing.
- Free market economy = resources allocated through price system.
- Centrally planned economy = resources allocated by planning officials.
- Mixed economy = resources allocated through free market and planning authorities.
- Microeconomics = study of household and firm's behaviour.
- Macroeconomics = study of whole economy.
- Marginal analysis = study of effects of one extra unit.
- Positive statement = based on fact.
- Normative statement = based on opinion.
- *Ceteris paribus* = other things remaining unchanged.

Data questions

Task 1.1   Obituary notice for old-style economics

Economists are increasingly discontented with economics. They are embarrassed by its forecasting failures. They are uncomfortable that its theories seem less and less able to describe the real world. They regret that quite modest mathematical prowess has become more important than original economic thinking. Things, they know, need to change.

The discontent is spreading. The Organization for Economic Cooperation and Development (OECD), reviewing the results of 5 years of economic forecasts from leading governments and multinational institutions, including itself, concluded that as reliable a benchmark would be simply to assume that next year will be the

Table 1.1 *Leisure and tourism sources*

Publication	Publisher	Publication	Publisher
Journals		**Magazines/reviews**	
Annals of Tourism Research	Elsevier Science (UK/USA)	*Barclays Economic Review*	Barclays Bank
		Leisure Management	Dicestar Ltd. (UK)
International Journal of Hospitality Management	Elsevier Science (UK/USA)	*Tourism Management*	Elsevier Science (UK)
Museums Journal	Museums Association (UK)	*Tourism Marketplace*	AMS Publishing (UK)
		Travel GB	
Journal of Sustainable Tourism	Channel View Books (UK)	*Travel Trade Gazette*	
		Travel Weekly	
Journal of Leisure Research	National Recreation and Parks Association (USA)	**Statistical sources**	
		Annual Abstract of Statistics	Central Statistical Office (UK)
Journal of Travel Research	Travel and Tourism Research Organization (USA)	*Compendium of Tourist Statistics*	World Tourism Organization (Spain)
Tourism Economics	Print Publishing Ltd.	*Digest of Tourist Statistics*	British Tourist Authority (UK)
Reports		*Economic Trends*	Central Statistical Office (UK)
International Tourism Reports	Economist Publications (UK)	*Employment Gazette*	Central Statistical Office (UK)
Leisure Forecasts	Leisure Consultants (UK)	*Social Trends*	Central Statistical Office (UK)
Leisure Futures	Henley Centre for Forecasting (UK)	*General Household Survey*	Central Statistical Office (UK)
Retail Business	Economist Publications (UK)	*Family Expenditure Survey*	Central Statistical Office (UK)
Travel and Tourism Analyst	Economist Publications (UK)	*Tourism Intelligence Quarterly*	British Tourist Authority/English Tourist Board

same as this – and ignore the forecasts. It is difficult to find a reflective economist who is happy with matters as they are. Professor Paul Ormerod has gone one step further. In *The Death of Economics*, published by Faber, he brings together the simmering discontents of economists over the past quarter of a century, and launches a comprehensive attack. Economics' core axioms do not and cannot correspond to any known reality, he says; economists know this but none the less close their eyes because of the intellectual elegance of their theories if they did work.

Paul Ormerod's prime target is the intellectual tools that economics have developed in order to permit mathematical rigour. To make the laws of supply and demand produce predictable outcomes, economists suppose a point of stable balance where the marginal gain from some branch of activity is exactly cancelled out by an equivalent marginal loss.

Prof. Ormerod lays into marginalism with relish. His charge is that it supposes a trajectory of costs and rewards that does not exist in the real world as extensively as economists need to make their theories work. The first problem has been known to economists since the advent of mass production: that the marginal costs of increasing output can fall continually so that there is no limit to firms' expansion. In other words, there need not be a point where, necessarily, marginal costs exceed any marginal gain. Prof. Ormerod cites Alfred Chandler's *magnum opus*, *The Scale and Scope of Industrial Capitalism*, which demonstrated how that once large companies had achieved a lead over their competitors they generally retained it – and costs continually fell. Quaker Oats, Campbell Soup, Heinz, Procter and Gamble, Eastman Kodak, Union Carbide and a host of other companies defied the laws of economics by making huge investments in product-specific marketing, distribution and purchasing networks, and establishing unassailable positions which allowed their costs to carry on falling.

Nor need gains fall at the margin, either. A third car, for example, will add little to the mobility of most families, or a fourth television set to their viewing habits. Yet, what drives such consumption is not a careful calculus of the marginal usefulness of additional purchases, but, as Thorstein Veblen argued in *The Theory of the Leisure Class*, by more human impulses – the more one has, the more one wants, and the greater the satisfaction obtained from getting it.

A world of conspicuous consumption and increasing returns to companies has no fine points of balance at all. But this is only the beginning. Can economic agents be rational in the sense that economists need them to be?

Source: *Guardian*, 21 March 1994 (adapted).

Questions

1 If '[economic] theories seem less and less able to describe the real world', what does this mean for economic models and scientific method in economics?
2 Why do economists study marginal behaviour? How have traditional assumptions about marginal behaviour been challenged?
3 Explain the relevance of Thorstein Veblen's *The Theory of the Leisure Class* to the economic problem of scarcity and choice.
4 What is meant by rational behaviour and why is it necessary for economics?

Task 1.2   *Tsar crossed city*

Seven o'clock on a brisk winter's evening on Nevsky Prospekt. The pavements near Gostiny Dvor station are crowded with last-minute shoppers. Hawkers line up to ply their wares at the entrance to Estée Lauder. It is hard to believe this is St Petersburg.

I first came to the city 10 years ago. Then it was called Leningrad. The year was 1984. I was there for the New Year: just after midnight on 1 January, I stood in a room at the top of the grim old Leningrad Hotel. Today, a decade on, the view from the hotel is just as breathtaking, but politically things could not be more different. With the fall of communism 3 years ago, St Petersburg has rushed to espouse capitalism.

St Petersburg has always been a beautiful city caught in the shadow of its history, a tantalizing prospect locked out of sight. Visitors' St Petersburg, the extraordinary baroque waterside complex of canals, bridges, palaces and cathedrals, has survived remarkably well. Not for nothing has it been compared to Venice.

And its real interest today is not in its past, but in how it is coming to terms with the new post-communist order. It is a mixed bag. Where once Russians queued for oranges, the shops are full of goods they can scarcely afford. Western chain stores and fashion houses have moved in – but so have the Russian mafia.

Where to eat? You will be surprised by the quality and range of restaurants. Forget the old tales of indigestible food, surly service and bortsch with everything. You can now dine out in style and find Russian, Ukrainian or Georgian, not to mention French, Indian, Chinese, even Korean and Vietnamese cuisine. Most are 'dollar' restaurants aimed at tourists and businessmen, charging anything from $20 to $50 a head. There are still plenty of grim Soviet-style cafés and restaurants, where the food is from the Brezhnev era and the service is according to a 5-year plan. Best avoided – like the German beer kellers, Italian pizza joints and English pubs.

Getting about? All the main attractions in the city centre are within walking distance of Nevsky Prospekt metro. The metro (underground) is fast, efficient, incredibly cheap, and reaches most other parts of the city you will want to visit. Buy a brass metro token at the kiosk in the booking hall (25 roubles – less than 2p). Write down in Cyrillic the name of the station you are heading for, and count the number of stops along the way because the name may not be very obvious when you get off.

Shopping? Most shops sell at fixed prices, unlike restaurants, hotels and taxis, which are more expensive for foreigners. Although prices are reaching western levels, there are still some bargains, especially for souvenirs, books, records and clothes. You may have to queue three times – once to order the goods, again to pay, and then to pick up your purchase. The old-fashioned abacus is only gradually being replaced by the cash register and supermarket check-out.

Currency exchange? Every other shop on Nevsky Prospekt seems to be a currency exchange. Take dollar bills and traveller's cheques. Don't change money on the street. Russian money changers are past masters at fleecing tourists – you may find you have just exchanged your dollars for a wad of toilet paper.

Where to stay? Russian hotels vary from the frankly dismal to the splendidly luxurious. Travel agents do not advise staying in the cheapest hotels, which are often gangster-infested and liable to robbery. Russia is not yet a country for backpackers on a budget. Top-range hotels include the Grand Hotel Europe, Mikhailovskaya Ulitsa 1–7 (312 0072). Top-class hotel, reputedly Russia's finest, with décor, comfort and standards to rival the west – and prices to match. Double room from $325 a night. Budget hotels include the Mir, Gastello Ulitsa 17 (108 5166). Dire and decrepit, but one of the only rouble hotels without a serious mafia problem. Not recommended. Around $20.

Source: *Observer*, 16 January 1994 (adapted).

Questions

1 Why does the writer of this article find: 'It is hard to believe this is St Petersburg'?
2 Contrast the system of resource allocation in Russia under the communist and free market eras.
3 Comment on the impact of the fall of communism for tourism in St Petersburg.
4 Comment on the fall of communism for the inhabitants of St Petersburg.

Task 1.3

Question

Table 1.2 lists organizations that operate in the leisure and tourism sector. Classify these organizations according to the industry structure illustrated in Figure 1.5, adding to or amending the structure where necessary.

Table 1.2   *Leisure and tourism organizations*

Arts Councils	Carlton	Eurotunnel	Eurodollar
English Tourist Board	Eurocamp	Department for National Heritage	Alton Towers
British Tourist Authority	Chrysalis	Tate Gallery	British Rail
Lonrho	Forte	Sega	BSkyB
Ready Mixed Concrete	First Choice	Virgin	Camelot
Council for the Protection of Rural England	First Leisure	Lunn Poly	Center Parcs
	Reed Elsevier	Sony	Ladbrookes
Bass	Touche Rosse	Boeing	National Trust
Pearson	Airtours	P&O	Raleigh
British Airports Authority	Qantas	Air France	SNCF
Britannia	BTR plc	Henley Centre	Sports Council
BBC	Manchester Utd	Going Places	Thorpe Park
Capital Radio	Thomson	Disneyland Paris	Wembley
British Airways			

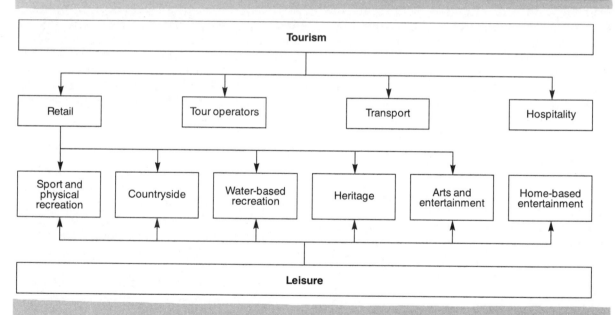

Figure 1.5   The leisure and tourism industry.

Short questions

1   What is the opportunity cost of watching television?

2   Explain in terms of marginal analysis at what point you will turn off the television.

3   Formulate a hypothesis that links the level of unemployment to the demand for video rentals. How would you test this hypothesis and what problems might you encounter?

4   Explain how the market mechanism responds to a change in consumer tastes or demand using an example from the leisure or tourism sector.

5   Distinguish between the kinds of problems which physics, biology, psychology and

economics might address in the area of sports. What similarities and differences in investigative methods are there between these disciplines?

Further reading

Beardshaw, J., *Economics*, Pitman, 1992.

Bull, A., *The Economics of Travel and Tourism*, Pitman, 1991.

Cooke, A., *The Economics of Leisure and Sport*, Routledge, 1994.

Eadington, W. and Redman, M., Economics and tourism, *Annals of Tourism Research* 1991; **18**, 41–56.

Gratton, C. and Taylor, P., *Economics of Leisure Services Management*, Longman/ILAM, 1992.

Medlik, S., *Dictionary of Travel, Tourism, and Hospitality*, Butterworth-Heinemann, 1993.

Parkin, M. and King, D., *Economics*, Addison Wesley, 1992.

Smith, S., *Tourism Analysis: A Handbook*, Longman, 1989.

Winnifrith, T. and Barret, C., *The Philosophy of Leisure*, Macmillan, 1989.

Part One

Organizations and Markets in Leisure and Tourism

2

Leisure and tourism organizations

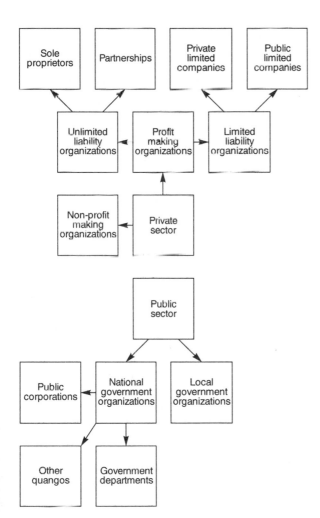

Objectives

In order to analyse and understand the behaviour of organizations in the leisure and tourism sector, we need to be able to clarify their aims and objectives. The National Trust for example will follow different policies to English Heritage which itself will have different policies to Alton Towers. The similarity between these three is that they all have historic houses open to the public. The key difference is in their forms of ownership – the first being a voluntary organization, the second a government-funded organization and the third a private sector organization.

By studying this chapter students should be able to:

- distinguish between private sector and public sector organizations
- understand the differences in finance, control, structure and objectives of organizations
- understand ways in which capital can be raised
- analyse movements in share prices
- analyse the effects of different organizational structures on organizational behaviour
- distinguish between operational management and strategic management

Public sector organizations

Public sector organizations are those owned by the government. This can be national government or local government.

Local government organizations

Leisure and tourism provision in the local government sector includes:

- leisure centres and swimming pools
- libraries
- arts centres
- parks and recreation facilities
- tourism support

It should be noted that some provision occurs in the commercial marketplace. For example, customers of arts centres and leisure centres have to pay for the services provided. On the other hand facilities such as parks and children's playgrounds are generally provided without charge.

Sources of finance

The finance of these organizations comes from:

- charges for services where applicable
- central government grants
- grants from other sources (e.g. the Arts Council of Great Britain)
- local government taxation (the council tax)
- local government borrowing

The ability of local government to provide the level of services it wishes has been severely curbed by government legislation in recent years. Local government no longer has the power to set its own level of spending but is regulated through a system of central government-determined expenditure targets, council tax capping and financial penalties for exceeding central government spending targets. Chapter 9 analyses factors influencing the level of government spending.

Ownership and control

In essence local government organizations are owned by the local population. Policy decisions or decisions of strategic management are taken on their behalf by the local council. Each local government area elects councillors or members to represent them. The political party which holds the majority of seats on the council will generally be able to dictate policy and such policy will be determined through a series of committees such as:

- libraries and arts
- recreation and leisure
- planning and resources

The planning and resources committee is a particularly powerful one as it determines the medium- to long-term strategy of the council and thus provides the financial framework within which the other committees must operate.

The day-to-day or operational management of local government-run services depends on the nature of the service being provided. The council officers are responsible for overall management and services which are spread out across a local government area, such as parks, will be run from the council offices. Larger services such as leisure centres will have their own management which in turn will be responsible to a service director at the council offices (see Chapter 7 for details of compulsory competitive tendering – CCT).

Aims and missions

The aims of local government and its organizations are largely determined by the political party or coalition of parties who hold the majority. This often means that leisure provision for example will vary between neighbouring local authorities which have different political parties in power. Administrations to the right of the political spectrum favour lower local taxes and market-driven provision. Those to the left favour public provision and subsidized prices.

To determine the differing aims of political parties we need to consult their manifestos as well as review their actual provision. However political parties do not operate in a vacuum. They will be influenced by:

- pressure groups
- trade unions

- local press
- national government

National government organizations

National government-owned organizations can be further subdivided into public corporations, other quangos and government departments.

Public corporations

There are few public corporations left after the privatization programme post 1979. Those privatized in the leisure and tourism sector included BA and BAA. The BBC remains in the public sector but it is increasingly being subjected to private sector objectives and management techniques.

Other quangos

There are a whole range of leisure and tourism organizations which are known as quangos – quasi autonomous non-governmental organizations. Their autonomy stems from the fact that they are not directly answerable to ministers or parliament. The 'non-governmental' description of them is only partially true as they are funded by government. They include organizations such as:

- the Sports Council
- the Arts Council of Great Britain
- the British Tourist Authority
- English Heritage
- the Forestry Commission
- the Countryside Commission

Government departments

There are a number of government departments which impinge on the leisure and tourism sector of the economy, including:

- the Department of National Heritage (DNH)
- the Department of Transport
- the Department of the Environment

Of these, the DNH is the most significant, having responsibility for:

- the British Tourist Authority
- the English, Welsh and Scottish Tourist Boards
- royal parks and palaces
- arts and libraries
- sport
- broadcasting and the press
- heritage sites

Exhibit 2.1 Preserving the past, shaping the future

The Department of National Heritage (DNH) has spent a small part of its £1bn-a-year budget on setting out its stall in its new publication *Preserving the Past, Shaping the Future*. In it, the DNH reveals its aims:

- to preserve the heritage of the past
- to help create the culture of today and add to the heritage for future generations
- to broaden opportunities for people to enjoy the benefits of their heritage and culture

The DNH, significantly, is headed by a minister of cabinet rank. (David Mellor was one-time holder of this post before his affair with an actress led to his sacking and the cruel *Sun* headline 'From toe job to no job'.) It brings together government responsibility for heritage, museums and galleries, libraries, arts, film, broadcasting, the press, sport, tourism and the national lottery. Thus its responsibilities include ensuring safety at sports grounds, broadcasting and press standards, subsidizing arts, and allocating national lottery proceeds. It performs these tasks by direct spending, legislation, through intermediaries such as regional arts boards and in conjunction with private sector providers.

But whilst the *Sun* was exercising its leader-writing skills on the sexual antics of the DNH minister, *The Times* (20.3.94) was conducting a more reflective debate. It cautioned against the recent obsession of value for money which has permeated almost every aspect of public spending. Instead it suggested that the priority ought to be money for values. In this it highlighted the danger of allocating DNH expenditure only where measurable economic effects such as urban regeneration or tourism revenue could be proven. It argued that arts expenditure needs to be informed by wider values.

Source: the author, from press cuttings, January 1995.

Exhibit 2.1 discusses the role of the Department of National Heritage.

Aims and missions

Before the 'Thatcher revolution' of the 1980s there was a much clearer difference between public corporations such as the BBC and private sector organizations. Public corporations tended to aim for public service and without the discipline of the profit motive were able to provide services that were loss-making. The rigours of efficiency and private sector management styles were rarely apparent. The old stereotypes are less true today. Public corporations have been subjected to efficiency targets, performance indicators, target rates of return on investment and citizen's charters, all of which have made them more closely mimic private sector organizations. The aims of public corporations are contained within their charters or constitutions. The BBC charter is due for renewal in 1996.

The aims of other quangos are specific to each organization. For example, the aim of the Countryside Commission is to promote the conservation and enhancement of landscape beauty and to encourage the provision and improvement in facilities in the countryside. The aim of the Sports Council is to promote the development of sport. In doing so it has developed a strategy which emphasizes participation and access. By its distribution of grants the Sports Council is able to encourage organizations which support its strategy. Both of these organizations support smaller, often voluntary organizations, and there is some tension between their government funding and their ability to support particular lobbies.

The aim of government departments is to carry out the policy of the government of the day and includes the planning, monitoring and reviewing of provision and legislation.

Sources of finance

National organizations in the public sector are financed in the main from:

- taxes
- trading income

There has been continuing pressure from the government for more contribution from sponsorship and trading activities. The dependence on tax funding makes public sector organizations subject not only to the whims of the government of the day but also to the state of the economy as a whole. Exhibit 2.2 records the cuts in funding faced by the English Tourist Board.

Exhibit 2.2 Staff fear more cuts as ETB funds diminish

Staff at the English Tourist Board (ETB) are awaiting the next round of job cuts.

The ETB has seen staff levels severed since the government announced drastic cuts in funding in 1992. Funding of £15.4m in 1992/93 is down to £13.9m in 1993/94 and will drop to £11.3m in 1994/95. In 1995/96 funding will be down to £10m – representing an investment of about 12p per domestic visitor.

Source: *Travel Trade Gazette*, 2 March 1994 (adapted).

Ownership and control

National government organizations are owned by the government on behalf of the population at large. However, each type of organization is controlled in a different way.

Public corporations are given some autonomy and have a legal identity separate from the government. An act of parliament outlines aims, organization and control for each industry. The basic structure is one where a board is established responsible for day-to-day running of the industry. The chair of the board and its other members are appointed by an appropriate government minister. Strategic decisions will be taken by the minister in consultation with the government.

Despite their non-governmental status, the government exerts considerable control over other quangos by its power of appointment. The Sports Council, for example, which meets four times a year has its chair, vice chair and members appointed by Under Secretary of State for National Heritage. Exhibit 2.3 reports on the frustrations articulated by the Arts Council over the bureaucracy created by government control.

Exhibit 2.3 Arts boss bound by bureaucracy

The Secretary General of the Arts Council has criticized the growing managerialist culture which the government is importing from industry as counterproductive.

He complained that a succession of ministers had insisted on structural changes, internal reviews and performance monitoring, so that he and other senior staff spent more time in meetings than in attending the arts events.

Source: the author, from news cuttings, February 1994.

Government departments are headed by a minister and staffed by civil servants. The degree of political control is thus more direct than for public corporations and other quangos.

Private sector organizations

Private sector organizations are those which are non-government-owned. They can be further subdivided into profit-making organizations and non-profit-making organizations.

Profit-making organizations

Profit-making private sector organizations consist of sole proprietors, partnerships, private limited companies and public limited companies. There is an important distinction between these types of company in terms of the liability of investors.

Limited and unlimited liability

Sole proprietors and unlimited liability partners both operate under conditions of unlimited liability. Unlimited liability means that the owners of such companies face no limit to their contribution should the organization become indebted. Most of their personal assets can be used to settle debts should the business cease trading. This includes not only the value of anything saleable from the business, but also housing, cars, furniture, stereos – the only exceptions being a person's 'tools of the trade' and a small amount of bedding and clothes. In contrast to this, limited liability places a limit to the contribution by an investor in an organization to the amount of capital that has been contributed. This applies to private and public limited companies as well as some partners who enjoy limited liability. Should one of these organizations cease trading with debts, an investor may well lose the original investment, but liability would cease there and personal assets would not be at risk.

Sole proprietors

Because of the discipline that unlimited liability brings, there are very few formalities required to start trading as a sole proprietor. The main requirement dictated by the Business Names Act 1985 is that the name and address of the owner must be displayed at the business premises and on business stationery.

The advantages of the sole proprietor include:

- independence
- motivation
- personal supervision
- flexibility

The problems of the sole proprietor include:

- unlimited liability
- long hours of work
- lack of capital for expansion
- difficulties in case of illness

Partnerships

The usual maximum number of partners is 20. A Deed of Partnership is generally drawn up to determine contribution of capital and sharing of profits. The Limited Partnership Act 1907 permits the admission of partners with limited liability as long as they do not take part in the management of the firm and as long as at least one partner retains unlimited liability.

The advantages of partnerships include:

- more capital available
- more expertise available
- flexibility
- motivation

The problems of partnerships include:

- unlimited liability
- disagreements

Private and public limited companies

The main difference between these is that public limited companies must have a minimum share capital and that shares in the private limited companies can only be transferred with the consent of other shareholders. Shares in public limited companies can be freely traded on the stock market. The similarities between the company forms are that they are bound by closer rules and regulations than are unlimited liability organizations. Recent examples of leisure and tourism sector organizations that have been floated on the stock market (i.e. changed from private to public limited companies) include:

- Eurodollar (car hire) 1994
- Servisair (aircraft handling) 1994
- BSkyB (satellite TV) 1994
- Telewest (cable TV) 1994
- Sunset Holidays (tour operator) 1994

Exhibit 2.4   Trade weighs taking the plunge

Airtours profits have rocketed from £2m in 1987 to £45m in 1993 – that could never have happened without Airtours floating on the stock market. Perhaps that explains why travel companies continue to make cash calls on the City either by going public or seek venture capital investment.

One person who believes more holiday companies should float has just done it himself – Inspirations managing director Vic Fatah. 'If you float on the stock exchange you give up less than if venture capitalists come in', said Mr Fatah. Companies could also consider raising private funds. 'The advantage of venture capitalists is that you can get people in at an earlier stage of your development.' Another advantage in taking the private route is that a company does not have to pay fees to advisors such as merchant bankers, brokers, lawyers and public relations firms.

Expense is one reason why former Eurocamp group sales and marketing director Julian Rawel advises caution before opting to float. Mr Rawel helped steer Eurocamp through its flotation in 1991.

The demands on a quoted company are always great, says Chris Parker, who has taken Unijet to the brink of floatation on two separate occasions: 'A quoted company always has to perform in the short term, which can be very difficult in a volatile industry'.

Source: *Travel Trade Gazette*, 9 March 1994 (adapted).

Exhibit 2.4 illustrates some of the debate in the travel sector over moving from a private limited company to a public limited company. Airtours sees access to capital as being a key advantage of becoming a public limited company. On the other hand Eurocamp stresses the costs of flotation and Unijet voices concerns about the constant need to perform as a public limited company, and the possible loss of control. The extent of share ownership and lack of control on transfer of shares mean that it is more difficult to retain control of public than private limited companies.

To commence business, limited liability companies must obtain a Certificate of Incorporation and a Certificate of Trading from the Registrar of Companies.

The following must be provided:

- Memorandum of Association. The key points included in this are the name and address of the company, the objectives of the company, and details of share capital issued.
- Articles of Association. This details the

internal affairs of the company including procedures for annual general meetings, and auditing of accounts.

Incorporation confers separate legal identity on the company. This may be contrasted with the position of unlimited liability organizations where the owners and the organization are legally the same.

Sources of finance

Sources of finance available to sole proprietors and partnerships are limited to:

- capital contributed by the owners
- ploughed-back profits
- bank loans

This is a key reason why small firms remain small.

Companies are able to raise capital through the additional routes of:

- shares (equity)
- debentures

Shares can be seen from the shareholder and company perspective. From the company point of view, share capital is generally low-risk since if the company doesn't make any profits then no dividends are issued. Shareholders seek dividend payments as well as growth in the value of shares. Debentures can be seen as a form of loan as they carry a fixed rate of interest. Thus to the company they pose a problem when profits are low, but their fixed interest rate is attractive when profits are high. Debenture holders get a guaranteed rate of return.

Several points emerge from Table 2.1 on the financing of Eurotunnel. First, Eurotunnel's capital represents a mixture of loans from banks which carry interest payments until they are repaid, and share issues which will not pay dividends until profits are earned. If profits from the tunnel are insufficient to repay loans and interest, the company may be forced into liquidation by the banks. The assets of the company would

Table 2.1 *Financing Eurotunnel*

1986	Concession to build the Channel Tunnel awarded to Eurotunnel
	£46m seed corn equity raised
	£206m share placing with institutions
1987	£5bn loan facility agreed with 200-bank syndicate
	£770m equity funding from public offer in UK and France
1990	£1.8bn additional debt from syndicate
	£300m loan from European investment bank
	£650m rights issue
1994	£700m raised from banks
	£850m rights issue, priced at 26 per cent discount and entirely underwritten

Source: *Guardian*, 27 May 1994 (adapted).

then be sold to repay the banks. Under this scenario, shareholders would get nothing. However because their liability is limited, neither would they stand to lose any personal assets. Under a more optimistic, high-profit scenario, payments to the banks are limited to previously negotiated rates, leaving substantial profits to be distributed in the form of high dividends to shareholders.

Second, three different forms of share issue are illustrated:

- A placing in 1986. This is where Eurotunnel's shares were placed directly with institutions such as pension funds and insurance companies.
- An offer for sale in 1987. This is where shares are advertised and offered to the public.
- A rights issue in 1990 and 1994. This is where existing shareholders are able to buy new shares at a discount.

Finally, the underwriting of share issues means that insurance has been taken out against the eventuality of shares remaining unsold.

Share prices and the stock market

Shares which are sold on the stock market are second-hand shares and thus their purchase doesn't provide new capital to companies. Prices of shares are determined by supply and demand. The stock market approximates to a perfect market (see Chapter 3) and thus prices are constantly changing to bring supply and demand into equilibrium. The demand for and the supply of shares depend upon the following:

- price of shares
- expectations of future price changes
- profitability of firm
- price of other assets
- interest rates
- government policy
- tax considerations

Aims and missions

Objectives in the private sector are generally to maximize profitability. Many organizations have elaborated their aims into mission statements, and exhibit 2.5 illustrates the mission statement of BAA.

Exhibit 2.5   BAA's mission statement

'Our mission is to make BAA the most successful airport company in the world.'
   This means:

- always focusing on our customers' needs and safety
- seeking continuous improvements in the costs and quality of our services
- enabling our employees to give of their best

Source: BAA (1994).

Ownership and control

Understanding small business organization is straightforward. The owner is the manager. This may mean that profit maximization is subject to personal considerations such as environmental concerns or hours worked.

For companies, size of operations and number of shareholders make the picture more complex. Companies are run along standard lines: the managing director is responsible for directing managers in the day-to-day running of the organization. The board of directors is responsible for determining company policy and for reporting annually to the shareholders. This can lead to a division between ownership (shareholders) and control (managers) and a potential conflict of interests. Shareholders generally wish to see their dividends and capital gains, and thus company profits, maximized. Managers will generally have this as an important objective since they are ultimately answerable to shareholders. However, they may seek other objectives – in particular, maximizing personal benefit – which may include kudos from concluding deals, good pension prospects and a variety of perks such as foreign travel, well-appointed offices and high-specification company cars.

Non-profit-making organizations

Non-profit organizations in the private sector vary considerably in size and in purpose. They span national organizations with large turnovers, smaller special interest groups, professional associations and local clubs and societies, and include:

- the National Trust
- the Council for the Protection of Rural England
- the Ramblers Association
- the Tourism Society
- the Institute of Leisure and Amenity Management
- the British Amateur Gymnastics Association

The National Trust

The National Trust is a charity and independent from the government. It derives its funds from membership subscriptions, legacies and gifts, and trading income from entrance fees, shops and restaurants. It is governed by an act of parliament – the National Trust Act 1907. Its main aim is to safeguard places of historic interest and natural beauty.

Aims and missions

Aims and missions of voluntary groups include protection of special interests, promotion of ideas and ideals, regulation of sports and provision of goods and services which are not catered for by the free market.

Review of key terms

- Public sector = government-owned.
- Private sector = non-government-owned.
- Council member = elected councillor.
- Council officer = paid official.
- Private limited company = company with restrictions governing transfer of shares.
- Public limited company = company whose shares are freely transferable and quoted on stock market.
- Public corporation = public sector commercial-style organization.
- Dividend = the distribution of profits to shareholders.
- Limited liability = liability limited to amount of investment.
- Strategic management = long-term policy making.
- Operational management = day-to-day management.
- Floatation = floating a private limited company on the stock market, thus becoming a public limited company.

Data questions

Task 2.1 Invasion of the outsiders

Recently a senior BBC correspondent said to me [John Tusa]: 'We're not correspondents any more, we're scarcely even reporters. We have become reprocessors. There is no time for digging up the news.' It is the tension between the subjective, instinctive activity of journalism and broadcasting and the purportedly objective methods of some schools of modern management that I wish to explore.

The new managerial techniques and the pressures and disciplines that flow from them blow coldly and indifferently on all parts of Whitehall and the public sector. These new disciplines were only those that the private sector had used for years. That in no way diminished the sense of shock when they were introduced into the public sector.

BBC participants in early management courses rebelled – these serious and competent people needed persuasion that the new and wholly untried and untested vocabulary of objectives, performance, goals, mission statements and so on was first something they could understand, second something they could respect; and third, something they could usefully apply to the work they were already doing rather well but might do better as a result.

The conclusions that I draw from this review of the sources of the new management drive in the public sector are that those involved were properly sensitive to the difficulty of what they were doing. They realised that there was not an exact fit between their chosen methodology of change and the Civil Service and public sector to which it was about to be applied. They knew, in other words, in the shorthand of journalism, that programmes are not products. Systems of management control that tend to treat programmes like products can only end up defeating the very activity they claim to protect.

Source: *Guardian*, 15 June 1994.

Questions

1 The BBC is a public corporation whilst Channel 4 is in the private sector. What are the essential differences in objectives, structure and finance of these organizations?
2 Why is the BBC being subjected to 'new management techniques and disciplines'?
3 'Systems of management control that treat programmes like products can only end up defeating the very activity they claim to protect.'

(a) What is meant by this statement?

(b) Do you agree with this statement?

Task 2.2 SkiBound eyes flotation to bolster growth ambitions

Top ski specialist SkiBound wants to fund ambitious growth plans with a summer flotation on the stock exchange.

UK country cottage operator Country Holidays is also poised to decide within the next month whether it will go public. Disclosure of the plans comes amid a flurry of activity by the trade reflecting renewed confidence in the travel sector. Inspirations floated on the unlisted securities market last December and *Travel Trade Gazette* revealed exclusively that Sunset Holidays intends to float by the end of the year. Other firms considering going public are Holiday Autos, Unijet and Panorama Holidays.

Brighton-based SkiBound may use cash generated by a listing to pursue its goal of buying a summer operator to balance its winter-heavy business.

Source: *Travel Trade Gazette*, 27 April 1994 (adapted).

Questions

1 What kind of a company is SkiBound at the date of the article?

2 How does a flotation occur?

3 What are the major benefits to SkiBound and the other organizations mentioned of flotation?

4 What are the main problems to SkiBound and the other organizations mentioned of flotation?

Task 2.3 MP claims quangos encourage corruption and fraud

The Labour party has launched a stinging attack of government policy in the House of Commons. Michael Meacher, the shadow Citizen's Charter Minister, opened the debate which sought to expose 'the progression towards an unelected state'.

He told MPs, 'The government's policy of privately appointed bodies, with secret meetings, privately arranged audit, and absence of surcharge facilitates – even encourages – corruption and fraud'. His speech accused ministers of eliminating from all public bodies everyone who was not of Conservative persuasion. Michael Meacher estimated that the growth of these bodies meant that they would be responsible for about £54bn of public spending, some one-fifth of the total.

William Waldegrave, the Citizen's Charter Minister, countered that there had been a 36 per cent reduction in quangos since 1979, saying, 'Virtually all of the great state industrial apparatus had been returned to the private sector'. He added that much of the expenditure of such bodies was accounted for by housing associations and National Health Service trusts.

The Labour motion was defeated by 308 votes to 263.

Source: the author, from *Hansard*, 24 February 1994.

Questions

1 Identify the main quangos in the leisure and tourism sector.

2 Explain the nature of Mr Meacher's attack on quangos.

3 How could these criticisms be addressed?

4 Explain and evaluate the basis of Mr Waldegrave's reply to Mr Meacher.

Task 2.4 Countryside cuts feared

The government has published plans for a merger of English Nature and the Countryside Commission. English Nature has responsibility for the protection of wildlife habitats, while the Countryside Commission advises on landscape use and management.

The green lobby is sceptical. Fiona Richards, director of the Council for the Protection of Rural England, expresses general fears that the Treasury will use the merger as a way of cutting spending on the countryside. She said, 'We would be very concerned if this is just a cost-cutting exercise. The only justification for the merger would be if it produces something better'.

Source: the author, from news cuttings, January 1994.

Questions

1 What are the main distinguishing features between the organizational forms of the Countryside Commission and the Council for the Protection of Rural England?
2 Research recent issues that have involved these organizations and consider whether the apparent aims of the organizations differ.
3 Is it necessary to have both of these organizations?

Task 2.5 Wonders of creation: the record label that gave us the Jesus and Mary Chain is 10 years old – Ben Thompson

Alan McGee – jet-setting Glasgow exile, British Rail clerk turned indie-music mogul – sits in the corner of a London brasserie, sipping a cappuccino in the refined manner of his hero, Paul Weller.

McGee is affable in the extreme. He has good reason to be. Creation Records, the 'Motown in leather trousers' he founded 10 years ago on a £1000 bank loan, has looked bankruptcy in the face on several occasions. But this year it has an expected turnover of £8–10m, and a complex and lucrative deal with Sony has brought new and unprecedented stability. Perhaps more importantly, all this has been achieved with no dilution of the label's mystique. 'We've always been brilliant at the music,' McGee observes

modestly, 'but we've had to learn the business part as we've gone along.' McGee's sharp eyes and ears have always been the label's greatest assets.

The Cramps, Creation's offices, are still in less-than-salubrious E8, just south of London Fields, but they have expanded to take over another floor.

'We are never going to be too big,' McGee insists. 'We'll always be what the business calls a "boutique" independent, reflecting one man's tastes.' These range 'from Lynryd Skynryd to the Orb, from Miles Davis to Willie Nelson'. It was Creation's long overdue and patently drug-induced embrace of dance culture in 1989–90 that eased their way into the pop mainstream. Primal Scream, led by McGee's schoolfriend Bobby Gillespie, were the key players here – and their new album, already the subject of furious debate in the music press 2 months prior to release, will be the key to Creation's 11th year. 'I took Bobby to his first concert,' McGee remembers, 'I was 2 or 3 years older than him and his dad wouldn't let him go to concerts.'

Which concert was it? 'Thin Lizzy in 1975.'

Source: *Independent on Sunday*, 30 January 1994 (adapted).

Questions

1 Creation Records is a private limited company. How suitable do you think this type of business organization is for its purposes?
2 If you were setting up a record company today on £10 000, what form of business organization would be most appropriate?

Short questions

1 Distinguish between the public sector, public limited companies and public corporations.
2 What is the major benefit of incorporation?
3 Who determines strategic policy for:
    (a) local government organizations?
    (b) public limited companies?
    (c) public corporations?

4 What conflicts of aims might occur in:
   (a)   public limited companies?
   (b)   quangos?
5 Identify four public limited companies in the leisure and tourism sector.
   (a)   Research and record movements in their share prices over the past 24 months as well as those of the *Financial Times*-Stock Exchange (FT-SE) index.
   (b)   Suggest reasons for the movements in these share prices.

Further reading

Adams, I. *Leisure and Government*, Business Education Publishers, Tyne and Wear, 1990.

Company annual reports.

Department of National Heritage, *Preserving the Past, Shaping the Future*, DNH, 1994.

Gratton, C. and Taylor, P., *Leisure Industries – An Overview*, Comedia, 1987.

Pearce, D., *Tourism Organisations*, Longman, 1992.

3

The market for leisure and tourism products

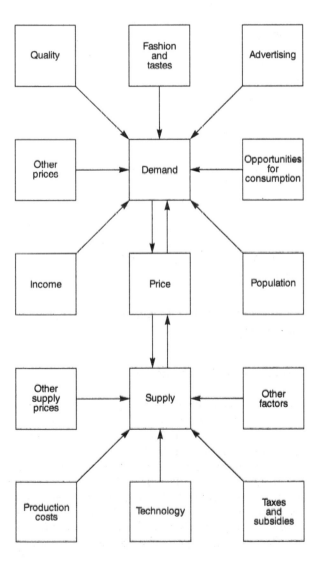

Objectives

Prices in a market economy are constantly on the move. For example, the price of package holidays has fallen considerably in real terms over the last decade, whilst the price of foreign currency changes many times in a single day. Price has a key function in the market economy. On the one hand it signals changes in demand patterns to producers, stimulating production of those products with increasing demand and depressing production of those products where demand is falling. At the same time price provides an incentive for producers to economize on their inputs. This chapter will investigate how price is formed in the market. It will investigate the factors which determine the demand for and the supply of a good or service and see how the forces of demand and supply interact to determine price.

After studying this chapter students will be able to:

- identify a market and define the attributes of a perfect market
- analyse the factors that affect the demand for a good or service
- analyse the factors that affect the supply of a good or service
- understand the concept of equilibrium price
- analyse the factors that cause changes in equilibrium price
- relate price theory to real world examples

Definitions

Effective demand

Effective demand is more than just the wanting of something, but is defined as 'demand backed by cash'.

Ceteris paribus

Ceteris paribus means 'all other things remaining unchanged'. In the real world there are a number of factors which affect the price of a good or service. These are constantly changing and in some instances they work in opposite directions. This makes it very difficult to study cause and effect. Economists use the term *ceteris paribus* to clarify thinking. For example, it might be said that a fall in the price of a commodity will cause a rise in demand, ceteris paribus. If this caveat were not stated then we might find that, despite the fact that the price of a commodity had fallen, we might observe a fall in demand, because some other factor might be changing at the same time – a significant rise in income tax, for example.

Perfect market assumption

A market is a place where buyers and sellers come into contact with one another. In the model of price determination discussed in this chapter we make a simplifying assumption that we are operating in a perfect market. The characteristics of a perfect market include:

● many buyers and sellers
● perfect knowledge of prices throughout the market
● rational consumers and producers basing decisions on prices
● no government intervention – e.g. price control

The stock exchange is an example of a perfect market – equilibrium price is constantly changing to reflect changes in demand and supply.

Table 3.1 *The demand for Matashi 21" colour televisions*

Price (£)	220	200	180	160	140	120	100
Demand (per week)	2000	2400	2800	3200	3600	4000	4400

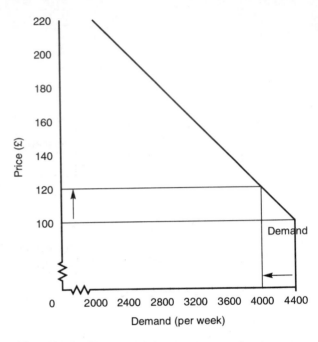

Figure 3.1 The demand curve for Matashi 21" colour televisions.

The demand for leisure and tourism products

Demand and own price

Generally, as the price of a good or a service increases, the demand for it falls, *ceteris paribus*, as illustrated in Table 3.1. This gives rise to the demand curve shown in Figure 3.1.

The demand curve slopes downwards to the right and plots the relationship between a change in price and demand. The reason for this is that as prices rise consumers tend to economize on items and replace them with other ones if possible. Notice that as price changes we move along the demand curve to determine the effect on demand so that in Figure 3.1 as price rises from £100 to £120, demand falls from 4400 units a week to 4000 units a week.

The main exceptions to this are twofold. Some goods and services are bought because their high price lends exclusivity to them and thus they become more sought after at higher prices. Also, if consumers expect prices to rise in the future, they might buy goods even though their prices are rising.

Demand and other factors

The following factors also affect the demand for a good or service:

- income
- other prices
- comparative quality/value added
- fashion and tastes
- advertising
- opportunities for consumption (e.g. leisure time)
- population

Since the demand curve describes the relationship between demand and price, these other factors will affect the position of the demand curve and changes in these factors will cause the demand curve to shift its position to the left or the right.

Disposable income

Disposable income is defined as income less direct taxes but including government subsidies. The effect of a change in disposable income on the demand for a good or service depends on the type of good under consideration. First, for normal or superior goods, as disposable income rises, so does demand. This applies to holidays abroad, CDs and membership of leisure clubs. However some goods or services are bought as cheap substitutes for other ones. These are defined as inferior goods and examples might include holidays in the UK, black-and-white TVs, cheap-

range hi-fi systems, or trainers without a leading brand name. As income rises the demand for these goods and services declines. Exhibit 3.1 shows that Morecombe can be classified as an 'inferior' destination in economic terms.

Exhibit 3.1 Boom and bust: a tale of two resorts: Blackpool and Morecambe – Elizabeth Heathcote

Blackpool and Morecambe lie back to back on the north-west coast of England, but while Blackpool has made good since tourism was shattered in the early 1970s by the introduction of cheap package holidays, Morecambe has continued to suffer.

Between 1970 and 1987, long holidays taken abroad increased from just over 5 million to 20 million; the number spent in the UK fell by a quarter. Morecambe has one of the most beautiful settings of any resort in the UK, but since 1974 visitor spending – adjusted for inflation – has fallen from £43.6m to £6.5m. The derelict pier has been demolished, all the town's cinemas have closed and there has been a 61 per cent reduction in the resort's holiday accommodation.

Source: *The Independent*, 3 August 1992 (adapted).

An income consumption curve shows the relationship between changes in income and changes in the demand for goods and services and Figure 3.2 shows the different income consumption curves for superior and inferior goods. As income rises from A to B, the demand for superior goods rises from C to E, whilst the demand for inferior goods falls from C to D.

Price of other goods

Changes in the prices of other goods will also affect the demand for the good or service in question. In the case of goods or services which are substitutes, a rise in the price of one good will lead to a rise in the demand for the other. In the skiing market, for example, Cervinia in Italy, Kitzbühel in Austria, and Valmorel in France are to some extent substitutes for each other and changes in relative prices will cause demand patterns to change. A similar picture holds for

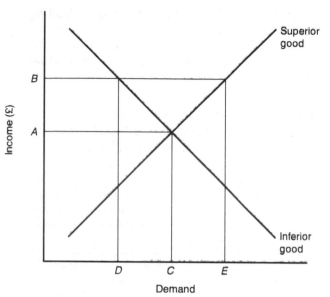

Figure 3.2 Income consumption curves for superior and inferior goods.

national newspaper titles, as illustrated by exhibit 3.2.

Exhibit 3.2   Price war among nationals hurts United Newspapers: falling circulation at Express titles holds back group profits – Gail Counsell

United Newspapers' national titles barely pushed up profits enough to cover inflation last year as the price war launched by Rupert Murdoch's News International and higher spending on new supplements took their toll.

In the face of stiff competition from the price-cutting *The Times* and *Sun*, sales of the *Daily Express* and *Sunday Express* fell by around 6 per cent to 1.35 million and 1.6 million respectively. That compared with a slightly higher fall of 6.4 per cent at the *Daily Mirror* – though to a bigger circulation of 2.4 million – while the *Daily Mail* held the decline to 1.3 per cent at 1.7 million copies.

Graham Wilson, United's managing director, said: 'I don't think we can deny that *The Times* price-cutting has had an effect on our circulation and that of all the middle-market popular newspapers'.

Source: *The Independent*, 25 March 1994 (adapted).

Some goods and services are complements or in joint demand. In other words, they tend to be demanded in pairs or sets. In this case an increase in the price of one good will lead to a fall in the demand for the other. Examples of such goods include CDs and CD players, and exhibit 3.3 reports on the link between currency values and demand for tourism destinations.

Exhibit 3.3   Florida doldrums threaten winter

The pain in Florida looks set to continue next winter, as operators struggle to overcome its negative image and the decline of the pound against the dollar.

An indication of how things are going is revealed by Jetsave's sales and marketing director John Standley who explained: 'Its a lousy summer in Florida. We have cut back capacity by 25%'.

Source: *Travel Trade Gazette*, 15 May 1994.

Comparative quality/value added

Consumers do not just consider price when comparing goods and services – they also compare quality. Improvements in the quality of a good or service can be important factors in increasing demand and exhibit 3.4 describes how BA is improving quality in its business class.

Exhibit 3.4   Special report on long-haul travel – David Richardson

Seasoned travellers may think they know all about business travel, especially on the busiest long-haul routes to the USA. They have been taught by business travel magazines to be super-choosy and to go for the airline with a one-inch longer seat or an extra prawn on the platter.

BA has a new focus on the inner man, but the outer man gets the most of the £100m investment. Seat-back videos have been introduced in Club World, while in first class a new sleeper service offers sheets, duvets and cups of hot chocolate. 'Fast-track' lanes through passport and security are also new.

Source: *The Independent*, 23 April 1993 (adapted).

This is an important consideration for airlines' strategies for increasing market share and is developed further in Chapter 6.

Fashion and tastes

Fashion and tastes affect demand for leisure goods and services as in other areas. For example, the demand for tennis facilities and accessories rises sharply during Wimbledon fortnight. Similarly, holiday destinations move in and out of fashion. In recent years Turkey, Florida, Spain and Greece have moved in and out of fashion. Goods and services are particularly prone to sudden changes in popularity in the age of mass, instantaneous communications. Florida has been affected by bad publicity surrounding the violent mugging of tourists, as exhibit 3.5 shows.

Exhibit 3.5 Dangers that go beyond adventure

For many people an element of adventure, and therefore of danger, gives a holiday extra zest. What is not acceptable is a well-above-average risk of being severely mugged, or even murdered. Yet as the world becomes more drug-, crime- and violence-ridden, the chances of either or both happening are rising.

The savage murder of a British jazz enthusiast in New Orleans – the second in a year – comes after a spate of such killings in US cities. Six tourists have been murdered in Florida since October, where no fewer than 35 000 visitors were robbed, assaulted or raped in 1991. When a German woman was murdered in Miami earlier this month, the German consul said that of 300 000 German visitors to Florida in the past year, 1200 had reported being a victim of some form of crime – roughly one per planeload.

Source: *The Independent*, 13 April 1993 (adapted).

Advertising

The aim of most advertising is to increase the demand for goods and services. The exception to this is advertising that is designed to inhibit the demand for some goods and services. For example, Health Education Council advertising includes campaigns to inhibit the demand for cigarettes and drugs. Exhibit 3.6 reports on the extent of the advertising campaign to launch Radio 5.

Exhibit 3.6 £1 Million fanfare helps to launch Radio 5 Live

The launch of the BBC's new 24-hour station, Radio 5 Live, at 5 a.m. next Monday will be heralded by a £1m advertising campaign. Television and radio trailers, posters, jingles, a campaign bus and 7 million leaflets are all part of the drive to alert listeners to the new network. It expects to start life with Radio 5's audience of 3 million but make 'substantial' improvements by the end of the first year. The controller, Jenny Abramsky, predicts that listeners will come from commercial stations, particularly music-based ones, and some will be new to radio.

Source: *The Independent*, 22 March 1994 (adapted).

Opportunities for consumption

Unlike many sectors of the economy, many leisure and tourism pursuits require time to participate in them. Thus the amount of leisure time available will be an important enabling factor in demand. The two main components here are the average working week and the amount of paid holidays. The level of unemployment is also an important consideration, but the unemployed lack effective demand. Table 3.2 illustrates free time availability.

Population

Demand will also be influenced by the size of population as well as the composition of the population in terms of age, sex and geographical distribution. Population is discussed in more detail in Chapter 10.

The supply of leisure and tourism products

Supply and own price

Generally as the price of a good or a service increases, the supply of it rises, *ceteris paribus*.

Table 3.2 *Time use in a typical week 1992–1993*

	Male employees	Female employees	Male retired	Female retired
Free time (hours)	46	31	92	71

Source: Various.

Table 3.3 *The supply of Matashi 21" colour televisions*

Price (£)	220	200	180	160	140	120	100
Supply (per week)	4400	4000	3600	3200	2800	2400	2000

This gives rise to the supply curve which is illustrated in Table 3.3 and Figure 3.3.

The supply curve slopes upwards to the right and plots the relationship between a change in price and supply. The reason for this is that, as prices rise, the profit motive stimulates existing producers to increase supply and induces new suppliers to enter the market. Notice that as price changes we move along the supply curve to determine the effect on supply so that in Figure 3.3, as price rises from £100 to £120, supply rises from 2000 units a week to 2400 units a week.

Supply and other factors

The following factors also affect the supply of a good or service:

- prices of other goods supplied
- changes in production costs
- technical improvements
- taxes and subsidies
- other factors (e.g. industrial relations)

Since the supply curve describes the relationship between supply and price, these other factors will affect the position of the supply curve and changes in these factors will cause the supply curve to shift its position to the left or the right.

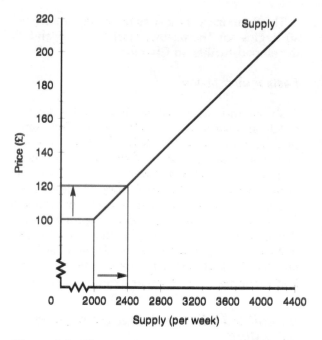

Figure 3.3 The supply curve for Matashi 21" colour televisions.

Prices of other goods supplied

Where a producer can use factors of production to supply a range of goods or services, an increase in the price of a particular product will cause the producer to redeploy resources towards that particular product and away from other ones. For example, the owners of a flexible sports hall will be able to increase the supply of badminton courts at the expense of short tennis, if demand changes.

Changes in production costs

The main costs involved in production are labour costs, raw material costs and interest payments. A fall in these production costs will tend to stimulate supply, whereas a rise in production costs will shift the supply curve to the left.

Technical improvements

Changes in technology will affect the supply of goods and services in the leisure and tourism

Table 3.4 *The effects of the imposition of a tax on supply*

Price (£)	220	200	180	160	140	120	100
Original supply (per week; S0)	4400	4000	3600	3200	2800	2400	2000
New supply (per week; S1)	4000	3600	3200	2800	2400	2000	

sector. An example of this is aircraft design: the development of jumbo jets has had a considerable impact on the supply curve for air travel. The supply curve has shifted to the right, signifying that more seats can now be supplied at the same price. Technology has had a large impact on the production of leisure goods such as TVs, video cassette recorders (VCRs), personal computers (PCs) and video cameras. The supply curve for these goods has shifted persistently to the right over recent years, leading to a reduction in prices after allowing for inflation.

Taxes and subsidies

The supply of goods and services is affected by indirect taxes such as VAT and excise duty, and also by subsidies. In the event of the imposition of taxes or subsidies, the price paid by the consumer is not the same as the price received by the supplier. For example, if the government were to impose a £20 tax on televisions at the price to the consumer of £200, the producer would now only receive £180, so the supply curve will shift to the left since the supplier will now interpret every original price as being less £20. Table 3.4 shows the effects of the imposition of a tax on the original supply data.

The effects of an imposition of a tax are illustrated in Figure 3.4. Notice that the supply curve has shifted to the left. In fact the vertical distance between the old (S0) and the new (S1) supply curves represents the amount of the tax.

Similarly, the effects of a subsidy will be to shift the supply curve to the right.

Other factors

There are various other factors which can influence the supply of leisure and tourism goods

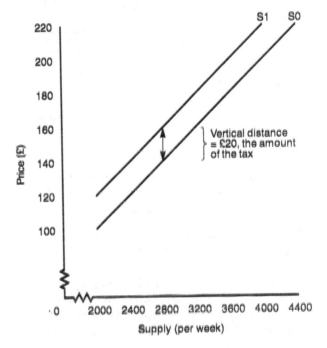

Figure 3.4 The effects of the imposition of a tax on supply.

and services, including strikes, wars and the weather.

Equilibrium price

Equilibrium is a key concept in economics. It means a state of balance or the position towards which something will naturally move. Equilibrium price comes about from the interaction between the forces of demand and supply. There is only one price at which the quantity that consumers want to demand is equal to the quantity that producers want to supply. This is the equilibrium price. Figure 3.5 uses the demand

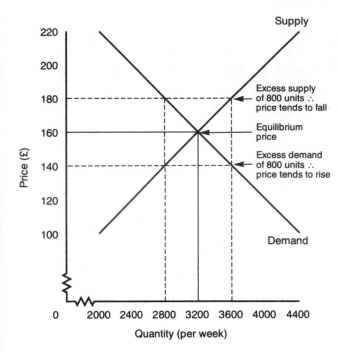

Figure 3.5 Equilibrium price in the market for Matashi 21″ colour televisions.

schedule from Table 3.1 and the supply schedule from Table 3.3. The equilibrium price in this case is £160, since this is where demand equals supply, both of which are 3200 units per week.

It can be demonstrated that this is the equilibrium by considering other possible prices. At higher prices supply exceeds demand. In the example, at a price of £180 there is excess supply of 800 units a week. Excess supply will tend to cause the price to fall. On the other hand, at lower prices demand exceeds supply. At a price of £140 there is excess demand of 800 units a week. Excess demand causes the price to rise. Thus the equilibrium price is at £160, since no other price is sustainable and market forces will prevail, causing price to change until the equilibrium is established.

Changes in equilibrium price

Equilibrium does not mean that prices do not change. In fact, prices are constantly changing in markets to reflect changing conditions of demand and supply.

The effect of a change in demand

We have previously identified the factors that can cause the demand curve to shift its position. Table 3.5 reviews these factors, distinguishing what will cause the demand curve to shift to the right from that which will cause it to shift to the left.

Table 3.5 *Shifts in the demand curve*

Demand curve shifts to the left	Demand curve shifts to the right
Fall in income (normal goods)	Rise in income (normal goods)
Rise in income (inferior goods)	Fall in income (inferior goods)
Rise in price of complementary goods	Fall in price of complementary goods
Fall in price of substitutes	Rise in price of substitutes
Fall in quality	Rise in quality
Unfashionable	Fashionable
Less advertising	More advertising
Less leisure time	Increased leisure time
Fall in population	Rise in population

Table 3.6 *A shift in demand for Matashi 21" colour televisions*

Price (£)	220	200	180	160	140	120	100
Original demand (per week; D0)	2000	2400	2800	3200	3600	4000	4400
New demand (per week; D1)		2000	2400	2800	3200	3600	4000
Supply (per week; S0)	4400	4000	3600	3200	2800	2400	2000

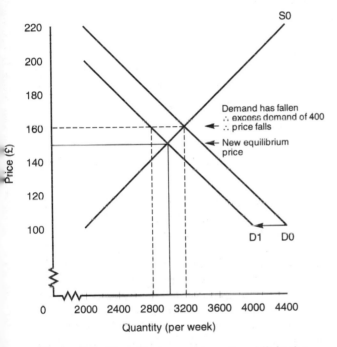

Figure 3.6 The effects on price of a shift in the demand curve.

In the example of Matashi TVs, a fall in the price of substitutes, for example Sony TVs, will cause the demand curve to shift to the left from D0 to D1. The supply curve will remain unchanged at S0. This is illustrated in Table 3.6.

Figure 3.6 shows the effect of this on equilibrium price. The original price of £160 will no longer be in equilibrium, since demand has now fallen to 2800 units a week at this price. There is now excess supply of 400 units per week, which will cause equilibrium price to fall until a new equilibrium is achieved at £150 where demand is equal to supply at 3000 units a week.

Similarly, if the demand curve were to shift to the right as a result of an effective advertising campaign, for example, the excess demand created at the original price would cause equilibrium price to rise.

The effect of a change in supply

The factors which cause a leftward or rightward shift in supply are reviewed in Table 3.7.

In the example of Matashi TVs, the effect of the imposition of a tax is shown in Table 3.8.

A tax will cause the supply curve to shift to the left from S0 to S1 but the demand curve will remain unchanged at D0, as illustrated in Figure 3.7.

The original price of £160 will no longer be in equilibrium, since supply has now fallen to 2800 units a week at this price. There is now excess demand of 400 units per week, which will cause equilibrium price to rise until a new equilibrium is achieved at £170 where demand is equal to supply at 3000 units a week.

Similarly, if the supply curve were to shift to the right as a result of an improvement in technology, for example, the excess supply created at the original price would cause equilibrium price to fall.

The price mechanism in action

Maximum prices and black markets

It is common in the leisure sector to interfere with free market pricing. The effects of this are

Table 3.7 *Shifts in the supply curve*

Supply curve shifts to the left	Supply curve shifts to the right
Rise in price of other goods that could be supplied by producer	Fall in price of other goods that could be supplied by producer
Rise in production costs	Fall in production costs
Effects of taxes	Effects of subsidies
Effects of strikes	Technical improvements

Table 3.8 *A shift in supply of Matashi 21" colour televisions*

Price (£)	220	200	180	160	140	120	100
Original demand (per week; D0)	2000	2400	2800	3200	3600	4000	4400
Original supply (per week; S0)	4400	4000	3600	3200	2800	2400	2000
New supply (per week; S1)	4000	3600	3200	2800	2400	2000	

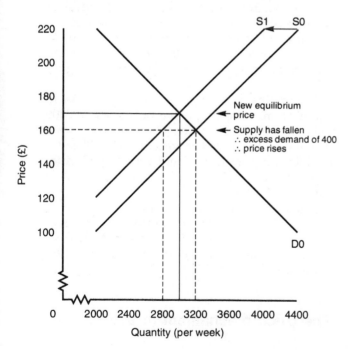

Figure 3.7 The effects on price of a shift in the supply curve.

particularly evident at prestige sports and music events where the capacity of the stadium is fixed, as illustrated in Figure 3.8.

The capacity of the Rugby Football Union (RFU) ground at Twickenham for example is about 70 000, and thus the supply curve (*S*) is fixed and vertical at this point. The demand curve for tickets is downward-sloping (*D*).The RFU fixes a price (*P0*) which is considerably below the equilibrium price (*P1*). At the RFU official price there is considerable excess demand (*a b*). Equilibrium is restored through the activities of ticket touts in the black market. Prices charged by touts rise and the effects of this can be shown by moving along the demand curve (*b* to *c*) until demand falls sufficiently to match supply.

Exhibit 3.7 reports on how ticket touts are well aware of elementary economics.

Exhibit 3.7 Rugby Union: ticket prices hit new heights – Steve Bale

Black market tickets for Saturday's England–Scotland match at Twickenham are in such unprecedented demand and such short supply that the price of

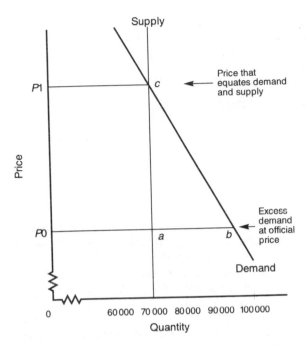

Figure 3.8 The effects of setting a maximum price below equilibrium price.

two together in a decent spot has reached the mind-boggling level of £2000.

But there are no plans for an increase, even when a completed new east stand increases Twickenham's capacity from 54 000 to 67 000 for the New Zealand match in the autumn.

Source: *The Independent*, 4 March 1993 (adapted).

Review of key terms

- Effective demand = demand backed by cash.
- Perfect market = many buyers and sellers, rational players, perfect knowledge, no interference.
- Normal good = demand rises as income rises (also called superior good).
- Inferior good = demand falls as income falls.
- Equilibrium price = where demand equals supply.

Data questions

Task 3.1

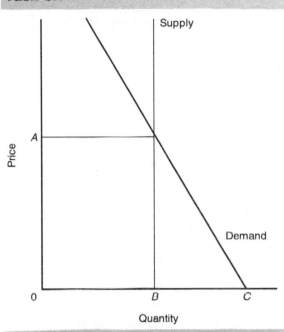

Figure 3.9 The demand and supply curves for tennis courts.

Questions on Figure 3.9

1 If a local authority decided to build OB tennis courts, what would happen if they decided to make these free?
2 If the authority wished to create a market equilibrium, what price should they charge?
3 What problems arise from charging an equilibrium price?
4 How would the courts be allocated if they were provided free of charge?

Task 3.2

Question

Discuss the factors that influence the figures given in Table 3.9.

Table 3.9 *Household expenditure in real terms on selected leisure items (£ per week at 1992 prices)*

	1986	1991	1992	19	19
Alcoholic drink consumed away from home	08.40	07.85	07.79		
Home computers	00.23	00.54	00.61		
Holidays	07.61	10.21	11.21		
Cinema	00.14	00.19	00.19		

Source: Central Statistical Office, *Social Trends.*

Task 3.3 What am I bid for a week in the sun?

The reporter for a TV holiday programme was looking pleased with himself as he sipped a cocktail on a Caribbean beach. He'd managed to book a week in Cuba's winter sun for couple of hundred pounds, and he was keen to make a point.

It wasn't long before his camera crew had found a couple to gloat over. Gill and Tom had paid over £500 each for an identical holiday, and they had booked several months before.

Enter camera left a man who stole the show: £110 – *for two weeks.*

So how can the price of the same holiday go up and down like share prices and currencies? The answer lies back in the UK where the late bookings section of Airtours, the UK's second biggest tour operator, resembles a share dealing room with banks of flickering screens. Here analysts change holiday prices several times a day. They are not alone – Thomson, the industry number one and First Choice, the industry number three, change their holiday prices every day too.

Each uses the latest information on their competitors' prices to adjust their own prices to maximize profits. First Choice gets much of its information on competitors' prices through its ownership of Going Places.

When demand for their products is strong and supply is tight, the companies push up prices. However, faced with a half-empty plane departing in 2 days' time, prices plummet as the team tries to get bums on seats that would otherwise earn nothing at all.

The First Choice team have developed some ground rules for pricing. There's nothing like grey skies and rain at home to move prices up on the day.

Somehow in the face of all this Gill and Tom managed to keep their smiles fixed.

Source: the author, adapted from news cuttings, January 1995.

Questions

1 Illustrate, using demand and supply diagrams, how the Airtours late bookings section sets prices.
2 Why is it difficult to keep to the prices printed in brochures?
3 How does a plane with empty seats represent market disequilibrium and how does Airtours attempt to restore equilibrium?
4 What is the significance of information and knowledge to market prices?

Task 3.4

Questions on Table 3.10

1 Using demand and supply theory, account for the difference in prices between running shoes.

Table 3.10 *Retail prices for men's running shoes (1994) and advertising expenditure on sports footwear (1993)*

	£
Retail prices	
Adidas Tubular 2	88.00
Nike Air Max	79.50
Reebook Ventilator HXL	60.00
Puma Prevail	44.00
Hi-Tec Classic	20.00
	£000s
Advertising expenditure	
Adidas	400
Nike	3000
Reebok	1500
Puma	1000
Hi-Tec	0

Source: Various.

2 What effect does advertising have on the demand and supply curves for the market for a particular shoe?

Short questions

1 Distinguish between the factors which cause a movement along a demand curve, and those which cause a shift of the curve.
2 'An increase in the price of a good may arise from an increase in the price of its substitute, *ceteris paribus*'. Explain this statement.
3 Distinguish between a normal and an inferior good using examples from the leisure and tourism sector.
4 What is the likely effect of setting the maximum price of a good below its equilibrium price?

4

Demand: choice, elasticity and forecasting

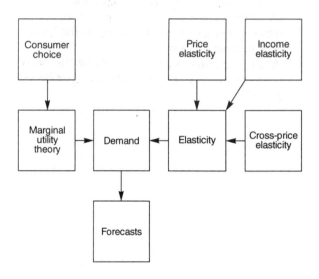

Objectives

This chapter looks in more detail at the demand curve. It considers consumer theory and the part it plays in explaining consumer behaviour, and the choice between leisure and work. Various concepts of demand elasticity are explained and the importance of these concepts to the leisure and tourism sector examined. Finally the chapter considers some techniques of demand forecasting, their uses and shortcomings.

By studying this chapter students will be able to:

- understand the concept of consumer equilibrium

- utilize marginal utility theory
- understand and apply the concept of price elasticity of demand
- understand and apply the concept of income elasticity of demand
- understand and apply the concept of cross-price elasticity of demand
- describe simple methods of demand forecasting
- evaluate techniques of demand forecasting

Consumer theory

Consumer theory attempts to explain consumer behaviour, and investigates consumer choice in consuming goods and services. It assumes first that consumers have limited income, second that consumers act in a rational manner, and third that consumers aim to maximize their total satisfaction, subject to the constraint of limited income.

Consumer equilibrium will occur when purchases are arranged so as to maximize a consumer's total satisfaction. In other words a consumer cannot rearrange purchases and be better off. Thus in order to analyse consumer equilibrium, the idea of satisfaction needs to be investigated.

Marginal utility theory

Utility is the term economists use to measure a person's satisfaction from consuming a good or

Table 4.1 *Total utility and marginal utility from visits to theatre and fitness centre*

Visits to fitness centre			Visits to theatre		
Quantity per month	Total utility	Marginal utility	Quantity per month	Total utility	Marginal utility
0	0	–	0	0	–
1	25	25	1	37	37
2	44	19	2	57	20
3	60	16	3	74	17
4	74	14	4	88	14
5	86	12	5	100	12
6	96	10	6	110	10
7	105	9	7	119	9
8	112	7	8	127	8
9	118	6	9	134	7
10	123	5	10	140	6

service. In fact it is not possible to measure utility precisely, but predictions can be made about how utility changes with consumption. Marginal utility theory can be used to explain consumer choice in a simple model.

Assume a person has a monthly income of £60, and spends all of it on two services – visits to a fitness centre which cost £6 each and visits to the theatre which cost £12 each. To see how this person will divide income between the two services the concept of total utility must first be considered.

Total utility

Total utility is defined as the total benefit or satisfaction a person gets from the consumption of goods and services. Generally a person's total utility increases the more of a good or service they consume. Table 4.1 shows the total utility associated with different levels of consumption of fitness centre and theatre visits.

Notice that where consumption is zero no utility is derived, but as consumption of each service increases, so does total utility. However, closer examination of the data reveals that total utility does not rise at a uniform rate, and this can be revealed by studying marginal utility.

Marginal utility

Marginal utility is defined as the utility gained from consuming one extra unit of a good or service. This can be calculated from the total utility data: for example, two visits to the fitness centre resulted in a total utility of 44 units and three visits resulted in 60 units, so the marginal utility of the third visit is 16 units. Table 4.1 also shows the marginal utility of visits to the theatre and fitness centre.

The information shows that marginal utility falls as consumption rises. This is known as the principle of diminishing marginal utility. The extra satisfaction consumers derive from successive consumption of a good or service tends to diminish. The freshness or novelty of a good or service wears off a little the more of it is consumed.

Maximizing utility (1)

In the above example, a person has a monthly income of £60 which is spent on consuming two services. Table 4.2 shows the various combinations of theatre and fitness centre visits that can be obtained from this income. In addition it shows the total utility obtained from each of the

Table 4.2 *Combinations of theatre and fitness centre visits possible from monthly income of £60, and total utilities of each combination*

Visits to fitness centre (£6)			Visits to theatre (£12)			Combined total utility
Total utility	Expenditure	Quantity	Quantity	Expenditure	Total utility	
123	60	10	0	0	0	123
112	48	8	1	12	37	149
96	36	6	2	24	57	153
74	24	4	3	36	74	148
44	12	2	4	48	88	132
0	0	0	5	60	100	100

Table 4.3 *Marginal utility per pound spent on theatre and fitness centre visits*

Visits to fitness centre (£6)			Visits to theatre (£12)		
Quantity	Marginal utility (MU)	MU/£ spent	Quantity	Marginal utility (MU)	MU/£ spent
10	5	0.83	0	–	
8	7	1.17	1	37	3.08
6	10	1.67	2	20	1.67
4	14	2.33	3	16	1.33
2	19	3.17	4	14	1.17
0	–		5	12	1.00

possible combinations of theatre and fitness centre visits.

The consumer will be in equilibrium when total utility is maximized. This occurs with a combination of six visits to the fitness centre (total utility = 96) and two visits to the theatre per month (total utility = 57), giving a combined total utility of 153. The consumer cannot rearrange purchases and be better off.

Maximizing utility (2)

It is also possible to find the combination which maximizes utility by calculating and comparing the marginal utility per pound spent on different goods and services. Table 4.3 shows these calculations for the example under consideration, listing the possible combinations of visits to the fitness centre or theatre that could be purchased with a limited monthly income of £60.

The consumer can again be seen to be maximizing satisfaction by purchasing six visits to the fitness centre and two visits to the theatre, since this is where the marginal utility per pound spent is equal for each (MU/£ = 1.67). This can be seen to be maximizing satisfaction by looking at other possible choices.

Consider a choice with less fitness centre and more theatre visits. Four fitness centre visits (MU/£ = 2.33) and three theatre visits (MU/£ = 1.33) could be purchased. However, since the fitness centre visits are giving more marginal utility per pound spent than theatre visits, the consumer can increase satisfaction by switching spending away from theatre towards fitness. Similarly, eight fitness centre visits (MU/£ ≐ 1.17) and one theatre visit (MU/£ = 3.08) could be purchased. However, since the fitness centre visits are giving less marginal utility per pound spent than theatre visits, the consumer can increase satisfaction by switching spending away from fitness towards theatre. Thus it is only where the consumer equates the marginal utility per pound spent for each good and service consumed that utility is maximized. This can be expressed for more general cases as:

Consumer equilibrium = $MUa/Pa = MUb/Pb = MUn/Pn$

where: MU = marginal utility; P = price; and a, b, n = individual goods and services.

Free goods and maximizing utility

Some goods and services are provided free to consumers (for example, roads, parks and beaches). People will consume such goods and services to the point where their marginal utility equals zero. This is because consuming extra units has no cost in terms of other goods which could have been bought with limited income, but will add to total satisfaction as long as marginal utility is positive. This point has important implications for providers of such 'free' goods and services as national parks. There is considerable scope for extra consumption of these services since existing levels of consumption do not take many users to the point where MU = 0. Figure 4.1 illustrates this point.

Consumers of free services using quantity OQ1 derive positive marginal utility of OMU1 from this level of usage. However they may extend their usage to OQ2 and up to OQ3 at no extra cost to themselves whilst adding to their total satisfaction, since the marginal utility of using the service is positive throughout this range.

Utility: a postscript

The term utility raises many questions in considering consumer behaviour: what factors generate utility in a good or service for consumers? The answers to these questions may be found by using analysis from other disciplines, particularly

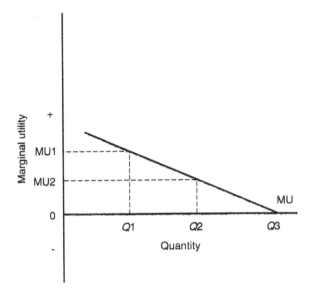

Figure 4.1 Marginal utility (MU) and demand for free goods/services. Q = Quantity.

psychology and sociology. Psychology, for example, investigates personal motivation in consumption, and considerable research has taken place in motivation of tourists.

Derivation of demand curve

Marginal utility theory confirms that demand curves slope downwards to the right and that as price falls demand rises. This can be shown using the data from Table 4.3 as a starting point. At the price of £12 per visit to a theatre, the consumer in our example will demand two visits per month. What happens if the price falls to £6 per visit? Table 4.4 shows the new possible combinations of fitness centre and theatre visits from a limited income of £60 monthly using data from the Tables 4.1–4.3.

Examination of the new calculations of marginal utility per pound spent reveals that the consumer will maximize utility at the point of five theatre visits and five visits to the fitness centre since this is where the marginal utility per pound spent is equal for each (MU/£ = 2.00). Thus there are now two points that can be used

Table 4.4   *Effects of a fall in price on consumer choice*

Visits to fitness centre (£6)			Visits to theatre (£6)		
Quantity	Marginal utility (MU)	MU/£ spent	Quantity	Marginal utility (MU)	MU/£ spent
10	5	0.83	0	–	
9	6	1.0	1	37	6.16
8	7	1.17	2	20	3.33
7	9	1.5	3	17	2.83
6	10	1.67	4	14	2.33
5	12	2.0	5	12	2.0
4	14	2.33	6	10	1.67
3	16	2.67	7	9	1.5
2	19	3.17	8	8	1.33
1	25	4.17	9	7	1.17
0	–	–	10	6	1.0

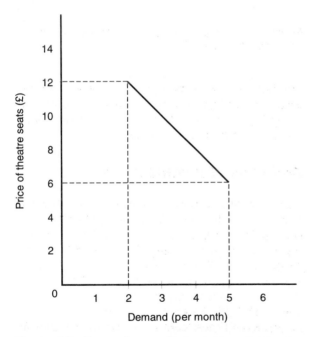

Figure 4.2   Demand curve for consumer for theatre seats

to construct a demand curve for this consumer for theatre visits: at seat price £12, demand equals two seats per month and at seat prices £6, demand equals five seats per month. On this basis, the demand curve in Figure 4.2 is constructed.

Market demand

A market demand curve is found by adding together the individual demand curves for a particular good or service.

The demand for leisure

Leisure time represents an element in the choice set available to consumers, and maximization of consumer utility will therefore also involve choice about how much leisure time to take. Just as when choosing between other goods and services, consumers will consider the extra utility or satisfaction they derive from leisure time against the price or cost of leisure time.

Consumers face the problem of limited time. There are only 24 hours in a day, and thus the most fundamental choice that consumers face is whether to devote their limited time to leisure or work.

We can consider the cost or price of leisure time as its opportunity cost – what has to be given up in order to enjoy leisure time? The opportunity cost of leisure time is clearly earnings that are lost through not working. What will happen to the trade-off between work and leisure when prices change? The key 'price' in this case is wages, and if wages increase there are two potential effects on the demand for leisure time.

First, an increase in wages means an increase in the price of leisure time, in terms of loss of earnings. Therefore consumers will tend to demand less leisure time as its price has increased. This is a substitution effect. Consumers will tend to substitute work for leisure to reflect their new relative prices. But the increase in wages will also lead consumers to have more income and spending power. Leisure can be classed as a 'normal service', and in common with other 'normal' goods and services, as income increases more will be demanded. This is called the income effect. There are clearly a complex set of forces which will determine whether the income or substitution effect is greater. One consideration is that as income increases, consumers have the ability to get more satisfaction out of their leisure time, thus resulting in a strong income effect. The utility derived from labour is also influenced by psychological and social factors. Some individuals may favour long leisure hours which they can happily fill with cheap or free activities such as reading, watching television, sleeping or walking. Other individuals may have a low boredom threshold and thus have a low marginal utility from leisure time. Equally there are cultural influences at work. There appears to be a greater work ethic in countries such as Germany and Japan than in other countries, particularly those with warmer climates.

Choice or rigidity?

The extent to which choice can actually be exercised in the work/leisure trade-off depends on flexibility in the labour market. When choosing between most goods and services, consumers can readily vary the amounts consumed in response to changing relative prices. Consumers generally have less choice in their participation in labour markets. Many jobs have standardized hours where individuals cannot choose to add or subtract hours in response to changes in wages. However workers can express their general pre-

ferences through trade unions and staff associations and these may be taken into account in determining the overall work package of pay, hours and holiday benefits.

Some jobs offer flexibility in offering overtime provision, and some individuals may have extra employment in addition to their main job. In these cases individuals will be in a position to exercise more precisely their choice between work and leisure.

Finally the unemployed are generally not acting out of choice but by lack of opportunity in their allocation of leisure time. However there has been considerable debate regarding social security benefits and incentives to work. Right-wing economists argue that benefit levels are distorting the labour market so that some unemployed maximize their total utility by remaining unemployed rather than entering the labour market.

Trends in work and leisure

There are several ways of examining these trends including analysis of:

- unemployment data
- holiday entitlement
- hours worked

Unemployment data

Recent data and trends in unemployment are discussed fully in Chapter 9.

Holiday entitlement

There has been a steady increase in paid holiday entitlement in the post-war period. For example, for manual workers the average holiday period has risen from 2 weeks in 1951 to 4–5 weeks by 1991.

Hours worked

Table 4.5 shows data for average working hours in European Union countries. It can be seen that

Table 4.5 *Average hours usually worked per week in European Union countries, 1992 (excludes meal breaks, includes overtime)*

Country	Hours per week
Portugal	40.6
Greece	40.0
Spain	39.5
Luxembourg	38.4
Irish Republic	38.2
Italy	37.8
France	37.4
UK	37.1
Germany	35.7
Belgium	34.1
Denmark	32.1
EU average	37.2

Source: Eurostat/*Social Trends*, CSO.

the UK total is close to the European Union average, with Portugal having the highest number of hours.

Price elasticity of demand

Price elasticity of demand measures the responsiveness of demand to a change in price. This relationship can be expressed as a formula, and exhibit 4.1 shows a worked example for calculating price elasticity of demand.

$$\frac{\text{Percentage change in quantity demanded}}{\text{Percentage change in price}}$$

Exhibit 4.1 Price elasticity of demand: a worked example

When the price of Matashi 21" colour TVs rose from £160 to £180, demand fell from 3200 to 2800 sets per week. Calculate elasticity of demand:

1 To calculate percentage change in quantity demanded, divide the change in demand ($\Delta Q = 400$) by the original demand ($D0 = 3200$) and multiply by 100:

Numerical value	Graph	Explanation	Term
0		Demand is unresponsive to a change in price	Perfectly inelastic
> 0 < 1		Demand changes by a smaller proportion than price	Inelastic
1		Demand changes by the same proportion as price	Unit elasticity
> 1 < ∞		Demand changes by a larger proportion than price	Elastic
∞		Any increase in price causes demand to fall to zero	Perfectly elastic

Figure 4.3 Elasticity of demand.

2 $400 \div 3200 \times 100 = 12.5$
3 To calculate percentage change in price, divide the change in price ($\Delta P = 20$) by the original price ($P0 = 160$) and multiply by 100:
4 $20 \div 160 \times 100 = 12.5$
5 Elasticity of demand = $12.5 \div 12.5 = 1$

Where demand is inelastic it means that demand is unresponsive to a change in price, whereas elastic demand is more sensitive to price changes. The range of possible outcomes is summarized in Figure 4.3. It should be noted that, since a rise in the price of a good causes a fall in demand, the figure calculated for price elasticity of demand will always be negative. Economists generally ignore the minus sign.

Note that the demand curve, which has elasticity of demand of 1 throughout its length, is a rectangular hyperbola.

Factors affecting price elasticity of demand

The following are the main factors which influence price elasticity of demand:

- necessity of good or service
- number of substitutes
- addictiveness
- price and usefulness
- time period
- consumer awareness

Necessity of good or service

Goods and services which are necessities generally have a lower price elasticity of demand than goods which are luxuries.

Number of substitutes

Goods and services which are provided in conditions of near monopoly tend to have inelastic demand, since the consumer cannot shop elsewhere should prices increase. Competition in a market makes demand more elastic.

Addictiveness

Goods such as cigarettes which are addictive tend to have inelastic demand.

Price and usefulness

Cheap and very useful goods and services tend to have inelastic demand since an increase in a low price will have little impact on consumers' purchasing power.

Time period

Demand elasticity generally increases the more time is allowed to elapse between the change in price and the measurement of the change in demand. This is because consumers may not be able to change their plans in the short run. For example, many holiday-makers book holidays 6 months in advance. Thus a fall in the value of the US dollar might have limited effect on the demand for US holidays in the short run since consumers have committed holiday plans. It may not be until the next year that the full effects of such a devaluation on demand can be measured.

Consumer awareness

Package holidays represent a bundle of complementary goods and services which are bought by consumers, and consumers may be attracted to the bottom-line price of a holiday. Consumers may be unaware of destination prices. For this reason, elasticity of demand for services such as ski passes may be inelastic for UK holiday-makers due to lack of information.

Elasticity of demand and total revenue

The concept of price elasticity of demand is useful for firms to forecast the effects of price changes on total revenue received from selling goods and services, as well as for governments wishing to maximize their tax receipts. Total revenue is defined as:

Total revenue = price × quantity sold

Consider a rise in the price of a good by 10 per cent. If demand is elastic, quantity sold will fall by more than 10 per cent and thus total revenue will fall. However, if demand is inelastic it will fall by less than 10 per cent and thus total revenue will rise.

Similarly, a fall in the price of a good will lead to a rise in total revenue in the case of elastic demand and a fall in total revenue where demand is inelastic. Exhibit 4.2 illustrates the application of these principles to the pricing of admission charges to royal palaces.

Exhibit 4.2   Polishing the crown jewels – David Bowen

Next week, the Queen opens the new Jewel House. The new Jewel House, which has cost £10m, will be run by Historic Royal Palaces (HRP), HRP was set up in 1989 as a 'next steps' agency to look after the Tower, Hampton Court Palace, Kensington Palace state apartments, the Banqueting House, Whitehall and Kew Palace. The agency's staff are civil servants but are not supposed to behave like them.

In 1989, the palaces were generating £11m in revenue, which was topped up with £10m from the taxpayer. This year, despite the recession, turnover is £26m and only £6m is coming from taxes. The trick has been to apply modern management methods to what is, after all, a substantial business. The first stage was market research. This revealed that tourists were not going to boycott the palaces for the sake of a couple of quid, so HRP has increased entrance fees by 50 per cent.

Source: *Independent on Sunday*, 20 March 1994 (adapted).

Exhibit 4.2 implies that market research was used to estimate elasticity of demand for royal palaces, and since it was found to be inelastic, prices were increased. Several other studies have been made into price elasticity of demand in the leisure and tourism sector of the economy. Boviard and colleagues (1984) researched elasticity values for National Trust sites. Time series analysis was used and changes in visitor numbers were compared with changes in admission prices, with account being taken of other factors such as changes in the weather, travel costs, unemployment and inflation. Using data from 1970 to 1980, estimates for price elasticity varied from 0.25 at Wallington to 1.05 at Hidcote, but with most results lying in the inelastic range.

Income elasticity of demand

Income elasticity of demand measures the responsiveness of demand to a change in income. This relationship can be expressed as a formula:

$$\frac{\text{Percentage change in quantity demanded}}{\text{Percentage change in income}}$$

Calculation of income elasticity of demand enables an organization to determine whether its goods and services are normal or inferior.

Normal or superior goods are defined as goods whose demand increases as income increases. Therefore their income elasticity of demand is positive ($+/+ = +$). The higher the number, the more an increase in income will stimulate demand.

Inferior goods are defined as goods whose demand falls as income rises. Therefore their income elasticity of demand is negative ($-/+ = -$).

Knowledge of income elasticity of demand is useful in predicting future demand in the leisure and tourism sector. It also helps to explain some merger and take-over activity as organizations in industries with low or negative income elasticity of demand attempt to benefit from economic growth by expanding into industries with high positive income elasticity of demand. Such industries show market growth as the economy expands. Examples of this include Pearson plc. Pearson owns the Financial Times Group Ltd. (low income elasticity of demand), and has bought into BSkyB Ltd. (high income elasticity of demand). Similarly, First Choice has bought into the cruise market, which promises high income elasticity of demand.

Cross-price elasticity of demand

Cross-price elasticity of demand measures the responsiveness of demand for one good to a change in the price of another good. This relationship can be expressed as a formula:

$$\frac{\text{Percentage change in quantity demanded of good A}}{\text{Percentage change in price of good B}}$$

Cross-price elasticity of demand measures the relationship between different goods and services. It therefore reveals whether goods are substitutes, complements or unrelated.

An increase in price of good B will lead to an

increase in demand for good A if the two goods are substitutes. Thus substitute goods have a positive cross-price elasticity of demand $(+/+ = +)$.

For goods which are complements or in joint demand, an increase in the price of good B will lead to a fall in demand for a complementary good, good A. Therefore complementary goods have negative cross-price elasticity of demand $(-/+ = -)$.

An increase in the price of good B will have no effect on the demand for an unrelated good, good A. Unrelated goods have cross-price elasticity of demand of zero $(0/+ = 0)$.

Demand forecasting

The supply of leisure goods and services cannot generally be changed without some planning. The supply of capital goods such as aircraft requires long planning cycles. Tour operations require considerable planning to book airport slots and hotel accommodation. Equally, leisure and tourism services are highly perishable. It is not possible to keep stocks of unsold hotel rooms, aircraft and theatre seats, or squash courts. Whilst the supply of some leisure goods, such as golf balls and tennis rackets, can be more readily changed, and stocks of unsold goods held over, there is clearly a need for forecasting of demand for leisure and tourism goods and services.

Exhibit 4.3 reports on forecasts from Boeing for aircraft demand.

Exhibit 4.3 Boeing set for take-off

The US-based Boeing Corporation has painted an optimistic picture for the future of the airline industry in its annual civil aviation market outlook. The report forecasts demand for new aircraft of $980bn (£610bn) over the next 20 years. Of this, $731bn-worth of aircraft would be needed to extend airline fleets to meet future passenger growth, whilst $249bn would be needed to replace aircraft which are wearing out.

Boeing, the largest manufacturer of commercial aircraft in the world, bases this figure on its forecast of passenger growth for air travel of around 5 per cent per year over the next 20 years.

This year's outlook represents an important turning point for the industry. Global airline losses, economic recession, the Gulf war and Chernobyl all contributed to a 4-year slump in aircraft sales. But an upbeat spokesman, Mr Richard James, Boeing's vice president of marketing, said that the second half of the 1990s looked more promising.

'The recovery is already well under way in the USA, and the widely held expectation is that Europe is on the road to recovery,' he said. In fact Boeing expects the biggest growth in passengers to take place in Asian markets. Although the Japanese economy is still suffering, the rest of Asia was witnessing a period of strong growth.

Boeing is the largest manufacturer of commercial aircraft in the world.

Source: author, adapted from *Annual Civil Aircraft Market Outlook*, Boeing, May 1994.

Methods for forecasting demand include:

- naïve forecasting
- qualitative forecasts
- time-series extrapolation
- surveys
- Delphi technique
- models

Naïve forecasts

Naïve forecasting makes simple assumptions about the future. At its simplest, naïve forecasting assumes that the future level of demand will be the same as the current level. Naïve forecasting may also introduce a fixed percentage by which demand is assumed to increase, for example 3 per cent per annum.

Qualitative forecasts

Qualitative forecasts consider the range of factors which influence the demand for a good or service, as discussed in Chapter 3. These factors are then ranked in order of importance and each of them is in turn analysed to reveal future trends. Although statistical data may be consulted at this stage, no attempt is made to construct a mathematical formula to describe precise relationships between demand and its determinants. Such forecasts rely on a large measure of common sense and are likely to be couched in general terms such as 'small increase in demand' or 'no change in demand envisaged'.

Time-series analysis

A time series is a set of data collected regularly over a period of time. An example of such data is given in Table 4.6.

Table 4.6   *Time series of sales of a product*

Year	Q1	Q2	Q3	Q4	Total
1	112	205	319	421	1057
2	124	220	350	460	1154
3	90	245	383	503	1221
4	138	267	412	548	1365
5	160	285	450	595	1490

Note: Q1, Q2, etc. = year quarters.

First this data can be seen to exhibit seasonal features. Sales of this product rise within each year to a peak in the fourth quarter and drop back sharply in the first quarter of the next year. Second there seems to be a trend. The figures for each quarter and the yearly totals nearly all display an upward movement. Third, the figure for the first quarter in year 3 does not fit in with the rest of the data and appears as an unusual figure. This may well have been caused by a random variation such as a strike or war or natural disaster.

Forecasting using time-series data first averages seasonal and random variations from the data, to reveal the underlying pattern or trend. The trend can then be used to predict future data, for general yearly totals and adjusted to indicate future seasonal totals. This is illustrated in Figure 4.4 and is a process known as extrapolation.

Time-series forecasting is useful in predicting future seasonal demand and adjusting supply to anticipate seasonal fluctuations. This is particularly important in the leisure and tourism sector where demand tends to be very seasonal (tennis

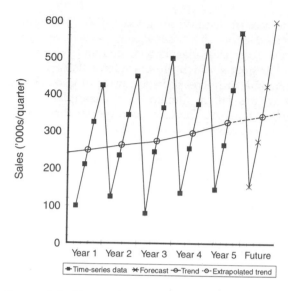

Figure 4.4   Time-series data, trend and forecast.

equipment in early summer, leisure centre use after work and at weekends, and holiday demand).

However care must be taken in using time-series data. Planning ski holiday capacity using time-series data may be useful in predicting market growth, but seasonal fluctuations due to school holidays are not best predicted from past events (which would give the average date) but by looking to see when Easter falls to find the precise date. Equally it is random events that can cause significant changes in the demand for ski holidays. Clearly snowfall and exchange rates are two key factors that cannot be forecast using time-series analysis. It is important therefore that time-series analysis should be used as part of a package of forecasting techniques.

Surveys

Surveys may be carried out by the organization itself or contracted out to a specialist market research organization. Alternatively use may be made of published forecasts constructed using surveys. Surveys can be useful ways of forecasting demand for new or revised products where no time-series data exist. However, survey results are only as valid as their underlying methodology, so care must be taken to ensure that the sample used for the survey is a true reflection of an organization's potential customers, and is of a large enough size to be valid. Additionally a pilot survey needs to be conducted and analysed to iron out any problems of interpretation of words or leading questions. In fact, surveys turn out to be more useful for testing ideas such as advertising campaigns or design, where respondents are asked to choose between real and concrete alternatives. Hypothetical questions are generally used in demand forecasting, and respondents' answers may not necessarily reflect what they would actually do if they had to spend money.

Delphi technique

The Delphi technique is a method of forecasting which attempts to harness expert opinion on the subject. Questionnaires are used to discover opinions of experts in a particular field. The results of the forecasts are then fed back to the participants with the aim of reaching a consensus view of the group.

Modelling

More complex forecasting methods attempt to describe accurately the relationship between demand for a product and the factors determining that demand. They consider a number of variables, and use statistical techniques of correlation and regression analysis to test relationships and construct formulae. Some include econometric techniques which forecast key economic variables such as growth rates, interest rates and inflation rates to construct a comprehensive model which relates general economic conditions to the factors affecting demand for a particular product to the demand forecasts for that product.

Problems with forecasts

There are several problems which arise from using forecasts. First the forecasts are only as good as the assumptions of the model being used. For example. the assumption that the past is a good guide to the future limits the validity of extrapolation using time-series analysis. However, there are equally questionable assumptions included in some very complex models. It is important to know what these assumptions are so that should any of these assumptions prove to be incorrect, forecasts can be re-evaluated.

The major problem, however, is the unpredictability of economic trends and outside events such as wars or strikes or disasters. For example, the recession of the late 1980s undermined the accuracy of many forecasts and caused severe financial problems to those who had relied on overly optimistic predictions of future levels of demand. This does not mean that forecasts are useless, but that those who use them should be constantly monitoring their operating environment to detect any factors which will upset the forecasts they are using.

Sources of forecasts

The following list gives an idea of the range and content of specialist and general sources of forecasts.

Barclays Economic Review (Barclays Bank)

This quarterly review offers a concise forecast for general economic conditions. It contains an economic outlook for the UK, and an international outlook, with forecasts of key economic variables such as exchange rates, income levels, inflation and interest rates for the next 2 years.

Leisure Futures (the Henley Centre for Forecasting)

The Henley Centre provides forecasting services, making particular use of market research. For example, in a 1994 forecast it predicted that the 'rave' music scene would cost the drinks and leisure industry £2bn per year in lost revenue.

Table 4.7   *Forecasts of local entertainment visits (UK adults, millions)*

	1995	1996	1997	1988	1999
Cinema	125	128	133	138	141
Dances/discos	226	228	230	230	231

Source: Leisure Consultants.

Retail Business *(Economist Intelligence Unit)*

Retail Business, published monthly, conducts market surveys, including those in the leisure and tourism sector. For example, its 1994 forecasts for sales of sports footwear predict a rise in sales from £928m in 1995 to £1076m in 1997.

Tourist Intelligence Quarterly *(British Tourist Authority/English Tourist Board (BTA/ETB) Research Services)*

Tourism Intelligence Quarterly provides data and comment on trends in tourism in the UK as well as forecasts. Its estimates for tourist visits to the UK for example are based on a mixed method. Firstly, time-series data are analysed and extrapolated. These are then adapted in the light of the wider knowledge of BTA research staff.

Leisure Forecasts *(Leisure Consultants)*

Leisure Forecasts is an annual two-volume publication which reviews changes in the leisure sector and makes 4-year forecasts with recommendations for action in each market. Table 4.7 illustrates Leisure Consultants' forecasts for cinema and disco visits.

Review of key terms

- Consumer equilibrium = when a consumer's purchases are arranged so as to maximize a consumer's total satisfaction.
- Utility = satisfaction.
- Diminishing marginal utility = the extra satisfaction consumers derive from successive consumption of a good or service tends to diminish.
- Market demand = sum of individual consumers' demand.
- Income effect = change in demand caused by change in income.
- Substitution effect = change in demand caused by change in relative prices.
- Price elasticity of demand = the responsiveness of demand to a change in price.
- Inelastic demand = demand is unresponsive to a change in price.
- Elastic demand = demand is responsive to a change in price.
- Income elasticity of demand = the responsiveness of demand to a change in income.
- Cross-price elasticity of demand = the responsiveness of demand for one good to a change in the price of another good.
- Time series = a set of data collected regularly over a period of time.
- Seasonal variation = regular pattern of demand changes apparent at different times of year.
- Extrapolation = extending time-series data into the future based on trend.
- Delphi technique = finding consensus view of experts.

Data questions

Task 4.1   Teleworking

An office worker who works for 48 weeks a year and has a 90-minute journey to and from work clocks up some alarming statistics. An average of 720 hours each year are spent on commuting. That's 30 whole days.

Over the last decade, commuting has reached new heights, largely because of high inner-city house prices and motorways. Cheaper house prices in out of city locations, together with the development of a comprehensive network of motorways, have encouraged people to increase their time spent on commuting and to cast a wider net in search of well-paid employment.

It may be, though, that we are nearing the peak of commuting. The technological revolution in the office means that the possibility for people to work from home is becoming a reality. Why spend a fortune in time and money sending people to the office, when the office can be sent to the people? The fax, digitalization of information, the telephone network, PCs, modems and video-conferencing are all enabling the spread of teleworking. Meanwhile environmental concerns have encouraged the government to increase taxes to curb the use of car journeys.

Almost half of major UK companies are experimenting with teleworking schemes. This has resulted in the creation of a new class of over half a million full-time teleworkers.

British Telecoms (BT) is a major potential benefactor of increased teleworking, since teleworking means more use of datalinks. However, BT also uses the scheme itself. Directory enquiries operators can now work at home where they have databases with telephone numbers installed on PCs and calls rerouted. To the customer there is no apparent change in service.

The Henley Centre for Forecasting has estimated that more than 15 per cent of hours worked in the UK will be worked from home in the mid 1990s, which translates into a figure of over 3 million people.

The choice for workers looks fairly straightforward. It has been estimated that the overall benefit to a £25 000-a-year employee who is able to work at home for 4 days a week and cut commuting to 1 day a week is of the order of £7080 a year. This is calculated mainly in terms of increased leisure time, priced at £6335.

To these benefits employees can add more flexibility in terms of house location and hours worked, and less commuting stress. On the other hand some psychologists have pointed out the important functions that a place of work may fulfil, particularly pointing to the friendship factor, and the benefits of a physical separation of work and home.

A key question posed by the release of commuting time is how it will be spent. Will people choose to use it as leisure time, or might they instead seek to increase their earnings by working more hours?

Source: the author, from news cuttings, 1994.

Questions

1 Consumer choice theory assumes people act rationally and maximize their total utility. Explain this proposition and discuss whether people who spend 30 days a year commuting fulfil these assumptions.
2 'For individuals, the advantages of teleworking are usually believed to have more to do with quality of life than with economics.' Does consumer choice theory consider the quality of life?
3 The value of the extra leisure time made available to the employee cited above is £6335.
   (a) How might this calculation be made?
   (b) What factors will determine what the person will do with the extra leisure time?
4 If the benefit to individuals of teleworking is so clear, why do not more people telework?

Task 4.2   Elasticity

Table 4.8 records elasticity figures for selected leisure goods and services suggested from recent studies:

Questions

1 Classify these goods as elastic/inelastic/inferior/normal goods.
2 Comment on your findings.
3 What implications do these figures have for policy-makers in organizations in these areas?
4 Devise a method of estimating price and

Table 4.8 *Suggested elasticities for newspapers and recreational goods*

	Price elasticity	Income elasticity
Newspapers	(−)0.34	−0.21
Recreational goods	(−)0.67	1.99

Source: Deaton (1975).

income elasticity of demand for cinema attendance, explaining any problems foreseen.

Task 4.3 Partying 18–30s set to rock the boat

New forecasts talk of 'revolutionary' growth in the cruise market, with passenger numbers and revenues soaring in the next 5 years while prices and holiday-makers' ages drop. Deck quoits are out, discos are in.

Only 80 000 Britons took a cruise 10 years ago, a figure which according to new estimates is set to quadruple to 320 000 this year and more than double again by the year 2000. Figure 4.5 illustrates these trends and forecasts.

The average age of the cruise passenger has already dipped. Forty-somethings are replacing over-60s as the main age range and new ships are being designed with the family in mind. It is the new, younger cruise fans who are putting capacity and revenue projections on full steam ahead.

High-street travel agent Lunn Poly predicts that if, as expected, more than 750 000 UK holiday-makers set sail in 2000, at an average price of £1500 cruising will generate around £1.12bn in revenue. That exceeds the entire non-ski winter overseas holiday market from the UK, which is 3 million strong and generates £1.08bn in revenue.

Cruise giants P&O and Cunard enjoy around 30 per cent UK market share each. The UK's second largest tour operator, Airtours [First Choice] bought a ship from Kloster Cruises ear-

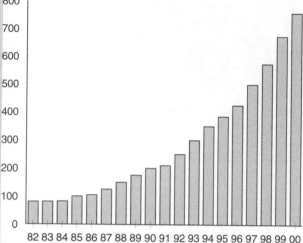

Figure 4.5 UK cruise growth (thousands of passengers), 1982–2000. Source: Lunn Poly.

lier this year and has a competitive 1995 cruise brochure.

Source: *Observer*, 28 August 1994 (adapted).

Questions

1 What additional information would you like before trusting 'new estimates' on cruise market growth?
2 What factors would be taken into account in preparing demand forecasts for the cruise industry?
3 Which organizations will use the above forecasts, and why?
4 What factors might cause the forecasts to be inaccurate?

Task 4.4 Airport traffic reaches new heights

The Department of Transport has published its latest forecasts for air travel up to the period 2010.

Figures for domestic and international

passengers are expected to rise from 106 million in 1992 to around 280 million by 2010. Over the same period, air traffic is expected to grow by up to 163 per cent at an annual rate of between 3.1 and 5.5 per cent, assuming that airport and airspace capacity can meet demand.

The distribution of this growth is likely to reflect faster growth at regional airports such as Manchester, rather than London, and of business rather than leisure passengers.

Source: the author, from Department of Transport Forecasts, 1994.

Questions

1 Evaluate the different methods by which forecasts such as the above can be made.
2 To what extent is it true that forecasts are 'a load of old crystal balls'?
3 Which organizations will find airport traffic surveys useful?

4 What degree of income elasticity of demand would you expect for summer holiday breaks in Bognor?
5 What cross-price elasticity of demand would you expect to find between:
   (a) price of pesetas/holidays in Spain?
   (b) holidays in Spain/holidays in Greece?
   (c) Nintendo games consoles/Nintendo games cartridges?
6 What is meant by extrapolation?

References

Boviard, A., Tricker, M. and Stoakes, R., *Recreation Management and Pricing*, Gower, 1984.
Deaton, A., The measurement of income and price elasticities, *European Economic Review*, 6, 1975.

Further reading

Bomhoff, E., *Financial Forecasting for Business and Economics*, Dryden, 1994.
Henley Centre for Forecasting, *Leisure Futures*, Henley Centre, London, Quarterly.
Johnson, P. and Thomas, B., *Choice and Demand in Tourism*, Mansell, 1992.
Leisure Consultants, *Leisure Forecasts 1993–1997*, from Leisure Consultants, 1993.
Smith, S., *Tourism Analysis*, Longman, 1989.

Short questions

1 What is meant by consumer equilibrium?
2 What is diminishing marginal utility? Are there any exceptions to this?
3 When will a consumer no longer demand a free good?

5

Supply and costs

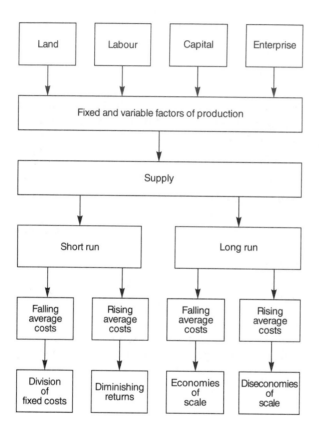

Objectives

Shuttle services such as BA's London to Belfast service operate on a turn-up-and-fly principle, so BA's operations division has to be able to provide a flexible service in order to meet sudden changes in demand. Air traffic control routes across Europe on the other hand are fairly inflexible – they are sometimes unable to cope with sudden surges in demand and this can lead to long delays in peak times of the year. This chapter looks behind the supply curve at issues such

as these. It investigates how easily the supply of leisure and tourism products is able to respond to changes in demand, using models of elasticity. It also considers how an organization's costs respond to changes in output and distinguishes between private costs and social or external costs.

By studying this chapter students will be able to:

- understand and utilize the concept of elasticity of supply
- identify the factors of production
- distinguish between fixed and variable factors of production
- analyse the relationship between costs and output in the short run and long run
- establish the relationship between costs and the supply curve
- understand the reasons for economies of scale
- identify methods and rationale for growth
- distinguish between social and private costs

Price elasticity of supply

Elasticity of supply measures the responsiveness of supply to a change in price. This relationship may be expressed as a formula:

$$\frac{\text{Percentage change in quantity supplied}}{\text{Percentage change in price}}$$

Exhibit 5.1 shows a worked example of how to calculate elasticity of supply.

Exhibit 5.1 A worked example

When the price of Matashi 21″ colour TVs rose from £160 to £180, supply rose from 3200 to 3600 sets per week. Calculate elasticity of supply:

Numerical value	Graph	Explanation	Term
0	P | S	Supply is unresponsive to a change in price	Perfectly inelastic
> 0 < 1	P S	Supply changes by a smaller proportion than price	Inelastic
1	P S S	Supply changes by the same proportion as price	Unit elasticity
> 1 < ∞	P S	Supply changes by a larger proportion than price	Elastic
∞	P S	Suppliers can supply any amount at the current price but none if price falls	Perfectly elastic

Figure 5.1 Elasticity of supply.

1 To calculate percentage change in quantity supplied, divide the change in supply ($\Delta Q = 400$) by the original supply ($S0 = 3200$) and multiply by 100:
2 $400 \div 3200 \times 100 = 12.5$
3 To calculate percentage change in price, divide the change in price ($\Delta P = 20$) by the original price ($P0 = 160$) and multiply by 100:
4 $20 \div 160 \times 100 = 12.5$
5 Elasticity of supply = $12.5 \div 12.5 = 1$

Where supply is inelastic it means that supply cannot easily be changed, whereas elastic supply is more flexible. The range of possible outcomes is summarized in Figure 5.1.

Note that any straight line supply curve passing through the origin has supply elasticity of 1.

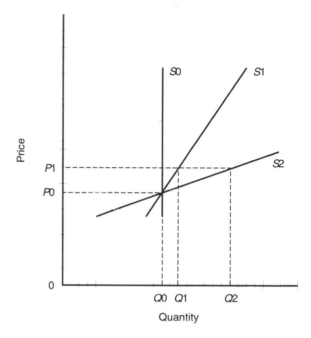

Figure 5.2 The effects of time period on elasticity of supply.

Factors affecting price elasticity of supply

The following are the main factors which influence price elasticity of supply:

- time period
- availability of stocks
- spare capacity
- flexibility of capacity / resource mobility

Time period

Generally the longer the time period allowed, the easier it is for supply to be changed. This is illustrated in Figure 5.2. In the immediate time scale, it is difficult to change supply and thus supply is relatively inelastic, and a change in price of $P0$ to $P1$ results in supply being unchanged at $Q0$ on curve $S0$. In the short run it may be possible to divert production or capacity from another use and thus supply becomes more elastic. This is shown by supply curve $S1$, where a rise in price from P0 to P1 results in a small rise in supply from Q0 to Q1. In the long run it is possible to vary fixed factors of production and increase capacity. Supply is thus more elastic during this time period, as shown by curve S2, where a rise in price from P0 to P1 results in a rise in supply from Q0 to Q2.

Availability of stocks

For manufactured goods the availability of stocks of goods will enable supply to be more flexible and more elastic. Modern 'just-in-time' methods of production are geared towards enabling manufacturing to be more sensitive to market needs without recourse to large stocks.

Spare capacity

The existence of spare capacity either in terms of service capacity or manufacturing capacity will make supply more elastic.

Flexibility of capacity/resource mobility

Flexibility of capacity means that resources can easily be shifted from provision of one good or service to another. Flexible sports halls, for example, enable capacity to be shifted from one leisure service to another to reflect market conditions and thus make supply more elastic. Flexibility of the labour force is also a key factor here.

Changing the supply of specialist goods or services may require the use of specialist skills or machines. These may be difficult or expensive to hire in the short period and hence will tend to make supply inelastic.

Significance of price elasticity of supply to leisure sector

The supply of some tourist attractions is totally inelastic. For example, there is only one tomb of Chairman Mao in Beijing, there is only one Sistine Chapel, and there is only one home of Sir Winston Churchill at Chartwell. It clearly is not possible to replicate these sites as it is for other popular attractions such as Disneyworld.

Considerable thought therefore has to be given to managing such sites. The market could establish an equilibrium if prices were allowed to fluctuate, but the heritage aspect of such sites generally precludes such a solution since they are generally meant to be universally accessible. Inevitably, then, there is excess demand for these sites at the given price and this problem is managed differently at each site. At Mao's tomb, capacity is raised substantially by having the queue divide into two to pass each side of Mao's body. White-gloved attendants furiously wave people by and thus queuing is kept to a minimum despite free admission. At the Sistine Chapel large queues do form, but they are accommodated in an imaginative way by making the detour, through the Vatican museum, to the Sistine Chapel progressively more and more circuitous. The problem of inelastic supply and excess demand at Chartwell is addressed by issuing timed tickets to visitors.

In general terms, price elasticity of supply determines the extent to which a rise in demand will cause either a change in price or shortage. Tour operators generally have relatively fixed capacity in ski resorts, and thus the supply curve is inelastic. When demand rises, for example, during school holiday periods, supply is unable to expand to meet the increased demand and so price changes considerably.

Supply and costs

Leisure and tourism outputs

We need to distinguish between different forms of output in the leisure and tourism sector. Where manufacturing of a product takes place, for example in the production of sports clothing, then output is measured in terms of physical product. Where the provision of a service takes place, output is measured in terms of capacity.

Leisure and tourism inputs

Inputs are classified in economics under the following general headings.

- Land – includes natural resources such as minerals, and land itself and can be divided into renewable and non-renewable resources. Land is a significant resource for tourism.
- Labour – includes skilled and unskilled human effort.
- Capital – includes buildings, machines and tools.
- Enterprise – is the factor which brings together the other factors of production to produce goods and services.

Factors of production are further classified as:

- fixed factors
- variable factors

Fixed factors of production are defined as those factors which cannot be easily varied in the short run. Examples of fixed factors of production in the provision of leisure and tourism services include the actual buildings of theatres and hotels, whilst factories and complex machinery are examples in leisure manufacturing.

Variable factors of production on the other hand can be changed in the short run and include unskilled labour, energy (e.g. electricity, gas, oil) and readily available raw materials. The existence of fixed and variable factors of production means that changes in output will be achieved by different means in the short run and the long run.

Production

Entrepreneurs bring together factors of production in order to supply goods and services in the market and maximize their profits. There are generally several possible ways to produce a given level of output or to provide a service. Profit maximization implies cost minimization and thus entrepreneurs will seek to combine inputs to produce the least-cost method of production.

Input prices themselves are constantly changing to reflect changing conditions in their markets. As input prices change, entrepreneurs will adapt production methods to maintain lowest costs, substituting where possible factors of production which are rising in price with cheaper ones.

Short-run costs

Fixed costs

The existence of fixed factors of production means that the costs associated with that factor will also be fixed in the short run. Such costs are sometimes called indirect costs or overheads since they have to be paid irrespective of the level of production. So, for example, whether a plane flies to New York empty or full, its fixed costs or overheads are the same. Exhibit 5.2 illustrates fixed costs for art galleries.

Exhibit 5.2 Art blossoms out despite bleak picture – Angela Flowers

Nobody could pretend that these have been anything other than terrible times for art galleries. The large buyers have gone into hibernation and there is an endless list of galleries that have gone bust.

There are some frighteningly high fixed costs that have to be paid for before the first painting is sold. Rent and rates have risen dramatically since 1970 and have probably been the main cause of many galleries going out of business. A typical gallery has to budget for three or four catalogues a year at about £12 000 each.

Source: *The Independent*, 16 August 1993 (adapted).

Variable costs

Variable costs are those costs which vary directly with output. They are sometimes called direct costs. For the production of leisure goods they would include raw materials, energy and unskilled labour costs, but for the provision of services such as air transport they are proportionately small and would include such items as meals and passenger handling charges.

Total costs

Total costs are defined as total fixed costs plus total variable costs. This distinction is an important one when deciding whether to continue to operate facilities out of season. A firm which is not covering its costs is making a loss and in the long term will go out of business. However in the short run a firm which is covering its variable costs and making some contribution to its fixed costs may stay in business. This is because it has to pay for its fixed costs anyway in the short run and thus some contribution to their costs is better than none at all.

Average costs

Average costs are defined as total costs divided by output.

Marginal costs

Marginal costs are defined as the cost of supplying one extra unit of output.

Relationship between output and costs in the short run (production)

Figure 5.3 shows a typical short-run average cost curve for the production of goods in the short run.

If a manufacturer has planned for a level of output $OQ0$, then $OC0$ represents the average costs of production. These will represent the least-cost method of production and combination of factors of production, since profit maximization is assumed. However, if the level of output should subsequently be changed in the short run, then by definition only variable factors of production can be changed and fixed factors remain constant. Average costs will therefore rise as the mix of inputs resulting in the least-cost method of production cannot be maintained.

Consider first a fall in output to $OQ1$. Average costs (AC) will rise to $OC1$. This is because the fixed costs will now be borne by a smaller level of output. Similarly, if output rises to $OQ2$, average costs rise to $OC1$. The fixed factors of production

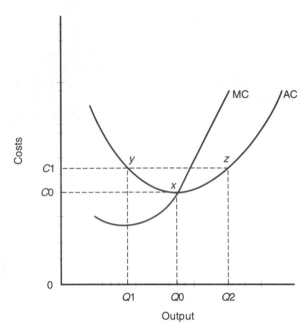

Figure 5.3 Short-run average costs (AC) and marginal costs (MC) for typical manufacturing firm.

become overcrowded and production less efficient. This is related to the law of eventual diminishing returns. The marginal cost curve MC is drawn to fit the above analysis. For mathematical reasons AC is always falling when $MC < AC$; AC is always rising when $MC > AC$, and thus the MC curve always cuts the minimum point of the AC curve.

Relationship between output and costs in the short run (services)

The provision of services often involves different cost relationships from the provision of goods. For a hotel, a theme park or a theatre, for example, fixed costs represent a large proportion of costs in the short run. There also exist some costs which can be termed semivariable costs. These represent capacity that is available only in blocks, such as putting on an extra plane. Variable costs for extra visitors to a theme park or a theatre are negligible up to the capacity level.

Figure 5.4 illustrates typical cost curves for the provision of a service with high fixed costs.

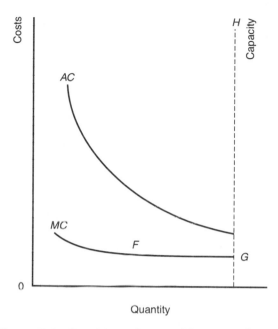

Figure 5.4 Costs for a firm providing a service with high fixed costs. AC = Average costs; MC = marginal costs.

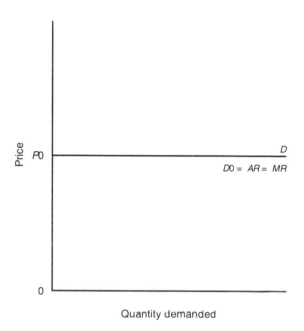

Figure 5.5 Revenue curves under conditions of perfect competition. AR = Average revenue; MR = marginal revenue.

Notice that the average cost curve falls all the way to short-run capacity and that for much of its range the marginal cost is low and constant. The existence of low or sometimes zero marginal costs explains some marketing activity for the service sector. Theatres sell standby seats to students at low prices but students still have to pay full prices for ice creams.

The short-run supply curve under perfect competition

Firms in the private sector will seek to produce at a level of output where profit is maximized. Knowledge of marginal costs and marginal revenue informs this decision. We have already derived a short-run marginal cost curve. Under perfect competition the marginal revenue curve is easily deduced.

A competitive firm will face a perfectly elastic demand curve. This is because, if the firm raised prices, consumers would make their purchases from competing firms. A perfectly elastic demand curve, D0, is illustrated in Figure 5.5.

This shows that the firm can sell as much as it wants at the prevailing market price of P0. This also derives from the fact that, under perfect competition, there are many small firms, none of which are big enough significantly to affect total supply. Therefore if one of these firms increases supply there will be no impact on market price.

Table 5.1 calculates revenue data for a typical firm under perfect competition. As explained above, price remains the same irrespective of output. Recapping, total revenue equals price multiplied by quantity sold, average revenue equals total revenue divided by output and marginal revenue equals the revenue earned from selling one extra unit of output. Thus, if price is £10 per unit, the total revenue from selling three units is £30 and for selling four units is £40, and both average revenue and marginal revenue for selling the fourth unit are £10. It can be calculated that average revenue equals marginal revenue at all levels of output.

Table 5.1   *Revenue for competitive firm (£)*

Output	Price	Total revenue	Average revenue	Marginal revenue
0	10	0	0	–
1	10	10	10	10
2	10	20	10	10
3	10	30	10	10
4	10	40	10	10
5	10	50	10	10

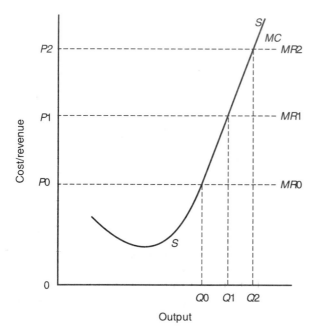

Figure 5.6   Profit-maximizing level of output and supply curve for typical manufacturing firm.

Thus, in Figure 5.5, the demand curve $D0$ is the same as the average revenue curve AR and the marginal revenue curve MR.

Figure 5.6 shows the cost and revenue curves for a typical manufacturing firm operating under conditions of perfect competition. We can now deduce where a profit-maximizing firm will seek to operate. $MR0$ represents marginal revenue at price $P0$ and MC represents marginal costs. At any level of output below $OQ0$, marginal revenue will exceed marginal cost and thus the firm can increase profit by increasing output since extra output is profitable. However, if output is increased beyond $OQ0$, marginal costs exceed marginal revenue, so the firm is making a loss on extra units produced and sold. Thus the profit-maximizing level of output will be at $OQ0$ where marginal costs equal marginal revenue ($MC = MR$).

We can now derive the firm's supply curve. At $P0$, the marginal revenue curve is at $MR0$ and the firm will produce at $Q0$ ($MC = MR0$). At $P1$, the marginal revenue curve rises to $MR1$ and the firm will produce at $Q1$ ($MC = MR1$). At $P2$, the marginal revenue curve rises to $MR2$ and the firm will produce at $Q2$ ($MC = MR2$). Thus the supply curve for a firm operating under conditions of perfect competition is the upward sloping part of its marginal cost curve – SS in Figure 5.6.

Similarly, in Figure 5.4, the curve FGH represents a typical supply curve for a firm providing a service with high fixed costs. The supply curve is elastic up to the point of capacity, when it becomes totally inelastic.

Long-run costs

In the long run all factors of production are variable and so organizations are not faced with the problems of fixed factors or diminishing returns. Output can be satisfied by the most suitable combination of factors of production. Figure 5.7 illustrates three possible ways in which average costs of production may vary with output in the long run.

In curve LRAC1, average costs fall for the entire range as output rises, illustrating economies of scale. In the case of LRAC2, the curve flattens out after point A when constant returns of scale are achieved. For the curve LRAC3, average costs begin to rise again after point A where diseconomies of scale begin to set in.

Internal economies of scale

Economies of scale arise from increases in the size of an organization and can be summarized as follows:

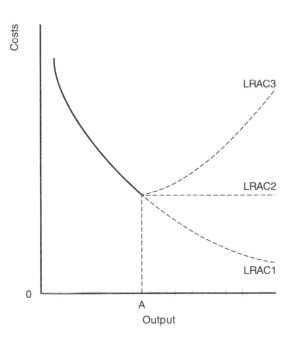

Figure 5.7 Long-run average costs (LRAC).

- financial
- buying and selling
- managerial/specialization
- technical
- economies of increased dimensions
- risk-bearing

Financial

Large organizations tend to have bigger assets. When they borrow money, they often raise large amounts and these two factors lead to financial economies. Borrowing from banks is likely to be at preferential rates of interest reflecting the security offered by large organizations and the amount borrowed. Additionally, larger organizations have the option of raising funds directly from capital markets by, for example, a rights issue of shares which can be an economical method of financing large projects.

Buying and selling

Buying and selling economies arise from buying and selling in bulk. On the buying side this leads to bulk purchase discounts, and on the selling side costs such as advertising are spread out over a large number of sales.

Managerial/specialization

As firms grow the potential for managerial and specialization economies becomes greater. The proprietor of an independent travel agency, for example, will have to act across a range of managerial functions and may lack specialist knowledge. Large travel agency chains such as Going Places, however, will have the scope for employing experts in functional areas such as accounting marketing and personnel.

Technical

Technical economies are also possible as firms grow. These relate in particular to the utilization of complex and expensive technology and machinery. A large hotel may employ a computerized reservations and accounting system since the cost per guest per year will be relatively insignificant. A small boarding house however may have insufficient business to justify the capital outlay.

Economies of increased dimensions

Economies of increased dimensions are well-illustrated by the example of jumbo jets. Although these have the capacity of perhaps three conventional jets, they do not cost three times as much to buy, or staff, or run. Thus the cost per seat of a jumbo jet is less than that in a conventional jet – costs rise proportionately less than capacity.

Risk-bearing

Risk-bearing economies derive from the ability of large organizations to weather setbacks. This arises from two factors. First many large organizations have diversified interests and thus a fall in demand in one area can be compensated for by business elsewhere. Second, large organizations with substantial assets are able to sustain short term losses from their reserves.

External economies of scale

External economies of scale result not from the size of an organization but from the concentration of similar organizations in a particular location. For example, hotels in a particular resort benefit from resort as well as their own advertising, and may attract visitors on the strength of complementary attractions supplied by neighbouring organizations.

Diseconomies of scale

Internal diseconomies

The main reason for the occurrence of diseconomies of scale is managerial capacity. For some organizations, it becomes difficult to manage efficiently beyond a certain size and problems of control, delegation and communications arise. These may become significant enough to outweigh economies of scale generated in other ways. Diseconomies of scale may also arise from growth due to mergers when the two firms find that there is insufficient fit between themselves in terms of systems of management or organizational culture. Exhibit 5.3 illustrates economies and diseconomies of scale at work in leisure industries. Reed Elsevier, incidentally, owns the publishers of this text.

Exhibit 5.3   The perfect couple? – Patrick Hosking

Mergers of equals rarely work. Look at the ghastly marriages of the Nationwide and Anglia building societies, or the Payless and Do It All do-it-yourself chains. Whatever the supposed cost savings and synergies, these are usually outweighed by the culture clash, the communication gap and the messy panic of two lots of managers trying to protect their empires and their jobs.

So I was pretty sceptical when Reed International announced in 1992 that it was merging all its operations with Elsevier of the Netherlands. The new grouping, Reed Elsevier, would have £3bn of sales, producing everything from *Woman's Own* to the *Lancet*. When I put my doubts at the time to Pierre Vinken,

the chairman, he told me this was not the bolting together of two supertankers but 'the mingling of two fishing fleets'. Pretty words, I thought, and waited for the marital fireworks to begin. Irritatingly, all seems to have gone smoothly.

Last week Reed Elsevier announced a stonking set of first-year results. The company has started to exploit scale economies in areas such as paper buying, insurance and bank borrowing. There have been cost savings in the few cases of product overlap. Then there are the less tangible 'strategic benefits'. For example, the new group felt able to acquire a French legal publisher because the Reed people had the legal publishing expertise and their Dutch counterparts were old hands at doing business in France.

So far, so good. But I'm not completely convinced. Reed and Elsevier would still have produced great figures this year had they continued on their separate paths. And the £10m cost savings achieved to date are dwarfed by the £41m paid to the merchant bankers, accountants and lawyers who stitched the merger together.

Source: *Independent on Sunday*, 20 March 1994.

External diseconomies

The negative side of concentration of organizations in a particular area can be overcrowding and the associated congestion costs.

How firms grow

The main methods by which firms grow are by:

- internal growth
- mergers and take-overs

Internal growth is often a slow process and firms can accelerate their growth by mergers and take-overs. The difference between these is that mergers are a joint agreement for two organizations to join together whereas a take-over does not necessarily have the agreement of the target firm.

It is also useful to identify different types of integration:

- vertical integration
- horizontal integration
- conglomerate merger

Table 5.2 *The structure of the package holiday industry*

Britannia Airways	Airtours International	(Air 2000)	
Thomson Holidays	Airtours	(First Choice)	(Best Inspirations)
Lunn Poly	Going Places	(Thomas Cook)	(AT May)

Note: Brackets indicate partial ownership or alliances.

Table 5.2 shows the structure of the package holiday industry in matrix form. The vertical part of the matrix represents the different stages of the industry moving from suppliers at the top, through operators to retailers at the bottom. Note that Thomson and Airtours represent fully vertically integrated groups. The horizontal part of the matrix represents competing firms at each stage of the industry.

Vertical integration

This occurs when a firm takes over or merges with another firm in the same industry but at a different stage of production. It is termed backward integration when the merger is in the direction of suppliers, and forward integration when it is towards the consumer. Thomson Holidays demonstrates a vertically integrated organization with its ownership of a charter airline, Britannia, and travel agency chain, Lunn Poly.

Airtours purchased Pickfords retail travel in 1992 and the Hogg Robinson travel agency chain in June 1993 (see exhibit 5.4), subsequently renaming its acquisitions Going Places.

Exhibit 5.4   Airtours to buy Hogg agencies – Gail Counsel

Airtours is buying Hogg Robinson's leisure arm for £25m cash in a move that will create the UK's second largest travel agency. Last September the tour operator paid £16m for the 334-branch Pickfords travel division.

With 548 outlets Airtours-owned travel agencies will be within a whisker of Lunn Poly, the UK's largest travel agency network, which has more than 600 branches, and considerably larger than Thomas Cook, with only about 350 outlets.

Economies of scale, plus the advantages of being able to sell its own packages through the network, should mean Airtours will be able to boost profitability significantly.

Source: *The Independent*, 15 June 1993 (adapted).

The key motive in forward vertical integration is in ensuring a market for an operators' product. This may be offensive – selling your product at the expense of your rivals – or defensive – making sure your rivals do not monopolize retail outlets and thus block the selling of your product. Backward integration gives your organization control over suppliers, and means that you have better control over quality.

Horizontal integration

This occurs when a firm merges with another firm in the same industry and at the same stage. For example, in January 1993, Airtours made an unsuccessful hostile £215m bid for rival tour operator Owners Abroad. In July 1993 Airtours successfully took over Aspro – Britain's seventh largest tour operator (see exhibit 5.5), and in April 1994 it bought SAS Leisure – Scandinavia's leading tour operator.

Exhibit 5.5   Airtours pays £20m for Aspro Travel – John Shepherd

Airtours, which failed to take over Owners Abroad earlier this year, is paying £20m for Aspro Travel, the seventh-largest tour operator in the UK, with a 4 per cent market share.

David Crossland, chairman of Airtours, the second-largest operator behind Thomson, said: 'Aspro would complement our strengths. It is strong in the Southwest, Wales and number one in Northern Ireland.'

Airtours has more than 15 per cent of the summer holiday market, compared with 29.5 per cent for Thomson and 13.8 per cent for Owners. Aspro is family-run and based in Cardiff. It has 700 employees and sells 400 000 holidays a year.

Source: *The Independent*, 29 June 1993.

Economies of scale is a prime motive for horizontal integration. For example, advertising costs per holiday fall, and bulk purchase discounts can be maximized. Market share and market domination are also key motives. Horizontal acquisition can also occur to purchase firms operating in complementary areas. The interest of Skibound – a winter sport's operator – in taking over a summer holiday operator demonstrates the search for balance throughout the year. There is also scope for cost savings through rationalization of activity and closing down of sites which duplicate work. This has certainly been the case for the Going Places travel agency chain formed from Airtours' acquisitions of Hogg Robinson and Pickfords. Horizontal integration also buys into an existing market and its customers and can be an effective way of reducing competition. One of the arguments made by Stenna Sealink and P&O for merging was the potential for service improvement.

Conglomerate merger

A conglomerate merger or diversification occurs when a firm takes over another firm in a completely different industry. The motives for such activity may include first a desire to spread risks. Second growth prospects in a particular industry may be poor, reflecting a low or negative income elasticity of demand. In such circumstances diversification into an industry with high income elasticity of demand may generate faster growth. W.H. Smith started the Do it All chain of DIY stores for this reason. Third it may be possible to get benefits of synergy, where the benefits of two firms joining exceed their benefits when separate. W.H. Smith opened up W.H. Smith Travel centres within its stores to try to benefit from its captive stationery and newsagent customers. This was not a successful move

but River Island is trying a similar strategy, as illustrated in exhibit 5.6.

Exhibit 5.6   Fashion chain to launch high street travel sales

The River Island Fashion Chain is to be the first High Street retailer to sell an ABTA tour programme through non-travel outlets nationwide. An adventure holiday programme, put together by its sister company IHS travel, is to be sold through the chain's 300 stores. A brochure will carry the branding of the new company, River Island Expeditions.

Source: *Travel Trade Gazette*, 23 March 1994.

Declutter

A problem that may occur from diversification is that an organization may lose sight of its aims and objectives and find strategic management difficult. Under such circumstances 'decluttering' may take place, whereby an organization disposes of its fringe activities and concentrates on its core business.

Social and private costs

Private costs of production are those costs which an organization has to pay for its inputs. They are also known as accounting costs since they appear in an organization's accounts. However the production of many goods and services may result in side-effects. Violent videos may for example result in more violent and antisocial behaviour. A night-club may result in noise pollution. These are classed as external or social costs. They do not appear in an organization's accounts and do not affect its profitability, although they may well affect the well-being of society at large. These issues are discussed more fully in Chapters 7 and 18.

Review of key terms

- Price elasticity of supply = responsiveness of supply to a change in price.
- Factors of production = land, labour, capital and enterprise.

- Fixed factor = one that cannot be varied in the short run.
- Variable factor = one that can be varied in the short run.
- Average cost = total cost divided by output.
- Marginal cost = the cost of producing one extra unit of output.
- Vertical integration = merger at different stage within same industry.
- Horizontal integration = merger at same stage in same industry.
- Conglomerate merger = merger into different industry.
- Private costs = costs which a firm has to pay.
- Social costs = costs which result from output but which accrue to society.

Data questions

Task 5.1 Public services: turning over a new leaf – Cathy Aitchison

Local government officers across England are finalizing their submissions to the Local Government Commission (LGC) ready for the deadline for the counties in the first wave of the local government review. Since 1974, libraries have been the responsibility of the counties, except in London and the metropolitan districts, which are already single-tier, unitary authorities. Two major problems will face the new unitary authorities if library services are devolved to their control. First, whether and how to disaggregate, or split up, centralized resources which have been built up over the past 20 years; and second, how to run a service which is both as comprehensive and as cost-effective as possible.

The Library Association opposes the proposals that place library services under the control of smaller unitary authorities. 'There will be heavy costs of disaggregating specialist stocks, services and staffing, and in some areas, a need for capital investment in new buildings, plant and equipment,' says Ross Shimmon, chief executive of the Library Association. His view

is supported by results of a study of library authorities carried out by researchers at the University of Strathclyde. The researchers found that libraries run by authorities with populations of less than 250 000 are more expensive than those run by larger authorities. 'Our analysis demonstrated fairly consistent evidence of higher resources being necessary to provide broadly average levels of access and usage,' says Professor Arthur Midwinter. 'If a larger number of authorities emerged from the local government review, we would therefore expect to find a higher cost of providing an average service.'

'The Commission has two conflicting targets,' says Jim Miles of Oxford City Council, 'to be as close to the people as possible and to be as cost-effective as possible.' Somerset county librarian, Roger Stoakley, believes that the smaller unitary authorities would have difficulty finding the funds for large rebuilding programmes: 'A new library for Taunton has just been given the go-ahead at a cost of well over £2m – would the smaller organizations have the money to pay for that?'

Source: *The Independent*, 31 March 1994 (adapted).

Questions

1 What are the main arguments in favour of devolving library services to the new unitary authorities?
2 What are the arguments against devolving library services to the new unitary authorities?
3 Are there any ways in which libraries could still benefit from economies of scale even after devolution to the new unitary authorities?

Task 5.2 Branson takes to the airwaves: hopes are high as Virgin Radio begins broadcasting – Patrick Hosking

Two-fifths of business start-ups fail within 3 years. But not, it seems, when Richard Branson has a hand in them. It is hard to find anyone who thinks his new national radio station, Virgin 1215, which goes live at lunchtime tomorrow, will be anything but an airwave-jangling success.

New stations have done well recently. Classic FM guaranteed 2.8 million listeners, achieved 4.3 million and has been able to put up its rate card – the prices it charges advertisers. According to Robert Devereux, chairman of Virgin Radio, the station has already sold 50 per cent of its first-year budgeted airtime sales even before launch. 'I think that must be a record for a media launch', he says.

Virgin 1215 is highly leveraged in the sense that profits grow very quickly once the heavy fixed costs are covered. It is paying £1.8m annually to the Radio Authority plus 4 per cent of advertising sales. It will have spent £2m by this summer in transmission fees to the BBC and others and in improving the quality of the signal. Copyright fees – 'needle time' in DJ argot – are another significant cost. Then there are the 35 staff on the payroll and the costly fees of DJs like Dave Fanning, Chris Evans and Richard Skinner. The news service, bought off the peg from Chiltern Radio, is said to cost £50 000 a year.

The business plan has the station moving into profit in year three. 'I think that's very conservative,' Mr Devereux says. 'Maybe we'll move into profit towards the end of the second year.'

Source: *The Independent*, 29 April 1993 (adapted).

Questions

1 Distinguish between the fixed and variable costs of Virgin 1215.
2 What is the output of Virgin 1215?
3 'Virgin 1215 is highly leveraged in the sense that profits grow very quickly once the heavy fixed costs are covered.' Explain this statement using diagrams.
4 What economies of scale might be open to Virgin 1215, and how would these be achieved?

Task 5.3 Travel industry on journey into the unknown: Airtours' offer for Owners Abroad – Richard Thomson

Airtours announced a bid last Wednesday for its close competitor, Owners Abroad. The Airtours case for take-over is very persuasive. Together, the two companies would have about 27 per cent of the package tour market, representing the first genuine competitive threat to Thomson's dominant 32 per cent share. There ought to be substantial economies of scale and potential cost reductions across the airline and package tour businesses. With the extra market clout of 1.65 million customers a year, the combined company could negotiate lower hotel costs, increasing its profits. There is also a good geographical fit, because Airtours is strong in the north of England and Scotland while Owners is dominant in the south of England.

Owners currently finds itself squeezed within the industry: both Thomson and Airtours now own a package tour supplier, a charter airline to service it, and a chain of retail travel agents to sell the holidays. Owners has the first two, but no travel agency. Thomson's Lunn Poly chain has 25 per cent of the retail market, while Airtours' Pickford chain, acquired last year, has 10 per cent. The agencies sell each other's holidays as well as those of other tour operators, but they are above all captive outlets for the products of their owners. The number of Airtours packages sold through Pickfords, for example, has shot up by 34 per cent since it bought the agency. Of the big three travel companies, therefore, Owners looks by far the weakest – not just in terms of profits but in strategic positioning.

Source: *Independent on Sunday*, 10 January 1993 (adapted).

Questions

1 Distinguish between vertical and horizontal integration in the package tour industry.

2 What specific economies of scale might arise from Airtours' acquisition of Owners?
3 The article describes Owners' weakness as lack of forward vertical integration:
   (a) What does this mean?
   (b) What developments have arisen post-case in this respect?

Short questions

1 Why may an organization's average costs of production rise as output rises in the short run, but fall in the long run?
2 What is the marginal cost of selling an empty seat on a scheduled flight?
3 Distinguish between private costs and social costs in the provision of air travel.
4 How elastic is the supply of:
   (a) CDs?
   (b) Theatre seats?
   (c) Package holidays?
5 Distinguish between vertical and horizontal integration.
6 Why does an organization maximize profits when $MC = MR$?
7 Distinguish between fixed costs, variable costs, the short run and the long run.

Further reading

Lane, H., Marriages of necessity, *Cornell H.R.A. Quarterly*, **27**(1), 1986.
Lee, D., How they started: the growth of four hotel giants, *Cornell H.R.A. Quarterly*, **26**(1), 1985.
Pratten, C., *Economies of Scale in Manufacturing Industry*, Cambridge University Press, 1971.
Sloman, J., *Economics*, Harvester Wheatsheaf, 1994.

6

Pricing and marketing strategy in the real world

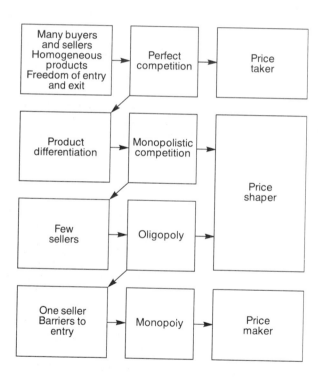

Objectives

In the real world it is often difficult to relate prices to the simple demand and supply analysis presented in Chapter 3.

For example, we find leisure centres and fitness centres offering similar services at vastly different prices. It has been said that an airline running a jumbo jet carrying 350 passengers will charge 350 different prices. Newspapers have been waging a price war that have dragged prices below production costs. Some shops have as many sale and offer days as normal trading days. This chapter investigates how prices are determined in the real world.

By studying this chapter students will be able to:

- understand how and why firms come to be price takers, price makers or price shapers
- analyse the pricing strategies that result from different market situations

Pricing in the private sector

Private sector organizations which seek to maximize profits will attempt to minimize their costs and maximize their revenue.

Revenue is composed of price multiplied by quantity sold, and the price that an organization can charge for its product depends largely on the type of market within which it is operating.

Price takers

Perfect competition

At one extreme, economic theory describes the model of perfect competition. Here firms have to

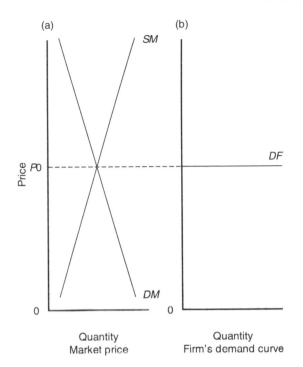

Figure 6.1 (a) The market and (b) the firm under perfect competition. See text for details.

accept the market price, since any attempt to increase their own price over and above market price will lead to consumers purchasing identical goods or services from competitor firms. This is illustrated in Figure 6.1.

Figure 6.1(a) shows the market demand curve *DM*, the market supply curve *SM* and the equilibrium price *P0*. Figure 6.1(b) shows the demand curve faced by an individual firm, *DF*, which is perfectly elastic. What do firms get for their labours in such markets? They get normal profits, defined as that level of return which is just sufficient incentive for a firm to remain in its present business. Any excess profits will lead new firms into the industry and this extra supply will drive prices down to the level where normal profits are restored.

However, whilst free market prices and normal profits are good for consumers, profit-maximizing producers will aim to increase and protect profits. Thus there are few examples in the real world of price takers, and if firms are

not in the fortunate position of being price makers they will generally take steps to become price shapers.

Price makers

At the other extreme from perfect competition, some firms exist in conditions of monopoly or near monopoly and thus have considerable control over prices.

Monopoly pricing

A monopoly is literally defined as one seller, and monopoly power is maintained by barriers to entry into the industry. Therefore the firm's demand curve is the same as the industry demand curve. Because of this, the monopolist is in a position to be a price maker.

There are examples of near-monopolies in the leisure and tourism sector. For example, there are only two car ferry services to the Isle of Wight and these operate on different routes, thus giving each operator some control over price. Unique tourist attractions also have some degree of monopoly power. There is no similar attraction to Madame Tussauds in London, although to some extent the main visitor attractions in London all compete with each other. Table 6.1 shows typical demand data for a unique attraction. It demonstrates the trade-off that a monopoly producer faces – the higher the price, the less the demand.

The price that maximizes total revenue for this organization is one of £5 when a total revenue of £250 per hour is generated. This is illustrated in Figure 6.2. In Figure 6.2(a), *D* represents the firm's demand curve, whilst in Figure 6.2(b), *TR* represents the firm's total revenue curve, found by multiplying quantity sold at each price. Price £5 generates total revenue of £250 per hour, whilst a higher price of £8 or a lower price of £2 causes total revenue to fall to £160.

This confirms the relationship between changes in price, changes in total revenue and elasticity of demand discussed in Chapter 4. Where

Table 6.1   *Monopoly attraction demand data*

Price (£)	Quantity demanded (visitors/hour)	Total revenue	Marginal revenue
10	0	0	
9	10	90	9
8	20	160	7
7	30	210	5
6	40	240	3
5	50	250	1
4	60	240	−1
3	70	210	−3
2	80	160	−5
1	90	90	−7
0	100	0	−9

Notes:
1   Total revenue = price × quantity sold.
2   Marginal revenue = the extra revenue gained from attracting one extra customer ($\Delta TR \div \Delta Q$), where TR = total revenue, and Q = quantity.

demand is inelastic a rise in price will cause an increase in total revenue. Where demand is elastic, a fall in price will cause an increase in total revenue. Profit maximization therefore occurs where demand elasticity is (−)1. In Figure 6.2 the demand curve is elastic in the range X to Y, inelastic in the range Y to Z and has unit elasticity at point Y.

To summarize, monopolists can choose a price resulting in high profits, without fear of loss of market share to competitors. The actual price chosen will reflect both demand conditions and the firm's cost conditions. Exhibit 6.1 demonstrates BAA's market power at Heathrow.

Exhibit 6.1   BAA seeks to raise charges at Heathrow – Michael Harrison

BAA, the airports operator, is asking the government for authority to increase airline charges at Heathrow and impose restrictions on which aircraft may use the airport. BAA has proposed that it be allowed to 'premium price' at Heathrow to reflect its position as the world's busiest international airport. BAA announced

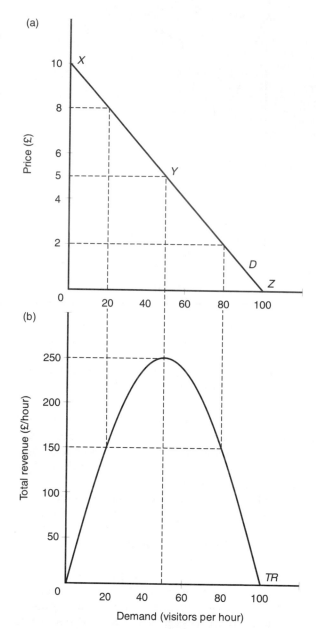

Figure 6.2   (a) Demand and (b) revenue-maximizing price for monopolist.

a near 50 per cent increase in pre-tax profits last year to £285m.

Source: *The Independent*, 8 June 1993 (adapted).

Price discriminating monopolist/yield management

Some firms sell the same good or service at different prices to different groups of people. For example, BA return fares from London to New York (summer 1995) are: £4026 (first class), £2208 (club class), £844 (standard economy), £438 (Super APEX), £84.40 (staff 10 per cent standby) and £0 (staff yearly free standby/holders of airmiles or frequent flyer miles).

In fact BA is not a monopolist since there is much competition on this route, but most fares are subject to International Air Transport Association (IATA) regulation and thus many firms are able to act as monopolists. It should also be recognized that the fare differential for club and first-class passengers is not strictly price discrimination since these represent different services with different costs. But since all economy-class passengers receive an identical service, why should BA charge different prices and why do passengers accept different prices?

The conditions for price discrimination to take place are:

- The product cannot be resold. If this were not the case, customers buying at the low price would sell to customers at the high price and the system would break down. Services therefore provide good conditions for price discrimination.
- There must be market imperfections (otherwise firms would all compete to the lowest price).
- The seller must be able to identify different market segments with different demand elasticities (for example, age groups, different times of use).

Figure 6.3 illustrates a typical demand curve for economy-class travel. If a single price of £500 is charged as in Figure 6.3(a), then 250 seats are

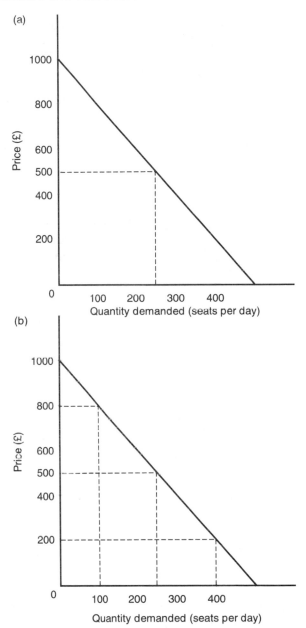

Figure 6.3 (a) Single price and (b) price discrimination.

sold and total revenue is £125 000. Figure 6.3(b) shows a situation in which three prices are charged. One hundred seats are sold at £800, the next 150 seats are sold at £500 and the next 150 seats are sold at £200, producing a total revenue of £185 000, an increase of £60 000 over the single-price situation.

Airlines must consider the behaviour of costs when price-discriminating. Once the decision has been taken to run a scheduled service, marginal costs are low up until the aircraft capacity, when there is a sudden large jump. Airlines are able to discriminate by applying travel restrictions to differently priced tickets. So, for example, full-fare economy tickets are fully refundable and flights may be changed at no cost. Cheaper tickets are non-refundable and have advance purchase and travel duration restrictions. Exhibit 6.2 describes a typical example of price discrimination.

Exhibit 6.2 Special report on business travel – John Law

The fare shown on a ticket for the 8000-mile round trip between Gatwick and Atlanta USA is £818, but over £600 was saved by buying it through a discount agent. And not a dodgy backstreet operation – £211 to Thomas Cook. If BA had not been prepared to discount so heavily, a dozen other carriers would have been prepared to sell a ticket for much less than the official fare.

Source: *The Independent*, 16 November 1993.

Yield management is a sophisticated form of price discrimination. Computer technology is able to identify patterns of demand for a particular product with its supply. A request for a hotel reservation or an airline ticket will result in the system suggesting a price that will maximize the yield for a particular flight or day's reservations.

Price shapers

Whilst firms operating under conditions of perfect competition are price takers and those operating under conditions of monopoly are price

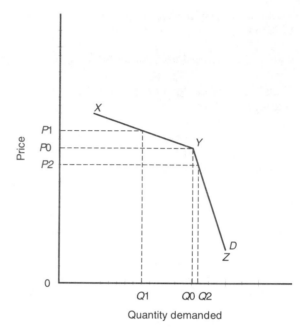

Figure 6.4 The kinked demand curve.

makers, firms operating in markets between these two extremes can exert some influence on price. The two main market types which will be examined are:

- oligopoly
- monopolistic competition

Oligopoly pricing

An oligopoly is a market dominated by a few large firms. An example of this is the cross-channel travel market. Oligopoly makes pricing policy more difficult to analyse since firms are interdependent, but not to the extent as in the perfectly competitive model. The actions of firm A may cause reaction by firms B and C, leading firm A to reassess its pricing policy and thus perpetuating a chain of action and reaction. For these reasons firms operating in oligopolistic markets often face a kinked demand curve. This is illustrated in Figure 6.4.

Consider the demand curve D, which might illustrate the demand curve for a cross-channel car ferry firm. The prevailing price is $P0$. Notice that the demand curve is elastic in the range X to Y. This is because, if a firm decides to increase its price, for example from $P0$ to $P1$, it will lose customers to its competitors and demand will fall sharply from $Q0$ to $Q1$ and the firm will suffer a fall in total revenue. On the other hand, if it should decide to reduce its price from $P0$ to $P2$, it is likely that its competitors will match the reduction in price to protect their market share, and there will be only a small increase in demand from $Q0$ to $Q2$, resulting in a fall in the firm's revenue. Thus the demand curve is inelastic in the range Y to Z, and the demand curve is kinked at point Y. In this situation it is clearly not in the interests of individual firms to cut prices, and thus such markets tend to be characterized by price rigidities.

Marketing and competition under oligopoly conditions are often based around:

- advertising
- free gifts and offers
- quality of service or value added
- follow-the-leader pricing – pricing is based on the decisions of the largest firm
- price wars occasionally break out if one firm thinks it can effectively undercut the opposition

Monopolistic competition

This is a common type of market structure, exhibiting some features of perfect competition and some features of monopoly. The competitive features are freedom of entry and exit and a large number of firms. However, firms which are operating in essentially competitive environments may attempt to create market imperfections in order to have more control over pricing, market share and profits.

It is competition from other sellers with homogeneous products that forces market prices down, and thus firms will often concentrate on these two issues in order to exert more market power. The more inelastic a firm is able to make its demand curve, the more influence it will have

on price, and thus firms will attempt to minimize competition by:

- product differentiation
- acquisitions and mergers
- cost and price leadership

Product differentiation

The rationale for product differentiation is to make the demand for a good or service less elastic, giving the producer more scope to increase prices and/or sales and profits. There are a number of routes to product differentiation.

The first is by advertising. One of the aims of persuasive advertising is to create and increase brand loyalty even if there are no major differences between a firm's product and that of its competitors.

The second route to product differentiation is through adding value to a good or service. This may include, for example, making improvements to a good or service or adding value somewhere along the value chain. The value chain can be thought of as all the interconnecting activities that make up the whole consumer experience of a good or service. Table 6.2 demonstrates aspects of the value chain for BA Club World.

Exhibit 6.3 shows how Virgin has opened a new lounge at Heathrow airport for its 'upper class' customers, thus adding value to, and differentiating, its product.

Exhibit 6.3 A better class of purgatory: airport lounges, don't you just hate them? – Jonathan Glancey

The airport lounge is the nearest most of us get to purgatory in this life. However, Richard Branson, the toothsome hero of the transatlantic hop, has devised a brand new breed of airport lounge. This week at Heathrow's Terminal Three, the Clubhouse opened for Virgin Atlantic's 'Upper Class' passengers. This is how the Clubhouse differs from limbo and purgatory.

It begins unpromisingly, as passengers climb stairs covered in carpet that has more power to distract than a Bridget Riley. One of a harem of Mandys in tight red takes your boarding card and points you to the

Table 6.2   *Value chain for BA Club World*

Pre-sales	Pre-check-in	Check-in	Flight	Arrival	Post-flight
Advertising	Valet parking	Dedicated check-in	Dedicated cabin	Rapid transit arranged to city centre	Frequent-flyer awards
		Express security/ passport route	Luxury meal Seat size		Complaints procedure
		Dedicated lounge	Increased staff ratio		

bar. By the time you are leaning against a bar top decorated with imitation Art Deco lamps, the barman not only knows your name but can mix you a real dry martini in a properly chilled glass. So far, you might think, so good.

Propping yourself up by the model railway, you take in the Virgin hot-air balloon making its way backwards and forwards across the ceiling. On the other side of the train set is a pinball machine, followed by a bank of video machines under a starry ceiling. Sit in an old dentist's chair and gawp at your choice of Mr Bean, The Stones in the Park, Captain Scarlett or Abba's Greatest Hits. Play one of a number of idiot games on computer screens opposite or climb a brown spiral stair laced with plastic ivy and plane-spot from a tiny observatory armed, courtesy of Mr Branson, with a pair of vintage T B Winter & Son binoculars and Virgin's *Flyer's Handbook*.

Back downstairs you can play chess or browse through shelves of second-hand books in the library. There is art everywhere and all of it is for sale. If you want a rest, have a real one, with a massage under soft blue light to the sound of whale song. Now, head past a 'Manneken-Pis' fountain to the lavatories. These are grand in a Grand Hotel way, and not a little over the top. Next stop, the telephone. Calls can be made using the latest technology while lying on a daybed. There are antique desks to work at in the study along past the bar (time for a whisky sour) and fax machines galore. And finally, after a spell at work, you flop out in the music room.

Source: *The Independent*, 27 February 1993.

The point of adding value and differentiating product is that it enables firms to charge a premium price but still retain customers.

Acquisitions and mergers

These are discussed in detail in Chapter 5, but they are an important consideration in pricing strategy as they can:

- reduce competition (and thus reduce downward pressure on prices)
- lead to economies of scale (which can underpin price leadership strategies)

Cost and price leadership

Another key strategic move to increase market share and profitability is through cost and price leadership. Cost leadership involves cutting costs through the supply chain – squeezing margins from suppliers, and economizing where possible in the production of goods or provision of services by stripping out unnecessary frills. The aim of cost leadership may be to increase margins but this is unlikely to be achieved since consumers are likely to resist lower quality of goods or services without any compensation in price.

Equally it is difficult to maintain cost leadership since other firms will attempt to achieve similar cost reductions. However, where cost leadership is translated into low prices it may be possible to increase market share. This can then lead to the creation of a virtuous circle where increased market share leads to economies of scale which enable lower costs and thus lower prices to be maintained ahead of rival firms. There has been a considerable battle for market share in the package holiday industry, as illustrated in exhibit 6.4.

Exhibit 6.4   Thomson promises to remain cheapest until 21st century

Thomson has sent out a clear warning to nearest rivals such as Airtours that it will never be beaten on price over the next decade.

Although not specifically mentioning closest rival Airtours, managing director Mr Newbold said: 'To those competitors which think that Thomson's low prices in 1994 are just a short term measure and the umbrella of high prices will return, think again. Thomson's low prices are here to stay. We intend to be the number one choice well into the 21st century'.

Source: *Travel Trade Gazette*, 4 May 1994.

Exhibit 6.5 reports Compaq Computer's price leadership strategy for raising profits.

Exhibit 6.5   Price war pays off as Compaq doubles sales – Larry Buck

New York – Compaq Computer emerged as one of the few victors from the price wars raging in the personal computer industry yesterday, reporting sharply higher second-quarter profits on sales that were double their year-ago turnover. The Houston-based manufacturer earned $102m, or $1.21 a share, compared with $29m, or 35 cents a share, for the same period in 1992.

Compaq started the price war almost two years ago, aggressively cutting its own production costs in a bid for greater market share. Yesterday it reiterated its goal of becoming the world's Number One PC manufacturer. 'The PC industry continues to be highly competitive, but clearly Compaq's business strategy has positioned the company to be a winner in the current industry consolidation,' Eckhard Pfeiffer, chief executive, said in a statement.

Source: *The Independent*, 22 July 1993.

Pricing in the public sector

Prices of public sector goods and services will depend upon the market situation which pre-

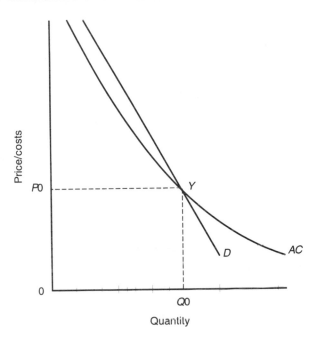

Figure 6.5   Break-even pricing.

vails in a particular industry as well as the objectives set for a particular organization. These might be:

- profit maximization
- break-even pricing
- social cost/benefit pricing

Profit maximization

In the case of profit-maximizing aims, an organization's pricing policy will follow the pattern set out earlier in this chapter.

Break-even pricing

Break-even pricing aims at a price which is just sufficient to cover production costs rather than one which might take advantage of market imperfections and maximize profit. Figure 6.5 illustrates a firm with average costs of AC and a demand curve D. At price $P0$ total revenue is $0 - P0 \times 0 - Q0$, and total cost is $0 - P0 \times 0 - Q0$

and thus the firm is breaking even. Any price higher than *P*0 would result in extra profit and any price below *P*0 would result in losses.

Social cost/benefit pricing

Where the aim of public provision is to take fuller account of public costs and benefits, the supply will be subsidized to produce a price either lower than market price (partial subsidy) or at zero price (total subsidy). More detailed analysis of this can be found in Chapter 7.

Pricing and the macroeconomy

The condition of the economy at large also has an influence on firms' pricing policy. If the demand in the economy is growing quickly, there may be temporary shortages of supply in the economy and firms will take advantage of boom conditions to increase prices and profits. Similarly, during a recession there may well be overcapacity in the economy and demand may be static or falling. These conditions will force firms to have much more competitive pricing policies to attract consumers.

Review of key terms

- Price taker = a firm in a perfectly competitive market which cannot directly influence price.
- Price maker = a firm in a monopoly market which sets its desired price.
- Price shaper = a firm in an oligopoly or imperfectly competitive market which may seek to influence price.
- Perfect competition = many buyers and sellers, homogeneous products, freedom of entry and exit to market.
- Monopoly = one seller, barriers to entry.
- Oligopoly = a small number of powerful sellers.
- Monopolistic competition = many buyers and sellers, freedom of entry and exit, products differentiated.

- Product differentiation = real or notional differences between products of competing firms.
- Price discrimination = selling the same product at different prices to different market segments.

Data questions

Task 6.1　Is Eurotunnel in too deep?: The £10bn venture needs half the Channel traffic by 1996 – Patrick Hosking

The tunnel is dug, the track laid, the rolling stock ordered, the travel agents briefed, the tickets on sale. The Channel Tunnel is no longer a dream. Eurotunnel last week unveiled its eagerly awaited fare structure for Le Shuttle, but the biggest uncertainty remains – will the punters actually use the thing?

Eurotunnel has set itself ambitious targets. Not only does it plan to capture 50 per cent of the cross-channel cake by 1996, it also expects the very fact of its opening to enlarge the cake substantially. Customers will have to flock to the tunnel in droves. The fares for Le Shuttle, the train that will ferry motorists and their cars under the Channel, have been set higher than expected. They range from £125 return for a carload in winter to a peak price of £310. Most are a little higher than the equivalent ferry fare.

There was an almost audible sigh of relief from the Channel ports as Christopher Garnett, Eurotunnel's commercial director, outlined the structure; at least the tunnel was not trying to undercut the ferries. Asked by the *Independent on Sunday* whether Eurotunnel would respond if the ferries cut their fares, Mr Garnett said: 'We would not be following. We're not going to get involved with price wars. We're not going to get involved in discounting.'

Richard Hannah, an analyst with UBS and a close follower of Eurotunnel, is sceptical: 'I'm convinced there will have to be a price war because of the excess capacity created by the tunnel.' He said fares would have to come down sharply to generate the extra volumes needed to meet Eurotunnel's ambitious revenue targets. 'Even if Eurotunnel captured the entire existing cross-channel business from the ferry companies, it would still not generate enough revenues even to cover its costs.' He argued that Eurotunnel had to create a fresh wave of demand for cross-channel travel, and it could only do that by cutting prices.

The ferry companies, which have had years to ready themselves for the onslaught, are well-prepared and well-financed, and will not give up their customers – and £600m-plus of annual revenues – without a fight. Eurotunnel expects to earn its revenues from three main sources: Le Shuttle for car passengers; the Paris–London passenger service; and freight. Le Shuttle will be much the most important, accounting for well over half of all expected revenues. By 1996, Eurotunnel expects to carry 8 million car passengers and their vehicles across the Channel. That compares with the 18 million who made the trip by ferry last year from the Channel ports. In addition to Le Shuttle, British Rail and its French equivalent SNCF will operate high-speed trains between Paris and London under the Eurostar name. The railways hope to compete for business travellers, poaching passengers from the airlines. The third income strand for the tunnel – freight – will come from dedicated Le Shuttle freight trains, carrying lorries on flat cars, and ordinary freight trains run by the national railways.

Freight and Eurostar will make a useful contribution to Eurotunnel's coffers, but Le Shuttle will make or break the company. It is spending £25m advertising the service across Europe. Mr Garnett sees Le Shuttle's advantages over ferries as speed, convenience and reliability. But one independent survey suggests that most people in the UK are lukewarm and of 932 randomly selected adults half of them felt it could be a target for terrorists. On perceived safety, the tunnel came out roughly as risky as the ferries.

The other unknown quantity in the calculation is the response of the ferry companies and the ports. According to chairman Mr Dunlop, P&O has spent £400m over the past 5 years modernizing its fleet. 'We've revolutionized the ferry industry in the last 5 years, creating an attractive product.' Certainly its newer vessels, such as the Pride of Dover and the Pride of Calais, are a far cry from the shabby, vomit-smelling, beer-soaked, cramped, crowded tubs that used to ply their trade across the Channel. 'The ferry crossing is now part of the holiday,' said Mr Dunlop.

Under or over the Channel?

	Le Shuttle	Car ferry
Return fare in winter	£220	£126–139
Return fare in summer	£280	£139–220
Return peak season	£310	£289–320
Motorway to autoroute	1 hour	2 hours
Comfort	Own car seat	Lounges
Sea view	None	Yes
Frequency	Up to 4 per hour	Every 1½ hours
Reliability	Weatherproof	Weather worry
Booked trips	No	Yes
Restaurants	No (in terminal)	Yes
Shopping	No (in terminal)	Yes
Yob density	Middling	High
Social cachet	High initially	Negative

Source: *Independent on Sunday*, 16 January 1994 (adapted).

Questions

1 What degree of competition exists in the cross-channel market?
2 Explain why the Channel Tunnel's initial strategy is not price-based.
3 What elements of product differentiation strategy are illustrated?
4 What have been the key factors affecting

price in the cross-channel market since the date of this article?

Task 6.2   Repairing the damage of a discount disaster – Heather Connon

The deepest recession since the war – and particularly the slump in the housing market, on which much of its business depends – has left the do-it-yourself industry bruised and battered. Virtually all the leading players have been forced to re-examine their strategies in the hope of rebuilding their profits. The impact of the slump on the big companies was graphically illustrated in last week's results from Texas Homecare, the Ladbroke subsidiary. Operating profits slumped from £43.6m to £7.8m. Texas is not alone in its bad results but its rivals would say it is responsible for making things worse than they needed to be.

Two years ago, Texas started a fierce price war with the launch of discount weekends, offering shoppers 20 per cent off everything. Its aim was simple. Texas is the second-largest DIY retailer, with 9.7 per cent of the market, compared with 14.7 per cent for B & Q. It wanted to close that gap by stealing some of B & Q's market share. Not surprisingly, B & Q retaliated by offering still lower prices on its own discount weekends.

Profits and margins at both companies dropped, as did as those of smaller rivals – most notably Do-it-All, the joint venture between W.H. Smith and Boots – which were dragged into the fray. While it may have encouraged some shoppers to buy more than they needed in the short term, the long-term effect was damaging. John Coleman, who took over as managing director of Texas last September, believes the effects are still being felt. 'It has significantly devalued the market. Lots of our products are now cheaper than they were two years ago, even after inflation which, contrary to what the commentators say, has not disappeared.' He points to paint, where discounting was fiercest. 'Prices were hit very badly, but there has been no increase in volume.'

Texas is planning dramatic changes to restore the group's profits. These are likely to include re-examining its position in the market as well as its product range. Texas offers a wider range of soft furnishings and home improvement products, putting it at the softer end of the market compared with competitors like B & Q and Wickes. Mr Coleman expects to abandon up to a quarter of its current lines and is likely to drop some of its 350 suppliers.

Texas's troubles may be severe, but they are as nothing compared with Do-it-All's. Formed through the merger of Boots' Payless and W.H. Smith's Do-it-All four years ago, it has suffered from putting together two weak brands and from combining two different management styles. In the year to last March, it lost £28.8m and little improvement is expected in the current year. Like Texas, it is making strenuous efforts to improve its positioning. It is introducing 'new concept' stores, in which products are grouped by projects such as paving or patio-building, and expert advice is on hand. It is also planning to sell up to half of its stores which cannot be adapted to that approach.

B & Q has not been immune to the problems afflicting the industry. While it has remained profitable, the £81.1m earned in the year to January 1993 was 15 per cent below the 1991 peak, despite expansion in the number of stores. Like the others, it too is re-examining its strategy. It is attacking the market on two fronts. First, it is pioneering the strategy of everyday low pricing which its parent, Kingfisher, is introducing throughout its retail chains. That means permanent price reductions on 500 key products under the slogan Key DIY. The group hopes that price promise will gain it enough extra volume to compensate for the lower prices. Its other strategy has been imported from the US. It is opening superstores called Depot that are up to 90 000 square feet, double the size of its traditional stores, offer 50 per cent more items and have staff on hand to advise on everything from plumbing to carpentry. Most important of all, however, its prices are cheaper than traditional B & Q outlets because the scale of the business means it can be run more efficiently.

The efforts of B & Q, Texas and Do-it-All to differentiate themselves may be drawing on the example set by Homebase and Wickes, two of the most successful DIY chains. Both stayed out of the price war but the strength of their offer and knowledge of their target market meant they survived rivals' discounting relatively unscathed.

Homebase, the J Sainsbury subsidiary, is under no illusions about its position: 'We are very clear we are aiming at the home enhancement and gardening market, not at the builder,' said Ross McLaren, deputy managing director. It has placed great emphasis on gardening, which accounts for about 30 per cent of its sales, and has a number of concessions – like Laura Ashley and Sharps furniture – which give the stores a more upmarket feel than its rivals.

Wickes is at the opposite end of the scale. It aims for builders and serious DIY-ers and has only a limited range of products – fewer than 4000, compared with more than 40 000 at B & Q depots. Wickes also issues catalogues with prices that are valid for about eight weeks, making short-lived special offers difficult. 'Our prices have to be good, because we are giving them to competitors,' said Henry Sweetbaum, Wickes' chief executive. 'And we felt that if we did anything like discount weekends, we would have lost credibility with our core customers.'

Clive Vaughan of Verdict Research, the retail consultancy, believes that recovery in the housing market should be enough to guarantee the industry a few years of growth – at least 8 per cent for the next three years. Whether that will be enough to go round – particularly as Magnet is likely to re-emerge as a player following its acquisition by Berisford – remains to be seen.

Source: *The Independent*, 10 March 1994.

Questions

1 Describe and explain the strategies adopted by the main players in the DIY market.
2 Evaluate which of these strategies is likely to be successful.

Task 6.3 Fidelity can equal free flights – Simon Calder

My bank account may not be healthy, but I am heavily in credit with several organizations, reports Simon Calder. I have 52 593 Continental one pass miles, four United 5000-mile award cheques, 1100 Virgin freeway points and 1648 BA air miles. Frequent flyer miles are a simple concept. The more you travel with a particular carrier, the more you are rewarded for your loyalty. Usually the award is another flight. As far as the carrier is concerned, the idea is that you will fill a seat which would otherwise be empty.

The bottom line, for the passenger and the airline, is – do the schemes work? For passengers, the answer is a resounding 'yes': you can get something for nothing, though it might not be a flight at the ideal time. For the airlines, the rewards are harder to define. Now that most carriers operate a frequent flyer scheme, passengers just take whatever is offered by each carrier and travellers are becoming more fickle.

Source: *The Independent*, 23 April 1993 (adapted).

Questions

1 What are the short-run and long-run benefits to airlines of operating frequent flyer miles incentives?
2 What are the costs to airlines of operating such schemes?
3 Evaluate frequent flyer incentive schemes in relation to other marketing techniques for increasing airlines' profits.
4 Why was the Hoover free flights scheme a fiasco?

Task 6.4 Special report on long-haul air travel – David Richardson

There's nothing quite like the threat of increased competition to inspire lower fares and improved services on airlines.

Travellers to South Africa have benefited

more than most over the last year with the arrival of new carriers keen to secure a foothold in a market with real money-spinning potential. BA and South African Airways (SAA), the established operators out of the UK, have increased departures, upgraded their quality of service and slashed fares since the South African government opened its skies to other carriers.

They aim to counter bargain-basement fares offered by upstarts such as Air Namibia – and to nip in the bud Richard Branson's African ambitions. It is now possible to fly between London and Johannesburg for as little as £419 return on a discounted Olympic Airways ticket. Both BA and SAA are acknowledged as offering a good business-class product to South Africa. The published return fare is £1835, though this is available at a discounted £1605.

One airline the others are watching is Virgin Atlantic, which aborted its attempt to launch a South Africa route last November. 'We were not frightened off by the political situation, or by BA and SAA's announcement of some very startling fares in the month we were due to launch,' says Virgin's route planning director Ed Hullah. 'There simply were no slots available at Heathrow. We still want to operate to South Africa, though nothing is likely to happen until next year at the earliest.'

Source: *The Independent*, 23 April 1993 (adapted).

Questions

1 How has the market structure changed for UK–South Africa air travel?
2 Account for the different levels of fares on this route.

3 Why might BA and other carriers wish to exclude Virgin from this route? How might they attempt to exclude Virgin?

Short questions

1 What kind of market structures do the following operate in:
    (a) Package tour operators?
    (b) London five-star hotels?
    (c) Brewers?
    (d) McDonalds?
2 Explain the elasticity of demand of a kinked demand curve.
3 Why will a monopolist choose not to produce in the inelastic range of its demand curve?
4 Why are there so few examples of perfectly competitive markets?
5 Under what circumstances is price leadership likely to lead to increased profits?

Further reading

Economist Intelligence Unit, *Developing Strategies for the World's Airlines*, EIU, 1989.
Gialloreto, L., *Strategic Airline Management: The Global War Begins*, Pitman, 1988.
Johnson, G. and Scholes, K., *Exploring Corporate Strategy*, Prentice Hall, 1993.
Lickorish, L. and Jefferson, A., *Marketing Tourism*, Longman, 1991.
Middleton, V., *Marketing in Travel and Tourism*, Butterworth-Heinemann, 1994.
Scottish Sports Council, *Differential Charges*, Scottish Sports Council, 1992.

7

Market intervention

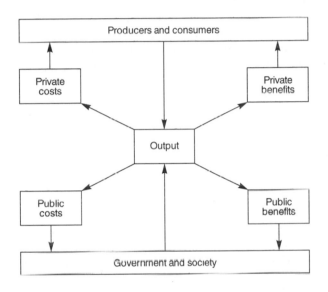

Producers and consumers

Private costs — Private benefits

Output

Public costs — Public benefits

Government and society

Objectives

The price mechanism as described in Chapter 3 seems to offer a simple yet effective system of signalling consumer demands to producers. It is often contrasted with systems of state planning – particularly as practised in former communist eastern Europe. Many commentators noted that the Berlin Wall was built to stop people escaping from eastern Europe to western Europe, not the other way round. The economic landscape of eastern Europe was characterized by queues for goods and services, empty shops, shoddy goods and service sector workers who exhibited indifference to their customers. Exhibit 7.1 illustrates some of the problems encountered by tourists to communist Cuba.

Exhibit 7.1 *Game for a fistful of dollars*

With their sandals, shorts and insect repellent, Ann and Tony Crossley booked into the El Paradiso hotel, in Cuba's premier resort. 'As a tourist, it's all right if you don't expect too much' said Tony, and since the British tour group arrived their Airtours representative had been filing complaints.

First the swimming pool was closed for 5 days. Then a pack of dogs invaded the dance floor and then there was the smell of rotten eggs – the byproduct of nearby oil exploration.

Source: *The Observer*, 26 June 1994 (adapted).

Free market economies, on the other hand, boast shops full of attractive consumer goods, few queues and a world of slick advertising. However critical analysis of the market mechanism raises issues of concern. Sex tourists to Thailand signal an effective demand for prostitution which suppliers satisfy. Similarly, the demand for snuff, and child pornography videos, and for addictive drugs is met by the operation of market forces. The market has also created the tower blocks of Benidorm.

The objectives of this chapter are first to examine whether leisure and tourism provision should be left to the free market, and second to consider reasons for, and forms of, market intervention.

After studying this chapter students will be able to:

- evaluate the benefits of the free market
- evaluate the problems of the free market
- understand the methods of market intervention

- justify market intervention
- understand recent developments in public sector provision

The free market

The benefits of free markets

Adam Smith wrote in *The Wealth of Nations* of the main benefits of the free market. He drew attention to the fact that people exercising choice in the market in pursuit of their own self-interest led to the best economic outcome for society as a whole. The concept that 'the market knows best' was also a central plank of the economic philosophy of the Thatcher government, post 1979. Indeed, Chancellor Nigel Lawson summed up this thinking as:

'The business of government is not the government of business'.

In particular, free markets have the potential to deliver:

- economic efficiency
- allocative efficiency
- consumer sovereignty
- economic growth

Economic efficiency

Economic efficiency means having the maximum output for the minimum input. Profit maximization and competition between firms both result in firms choosing least-cost methods of production and economizing on inputs, as well as using the best technological mix of inputs. Exhibit 7.2 illustrates how competition in the market place stimulates organizations such as BA into a drive for economic efficiency.

Exhibit 7.2   Cost cuts help BA double profits – Mary Fagan

BA more than doubled its pre-tax profits to £285m in 1991 from £130m in 1990. Heavy internal cost cutting, increased productivity and reduced fuel bills contrib-

uted to the strong performance. Sir Colin Marshall, chief executive, said that 'great dollops' of competition had emerged, with 17 more airlines joining the 70 existing carriers operating out of Heathrow.

Source: *The Independent*, 20 May 1992 (adapted).

Allocative efficiency

Allocative efficiency is related to the concept of Pareto optimality and means that it is not possible to reallocate resources, for example by producing more of one thing and less of another, without making somebody worse off. It results first from economic efficiency and second from consumers maximizing their own satisfaction and implies maximum output from given inputs and maximum consumer satisfaction from that output.

Consumer sovereignty

Consumer sovereignty means that consumers are able to exercise power in the market place. It implies that production will be driven by consumer demand rather than by government decisions. In a free market system, firms which survive and grow will be those which make profits by being sensitive to consumer demand.

Economic growth

Economic growth will be encouraged by the free market since those firms which are the most profitable will survive and flourish. Under conditions of competition, firms will compete to increase productivity and thus in the market system resources will be allocated away from unprofitable and inefficient firms towards those which are profitable and efficient, thus generating economic growth.

In summary, under a competitive free market system consumers will get the goods and services they want at the lowest possible prices.

Criticisms of free market solution

Criticisms of the free market focus on the following:

- the inappropriateness of the perfect market assumption
- reservations about consumer sovereignty
- externalities
- public goods
- realities of economic growth
- equity

Perfect market assumption

For free markets to deliver economic and allocative efficiency, perfect markets as outlined in Chapter 3 are assumed, i.e. many buyers and sellers, homogeneous products, perfect knowledge, freedom of entry and exit in markets, and no government interference. The existence of market imperfections will reduce the efficiency of the free market system. The Thatcher government in fact devoted considerable legislation to the removal of market imperfections, particularly in the labour markets.

However, in practice markets are far from perfect. Many markets are dominated by a few suppliers and considerable product differentiation occurs by producers attempting to make their goods or services different from the competition in order to minimize price competition. These factors mean that consumers may not get the benefits of lowest prices afforded by perfect markets.

Consumer sovereignty

There are a number of factors at work in market economies that undermine the concept of consumer sovereignty. The first is lack of information. In the complex world of competing goods and services – particularly for technical products – consumers may not have enough information about the range of goods available and may find it difficult to make comparisons beyond the superficial. Second consumers are subject to persuasive advertising from producers, the aim of which is to interfere with the consumers' exercise of free choice.

Externalities

It is also evident that free markets fail in their signalling function in some areas. For example there are some missing markets. There is no market for the ozone layer. There is no market for peace and quiet. There is no market for views and landscapes. It is difficult therefore for people to register their preferences in these areas.

Equally markets do not always consider the full range of costs and benefits associated with production, or consumption of certain goods and services. The selling of alcohol is associated with the private benefit of feeling happy but has the unwanted public cost of fighting and accidents.

Missing markets and externalities are closely linked. Consider a plan for a development of holiday apartments on a piece of farmland adjacent to the sea. In a free market situation the developer will have to consider the costs of the land, materials and labour. However the development will clearly have an impact on the landscape, the view and the tranquillity of the area. But no one owns these rights, so there is no market in them and there is no price associated with the using up of them to develop the site. In this case there is a clear difference between the private costs of development and the public or social costs of development.

In Figure 7.1, *MPC* is the marginal private costs of the development. This shows the additional private costs of supplying extra units and represents the supply curve, *S*. The demand curve, *D*, shows the quantity demanded at different prices and the marginal private benefit, *MPB*. In this case it is assumed that there are no external benefits to consumption and thus this curve also represents the marginal social benefit (*MSB*). A market equilibrium price is achieved at price *P0* and the development will go ahead with a quantity of *Q0*.

However, *MXC* represents marginal external costs, i.e. the costs in terms of amenities lost such as views and tranquillity. Adding *MPX* to *MPC* gives the marginal social cost curve *MSC*. In this case it can be seen that the external costs are such that no equilibrium is achieved in the market, since the marginal social costs exceed the

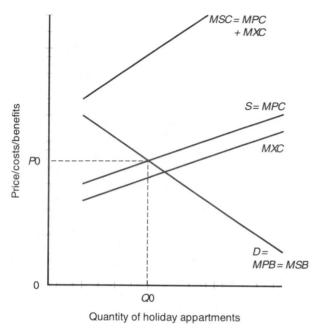

Figure 7.1 External costs and private costs: different equilibrium solutions. See text for details.

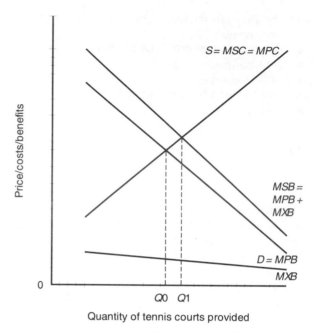

Figure 7.2 External benefits and private benefits: different equilibrium solutions. See text for details.

marginal social benefits at all prices. Thus we can see that the free market overproduces goods and services which have significant external costs.

A similar argument may be deployed to demonstrate that the free market underproduces goods and services which provide external benefits to society over and above the private benefits enjoyed by the consumer.

In Figure 7.2, *MPB* is the marginal private benefit derived from the use of tennis courts and represents the demand curve, *D*. *S* is the supply curve which shows the quantity supplied at different prices and the marginal private costs, *MPC*. In this case it is assumed that there are no external costs to provision and thus this curve also represents the marginal social cost *MSC*. A market equilibrium quantity is achieved at *Q0*. *MXB*, however, represents external benefits, i.e. the benefits to the community at large of the use of tennis courts which might include a fitter and more productive workforce and a reduction in petty juvenile crime. Adding *MXB* to *MPB* gives the marginal social benefit curve *MSB*. In this

case it can be seen that the equilibrium quantity rises to *Q1*.

Goods which include substantial external costs are sometimes termed demerit goods and goods which include substantial social benefits are sometimes termed merit goods.

Public goods

The market has an incentive to produce private goods or services because it can charge for them and make profits. It is very difficult to charge consumers for public goods and services and thus they are not provided in free markets. Signposts to tourist attractions are an example of a public good since:

- they are non-excludable (you cannot exclude people who do not want to pay for them from seeing them)
- consumption is non-rival (if I use the sign it does not prevent anyone else from using it – unlike a tennis court)

Economic growth

There is considerable debate as to whether the free market left alone will provide the fastest route to economic growth. Whilst it is true that the free market will naturally select profitable industries for survival, the free market is also subject to economic upswings and downswings which may hinder growth prospects.

Equity

Consumer sovereignty does not exist for those with insufficient purchasing power to influence a market.

Market Intervention

The following forms of market intervention are often proposed in order to address the problems inherent in a pure free market economy:

- central planning
- legislation and control
- taxes and subsidies
- public provision

Methods and benefits of market intervention

Central planning

The most drastic solution to market failures is the adoption of state or central planning of production. In this model, production decisions are made by state planning teams rather than in response to consumer demand and profitability. This is the main way in which resources are allocated in China and Cuba.

Legislation and control

There are a variety of ways in which the government exerts control over the market including:

- monopolies and mergers legislation
- laws, planning controls and permits

One of the aims of monopolies and mergers legislation is to protect the consumer from higher prices and the reduction in choice that may result from concentration of ownership in an industry. The key milestones of monopolies and mergers legislation have included the following:

- 1948 UK Monopolies and Restrictive Practices Act. This set up the Monopolies and Restrictive Practices Commission which could investigate any industry referred to it that had a market share of more than 30 per cent, and investigate whether the public interest was being served.
- 1956 UK Restrictive Trade Practices Act. This banned formal restrictive practices (e.g. price agreements between firms) that were not in the public interest.
- 1965 UK Monopolies and Mergers Act. This instigated a name change to the Monopolies and Mergers Commission and allowed examination of proposed mergers that might create a monopoly. Such mergers could be blocked.
- 1973 UK Fair Trading Act. This reduced the definition of monopoly to 25 per cent of market share.
- 1980 UK Competition Act. This widened the terms of reference of the Monopolies and Mergers Commission to include public corporations.
- European Union Article 85. This bans agreements and restrictive practices which prevent, restrict or distort competition within the European Union and affect trade between member states.
- European Union Article 86. This prohibits a firm from abusing a dominant position in the European Union which affects competition and trade between member states.
- 1990 European Union Merger Control Regulation. This gave the European Union Commission (as opposed to national government regulators) responsibility for control over large-scale mergers which have a significant European Union dimension.

The European Commission is able to fine firms up to 10 per cent of their turnover if they are found to be in contravention of Articles 85 or 86. The Commission recently exercised its powers to prevent mergers which would be detrimental to competition, by blocking the proposed take-over in 1991 by Aérospatiale of France and Alenia of Italy, of the Canadian aircraft manufacturer de Havilland. It was argued that the proposed new company would force up prices of certain aircraft, where it would control 76 per cent of the world market and 75 per cent of the European Commission market.

Investigations conducted by the UK Monopolies and Mergers Commission into firms in the leisure and tourism sector have included:

- the BA/British Caledonian merger
- P&O/Stenna Sealink merger
- the supply of package holidays
- Isle of Wight ferry services
- the price of CDs
- the brewing industry
- vertical integration in the package tour industry

Exhibit 7.3 reports the government withholding permission for a merger between P&O and Stenna Sealink, whilst exhibit 7.4 reports the government as satisfied that CD prices are not unduly high.

Exhibit 7.3 Ferry operators' merger refused: Channel services will have to compete individually with the tunnel – Michael Harrison

The government yesterday refused permission once more for the two biggest cross-Channel ferry operators to merge their services to compete with the Channel tunnel. This is the third time ministers have turned down requests from P&O European Ferries and Stenna Sealink to pool their short-sea operations between Dover and Calais.

In a further blow, Tim Sainsbury, the Industry minister, in effect told the two companies there would be no review of the ruling until autumn 1994 at the earliest. It was concluded that allowing a merger of the rival ferry services, which account for 80 per cent of passengers and freight on short-sea crossings,

would reduce choice, quality of service and price competition.

Source: *The Independent*, 16 July 1993.

Exhibit 7.4 CD prices ruling infuriates consumer group

Record companies and shops were yesterday cleared by the Monopolies and Mergers Commission (MMC) of allegations that they charge too much for CDs.

The Commission's report was condemned as 'astonishingly complacent and misguided' by the Consumers' Association.

The Office of Fair Trading ordered the Commission to investigate in May 1993, days after the high price of CDs was condemned in a report from the Commons National Heritage committee.

Graeme Odgers, the MMC chairman, said that the UK profits of EMI, Polygram Sony, Warner and BMG, which control 70 per cent of sales, were not excessive, even though CD prices are higher in the UK than in the USA. 'Excessive profits are not being made', he said. 'They are not ripping the consumer off – it is a highly competitive industry'.

Source: *Guardian*, 24 June 1994 (adapted).

The government often uses laws, planning controls and permits to prevent the free market from operation in some areas. For example, licensing laws limit the hours that licensed premises may open. Betting and gaming are regulated by the law. Similarly, some goods and services are banned outright. Possession of a whole range of drugs is illegal. Interestingly, legislating against something is not sufficient to prevent a market emerging and so black markets have arisen for the supply of drugs. Because of the risk involved in supplying drugs the market price reflects considerable profit.

Planning control affects new buildings and change of use and is largely the function of local government with the right of appeal to the Department of the Environment.

Taxes and subsidies

Taxes and subsidies may be used to encourage the consumption of merit goods and discourage the consumption of demerit goods.

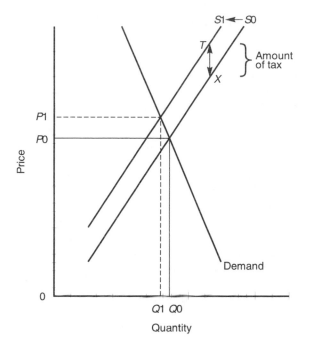

Figure 7.3 The effects of the imposition of a tax on the market for cigarettes. See text for details.

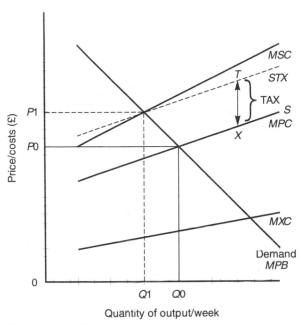

Figure 7.4 The use of taxation to restore optimal provision of goods with externalities. See text for details.

Cigarette smoking, for example, is subject to large taxes although it is not entirely clear whether the main purpose of taxation is to collect revenue, or to cut consumption.

The effect on the market is illustrated in Figure 7.3. Originally, equilibrium price is established at P0 where demand equals supply at Q0. The effects of the imposition of a tax of TX is to shift the supply curve to the left, the vertical distance between the two supply curves representing the amount of the tax. Equilibrium price rises to P1 and cigarette consumption has been reduced to Q1. Notice that the demand curve has been drawn to reflect the relative demand inelasticity for cigarettes and thus the effect of a tax on quantity bought and sold is relatively modest.

If it were possible to measure marginal external costs of provision of a good or service, it would be possible to restore an optimum level of output in a market by the imposition of a tax. This is illustrated in Figure 7.4. The equilibrium price is at P0 with an equilibrium quantity of

Q0. However the existence of external costs MXC establishes the marginal social cost curve MSC to the left of the supply curve S, which only reflects marginal private costs. This would suggest an optimal price of P1 and quantity of Q1, but since the marginal external costs are purely notional and do not actually affect the supply curve, overproduction of Q0–Q1 occurs. This could be remedied by the imposition of a tax which would shift the supply curve to STX and result in an equilibrium quantity of Q1.

An example of a tax on airlines to reduce the amount of noise pollution demonstrates that, whilst the problem can be addressed from an overall perspective (i.e. marginal social benefit equals marginal social cost), it is likely to be the government which benefits from the tax and not those who are directly affected by the noise.

Similarly, where there are significant marginal social benefits involved in the supply of a good or a service, a subsidy could be used to ensure that the market equilibrium occurred where marginal social costs equal marginal social benefits, rather than where marginal private benefits equal marginal private costs. This is the economic justification for the subsidy of arts and recreation, much of which is done via the Arts and Sports Councils, and such a policy results in more provision than would result from free market activity alone.

As exhibit 7.5 argues, there is a strong economic case for subsidies for public goods.

Exhibit 7.5   Follow Spitfire, not Concorde

Leaving the market to provide the impetus for research and development (R&D) is short-sighted and ignores the lessons of recent economic history. At a conference 10 days ago, organized by the Institute for Fiscal Studies and supported by the Economic and Social Research Council, it was painfully obvious that innovation was a complex phenomenon.

Above all it was clear that science and research are public goods. It is to support a public good that government involvement, in particular government finance, is imperative. Science ranks with law and order or defence as deserving public support. Indeed, Bronwyn Hall, a leading US economist, from Berkeley, declared that the social rates of return to R&D in industry and agriculture are demonstrably far above private rates of return – that a new invention had huge benefits beyond the gains capturable by an individual company. This, she said, was why there was a case for subsidy. Yes, subsidy, to raise the private rate of return to the social level.

Source: *Guardian*, 17 January 1994 (adapted).

Public provision

Public provision consists of supply through public corporations and local government ownership. The rationale for public ownership has included a mixture of political and economic aims. In the leisure and tourism sector, at a national level, BAA and BA have both been privatized whilst the BBC remains in public ownership. Around the world there are still many examples of nationalized airlines, Air France being a prime example. At a local level arts centres and leisure centres are commonly publicly owned. Economic

arguments for public ownership have included first:

● economies of scale
● rationalization
● avoidance of competitive costs

These arguments all stem from government ownership of a whole industry. The resulting size of operation leads to economies of scale including bulk purchasing. Rationalization – making processes and products uniform and cutting waste – is also then possible, and competitive costs such as advertising can be eliminated. These arguments were powerful reasons for maintaining state monopolies in water, gas and electricity production.

The second group of arguments in support of public ownership includes:

● control of monopoly power and excess prices
● consideration of externalities
● provision of merit and public goods
● employment provision

Under private ownership monopoly industries are able to charge high prices in the absence of competition, and profit maximization will encourage such industries to do so. State ownership enables non-profit-maximizing pricing strategies to be adopted. Price may be set for example to ensure that the industry breaks even to protect consumers from excess prices.

In the case of an industry supplying merit goods or public goods, price may be set below market price where marginal social cost equals marginal social benefit. Such a pricing strategy would involve the industry making an accounting loss (since total private revenue would be less than total private costs) and thus require government subsidy. The use of public sector industries to provide employment would also be based on wider economic considerations, including social costs and benefits, rather than the narrow considerations of private costs and benefits.

Problems of market intervention

Resource allocation in disequilibrium

Where goods and services are provided free of charge – changing the guard, roads, and children's playgrounds, for example – price is not able to bring demand and supply into equilibrium. The problem of excess demand often arises and therefore allocation of goods and services occurs in some other way. Queuing, first come first served, and ability to push are methods in which goods and services may then be allocated.

Public ownership: efficiency and culture

The profit motive engenders an organizational culture of efficiency and customer service. A criticism of public ownership is that lack of incentive leads to waste and poor service.

Side-effects of subsidies and taxes

The provision of subsidies to industry has to be paid for. Subsidies are financed from increasing taxes or from reducing government spending elsewhere, or from government borrowing. Increasing the level of taxes can reduce incentives in the economy and it is rarely prudent to pay for current expenditure by borrowing since this merely postpones the raising of taxes.

Loss of consumer sovereignty

In the extreme case of total state planning, consumer sovereignty is replaced by decision making by state officials, often leading to a mismatch between what consumers want and what the state provides. Government subsidies or ownership also reduce consumer sovereignty. Consumers' spending power is reduced by taxes, and government then makes decisions about how taxes will be spent.

Measurement of external costs and benefits

Private costs and benefits are easily measured since they all have market prices. On the other hand it is very difficult to measure social costs and benefits which are not directly priced – what is the cost of the loss of a view for example?

Government interference and changing objectives

A fundamental problem of state ownership of industry has been the lack of consistency of aims. As government policy and, indeed, as governments themselves change so public corporations are given different aims. Governments sometimes interfere in purchasing decisions for political reasons. Public corporations are also hypersensitive to the condition of the general economy. Governments may interfere with public sector pay to control inflation, and investment funds may suddenly disappear when public sector borrowing becomes too high.

Trends in public sector provision

Central planning

This has been abandoned by Eastern bloc countries and the two remaining significant examples of this – Cuba and China – are allowing the free market an increasing role in their economies.

Privatization

Since 1979, the scale of public ownership has been drastically reduced. Public corporations have been privatized, their shares floated on the stock exchange and their aims have become those of profit maximization. Those organizations remaining in the public sector have been subject to greater accountability Exhibit 7.6 reports on the privatization of the German airline Lufthansa.

Exhibit 7.6 With one bound Lufthansa is free

Lufthansa's privatization lifts off this week with a roar.
    Executive chairman Jurgen Weber's determination to ensure Lufthansa becomes a private and efficient competitor sends a hostile message to airline managers

in Brussels, Madrid, Athens, Dublin, Lisbon and, most controversially, Paris.

In a two-tier European aviation industry, Weber has taken a stand with the likes of BA, KLM and SAS in opposing state subsidies to rivals with bleeding balance sheets.

Source: *The Observer*, 11 September 1994 (adapted).

Citizen's charters

These have defined the rights, complaints procedures and compensation provision for customers.

Performance targets and indicators

Public sector organizations are increasingly required to define their provision in terms of measurable outcomes. These outcomes are often subject to interorganizational comparison – 'league tables', and targets for improvement from year to year.

Compulsory competitive tendering (CCT)

Leisure centre management, in common with a range of local government services, has been subject to CCT since 1993. The idea of CCT is an attempt to bring competitive market forces into areas of provision which were previously provided by government employees. The Thatcher government was convinced that local government provision of many services was subject to waste and inefficiency and that wage rates paid were uncompetitive and that restrictive work practices had arisen.

Bids are invited, by a process of open tender, to manage centres in line with a detailed contract. The successful bid is the one with the lowest cost. This is not privatization, since the buildings and policy objectives remain in local government hands. In many cases the local authority's own Direct Service Organization (DSO) bids for contracts, and in some cases they are the only bidder. In reality DSO contracts still form the majority of CCT contracts.

There are several advantages claimed for CCT. First, since the lowest-cost bid wins the contract, there is an inbuilt pressure to deliver services more efficiently. Inputs are used more economically, and cost-saving practices and technologies are encouraged. Second, the actual management of a facility gains autonomy and is not subject to interference from the local authority. Third, standards and performance indicators have to be established in order to monitor the effectiveness of services provided by third parties. This encourages more emphasis on quality than might otherwise have occurred. Fourth, savings generated by lower costs of services subject to CCT can result in lower taxes or more expenditure on services elsewhere. Fifth, the bureaucracy of local government is reduced and thus it has more time to devote to its core services and policies. Finally, firms which are successful in CCT and which win multiple contracts can achieve economies of scale and develop their expertise.

However, there are also some robust criticisms of CCT. Perhaps one of the key points is the hidden costs of CCT. A range of extra costs arise out of the process which were not necessary under direct provision. These costs include contract specification, and negotiation, regular monitoring of performance and any legal costs arising from disputes. Second, the drive to reduce costs leads to a deterioration of working conditions and wages of those employed. Third there arises an undue obsession with performance targets, since these are the measures by which contractors will be judged. In reality a service is greater than a collection of performance targets and contains a range of intangibles. Fourth there have been some conflicts of interest where persons with a direct link to councils have also acted on behalf of private sector tendering firms. Finally, services contracted to external suppliers must necessarily include a profit element that was not previously necessary. If the effects of CCT allow this profit to be met by increased efficiency of provision, there is a likely net gain, but it may be that the profit margin has to be met by shaving parts of the service.

Review of key terms

- Consumer sovereignty = goods and services produced according to consumer demand.

- Economic efficiency = maximum output from minimum input.
- Allocative efficiency = maximum output from given inputs and maximum consumer satisfaction form that output.
- Externalities = costs or benefits which have social significance.
- Merit goods = goods with external benefits.
- Demerit goods = goods with external costs.
- Public goods = goods which are non-excludable and non-rival.

Data questions

Task 7.1 Peacock proposes privatization of the arts

Sir Alan Peacock has recently made a plea for more public scrutiny over public arts expenditure even though, as he notes, government expenditure on creative performing and visual arts is a small part – less than 1 per cent – of total expenditure.

His argument is that those in receipt of public subsidy are loath to accept any objective measure of their success or failure. Theatre directors prefer to take the money without any strings, and where they are forced to account for subsidies their instinct is to judge success themselves.

The danger that Sir Alan sees in this approach is that those who are paying for the subsidies, the taxpayer, have little or no say in how their money is spent and often see little benefit from their contributions.

A major defence of public subsidy to the arts is that they deliver external benefits and that, if left to market forces, much arts provision would disappear, since it rarely makes a commercial profit, and these external benefits would be also be lost. Sir Alan questions the size of such benefits, noting that only a minority of people comprise the audience for the arts and that it is difficult to ascertain what benefits are received by the vast majority who do not attend concerts, plays and opera. He also points out that there is a disproportionate expenditure on the

arts in London, which leads to a further narrowing of its effects.

Some right-wing politicians favour a pure market approach to the arts and favour an immediate withdrawal of state support. Why support opera and not football? Let those who want to see opera pay the full costs of it. If Covent Garden can't turn in a profit, let its assets be released for a purpose that can. So run the arguments of the free marketeers.

Sir Alan does not propose the immediate cutting of state subsidy. His long-term goal is for the arts to be self-supporting, and responsive to consumer demand. What he therefore proposes is 'investment in life-time education in the arts' so that an improved public appreciation of the arts would create bigger audiences who are prepared to pay for what they want, rather than the present position where a majority pay for what they don't care about. In effect this seems a proposal for consumer re-education.

Source: the author, from news cuttings, 7 January 1994.

Questions

1 Where in the article are the marginal social benefits of the arts considered, and what are Peacock's views on the likely size of these benefits?
2 List what you consider to be possible social benefits of the arts. How would you seek to quantify these?
3 How does state subsidy of the arts affect consumer sovereignty?
4 Consider the case for privatizing the arts.

Task 7.2 Around the rugged rocks: quarries are scarring our national parks

Old Moor is being blown up and bulldozed away. One of Britain's most beautiful and best protected areas, in the Peak District National Park, is being destroyed for stone to build roads and to feed industry. Old Moor, along with the adjacent Tunstead quarry immediately outside the park boundary, is effectively England's first superquarry. Operated by Buxton Lime Industries along the southern edge of the park, it is one of the largest in Europe, covering more than a square mile and on course for producing 10 million tonnes of rock a year.

Huge, ugly and unnecessary, say its critics, it could become – according to a report published by the Council for National Parks yesterday – the face of future quarries. As demand for rock increases from the construction, road and other industries, so existing quarries will expand. In the Peak District, existing permissions enable limestone extraction to carry on at the current rate for the next 50 years. National parks, which cover nine per cent of England and Wales, already contain about 300 quarries which damage nature, destroy footpaths, generate traffic and – above all – scar the landscape.

The new report, prepared by environmental consultants Green Balance and part-funded by the government's Countryside Commission, reveals that nearly two thirds of national parkland with permission for mineral extraction has unsatisfactory arrangements for restoring the landscape. This is a legacy of planning permissions granted in the 1940s, 1950s and 1960s. The report calls on the Government to apply tougher criteria when deciding whether to allow further mineral development. The aim should be to achieve a decline in mineral extraction in the parks without simply shifting the problem elsewhere. This means using fiscal incentives to encourage the use of alternatives, the recycling of existing materials and the lowering of required material specifications. 'Planning permissions for mineral working at dormant sites in national parks should be revoked without compensation as a priority,' it says. 'Energy conservation and, recently, water conservation have entered the national consciousness and there is no reason why mineral conservation should not join them,' concludes the report.

In February, the Council for the Protection of Rural England called for a complete moratorium on all new planning permissions for quarrying over the next few years. It pointed out that permissions already existed to extract almost six billion tonnes of rock, although the government target was only to supply three billion tonnes by 2011.

Source: Guardian, 18 June 1993.

Questions

1   Explain how private costs and social costs of mineral extraction differ.
2   Illustrate, with appropriate diagrams, ways in which market intervention could reduce the impact of quarrying on national parks.
3   What problems might arise from market intervention?

Task 7.3   A slice of the auction

When leisure was added to the list of services to be privatized as part of the 1988 Local Government Act, the government made it clear to the industry that it saw local authorities as enablers and not service providers. The consensus outside the industry was that the private sector would fall over itself to get a piece of the action. But the leisure world is complicated and diverse. It was all too easy – then and now – to think that the public, with more leisure time on its hands than ever before, would flock to facilities that in private hands would be better funded, better managed and better marketed. Councils, it was thought by many, would be unable to compete for the new contracts in public auctions.

But those making the assumptions failed to understand that leisure, unlike cleaning and refuse collection, is a minefield because of the enormous range of facilities and the complexity of contract specifications in a non-statutory sector. Would-be private sector contractors found that managing local authority leisure facilities was anything but a licence to print money. The result was that they proceeded to cherry-pick the best contracts and many local authorities outside the south-east (particularly the metropolitan boroughs) found that all the initial interest in contracts melted away, leaving only their own sealed envelope to open. In the end council leisure services were shaken but largely stayed in the hands of in-house council teams. The private sector managed to field fewer than 20 companies to bid for more than 350 local authority contracts in England, and recent figures show that more than 80 per cent of contracts awarded went to local authority teams.

In its report *The Competitive Edge*, the Institute of Public Finance's CCT monitoring unit identified 223 leisure contracts across 203 local authorities at an estimated value of £140m. Only 42 of these contracts went to private contractors. City Centre Leisure and Serco Leisure emerged as the largest private contractors with six each, followed by Contemporary Leisure and Circa Leisure, both on five. Crossland Leisure, which was the largest contractor, collapsed in October 1991. Those who had maintained that council staff were the best people to run council facilities see the non-appearance of widespread competition for contracts as vindication of the work they have been doing. The government, meanwhile, has been eager to distance itself from the low number of take-ups and suggests that success should be measured in terms of the overall increased commercial acumen of councils.

As expected, there has been a mixed response to privatization, but most local authorities believe it has made municipal facilities more attractive to the public. A report from the then Polytechnic of North London suggested that the most negative result has been the worsening of pay and conditions for the staff that run venues. But those local authority leisure managers who have survived the all-out assault of CCT are now facing other pressures which threaten to wrench control of municipal facilities from their hands. In many cases the in-house teams have no access to funds and their ability to compete

effectively has been hampered by the second claw of the government's attack on local authorities – capital spending controls. This is the regulatory straitjacket designed to ensure that a large portion of the money raised from council's asset sales such as development land and housing is used to pay off local authority debt. The ability of the private sector to raise loans on the basis of future earnings gives outside contractors a significant edge over their in-house colleagues. If a local authority client is looking for more than management from a contractor, the in-house team is generally unable to compete. Consequently the private sector is likely to move in much more significantly when leisure contracts are put up for renewal. Local authorities may also lose control of municipal theatres and arts venues if the government decides to extend CCT to these facilities. The government so far has not tried to show that cost savings have been made. Councils would argue that the time spent restructuring departments and writing detailed specifications for consultants to evaluate bids has cost them dearly without real evidence of significant savings.

Meanwhile, many people in the industry are concerned that local authority leisure is in danger of disappearing into a supportive role under some other departmental head such as education. Considering that so many local authority leisure managers have risen to the challenge and now run their businesses as effectively as the commercial entrepreneurs, this would be grossly unfair.

Source: *Guardian*, 2 April 1993 (adapted).

Questions

1 What are the major benefits of CCT?
2 What are the major drawbacks of CCT?
3 What is meant by 'leaving [the councils] only their own sealed envelope to open'?
4 If a council DSO win the contract has any change occurred?

Short questions

1 Why might leaving provision of the arts entirely to the private sector lead to suboptimal resource allocation? Use a diagram to show how provision of a public subsidy to the Arts Council might restore optimal allocation and explain why achieving this aim might be difficult in practice.
2 Should children's playgrounds be provided free of charge?
3 Should opera be subsidized?
4 Should football admission be subsidized?
5 Should local authorities provide arts centres and what should their pricing policy be?
6 What problems arise from providing merit goods additional to those provided in the market?

Reference

Smith, A., *The Wealth of Nations*, Modern Library Random House, 1937.

Further reading

Adams, I., *Leisure and Government*, Business Education Publishers, 1990.

Hurl, B., *Privatisation and the Public Sector*, Heinemann, 1988.

Wilkinson, M., *Equity and Efficiency*, Heinemann, 1993.

Part Two

Leisure and Tourism Organizations and the External Environment

8

The competitive environment

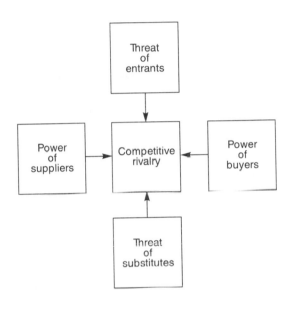

Objectives

The environment in which organizations operate is often now characterized by the four Ds:

- difficult
- dangerous
- dynamic
- diverse

In other words, the environment is constantly changing. It is this constant change that makes environment scanning important for leisure, tourism and other organizations. Organizations that remain static in a dynamic environment experience strategic drift and are likely to fail. Figure 8.1 illustrates the concept of strategic drift.

Between period $t0$ and $t1$, the operating environment is static, and the organization illustrated makes no policy change, so that by the end of the period, at $t1$, organizational policy at B is in tune with the environment at A. However, the period $t1$ to $t2$ represents a period of dynamic change in the operating environment. The organization, however, undertakes only marginal policy change so that by the end of the period it is experiencing strategic drift, represented by the distance CD.

Chapters 8–11 analyse the nature of the operating environment. This chapter considers the competitive environment, whilst Chapters 9–11 consider the political, economic, sociocultural and technological (PEST) environment, enabling a comprehensive opportunities and threats analysis to be undertaken in the second part of Chapter 11.

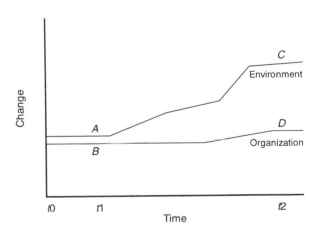

Figure 8.1 Strategic drift.

In his book *Competitive Strategy* (1980), Porter proposes the following model ('the five forces') for investigating the competitive environment:

1 the threat of entrants
2 the power of suppliers
3 the power of consumers
4 the threat of substitutes
5 competitive rivalry

Porter's model is used in this chapter to analyse the competitive environment.

By studying this chapter students will be able to:

● analyse an organization's competitive environment using 'five forces' analysis
● utilize strategic group analysis to identify competitive groupings

The threat of entrants

The threat of new entrants into an industry will have a significant effect on a leisure and tourism organization. New entrants may stimulate more price competition or more investment in product differentiation as they attempt to win market share and profits and existing firms seek to defend market share and profits. Chapter 6 analysed these effects of competition on pricing policy and strategy.

The extent of the threat of new entrants will depend upon barriers to entry such as:

● economies of scale
● capital and experience barriers to entry
● advertising barriers to entry
● availability of distribution channels (vertical integration)
● anticipated entry wars
● natural monopoly conditions
● product differentiation barriers

Clearly barriers to entry will represent a hurdle to be surmounted for organizations wishing to enter an industry or defences to be maintained and strengthened in the case of established organizations. Exhibit 8.1 reports the threat of new

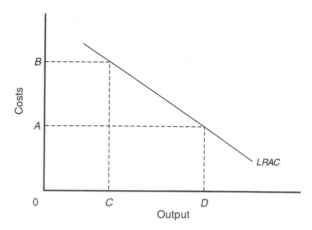

Figure 8.2 Economy of scale barriers to entry.

entrants on Scotland-to-USA air routes where entry barriers are low.

Exhibit 8.1 Edinburgh challenge to Glasgow's air supremacy

Ron Wallace, managing director of Edinburgh Airport, has ambitious plans for its growth and development. His latest success has been to help launch a new Aer Lingus daily flight to New York. Market research supports his plans, showing the airport's catchment area extends to East Kilbride.

All this is worrying news for Glasgow Airport and its transatlantic operators, BA, Northwest and American. Glasgow had previously picked up Edinburgh's US east coast trade, and this lucrative market now looks threatened.

BA is probably in the strongest position to resist the new competition as its New York flight is direct. But even with its change of planes and hour stop-over at Dublin, the new Aer Lingus route compares favourably with Northwest's route via Boston, and American's route via Washington.

Source: the author, from news cuttings, March 1994.

Economies of scale

Economies of scale, discussed in more detail in Chapter 5, result in reductions in average costs of production as the scale of production increases. Figure 8.2 illustrates the long-run average cost curve (LRAC) of an organization experiencing economies of scale.

An established organization producing at level of output 0*D* will experience significant economies of scale with long-run average costs at 0*A*. A new entrant to the industry will initially produce a low level of output, for example at 0*C* and lack of scale economies will result in high average costs of 0*B*. The established organization can therefore often outcompete the new entrant by passing these lower costs on in the form of lower prices or use higher profit margins to finance more added value of the product.

Capital and experience barriers to entry

For some areas of business the capital costs of entry are fairly modest. This is true for example for video rental stores, for dance and fitness classes, small hotels and guest houses and for tour guiding. Entry into such areas is thus relatively easy. On the other hand there are substantial capital costs in entering the airline or theme park industry and thus entry barriers are stronger in such industries. Exhibit 8.2 ascribes the lack of competition in domestic air travel to high costs and lack of access to distribution channels – in this case 'slots'.

Exhibit 8.2   Fares in UK sky: high

A 14-day APEX return flight between London Heathrow and Glasgow costs £138. It's about the same distance as Los Angeles–San Francisco, which costs only £51. That's not the worst comparison. Stanstead to Aberdeen is the same distance as Chicago to Kansas but at £192 costs three times as much. Why?

Some of the difference lies in costs. It costs more to run an airline in the UK than in the USA. But the main difference must lie in the competitive environment. People's Express, the now defunct US carrier, started the ball-rolling with its $49 New York–Miami fare. Recently there has been a huge growth in imitators of this service on the busy short-haul routes such as Los Angeles–San Francisco and Washington–New York. They offer no frills but low fares. You might have to lug your own bags to the far side of the runway (cheap aircraft parking), pack your own sandwiches and fly a propeller museum piece, but you won't have to dig too deep into your pocket.

Competition in the UK domestic air travel market is much more limited. Since the collapse of Dan-Air in 1992 there are only three major players: BA, British Midland and Air UK. A major problem for potential entrants is the UK's crowded skies and airports. There are few slots available for competitors at London.

Source: the author, from news cuttings, February 1995.

Similarly, an experience curve can be envisaged for the supply of complex goods and services. Established firms, having travelled along their experience curve, develop expertise that delivers lower costs and better service. Potential entrants will find themselves disadvantaged by being at the start of their experience curve.

Advertising barriers to entry

Advertising may be used to create an artificial barrier to entry. Successful brands can be underpinned by extensive advertising which makes it difficult for newcomers to break into the market. For example, extensive advertising on lager brands has the effect of minimizing the threat of new entrants.

Availability of distribution channels

Entry into some markets may be prevented or limited by access to distribution channels. There are many examples of this in the leisure and tourism sector. Many airlines would like to expand their operations into London Heathrow airport but are unable to do so because take-off and landing slots are either unavailable or are at inconvenient times. BA is able to maintain some of its market power because of its allocation of slots. On the other hand, BA has recently successfully opened up access previously denied to it at Orly airport in Paris, as reported in exhibit 8.3.

Exhibit 8.3   French forced to open air routes

The French government yesterday bowed to a European Court of Justice ruling by promising to open up two domestic air routes to other European airlines.

The Commission had argued that France was discriminating in favour of Air Inter by preventing other airlines from flying on the Orly–Marseilles and Orly–Toulouse routes. But France contended that Air Inter's monopoly on two profitable routes helped to subsidize loss-making routes elsewhere in France.

The Commission acted in response to a complaint by French airline TAT, which is 49.1 per cent owned by BA. TAT is now expected to operate on these routes, which are the most profitable domestic routes in France.

The Commission has already succeeded in forcing Paris to open up the London–Orly route, which BA has been serving since the summer.

Source: *Guardian*, 27 October 1994 (adapted).

One of the motives for vertical integration may be to discriminate against other suppliers by ownership of distribution channels, as discussed in Chapter 5. Thus Thomson's ownership of the Lunn Poly travel agency and Airtours' ownership of Going Places may represent a strategy to prevent competitors from increasing their market share.

The Monopolies Commission report on the brewing industry in 1989 found that vertical integration in the brewing industry was stifling competition and as a result brewers were set limits as to the number of pubs they could own and pub tenants were allowed to sell beer from an alternative brewery.

Ownership of distribution channels has led to similar debates about fair access to markets in the film and cinema, and satellite TV industries. In the video games market, Nintendo and Sega had cornered 70 per cent of world sales by 1994. This is because, having bought a particular game console, customers have then been forced to purchase games from Sega or Nintendo. However, with the price of PCs falling and their specifications rising, Nintendo sales are being threatened by games using floppy disk or CD-ROM technology.

Anticipated entry wars

Where entry into a market is likely to precipitate a strong reaction from established organizations, potential new entrants may be dissuaded from market entry. The example of SkyTrain is still a potent one. The arrival of this new service on transatlantic air routes led to price wars from BA and American carriers that were so intense that Laker Airways went out of business. The established companies had the financial muscle to cut prices deeper and for longer than Laker.

The arrival of Virgin Atlantic instigated similar entry wars that culminated in the infamous BA 'dirty tricks' campaign that allegedly poached Virgin customers by devious means. Exhibit 8.4 reports new developments in this saga.

Exhibit 8.4 More BA 'dirty tricks' claims

Allegations of more 'dirty tricks' tactics have been made against BA. Virgin is currently engaged in a $1bn lawsuit against BA in the USA, based on allegations of poaching passengers, and smears. One tactic used in the USA was to telephone Virgin passengers and offer them upgrades on BA flights. In the UK private detectives were hired to provide information for a disinformation campaign against Virgin.

New allegations involve American Airlines, Air France and Lufthansa whose passengers were poached by 'the ambush'. This involved business travellers arriving at Gatwick, who would be approached, often by young women, and offered a range of incentives to change their booking to BA. These teams, who were coordinated by radio handsets, were nicknamed 'Maude's marauders', after a Heathrow sales manager, Chris Maude. The reward for a successful maraud was a £5 gift voucher.

These allegations have called into question the notion of good faith and confidentiality, since many competing airlines have hired space on BA computers, and are now suspicious that BA may have used their passenger lists as a way of pirating passengers.

Source: the author, from news cuttings, March 1994.

Natural monopoly conditions

A natural monopoly exists where it is not technically feasible or desirable to have many competing services. For example, it is only feasible to have one water pipe connecting each house, otherwise streets would be a tangle of competing pipes.

Telecommunications were also held to be a natural monopoly for similar reasons, but there is now increasing competition to provide datalinks. Thus, although BT still owns most of the local lines into residential properties, cable has now established an alternative service and other companies such as Mercury have been given access to the telephone network. Technology thus allows competition into an area that was previously a natural monopoly. This has led to strong price competition in telecommunications.

The power of suppliers

Supplier power is another important aspect of the competitive environment. Suppliers of inputs have a key impact on prices and quality and the greater the power of suppliers, the lower margins will be. Supplier power is increased by the degree of monopoly or oligopoly in the supplying industry, and if there are high costs of switching suppliers. Supplier power is diminished where the organization buying inputs has large purchasing power.

Credit card companies supply credit facilities in an oligopolistic market. There is little competition between the key players, Visa, Mastercard and American Express. This has led to considerable battles over their charges. Large organizations such as Holiday Inn International, BA and Lunn Poly can negotiate favourable deals because of the size of their turnover, but smaller organizations face an unequal struggle and supplier power forces them to accept high commission rates.

Similarly, centralized reservation systems such as SABRE and Amadeus supply a booking service for hotels, airlines and car hire companies. A similar picture emerges of strong supplier power that is resisted most successfully by large users of the services.

Backward vertical integration is a route to avoiding supplier power by take-over of the supplying organization. Thomson's ownership of its carrier Britannia and Airtour's ownership of Airtours International mean that they can dictate the level of service and its price. The latter is particularly important when demand is buoyant and airlines find their bargaining position enhanced.

Similar issues of supplier/buyer power can be found between Eurotunnel and its customers Eurostar and Le Shuttle, Railtrack and rail operators, and owners of the information superhighways and their commercial users.

The power of buyers

Where the buyer is a monopsonist (single buyer) or a near monopsonist, considerable power can be exerted over the selling organization. For example, in Spanish resorts where hoteliers have become dependent upon one or two UK tour operators, room rates are negotiated with very slim margins for the hoteliers.

Competition between suppliers is a key factor that increases buyer power. This is evident for air travel where there is intense competition on routes, for example London–New York fares are very competitive, but where a route is served by a single operator price per kilometre flown increases sharply.

The level of buyer knowledge is another important factor. In order to exercise buyer power, customers need information about goods and services on offer and prices of competitors. In some areas of leisure and tourism this is difficult. Customers do not always have full information when booking a hotel room for example and it is often a transaction undertaken sight unseen. National and international hotel chains often standardize their product to remove this kind of consumer uncertainty. Similar uncertainty exists for customers of restaurants. For standardized, mass-produced goods and services, buyer power is sometimes increased by the existence of specialist publications such as *What Hi Fi?* and *What PC?* which compare quality and prices.

Finally, the overall state of the market is important in determining the relative balance of buyer and supplier power. When the economy is growing strongly, there may be shortages of supply and supplier power becomes stronger. In conditions of recession there is often a shortage of customers and buyer power increases.

The threat of substitutes

Substitutes can take several forms. First a new product or service may make a current one obsolete. Word processors and CD players have made the typewriter and the turntable obsolete. Second a substitute may result in a new product or service competing closely with existing ones. Exhibit 8.5 reports on Camelot's winning bid to operate the national lottery.

Exhibit 8.5   Camelot takes lottery prize

The 7-year licence to run the national lottery from November 1994 has been won by Camelot. The turnover of the lottery is estimated at an average of £4bn a year.

Camelot Group is a consortium of companies including Cadbury Schweppes, Racal Electronics, De La Rue, ICL and GTECH, an American lottery operator. Its main rival was in the form of Richard Branson who had tried to out-manoeuvre Camelot by his promise to distribute lottery profits to good causes.

The lottery is run on behalf of the Department of National Heritage, who will coordinate the distribution of a lottery funds to five good causes. These are the arts, sports, heritage, charities and the Millennium Fund whose role is to support projects which will celebrate the year 2000. Over £300m should be available to each of these causes at the peak of the lottery.

Source: the author, from news cuttings, 26 May 1994.

The national lottery has resulted in increased competition for pools firms, bingo and betting shops.

Finally, to some extent all goods and services compete for consumers' limited incomes and thus new products even in distant markets may have some impact on a variety of unrelated organizations.

Organizations faced with the threat of substitutes may react in several ways. These include:

- price leadership strategies
- differentiation strategies
- withdrawal or diversification strategies
- creating switching costs to prevent loss of customers

Exhibit 8.6 examines the impact of the channel tunnel on existing service providers and considers their respective strategies.

Exhibit 8.6   Virgin rails against competition

Competition is hotting up on short-hop routes from England to France as the Channel Tunnel offers direct competition to airlines and ferries with its Eurostar and Le Shuttle services.

The airlines are taking different approaches to this new threat. BA has recently relaunched its Club Europe services to keep its business passengers content, and has started a new service from London to Orly (in the south of Paris) to provide more choice and flexibility. Not to be outdone, British Midland has also introduced a London–Orly service, and in a key strategic move has announced new routes away from the direct competition of the tunnel.

Virgin boss Richard Branson has taken altogether a different route. His transcontinental services suffer from having no feeder services from within mainland Europe and his characteristic lateral style of thinking sees a rail rather than air solution to this problem. He said, 'We have no intention of expanding in the short-haul European airline business, but trains would give us a big foothold in the market'.

It is not difficult to picture the Virgin concept: stylish interiors, wacky waiting rooms, entertainment consoles and a full range of business facilities.

Branson might just win a Railway Cup to add to his Airline of the Year trophies.

Source: the author, adapted from news cuttings, January 1995.

Clearly Eurostar provides a close substitute for London–Paris air services. Different responses to the threat can be detected. BA is to seek to differentiate its product by adding more value to its Club Europe business class. British Midland is to diversify into services not directly affected by the tunnel. Virgin, however, is in a different position since it does not have an air route from London to Paris and is thus seeking to provide its own trains on the London–Paris route.

The degree of competitive rivalry

Competitive rivalry within an industry is increased by the threat of new entrants and the threat of substitutes, but it is also influenced by current conditions in the industry. These include:

- whether competitors can cross-subsidize
- degree of market leadership and number of competitors
- changes in capacity
- high storage costs/perishability

Whether competitors can cross-subsidize?

Cross-subsidization occurs where an organization uses profits from one sector of its business to subsidize prices in another sector. This can lead to intense competition in the markets for some goods and services. The newspaper price war described in Chapter 3, where *The Times* dropped its cover price to 30p and then to 20p when the *Telegraph* retaliated, is made possible by cross-subsidization. News Corporation, the owners of *The Times*, and the *Telegraph* group both have extensive and profitable global interests from which to finance cross-subsidies. The motive behind cross-subsidization is to win market share by low prices, and for newspapers this leads to economies of scale and big increases in advertising revenue.

Degree of market leadership and number of competitors

Clearly monopoly or near monopoly supply means little competitive rivalry. Oligopoly conditions can lead to competitive rivalry, but since, as Chapter 6, explains rivalry reduces profits all round, organizations may choose to follow the lead of the dominant firms in such circumstances. Competitive conditions of supply are likely to lead to a state of constant rivalry. Firms may attempt to insulate themselves from such rivalry by differentiating their product from other products.

Changes in capacity

Where the supply of a good or service is subject to large increases in capacity, competitive rivalry is likely to become more intense. For example, the opening of the channel tunnel has led to a sudden increase in the capacity for cross-channel traffic. Exhibit 8.7 illustrates the effects of an increase in local capacity of hotel accommodation in Glasgow.

Exhibit 8.7   £3m Investment despite tough competition

The 21-year-old Forte Crest Hotel is surrounded by newly built rivals: the Marriot, the Hospitality Inn, Moat House International and the most recent arrival, the £42m Hilton International.

The opening of the Hilton led to a difficult time last year. A price war broke out in an attempt to fill empty rooms. The result was evident more in terms of lost revenue than in extra reservations, and Alberto Laidlaw, the manager of the Forte Crest, lost his job. A Forte spokesperson explained his sacking in terms of 'changes in the competitive environment'.

Despite this temporary blip in the hotel's fortunes, it has generally survived the ravages of the recession. A new manager, John Millar, has been appointed and profitability has been improved. The price war has been replaced with marketing-led competitive strategies to fill spare capacity.

Forte have confirmed their faith in the hotel's future by announcing a £3m investment programme over the next 3 years.

Source: the author, from news cuttings, May 1994.

Similarly, some firms face substantial exit costs to leave an industry. These might be redundancy costs or a low scrap value of specialized buildings, machinery or equipment. In such cases, firms may stay in an industry despite falling demand, adding to overcapacity. Such conditions will often create the conditions for competitive

Table 8.1   *Checklist of characteristics for identifying strategic groups (adapted from Porter, 1980)*

Geographical coverage	Financial strength	Market segment served	Product range
Extent of branding	Vertical integration	Cost position	Size
Ownership	Quality	Marketing strategy	Technological position
Distribution channels used	Pricing policy	Research and development position	

rivalry. There is often overcapacity of rooms in resorts facing falling demand. This can be recognized in many UK seaside resorts and some of the older resorts in Spain.

High storage costs/perishability

Some goods and services have high storage costs or are highly perishable. Aircraft seats, hotel rooms, hire cars and theatre seats are highly perishable. There is always the prospect of intense last-minute competition to sell such services, but in reality competition here is carefully orchestrated so that an organization's main market is not disrupted. For example, tour operators want to encourage advance bookings at brochure prices and therefore do not make big advertising capital over the last-minute bargains that can be obtained.

Strategic group analysis

The notion of 'an industry' or 'an organization' may be too generalized and blurred to allow useful analysis of competition. For example, it is difficult to determine the competitive position of Pearson plc because it is an organization with diverse interests in newspapers, books, television and leisure. Instead it is necessary to look at competition in a particular area of operations such as newspapers. Similarly, the package tour industry is a diverse industry comprising, for example, domestic tours, coach tours, air tours, ski packages, winter sun, specialist and summer sun.

The concept of strategic grouping has been

developed to define areas of competition. Analysis of characteristic groupings will identify firms competing in similar areas, and Table 8.1 illustrates a checklist developed by Porter.

Key characteristics are defined for a particular market and the competitive structure of that market can then be identified. For the newspaper industry, for example, the key characteristics include quality and geographic coverage. Figure 8.3 maps strategic groups using these criteria and this enables close competition to be identified.

Review of key terms

- Environment scanning = monitoring of operating environment.
- Strategic drift = failure of business strategy to keep abreast of environmental change.

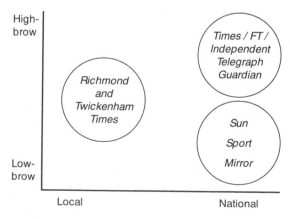

Figure 8.3   Strategic groups in the newspaper industry. *FT = Financial Times.*

- Operating environment = competitive and PEST environment.
- PEST = political, sociocultural, economic and technical environment.
- Barriers to entry = factors making entry into industry difficult.
- Monopsonist = single buyer.
- Cross-subsidization = using profits from one division to subsidize prices in another division.
- Strategic group analysis = determination of groups of competitors for a particular market.

Data questions

Task 8.1   Bingo knights arm against onslaught from Camelot – John Shepherd

Winning money comes a clear second to enjoyment for the 3 million adults who regularly play bingo in the UK. But coming a clear second to the national lottery would be far from fun for the country's 950 bingo clubs. As a result, the industry is gearing up for an intense lobbying campaign to enable it to compete.

No one knows what impact the lottery will have on bingo – or indeed on the rest of the UK's gaming and gambling industry – but the consensus is that some financial damage will be inflicted on the £1.4bn-a-year industry. As Mike Robinson, managing director of Top Rank and chairman of the Bingo Association of Great Britain, says: 'I don't know exactly what will happen. But the lottery will have some effect, perhaps 3 to 4 per cent could be taken away'.

Signs of concern are already visible in the industry's recent push to have the ceiling on its top prize on its national game raised from £75 000 to £250 000. But lobbying will probably focus on the 1968 Gaming Act. The bingo industry's main concerns about the lottery stem from the stiff regulatory requirements of the Act, from which the lottery is virtually exempt.

As a result, Camelot, the consortium that bid successfully for the lottery, will be allowed to advertise on television. Bingo cannot. Camelot will be able to publicize the identity of lottery winners and the sums they have won – as can football pools companies. Again, bingo cannot.

The industry can cite many examples worldwide where the introduction of a lottery has blown gaping holes in the bingo business: in Texas it prompted a 30 per cent decline in bingo stake money. However, bingo has also proved to be virtually recession-proof, a reflection of loyal players – mostly women, with an average age of 47 – who typically spend £12 on a night out.

The club culture is central to bingo's pulling power, and a key to its ability to generate revenues. The clubs incorporate diners, bars and banks of fruit machines – all targeted at the customer's pocket. Of the industry's annual £1.4bn turnover, only half is stake money. The rest comes from admission fees, drinks, food and fruit machines in the club.

Computer technology has become a useful marketing tool. Membership cards are electronically swiped at each visit – infrequent visitors are informed about the recent big winners at the club, and even invited to celebrate their birthday playing bingo.

Bingo operators – from the market leader Top Rank, part of the Rank organization, through to Gala Clubs, owned by Bass, newer entrants like First Leisure and Vardon, and a myriad of small independents – now want to take the national game a stage further.

Source: *The Independent*, 9 June 1994 (adapted).

Questions

1   Which of Porter's five forces of the competitive environment is exerting the strongest influence on bingo?
2   What other leisure and tourism organizations are likely to be affected by the national lottery?
3   Examine possible responses to the threat of the national lottery under the following headings:

(a)   Price leadership strategies
(b)   Differentiation strategies
(c)   Withdrawal or diversification strategies
(d)   Creating switching costs to prevent loss of customers

Task 8.2   Sabre's rattled in booking systems war

What have the following in common – Sabre, Galileo, Amadeus, Worldspan, and Abacus? They are all computer reservation systems (CRS). The prize they are fighting for? Global domination. If that sounds overdramatic, think of the similar technological battles which have been fought. The battle of the computers where Apples and Amigas rapidly lost ground as the IBM-based PC format became the emerging world standard. The battle of the videos where Betamax and Video 2000 struggled on with occasional price skirmishes before yielding to the eventual victor – VHS.

Sabre is currently the leading player in the CRS field. It runs its service from giant IBM computers in Tulsa, Oklahoma which process up to 150 million requests a day. The company has computer terminals in 26 000 travel shops spread over 184 countries and as well as selling air seats it can book the services of 200 hotel companies and 60 car-hire firms. Using the services of a CRS, a customer can walk into a travel shop in Paris and book a flight to New York. Prices, times and availability are all available on screen. Having booked a flight it is then possible to make other travel arrangements, booking a car hire, reserving a hotel room and buying tickets for a Broadway show at the same time.

Sabre is owned by American Airlines, the world's biggest airline. It charges $2.50 for each transaction and makes handsome profits. Main rival to Sabre is Galileo, the CRS owned by 11 airlines headed by BA and United. As yet the two giants have eyed each other up, but have maintained their distance in the market place.

This cosy coexistence may now be set to change as three smaller companies have entered talks to turn a loose alliance into a full-scale merger. The companies are Abacus (Cathay Pacific, All Nippon and Singapore Airlines), Amadeus (Air France, Lufthansa and Iberia), and Worldspan (Delta, Northwest and TWA). Their combined presence would outclass either Sabre or Galileo and there is already talk of an intensification of competition through a CRS price war.

At the same time some of the smaller users of CRS systems are complaining about the increasing power of the CRS owners. Sir Michael Bishop, chairman of British Midland, has lodged a complaint with the EC claiming to have been billed by Galileo for bookings that never materialized. He also complains of a lack of transparency in their pricing structure. His concerns are shared by many other regional airlines who say they are getting a bad deal from the two main CRS operators.

One market analyst clearly sees a change in the balance of power emerging, saying, 'There is a new player in town and a new honeymoon is about to begin'.

Source: the author, from news cuttings, April 1994.

Questions

1   Identify the buyers and suppliers of CRS.
2   Discuss the relative power of buyers and suppliers of CRS.
3   What degree of competitive rivalry exists in CRS?
4   Will the relative power of buyers and sellers in CRS remain constant?

Task 8.3   Skiing with Sega in the Arizona desert

Could it be that Sonic the Hedgehog will end up as a nasty squashed mess in the middle of the road of progress, flattened by the juggernaut of technology? Behind this gory vision lie some puzzling trading figures from Sega whose profit forecasts for the first quarter of this year are down from £423m to £113m.

What is going on? Has the games boom bust? The answer is no, but Sega realize that it won't keep them going for ever so the company has been investing heavily in leisure for the future. Hence the blip in the figures.

Sega is advancing its leisure empire on several fronts. On the one hand it has its sights set on Disney-style leisure parks. But whilst theme parks have traditionally involved large sites, sunny climates and bigger and better engineered rides, the Sega plan is for small, indoor settings for virtual adventures. Sega Virtualand is a recent manifestation of Sega's new thinking. It is an experimental virtual-reality arcade set within the Luxor Las Vegas Hotel. Visitors to the arcade can thrill to the excitement of downhill skiing or space travel to Mars just by stepping into small windowless capsules. Here computer-coordinated graphics and pneumatics combine to trick mind and body into new and exciting experiences.

Nick Alexander, chief executive of Sega Europe, explains the financial attractions of such developments. 'The great virtue of this kind of park is that it takes up only about 3 per cent of the space a traditional theme park requires. It means they can be built in densely populated areas and once the initial software development has taken place, they will be cheaper too.' Sega plans to open two virtual parks in Japan by the end of the year and to have a global network of up to 50 sites developed by 1997.

Whilst Sega's main competitor Nintendo has not yet followed suit, there are other companies pursuing similar strategies. The UK company Virtuality is also operating at the cutting edge of virtual-leisure technology and two virtual reality machines are to be found in the Trocadero centre in London's Piccadilly Circus.

Sega's other developing front? Enter Sega Channel TV. This is Sega's response to the communications revolution, which begins transmissions to American homes in the summer and will shortly be available in the UK. The concept is simple. The use of cartridges, disks and CDs for computer games is already yesterday's technology. Why not cut out the visit to the shops and download the game directly into your console from satellite or cable TV?

Source: the author, from news cuttings, 1994.

Questions

1 Define the markets in which Sega's new products will have a competitive impact using strategic group analysis.
2 Analyse the competitive environment of Sega channel TV, using Porter's five force analysis.
3 How easy will it be for Sega to protect its new products from the threat of new entrants?
4 To what extent can Sega be said to be suffering from strategic drift?

Short questions

1 How does strategic drift occur?
2 Which sectors of the leisure and tourism industry are currently secure from new entrants?
3 Where is supplier power high in the leisure and tourism industry?
4 What are barriers to entry? Identify entry barriers for airlines and hotels.
5 What factors tend to create a high degree of competitive rivalry?
6 Identify strategic groups in the hotel industry.

Reference

Porter, M., *Competitive Strategy: Techniques for Analysing Industries and Competitors*, Free Press, 1980.

Further reading

Gregory, M., *Dirty Tricks: British Airways' Secret War Against Virgin Atlantic*, Little Brown, 1994.
Porter, M., *Competitive Advantage*, Free Press, 1985.

9

The economic environment

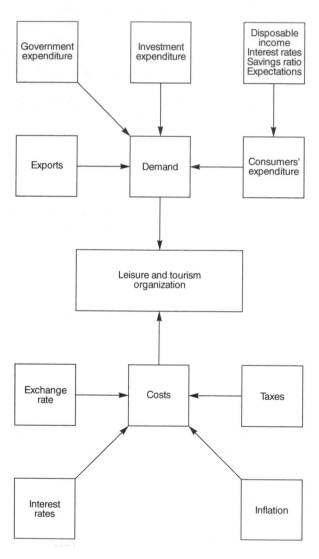

Objectives

The UK economy has a history of ups and downs. The last decade has witnessed the boom years of the mid 1980s – characterized by rising profits – as well as the profound recession of the early 1990s – characterized by rising bankruptcies.

Figure 9.1 charts the path of the UK economy over recent years. It is clearly important for organizations to monitor their economic environment carefully. Managers who read the rapid growth of the UK economy between points *A* and *B* as being normal and sustainable may well have instigated optimistic and expansionary strategic plans. These plans may have proved ruinous as the economy nose-dived between points *B* and *C*. This squeezed organizations from two directions as sales revenue fell, and increasing interest rates added to costs.

Exhibit 9.1 illustrates the effects of changes in the economy on key tourism attractions.

Exhibit 9.1   Leisure ups and downs

Tourism recession

The Tower of London and other leading attractions are suffering in the recession, the English Tourist Board reported. The tower was visited by 1.9 million people last year [1991], 16% fewer than in 1990.

Source: *The Independent*, 10 August 1992.

Pearson PLC: annual reports 1991–1993

1991: Tussauds Group had a tough trading year. The Gulf War, and the recession affected visits to tourist

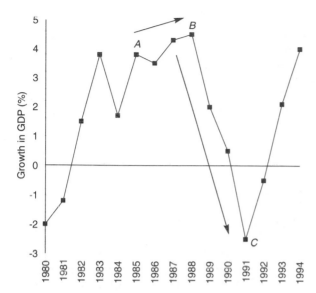

Figure 9.1 UK economic growth. Source: CSO, *Economic Trends*. GDP = Gross domestic product.

attractions and the spending of those who did visit was less than 1990 levels. For the group as a whole, attendances were therefore lower than in the previous year, and profits down 44 per cent to £8m.

1992: In spite of the prolonged UK recession, profits for the Tussauds Group were £10.5m, 35 per cent more than for 1991. Attendances at Alton Towers reached an all-time high. Attendances in London were affected by increasing levels of unemployment and the total number of visitors at Madame Tussauds was virtually unchanged from 1991.

1993: Attendances, turnover and operating profits of the Tussauds Group reached new heights in 1993. Operating profits reached £14.1m, an increase of 34 per cent. Attendances at Alton towers reached an all time high and there were improved attendances at Madame Tussauds in London. With continuing improvement in the UK economy, trading prospects for 1994 and beyond are encouraging.

Source: *Pearson Group Annual Reports*, 1991–1993.

This chapter considers the variables in the economy that affect leisure and tourism organizations and the causes of changes in these variables. It also peers tentatively into the future. It

will equip you with the skills to perform the 'E' part of PEST analysis.

By studying this chapter students will be able to:

- identify the key variables in the economy which affect leisure and tourism organizations
- identify and utilize information sources
- explain the impact of changes in economic variables on leisure and tourism organizations
- explain the interrelationship between key economic variables
- understand the causes of change in the economic environment
- understand government economic policy and the significance of the budget
- understand the global economic environment
- utilize economic forecasts with due caution

What are the key variables?

The economic environment affects organizations in the leisure and tourism sector in two main ways. First changes in the economic environment can affect the demand for an organization's products and second changes may affect an organization's costs. Additionally background factors such as property prices may affect organizations, particularly those in the accommodation sector. These three areas will be discussed in turn.

The economic environment and demand

The key macroeconomic factors affecting demand for leisure and tourism products are:

- consumers' expenditure
- export demand
- investment demand
- government expenditure

Consumers' expenditure

Consumers' expenditure can be defined as the total expenditure on goods and services for

Table 9.1   *Consumers' expenditure (£bn)*

Consumers' expenditure	1987	1988	1989	1990	1991	1992	1993	1994	1995
Current prices	265	299	327	347	365	382	406	428	
1990 prices	311	335	345	347	340	340	348	358	

Source: CSO, *Economic Trends.*

immediate consumption. Thus the level of consumers' expenditure is a key element in determining the demand for goods and services in the leisure and tourism sector.

Care needs to be taken in interpreting consumers' expenditure statistics. Table 9.1 shows two series for consumers' expenditure. The top row shows consumers' expenditure at current prices (sometimes referred to as 'money consumers' expenditure'), whilst the bottom row shows consumers' expenditure at 1990, or constant prices (sometimes referred to as 'real consumers' expenditure'). Notice that the data for consumers' expenditure at current prices rise throughout the recession of the early 1990s.

An organization basing its business planning on such data would draw false and overly optimistic conclusions about the state of the economy. This is because consumers' expenditure at current prices includes the effects of inflation on consumer spending. However, consumers' expenditure at constant prices has had the inflationary element removed and is therefore a more useful guide.

It can be seen from Table 9.1 that consumers' expenditure at constant prices rose strongly between 1987 and 1989 and then fell in the period following 1990. This burst of activity, followed by an abrupt halt, encouraged some organizations to expand recklessly only to suffer difficulties when the recession started to bite.

To understand fully movements in consumers' expenditure we need to consider its determinants. The main determinants of consumers' expenditure include:

- real disposable income
- interest rates
- expectations
- savings ratio

Real disposable income

The main determinant of consumers' expenditure is the amount of income earned. Figures for national income can be an important source here, but real disposable income provides a more useful guide.

To understand real disposable income we need to consider the meaning of the terms 'real' and 'disposable'. First, we are generally more interested in real income rather than money income since the former has had the effects of inflation removed.

Second, disposable income can be defined as the amount of income left after deduction of direct taxes (such as income tax and national insurance contributions), and the addition of state benefits (such as child benefit and unemployment benefit). In other words, it is the amount of income available for spending. Table 9.2 records recent data for personal disposable income.

The change in the income component of disposable income is determined by a number of factors. First income is related to the level of economic activity. Figure 9.2 illustrates the relationship between income and expenditure.

Households obtain income from selling factors of production (for example, labour) to firms. Firms use these factors of production to produce the goods and services that they sell. Thus as expenditure increases, more goods and services are sold which in turn creates demand for more factors of production such as labour. This in turn generates more income.

Changes in taxes and benefits can cause

Table 9.2 *Personal disposable income (£bn)*

	1987	1988	1989	1990	1991	1992	1993	1994	1995
Personal disposable income (current prices)	285	317	353	380	406	436	458	477	
Real personal disposable income (1990 prices)	335	355	372	380	378	388	394	400	

Source: CSO, *Economic Trends*.

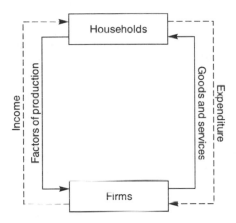

Figure 9.2 The circular flow of national income and expenditure.

significant changes to the disposable element of disposable income. Such changes are often used by the government to manage the economy. For example, in 1987, Chancellor Lawson cut the basic rate of income tax from 29 to 27 per cent. He followed this in 1988 with a further cut to 25 per cent and reduced the top rate of income tax to 40 per cent. The effects of these measures can be seen in Table 9.2. Real personal disposable income rose by 5.97 per cent between 1987 and 1988 and by a further 4.78 per cent by 1989. In 1993, however, the government was forced to raise tax levels in order to reduce its own borrowing requirement. National insurance contributions were raised by 1 per cent from April 1994, personal allowances were frozen and mortgage tax relief reduced.

Real disposable income shows how much consumers have at their disposal for potential spending. How much they actually spend depends on the following factors:

- interest rates
- expectations
- the savings ratio

Interest rates

Interest rates have an important effect on consumers' expenditure. In general, higher interest rates tend to depress consumers' expenditure for two reasons. First, at higher interest rates borrowing becomes more costly and thus consumer spending that is financed by credit is curbed. At the same time households with mortgages find their monthly repayments increasing, thus leaving less money available for spending. Second, high interest rates make savings more attractive and the savings ratio will tend to rise.

Table 9.3 illustrates recent changes in interest rates. It can be seen that in recent years interest rates peaked in 1989 and troughed in 1993. The impact of these changes on consumers' expenditure can be traced in Table 9.1. The growth in consumers' expenditure slowed dramatically in 1990 and went into reverse in 1991, whilst some growth was recorded again from 1993. Exhibit 9.2 illustrates the impact of lower interest rates on demand, and hence share prices in the leisure sector.

Exhibit 9.2 Stock market report

Amongst the market's best recent performers were leisure stocks as dealers pointed to the recovery

Table 9.3 *Bank base rates (%)*

	1987	1988	1989	1990	1991	1992	1993	1994	1995
Bank base rates	11	13	15	14	10.5	7.0	5.5	6.25	

Source: CSO, *Economic Trends*.

potential of the sector amid speculation of further cuts in interest rates.

Source: author/FTSE index, first quarter 1994.

The term 'interest rates' can be misleading since there are many interest rates in the economy. The bank base rate which is quoted in Table 9.3 is the rate to which many other interest rates are referenced. Taking 1993 as an example, bank base rate averaged 5.5 per cent. Rates paid to savers in building society ordinary share accounts would be around 2 per cent. Mortgage rates would be around 8 per cent, whilst interest charges on credit cards would be about 23 per cent. A change in the bank base rate will trigger a change in the whole structure of interest rates. The reasons behind changes in interest rates are discussed later in this chapter.

Expectations

Expectations refers to the degree of optimism or pessimism with which consumers and business people view the future. Expectations have a profound effect on the economy because they tend to deliver self-fulfilling prophecies. When consumers feel good about the economy they tend to spend more and they thus cause the economy to grow. Conversely, when they feel bad about the economy they tend to spend less and thus they may prolong the recession that is causing their pessimism. Expectations tend to be influenced by recent experience, by the mass media, and by the level of unemployment. Measuring expectations is often done by way of surveys, as illustrated in exhibit 9.3.

Exhibit 9.3   Low expectations

The most pessimistic level of confidence since April 1990 was revealed by a Gallup survey conducted in March 1994. Forty-two per cent of those questioned felt that their financial position would deteriorate over the next year.

Source: author from Gallup data.

Of course the government often attempts to influence expectations. Norman Lamont when Chancellor of the Exchequer famously attempted to 'talk up' the economy by his remarks about the 'green shoots of recovery'.

Savings ratio

The savings ratio is defined as that proportion of personal disposable income that is saved. The savings ratio is important to firms since, when it increases, consumers are saving more of their disposable income and consuming less of it. The main factors which affect the savings ratio are the rate of interest and expectations. As interest rates rise, *ceteris paribus* consumers will generally wish to save more and consume less, since savings will be more profitable and borrowing more costly. When consumers' expectations about the future are pessimistic they will generally increase their savings.

Table 9.4 shows that the savings ratio rose considerably between 1987 and 1992. The high savings ratio of 1991 certainly fuelled the recession.

Export demand

The economic environment will affect an organization's export demand in two main ways. First,

Table 9.4   *Personal savings ratio*

	1987	1988	1989	1990	1991	1992	1993	1994	1995
Personal savings ratio	7.1	5.7	7.2	8.6	10.1	12.3	11.5	10.4	

Source: CSO, *Economic Trends.*

Table 9.5   *Gross domestic fixed capital formation (private sector; £bn at constant 1990 prices)*

	1987	1988	1989	1990	1991	1992	1993	1994	1995
Gross domestic fixed capital formation	79	92	96	90	81	78	78	79	

Source: CSO, *Economic Trends.*

the exchange rate will affect the overseas price of exports and this is discussed in detail in Chapter 16. Second, analysis of the international economic environment can provide information on the level of economic growth in countries which are markets for an organization's products. The major banks publish regular reviews of economic prospects for our major trading partners and exhibit 9.4 illustrates the size and division of the global economy and predicts the growing strength of the Chinese economy.

Exhibit 9.4   Gross reality of global statistics

Shouldn't everyone, not just economists, know gross national product (GNP) statistics for their own country, global GNP, and also GNP for leading economies such as the European Union (EU) and Japan?

Here are a selection of such statistics:

Gross global product amounts to $24 trillion (£16 trillion). The GNP of the USA is $5.6 trillion (23.3 per cent); the EU $4.7 trillion (19.6 per cent), of which Germany's $1.25 trillion is 5.2 per cent of global product; Japan $2.4 trillion (10 per cent); China $2.4 trillion (10 per cent); India $1 trillion (4.2 per cent) and the UK $0.9 trillion (3.6 per cent).

Projections, possibly wayward, until 2010 are: the global economy $34 trillion, the USA $7.8 trillion (almost 23 per cent), the EU (present 12 members only)

$7.2 trillion (just over 21 per cent), Japan $3.8 trillion (11 per cent) and India $2.1 trillion (6 per cent).

The big question mark is China. If its economy grows as fast for the next 25 years as it has for the past 14, it could become the biggest in the world. Since the radical reforms of late 1978, real GNP has grown by an average of nearly 9 per cent a year. The economy is almost certainly four times bigger today than in 1978; and as early as 2002, it is projected to be twice as large again. This means that China will have matched the performances of Japan, Taiwan and South Korea during their fastest quarter-centuries of growth.

Source: *Guardian*, 2 May 1994 (adapted).

Investment

Some organizations do not supply goods and services to consumers, but specialize in supplying capital goods to other firms. Thus the aircraft manufacturer Boeing, selling to airlines and tour operators, finds demand for its products is sensitive to the level of investment in the economy.

Table 9.5 shows recent changes in gross domestic fixed capital formation in the private sector. This refers to the total amount of investment in new capital goods. The term 'gross' means that it covers all capital investment including the replacement of worn-out machines. The term 'net' would cover only investment over and above the replacement of worn-out machines.

Table 9.5 shows a considerable fall in investment from 1990 to 1993. The main determinants of investment demand are:

- consumers' expenditure
- expectations
- amount of spare capacity
- interest rates

It is therefore changes in the above factors that should be examined for an explanation of the fall in investment evident from Table 9.5 in 1990. In fact, all four factors contributed to the fall in investment. High interest rates had the double effect of reducing consumers' expenditure and increasing the cost of borrowing for investment projects. The fall in consumers' expenditure meant that suppliers were left with spare capacity in the form of empty planes, unused accommodation and idle machinery and thus there was little need for additional or replacement investment. Finally, as the recession deepened, people's expectations became more pessimistic and investment depends on optimistic expectations about future levels of income and expenditure.

It should be noted that lower interest rates will not necessarily, single-handedly, stimulate investment demand in a recession since there may already be spare capacity in the organization and expectations may remain pessimistic. Thus there was no immediate recovery of investment in 1992 when interest rates fell.

Exhibit 9.5 describes how the early 1990s recession affected aircraft manufacturers. The demand for aircraft depends upon the demand for air travel and this was hit by the recession. Note that it is the prospect of rises in disposable income that is likely to stimulate the demand for travel and thus in turn the investment demand for new aircraft.

Exhibit 9.5 £270bn dilemma for jet set: the aviation industry is banking on a tourism revival to help pay for new aircraft – David Black

A troubled aviation industry is pinning hopes on a massive upturn in the world tourist trade to ensure airline customers can continue to buy new jets.

Some 3200 jet airliners are on order from the big three plane makers – Boeing, Airbus and McDonnell Douglas. However, the recession and the aftermath of the Gulf War have conspired to knock the bottom out of the airline's biggest earner, the business traveller market. Tourist travel has also been hit. As a result, the huge backlog of airliners on order is under threat. The gravity of this situation has been slowly sinking in for the aircraft makers and the airlines over the past few months as the grim airline performance figures have filtered through. In November [1991], Boeing announced plans to cut production of 737 jets from 21 to 17 a month, and American Airlines said it was cancelling or deferring options on 93 aircraft worth $5.2bn.

Overall the number of passengers carried by airlines between January and September [1991] was a mere 67 per cent of 1990's figure according to the International Air Transport Association, which represents most of the world's airlines. The airlines desperately need traffic growth to recover their profitability. That profitability is vital to repay the debts they must incur to take delivery of their new generation of jets.

All is not doom and gloom according to the IBA, the International Bureau of Aviation, which specializes in advising financial institutions on all aspects of the aviation industry. Its view is distinctly upbeat.

So on what factors do the financiers base their optimism? Tourism, says the IBA. And it is not alone. The World Travel and Tourism Council calculated that 11.4 per cent of global consumer spending is on personal travel. As a result, the IBA concludes: 'Rises in disposable income will reinforce the trend towards the growth of tourism, which will increasingly become the largest revenue earner for the airline industry'.

Source: *The Independent*, 10 January 1992 (adapted).

Government expenditure

Leisure and tourism organizations which are sensitive to changes in government expenditure include the BBC, the Arts and Sports Councils, the BTA, and those organizations which depend on local government support.

The level and detail of government expenditure tend to reflect two things – the state of the economy (discussed later in this chapter) and the political party in power. The overall policy of Conservative governments since Mrs Thatcher's

Table 9.6 *Public spending plans 1994–1998 (£bn)*

	1994–95	1995–96	1996–97	1997–98
Department of the Environment, local government and other	30.0	30.3	30.9	30.8
National Heritage	1.0	1.0	1.0	1.0
Local government own spending	12.0	11.8	12.0	12.2
Total (excluding privatization receipts)	295.2	305.0	316.0	325.4

Source: HM Treasury, *The Red Book.*

coming to power in 1979 has been to reduce the level of government spending. Table 9.6 records projections for overall government spending and the details for local government and National Heritage. These are money figures and have not been adjusted for inflation. Assuming that there will be some level of inflation between 1994 and 1998, the real value of spending on National Heritage for example is set to fall. Similarly local government spending is projected to be tightly controlled over this period.

The economic environment and costs

The key macroeconomic factors affecting costs of leisure and tourism products are:

- interest rates
- inflation
- the exchange rate
- indirect taxes

The rate of interest

The effects of changes in interest rates have been discussed above with reference to consumers' expenditure and investment. However interest rates also affect firms' costs, particularly those with significant borrowings such as Eurotunnel, as illustrated by exhibit 9.6.

Exhibit 9.6   Debt floods the Chunnel

Yesterday's rescue package announced for the channel tunnel means that a total of nearly £10.6bn has been raised to fund the massive project – more than double the amount that was originally projected. Eurotunnel said that £1.5bn further projected cash requirements after May 6th [1994] mostly represented interest costs on the increased debt not covered by cash flow until the expected break-even of the project in 1998. Although this is the last cash call, there are numerous financial 'variables' which Graham Corbett, Eurotunnel's chief financial officer, set out, including the fact that around half of Eurotunnel's sterling borrowings are exposed to variable interest rates.

Source: *Guardian*, 27 May 1994 (adapted).

It is reported that around half of Eurotunnel's borrowing is exposed to variable interest rates. The variations in interest rates illustrated in Table 9.3 show how risky exposure to variable interest rates can be. Assuming borrowing rates of base rate +2%, the interest payments without any capital repayment would be £75 000 per year per £1m borrowed at 1993 interest rates. However, interest payments would rise to £170 000 per year per £1m borrowed at 1989 rates of interest.

Inflation

Inflation will affect the price of a firm's inputs. Table 9.7 shows the varying rates of inflation on leisure and tourism-related items and the

Table 9.7 *Retail prices in UK leisure and tourism-related items, February 1994*

	Percentage change over year
Restaurant meals	5.0
Beer	5.0
Leisure goods	0.2
Entertainment	8.0

Source: CSO: *Employment Gazette.*

importance of inflation is discussed more fully in Chapter 14.

The exchange rate

Where imports form a substantial component of a good or service, changes in the exchange rate can have an effect on production costs. A fall in the exchange rate of the pound against foreign currencies will make imports more expensive. For example, component costs for tour operators such as Thomson include foreign hotel costs, and a fall in the exchange rate will increase such costs. This issue is discussed more fully in Chapter 16.

Indirect taxes

Indirect taxes are taxes paid indirectly to the government. They are paid first to a third party – generally a retailer. VAT is a key indirect tax and indirect taxes have a direct effect on prices.

Exhibit 9.7 records the introduction of a tax on air travel which was announced by the chancellor in the autumn 1993 budget. There has been considerable protest from the airline industry over this new tax. In particular they fear that, since surface transport is not subject to such a tax, this may cause a loss of passengers. This is particularly likely on routes such as London to Paris, where Eurostar offers a close substitute to air travel.

Exhibit 9.7 Excerpt from 1993 budget speech

'This will be set at £5 for departures to anywhere within the UK and the European Union and £10 for departures to other destinations. The new duty will come into force next October [1994] and will raise some £330 million in a full year'.

Source: Kenneth Clarke's Budget speech to the House of Commons, 30 November 1993.

The provision of some goods and services in the leisure and tourism sector is currently zero–rated for VAT. This includes books and magazines, travel and overseas package holidays. However there is no guarantee that the government will not extend VAT to these items.

Background features in the economic environment

The labour market

The level of unemployment has several effects on firms in the leisure and tourism sector. High unemployment has a detrimental effect on consumer spending and confidence. Ironically, it provides individuals with more leisure time, but with reduced spending power to enter leisure markets. On the other hand, in terms of hiring labour, high unemployment means greater availability of labour at competitive wage levels. The extent of membership and power of trade unions also affects wage rates.

Property prices

The volatility of property prices in recent years has had a profound effect on many organizations in the leisure and tourism sector. During the property boom of the mid 1980s organizations such as Brent Walker, with substantial property holdings, were able to use the increased valuation of these assets as security for increased borrowing. On the other hand, firms which made large property acquisitions at the top of the property boom often found themselves in terminal difficulties as property prices fell sharply and interest payments rose.

Government and the economy

It is impossible to understand changes in the external economic environment without consideration of the government's role in the economy. This in turn can be understood in terms of aims and policies.

Government economic aims

The following aims are followed by most governments:

- low inflation
- low unemployment
- balance between government spending and income over the medium term
- balance between overseas earnings and expenditure
- economic growth

However, different governments have different priorities among these objectives. The Thatcher government for example put control of inflation and a balanced budget at the top of the list. It must also be recognized that these aims are sometimes conflicting and also that as elections occur, policy aims are generally distorted towards reducing taxation.

Government economic policy

Economic policy refers to a set of measures designed to affect the economy. The budget, in late autumn, is the traditional time for making changes to economic policy. Policies can be divided into:

- Fiscal policy. This uses changes in the level of taxation or government spending to influence the economy.

- Monetary policy. This uses changes in interest rates, and thus the cost of borrowing, to influence the economy.

Recent economic policy

Table 9.8 shows changes in the main indicators for the UK economy in recent years, and three distinct phases can be identified.

1985–1988: Boom

It can be seen that the UK economy grew strongly in the period 1985 to 1988, and unemployment fell. This was despite the fact that monetary policy was generally quite tight during this period. The purpose of tight monetary policy and high interest rates was to suppress inflation. The rationale behind this policy was first that high interest rates reduced consumer demand by making credit expensive, and second that import prices were kept low as high interest rates stimulated the demand for sterling and kept the exchange rate high.

However the chancellor reduced interest rates in 1987 and also made some adjustments to fiscal policy. The 1987 budget cut the basic rate of income tax to 27 per cent and the 1988 budget made a further cut in income tax to 25 per cent and scrapped higher rates of income tax from 60 to 40 per cent.

The result of this loosening of monetary and fiscal policy was that economic growth became unsustainable. By 1989 inflation had risen rapidly to nearly 8 per cent, and the UK's overseas trading account showed a deficit of £22bn.

1989–1992: Bust

The rapid deterioration in inflation and foreign currency earnings meant that the government had to apply the brakes to the economy. Monetary policy was designated for this task, and interest rates were progressively increased to 15 per cent in 1989. John Major, as chancellor of the exchequer, used the famous phrase, 'if it's not hurting it's not working' to explain the policy. What he

Table 9.8 *The UK economy: selected indicators*

	1985	1986	1987	1988	1989	1990	1991	1992	1993	1994	1995	1996
Growth (percentage change)	3.8	3.6	4.4	4.5	1.9	0.6	−2.5	−0.5	2.0	3.9		
Inflation (percentage change)	6.1	3.4	4.1	4.9	7.8	9.5	5.9	3.9	1.9	2.5		
Current balance (£bn)	2.2	−0.8	−5	−16	−22	−18	−7	−11	−10	−0.1		
Unemployment (m)	3.2	3.2	2.9	2.4	1.8	1.6	2.2	2.7	2.8	2.5		
Rate of interest (%)	15	13	11	13	15	14	10.5	7.0	5.4	6.25		
Public sector borrowing requirement (£bn)	7.4	2.4	−1	−12	−9	−2	13	37	46	39		
£/$	1.3	1.5	1.6	1.8	1.6	1.8	1.8	1.8	1.5	1.5		
£/DM	3.8	3.2	2.9	3.1	3.1	2.9	2.9	2.5	2.6	2.5		

Note:
1   Rate of interest = three-month interbank.
Source: CSO/Barclays Bank Review.

meant was that interest rates were going to be used by the government to slow down consumers' expenditure – mainly by making credit expensive – and that rates would continue to rise until consumers' expenditure was curbed.

Eventually the government's policy did work, but perhaps too successfully, since the economy slowed down and went into reverse, economic growth being a negative figure for both 1991 and 1992. As the recession took hold, unemployment rose quickly to reach 2.8 million by 1993.

During this period government policy got into a mess. The recession, and the consequent rise in unemployment, meant less tax receipts for the government and more spending on state benefits. Thus the public sector borrowing requirement (PSBR) increased sharply and the government had to borrow £37bn in 1992. The high PSBR meant that it was difficult to stimulate the economy by reducing taxes.

At the same time, the government had taken sterling into the exchange rate mechanism (ERM) of the European monetary system (EMS). Monetary policy was used to maintain sterling's agreed rate of exchange against European currencies. High interest rates were used to make sterling an attractive currency and thus maintain its value.

Thus the recession was prolonged by high interest rates, and tax cuts could not be used to stimulate consumer spending because of the high PSBR. Monetary policy and fiscal policy were both tight.

1992 and after: a lucky escape

Despite all the government's efforts (interest rates were raised from 10 to 15 per cent in one day), sterling was forced to leave the ERM in September 1992. This enabled the government to relax its monetary policy and interest rates were lowered in a series of moves from 10.5 per cent in 1991 to 7 per cent in 1992. This allowed the economy to recover, led by a rise in consumers' expenditure.

However, PSBR was still high, reflecting the effects of the recession in reducing government tax income and increasing benefit payments and in 1993 the government had to borrow £46bn. The budgets of 1993 and 1994 thus contained a series of measures to increase taxes (including the extension of VAT to fuels) to reduce government borrowing. They also maintained tight control on government expenditure and the £3.2m cut in the Arts Council of Great Britain's grant for 1994 can be seen in this light.

There was considerable debate as to whether the tax increases in the 1993 budget would stall the economic recovery, but the evidence from exhibit 9.8 suggests not.

Exhibit 9.8 Cost of living fails to halt holiday sales

Government tax hikes for this year and next will not dent booming holiday sales according to a new report.

Business forecaster Key Note predicted a healthy 11 per cent increase in air-inclusive tours this year to 15.7 million despite dearer mortgages, VAT on fuel and the introduction of air passenger duty in the autumn.

Source: *Travel Trade Gazette*, 1 June 1994 (adapted).

The future

An eminent professor of economics, the Lord Maurice Peston of Mile End, cautioned against blind faith in economic forecasting, suggesting that random typing of a monkey at a keyboard would result in equally useful forecasts as those produced by complex mathematical models. Equally, the 'flying by the seat of the pants' technique exercised by many in the late 1980s boom led to overly optimistic business decisions which, as Keynes said of the 1920s boom, 'discounted not only the future but the hereafter'. Economic forecasts are an essential part of business planning, but must be used with extreme caution, and the assumptions upon which they are made must be constantly monitored. Exhibit 9.9 illustrates general optimism about the prospects for the UK economy. However, the chancellor, Kenneth Clarke, pointed out that the UK had seen growth disappear into excessive inflation

three times in the last two decades and a leading newspaper commented that the experienced observer would wonder how things would be messed up this time.

Exhibit 9.9 Two views of the future

Accidental birth of a very British recovery

The British economic recovery at the macro level is a fact of life – or at least of the best statistics we have. From the point of view of the Treasury's Panel of Independent forecasters:

'The economy has continued to evolve favourably since . . . May, with robust growth, low inflation, falling unemployment and a much reduced trade deficit. We expect growth to continue at a healthy rate next year . . . inflation to remain within the Government's target range in the short term. In the very long term, with appropriate policies we think it should be possible for the economy to return to a low level of unemployment.'

Source: *Observer*, 13 November 1994.

UK economy

This year's overall economic performance is set to be much better than expected. Overall output should record an increase of at least 3.5 per cent, while inflation is now likely to end the year at around 2.5 per cent. At the same time, the balance of payments deficit, often viewed as a potential barrier to a sustainable recovery, has been on a clear downward trend.

[There] appears to be a healthy medium-term outlook, encompassing both a relatively strong and well-balanced recovery with low inflation and the restoration of sound public finances.

Source: *Barclays Economic Review*, fourth quarter 1994.

Review of key terms

- Real consumers' expenditure = money consumer expenditure adjusted for inflation.
- Disposable income = income – direct taxes + government benefits.
- Recession = two consecutive quarters of falling output.

- Savings ratio = proportion of income saved.
- PSBR = public sector borrowing requirement (excess of government spending over taxes).
- Gross investment = net (new) investment + depreciation (replacement investment).
- Final goods = goods bought by consumers.
- Capital goods = goods bought by firms to assist production, e.g. machines.
- GDP = gross domestic product = total value of output of an economy in a year.
- Fiscal policy = use of tax and government spending levels to influence the economy.
- Monetary policy = use of interest rates to influence the economy.

Data questions

Task 9.1   Learning how to make play pay – John Shepherd

'Much work is merely a way to make money; much leisure is merely a way to spend it.' Alas, that statement in C. Wright Mills' *Power, Politics and People* can today be turned on its head. There is not much work about, and those who have jobs are not spending. Against this background, leisure has been one of the hardest-hit of all industries by the recession. Many companies have gone to the wall and the accountancy profession now finds itself in the unenviable position of being one of the industry's largest participants, owning scores of hotels, discos and clubs picked up from companies that have gone into receivership.

The people and companies lured into leisure at the height of the property boom have been weeded out first, closely followed by established outfits that paid over the top for market share. The list of fallen names is long and star-studded; it includes George Walker at Brent Walker, Harry Goodman at International Leisure, Michael Ward at European Leisure and the Forsyth brothers at Leading Leisure.

Source: *The Independent*, 21 October 1992 (adapted).

Question

Conduct a CD-ROM search on the companies named in the above newspaper article and identify the major changes in the economic environment which were responsible for the difficulties which faced each organization.

Task 9.2   The UK recession 1990–92

A widely used definition of a recession, adopted in this article, is that of 'two or more consecutive quarters of falling output'. The latest recession was spread over seven quarters. Recessions can be caused by many different factors. The 1990–1992 recession in the UK followed a period of unsustainably fast growth during the late 1980s.

The anatomy of the 1990–1992 recession was as follows: manufacturing output fell by 7.5 per cent and output in the services sector fell by 2 per cent. The services sector includes retailing and wholesaling, hotels and catering, transport and communications, and businesses and financial services. The services sector amounted to over 60 per cent of gross domestic product (GDP) in 1990, whereas manufacturing only accounted for about 25 per cent, so its impact on total GDP is significant. Consumers' expenditure fell steeply in the 1990–1992 recession. Households built up debt rapidly during the boom years of the late 1980s; this led to a sharp retrenchment in their spending in 1990 and 1991 as they acted to reduce their debt in the face of high interest rates.

The initial impetus to recovery came mainly from consumer spending and exports. The substantial cut in interest rates over the past 3 years, and strong growth in real personal disposable income, boosted personal sector spending power. By the third quarter of 1993 most of the fall in consumer spending during the recession had been reversed.

As the recovery becomes more firmly established, businesses are likely to increase their spending as they become more confident that the pick-up in demand is sustained. The improvement in company finances and a modest increase in capacity utilization will also encourage investment in new and replacement stocks. These developments will help to broaden the recovery and strengthen growth.

Source: HM Treasury: *Economic Briefing*, February 1994 (adapted).

Questions

1 What evidence is there to support the assertion of 'unsustainably fast growth during the late 1980s'?
2 Why did 'unsustainably fast growth during the late 1980s' lead to a recession?
3 'The initial impetus to recovery came mainly from consumer spending. . .' Explain this statement by reference to the determinants of consumer spending.
4 'As the recovery becomes more firmly established, businesses are likely to increase their spending . . . and a modest increase in capacity utilization will also encourage investment in new and replacement stocks.' Explain which industries in the leisure and tourism sector are likely to benefit from this and what other factors are likely to encourage investment.

Task 9.3 Scenario planning

Organizations increasingly use the method of scenario planning to anticipate changes in the external environment. This enables them to plan considered responses.

Questions

1 Choose two firms in the leisure and tourism sector and analyse how they might be affected by the following scenarios:
   (a) a rise in interest rates of 6 per cent
   (b) a fall in unemployment of 500 000
   (c) a fall in the savings ratio
   (d) a fall in investment
2 Which two of these represent the most likely scenario for the next 2 years?

Task 9.4 Leisure profiles 1993–1994

Some of the leading leisure companies have recently reported on their profits and trading statements for 1993.

Rank Organization (bingo, casinos, Butlin's holiday camps, cinemas)

- pre-tax profits up from £125m to £276m
- cinema admissions up 10 per cent
- cinema prices: unchanged
- nightclub admissions up 13 per cent
- spending per head at nightclubs static
- bingo: spending per head up 6 per cent, admissions static
- casinos: spending per head up 4 per cent, admissions static

First Leisure (discotheques, bowling and tourist attractions

- pre-tax profits up 2.3 per cent to £31.8m
- turnover up 12.3 per cent to £121.8m
- discotheque admissions up 14 per cent
- discotheque admission prices: no change
- bowling: games played–unchanged
- bowling: spending per head down

Airtours (travel)

- pre-tax profits up 25 per cent to £46m
- bookings for summer 1994 up 56 per cent

Stakis (hotels and casinos)

- substantial increase in profits

Stanley Leisure (betting shops and casinos)

- substantial increase in profits

What are the prospects for 1994 and beyond? Stockbrokers Smith New Court's analyst for the leisure sector, Bruce Jones predicts that rising consumer expenditure will spill into the leisure sector. His views are echoed by general optimism amongst commentators in the sector.

Source: author/company reports/news cuttings, February 1994.

Questions

1   Using the exhibits in this chapter as a data source, explain why the leisure sector should have experienced some recovery in 1994.
2   Evaluate the opportunities and threats in the economic environment as they relate to the organizations discussed in the article.

Short questions

1   Consumers' expenditure at current prices rises from £100bn in year 1 to £110bn in year 2. Over the same period inflation is 10 per cent. What is the level of consumers' expenditure at constant (year 1) prices in year 2?
2   What is the definition and what are the characteristics of a recession?
3   What is the definition and what are the characteristics of a recovery?
4   Distinguish between fiscal and monetary policy.

5   What type of fiscal and monetary policy could be used to stimulate the economy in a recession?
6   What is the relationship between PSBR, taxation and government revenue?
7   What is the present outlook for the UK economy?
8   Explain the significance of the following to a named leisure or tourism sector organization:
    (a)   Interest rates
    (b)   Exchange rates
    (c)   Real disposable income
    (d)   Expectations

Further reading

Barclays Bank, *Barclays Economic Review*, Barclays Bank, quarterly.

Central Statistical Office, *Economic Trends*, Central Statistical Office, monthly.

Economist Intelligence Unit, *Travel and Tourism Analyst*, Economist Publications.

Henley Centre for Forecasting, *Leisure Futures*, Henley Centre for Forecasting, quarterly.

National Institute of Economic and Social Research, *The UK Economy*, Heinemann, 1993.

Smith, P. (ed.), *Keynote Market Review: UK Leisure and Tourism*, Keynote, 1993.

10

The political and sociocultural environment

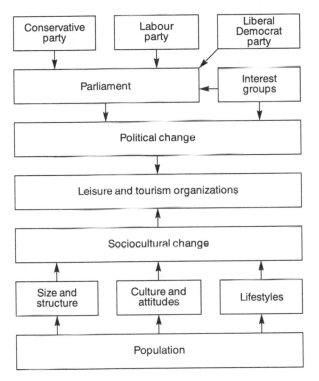

Objectives

This chapter continues the analysis of the operating environment focusing on the political and sociocultural parts of PEST analysis. It discusses the effects of political change on organizations and considers for example how leisure and tourism organizations might be affected by the results of the next election. The population is also

undergoing change in its size, structure and attitudes, each of which may affect leisure and tourism organizations.

The fox-hunting debate illustrates points of a political and cultural nature. In terms of cultural change, the League Against Cruel Sports has influenced public attitudes against the sport and its campaigns of hunt sabotage have affected hunts. In the political arena however, the Criminal Justice Bill has outlawed demonstrations which involve trespass and thus hunting may well expand again.

By studying this chapter students should be able to:

- define the scope of the political environment
- identify sources of information for the political environment
- identify political opportunities and threats to leisure and tourism organizations
- define the scope of the sociocultural environment
- identify information sources for the sociocultural environment
- identify sociocultural opportunities and threats to leisure and tourism organizations

The political environment

The political environment is shaped by those with political power, or the ability to influence events. A key player in this is the party in government for the immediate period until the next election.

Longer-term political trends are clearly difficult to predict since they depend largely upon which political party wins the next election. Although opinion polls give some indication of current party popularity they are likely to change considerably by the pre-election period and in any case do not have a good record of accuracy. The government itself will be subject to its own operating environment and thus policy will be shaped by the EU, the economy, international relations and interest group activity.

Given the range of possible directions of policy, scenario planning is likely to be used by organizations wishing to incorporate the political environment into their strategic planning. This involves analysing the impact of a range of possible political outcomes on an organization. Sources of information on changes in the political environment include:

- the queen's speech
- government reports
- party manifestos
- other reports and activity
- changes in the law

The queen's speech

The queen's speech sets out the government's parliamentary agenda for the coming year. It is read on behalf of the government by the queen at the state opening of parliament each autumn. Exhibit 10.1 reports on the parts of the Queen's speech of 16 November 1994 that relate to leisure and tourism.

Exhibit 10.1   Extracts from the queen's speech 1994

My government will continue with firm financial policies designed to support continuing economic growth and rising employment, based on permanent low inflation. Fiscal policy will continue to be set to bring the budget deficit back towards balance. My government will reduce the share of national income taken by the public sector.

Legislation will be introduced to equalize the state pension age between men and women and to improve security, equality and choice in non-state pensions.

My government will introduce a bill to tackle discrimination against disabled people.

Legislation will be introduced to authorize the construction and operation by the private sector of a high-speed rail link between London and the channel tunnel.

The delivery of environment policies will be strengthened by legislation to establish environment agencies for England and Wales and for Scotland.

Other measures will be laid before you. My Lords and members of the House of Commons, I pray that the blessing of Almighty God may rest upon your counsels.

Government reports

Government reports are a useful guide to policy. They set out detailed points which can affect specific organizations (for example, the Taylor report on football) and give clues about the general direction of government policy. The underlying support of the unregulated free market can be seen to permeate the 1985 report *Pleasure, Leisure and Jobs*, and the 1988 White Paper on broadcasting. However, the 1994 report on environmental pollution takes a much stronger interventionist line.

Pleasure, Leisure and Jobs: *the business of tourism (1985)*

This report underlined the government's belief in the importance of the leisure and tourism sector for the UK economy, but echoed the general Thatcher principles that instead of government intervention, there should be promotion of an enterprise economy. Specific proposals included:

- some merging of the activities of the BTA and the ETB
- encouragement of dispersal of tourists from London
- a new hotel classification system
- improvements in training

The 1988 White Paper: *broadcasting in the 1990s*

This set out government policy for the 1990s as being one of encouraging competition and choice in broadcasting whilst maintaining quality. Its main proposals included:

- maintenance of publicly funded BBC
- ITV franchises to be sold to the highest bidder subject to minimum quality standards
- authorization for channels 5 and 6 for terrestrial TV
- expansion of commercial satellite and cable TV
- new radio franchises

The results of this policy are likely to be a rapid expansion of TV and radio stations in the 1990s, but with a question mark over the quality of output.

The 1990 Taylor report

The Taylor report on football concluded the public inquiry set up after the 1989 Hillsborough disaster. It recommendations included:

- halting the proposed national identity scheme for football spectators
- football grounds to be converted to all-seat stadia by 1994 for top-division clubs and 1999 for the remainder of the league.
- making pitch invasions and the shouting of racial abuse a criminal offence

The 1994 Royal Commission on Environmental Pollution

This report concluded that current growth rates in road traffic, which are forecast to lead to a doubling in road traffic between 1995 and 2025, are neither socially nor environmentally acceptable. It made 110 recommendations to encourage 'a gradual shift away from lifestyles which depend on high mobility and intensive use of cars'. These included:

- a doubling of petrol prices in real terms between 1994 and 2004
- higher parking charges
- road pricing

- residential, commercial and leisure developments to be located to minimize car use
- switching investment from roads to public transport
- banning of super unleaded petrol
- ending of zero-rating of tax on aviation fuel

The local government commission

This examined the structure of local government and considered whether it was best served by unitary or two-tier administrations. For example, it recommended that two-tier structures in Bedfordshire and Buckinghamshire be replaced by unitary authorities. Two-tier authorities have been allowed to continue in other areas such as Oxfordshire and Cumbria.

Party manifestos

These identify policies which political parties will follow if elected to government. They are generally available in the period preceding a general election.

Other reports and activity

The following examples demonstrate different approaches to policy from the right-wing thinking of the Adam Smith Institute, to the centre-left thinking of the Social Justice Commission.

The Adam Smith Institute

This right-wing pressure group has produced numerous reports, including those advising on more privatization in leisure and tourism. For example, *Expounding the Arts* (1987) advocates the phasing-out of government subsidies to the arts, and that museums should be encouraged to become more commercially oriented. *Pining for Profit* argued for the privatization of the Forestry Commission. Exhibit 10.2 illustrates the main points from its recent report on the BBC, *What Price Public Service*?

Exhibit 10.2   Privatize 'smug' BBC call

The BBC should be privatized through a stock market flotation and the licence fee phased out over 10 years with advertising and sponsorship making up its funding, the free-market Adam Smith Institute proposes today.

The report – *What Price Public Service?* – is highly critical of the licence fee, saying: 'The mentality of the bottomless purse allows new finance to be sought by asking for increases in the licence fee. The BBC, with that guaranteed source of income, is not liable to any penalty for failure to provide what the general public wants to see; nor for that matter to reap the rewards'.

It dismisses a suggestion in the government's green paper on the future of the BBC that advertising might alter the range and quality of programmes, arguing that there is little difference between the output of BBC and ITV. The report says: 'Members of the public would jump at the chance to become part owners of the corporation, and it would make good sense to set aside about 10 per cent of the shares for the BBC's employees, at attractive prices'.

A new industry-wide regulatory body, called Ofcast, would promote competition, protect consumers and monitor standards, while competition would make BBC programmes 'more adventurous and more innovative', shaking the corporation out of its 'smug complacency', the institute says.

Source: *Guardian*, 9 February 1993 (adapted).

The Social Justice Commission (1994)

This commission, set up by the late labour leader, John Smith, produced a blueprint for the future of the welfare state and is likely to influence Labour party policy. It stresses the need for national renewal based on investment, education and fair taxation. Some of its key suggestions are:

- minimum wage
- subsidies to employers to take on staff
- new top rate of tax
- abolition of mortgage interest tax relief
- taxation of child benefit for higher earners
- creation of a learning bank to extend education opportunities

Changes in the law

The 1994 Sunday Trading Act

The passing of this act made lawful what had already been widely practised. Although large stores have their opening hours restricted to 6 hours, the act enables leisure and travel retailers to trade lawfully. DIY stores have a long track record for Sunday opening, and it remains to be seen whether the whole high street, including record stores and travel agents, opens on Sunday.

The 1994 Criminal Justice Act

This wide-ranging act included some new offences which are of direct relevance to the leisure and tourism sector. These include:

- the banning of ticket touts
- aggravated trespass
- public disorder

The banning of ticket touts is unlikely to stop the practice completely, as the underlying economic disequilibrium that allows touts to operate will not be removed. Touts are likely to operate more discreetly.

Aggravated trespass will make it a criminal offence to trespass with intent to disrupt anyone from engaging in a lawful activity, and is thus likely to limit the actions of hunt saboteurs.

Unlicensed raves will become liable to more focused police action as a result of the tightening of the law on public disorder.

The sociocultural environment

Sociocultural factors include the make-up of society, for example in terms of its population structure, levels of education, social class and attitudes.

Demographics

Demography is the study of population, and population trends are important for the leisure

Table 10.1 *Age and sex structure of the UK population (percentage and millions)*

| Year | Percentage of total in each age group | | | | | Millions |
	<16	16–39	40–64	65–79	>80	All ages
1961	24.9	31.4	32.0	9.8	1.9	52.8
1971	25.5	31.3	29.9	10.9	2.3	55.9
1981	22.3	34.9	27.8	12.2	2.8	56.4
1991	20.3	35.3	28.6	12.0	3.7	57.8
Males	21.4	36.7	29.0	10.6	2.3	28.2
Females	19.3	34.0	28.2	13.3	5.2	29.6
2001F	21.0	32.8	30.5	11.4	4.2	59.7
2011F	19.5	30.3	33.7	11.9	4.7	61.1
2021F	18.5	30.0	32.3	14.0	5.2	62.0
2031F	18.4	28.7	30.3	15.6	6.9	62.1
Males	19.0	29.7	30.9	14.9	5.5	30.7
Females	17.7	27.8	29.8	16.4	8.3	31.4

F = Forecast.
Source: CSO: *Social Trends.*

and tourism sector for two key reasons. First the population is an important factor in determining demand. So, for example, the leisure requirements of a country are likely to change considerably as the average age of the population increases. Football pitches may need to give way to bowling greens. The location of leisure facilities similarly needs to be tailored to the migration trends of the population. Tourism marketing also needs to be informed by relevant population data. The dramatic growth in extended winter sun breaks reflects the demands of an ageing population.

Second the population provides the labour force. Where there is a constant stream of school leavers entering the job market, recruitment and training are relatively straightforward. But when the proportion of the population in the working age group is shrinking, firms have to operate more worker-centred policies. Retention of the labour force (for example, by providing crèche facilities for working parents) and retraining of mature workers are likely to be important. Third an ageing population is likely to have a less progressive culture and adapt to change less easily.

It is therefore useful to have information about trends in the total population and its structure in terms of age, sex, geographic, and socioeconomic distribution.

Population: growth, age and sex structure

Table 10.1 details the age, sex structure and totals of the UK population.

The rate of growth of the population is determined by the birth rate, the death rate and net migration. The birth and death rates are generally expressed as crude rates, for example:

Crude birth rate = number of births per thousand population

The UK, in common with many developed countries, has a relatively stable population and Table 10.1 confirms that its population has only risen from 55.9 to 57.8 million in the period 1971 to 1991. This is because the birth rate and the death rate for the UK have both stabilized at similar levels.

Birth rates are linked with economic development and high per capita income countries tend to have low rates since women are more likely to want to be active in the labour market, the cost of upkeep of children is high, and birth control is widely practised. High birth rates in low per capita income countries need less explanation. In these countries there are fewer factors reducing the higher crude birth rate that is natural in humans. Children are seen as natural, as extra help and as an insurance in old age, and birth control is less widely adopted. Figure 10.1 illustrates the consequences of this for population sizes and growth rates in different countries.

Economic development tends to a lowering of death rates (which are partially determined by nutrition, hygiene and medical technology) earlier than birth rates, which are dependent on attitudes. Thus many countries are still witnessing rapid population growth. The population of India is forecast to grow by more than a third over the next 30 years, whilst that of Mali will more than double. The one important exception to this is China, where a strict one-child policy is enforced.

Analysis of the age structure of the UK population from Table 10.1 reveals an ageing population which is typical of many developed countries. In 1961, less than 12 per cent of the population were aged over 65. This proportion had risen to around 16 per cent by 1991, and is projected to rise to over 22 per cent by the year 2031. In contrast, the proportion of the population under 16 years is falling from 25 per cent in 1961 to a projected 18 per cent by 2031. Countries which are still experiencing rapid population growth have a much lower average age of their population.

Differing age groups of the population can be identified as having distinct demands for leisure and tourism. Table 10.2 illustrates characteristics and demands of distinct age groups.

Geographic and occupational distribution of the population

The UK population is mainly urban. Only 20 per cent of the population of England lives in the country, whilst the majority of the population lives in the major conurbations such as London, the West Midlands, South-east Lancashire, West Yorkshire and Merseyside. However the population is not static and Table 10.3 shows the major population migrations of recent years.

Some of the key trends that emerge are depopulation of city centres (in London there has been a population drift towards the outer commuter belt of the home counties), migration into the South-east, East Anglia and the South-west, and depopulation of Scotland.

Predicting the future population

There are some population predictions that are unlikely to be subject to much error. For example, predictions about the number of persons retiring, or entering higher education, in the next 10 years are fairly predictable since the people concerned are already born.

Predictions about future population totals have to make assumptions about the factors underlying population change. The birth rate has been stable for the UK in recent years but this cannot be guaranteed. The death rate could be reduced by discoveries which inhibit ageing, or might increase in the face of war or disease. Free movement of labour within the EC makes migration less predictable.

Lifestyles

J.K. Galbraith drew attention many years ago to the paradox of private affluence and public squalor. This was a description of society in the USA where many individuals were becoming richer and richer and yet public facilities were becoming run down. New York illustrates this point graphically. In the short walk along 42nd Street, the chic and stretched limo symbols of Broadway are soon replaced by the nightmare scenes of poverty in the Transit Authority terminal.

UK society has become increasingly polarized in the last two decades. Figure 10.2 illustrates how the rich have increased their share of national income whilst the share of the poor has declined. Unemployment, in particular, has led to the emergence of an 'underclass' in UK

(a)

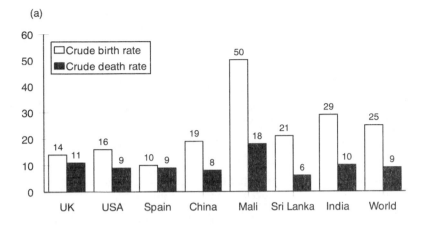

(b)

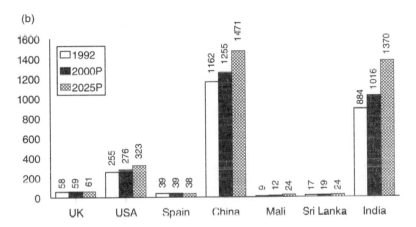

(c)

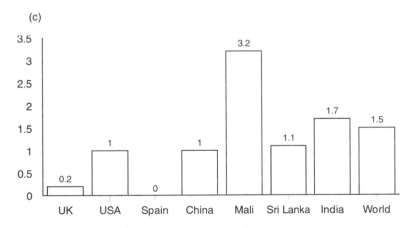

Figure 10.1 Population growth for selected countries. (a) Crude birth and death rates (per thousand per year 1992); (b) total populations in millions (P = projections); (c) average percentage yearly population growth (projection: 1992–2000).

Table 10.2 *Age characteristics*

Life stage	Characteristics	Leisure income	Leisure time
Child	Leisure decisions generally taken by parent	Low	High
Single	High propensity for leisure pursuits and travel. Independence asserted, budget travel popular, social aspects sought	Medium	Medium
Partnered	High leisure and tourism propensities underpinned by high income and free time	High	Medium
Full nest	Children become key preoccupation. Leisure and tourism must meet children's requirements. Costs per person important	Medium	Low
Empty nest	Children have left home. Opportunities for leisure and tourism increase. Exotic destinations and meaning of life sought	High	Medium
Old age	May lack partner, may suffer from infirmity. Safer leisure and travel pursuits sought, package holidays popular	Low	High

Table 10.3 *UK population: changes in regional populations, 1981–1992*

Region	Annual growth rates (%)
North	−0.1
Yorkshire and Humberside	0.2
East Midlands	0.5
East Anglia	0.9
South-east	0.4
Greater London	0.1
Rest of south-east	0.5
South-west	0.7
West Midlands	0.2
North-west	−0.1
Wales	0.3
Scotland	−0.1
Northern Ireland	0.4

Source: CSO: *Regional Trends.*

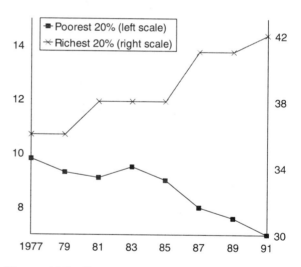

Figure 10.2 Percentage of total disposable income, adjusted for household size. Source: *Guardian.*

society. Thus the leisure and tourism demands of the rich have become ever more sophisticated, whilst access to the poor is ever more limited.

On the other hand, by 1990, two-thirds of households were owner-occupiers. The increase in home ownership has encouraged the growth of home-improvement leisure activities such as DIY and gardening. Television continues to exert a big influence on people's lives and 98 per cent of households have television sets. The total hours of television viewing have changed very little over the last 5 years, as shown in Table 10.4. There is, however, a marked division between social classes in their viewing habits.

Table 10.4 *UK television viewing by social class (hours/week)*

Social class	1986	1991	1992
AB	20	19	20
C1	23	24	25
C2	26	27	28
DE	34	32	32
All persons	27	26	27

Source: CSO: *Social Trends*.

By 1990 almost half of households had access to a car and the extension of the motorway network has extended the distance that can be reached within 3 hours of home. Out-of-town shopping and browsing has become a key leisure pursuit. Visitor attractions have benefited from increased mobility, and some parts of the countryside are becoming overwhelmed by their urban visitors.

Culture and attitudes

Culture refers to the dominant beliefs, values and attitudes of society, or a subgrouping in society. Changing beliefs, values and attitudes affect the way in which people perceive, demand and use leisure and tourism products, for example:

- The mass availability of visual and music media has led to a large upward revision of what is ordinary. This leads to an ever-desperate search for the extraordinary in leisure and tourism pursuits.
- Culture is organic. For example, materialism has replaced religion; feminism has made inroads into sexism; hedonism has become a dominant form of social behaviour. Leisure and tourism accommodate these changes with Sunday betting, women-only swimming sessions, and sex tourism in Bangkok.
- The population is becoming less culturally homogeneous and more culturally fragmented. Subcultures have particular leisure and tourism demands.
- Advertising is promoting leisure and tourism fantasies.

- Crime is increasing, as is fear of crime, and in this context exhibit 10.3 reports on attitudes to parks.

Exhibit 10.3 Parks hit by funding cuts and crime fear

Parks are neglected and fear of crime is deterring potential visitors, a conference on the future of urban parks was told yesterday.

Yet parks are still hugely popular. Forty per cent of the population regularly use a park according to the Audit Commission. However, fear of crime is increasingly deterring users. A survey last summer of more than 12 000 park-goers in 11 parks around the country found that two-thirds were men. Women rarely visited parks on their own, and the elderly were particularly under-represented. The number of places where parents would let their children go unaccompanied halved between 1970 and 1990.

One of the main complaints received by the survey consultants, Comedia, was that a decline in staff had increased the sense of insecurity. Graffiti, vandalism and poor maintenance also worried people, though fear of crime was out of proportion to the number of crimes committed in British parks.

Source: *Guardian*, 26 October 1994 (adapted).

Exhibit 10.3 reports that attitudes to crime are changing park use, with unaccompanied children, women and the elderly being under-represented as park users. If such attitudes harden it is easy to forecast future urban parks as becoming derelict rather than offering recreation for all.

Review of key terms

- Political power = the ability to influence events.
- Scenario planning = developing plans to cope with different views of future.
- The queen's speech = the government's parliamentary agenda for the coming year.
- Crude birth rate = number of births per thousand population.
- Ageing population = average age of population increasing.

Data questions

Task 10.1   Windermere is focus of fight for tranquillity — Malcom pithers

Windermere, one of the most popular stretches of water in Britain, will tomorrow become the focal point for a fierce debate about how people spend their leisure time. For the next two to three months hundreds of people will press home their views on whether the lake should forever be the tranquil place it once was or whether power-boats have a permanent place on the water. The outcome of the debate will have enormous consequences for tourists and residents alike and may well change the way National Parks are allowed to operate.

The Cumbrian issue is as straightforward as it is controversial: whether Windermere should be used for 'quiet enjoyment' and whether or not a by-law should be introduced to enforce a 10mph speed limit on the lake.

The move, proposed by the Lake District Planning Board, has triggered strong opposition, not just from boat owners but from water-ski enthusiasts and hundreds of people who run commercial operations around the lake. A 10mph speed limit would stop all high-speed water sports on the lake. More than 2000 people have written to oppose the plan. The planning board is being backed by the Friends of the Lake District, an umbrella title for those in favour of the ban. For the first time, individuals and organisations, including the Council for National Parks, the Ramblers' Association, heads of outdoor education centres and the Youth Hostels Association, are working jointly to support the imposition of the speed limit.

The board says that the phrase 'quiet enjoyment' has been adopted as an 'object of policy' in National Parks. So much so that where conflict between public enjoyment and the preservation of natural beauty is 'irreconcilable', then 'precedence should be given to preservation and enhancement'. For years there has been a strong lobby within National Park authorities claiming that high-speed boating and water ski-ing are not reconcilable with the peace, beauty and tranquillity expected. The problem has always been how to attract visitors and bring in much-needed income without damaging or significantly altering the environment. The boating fraternity argues that a minority of people with power craft, who have not paid proper attention to noise or safety, have hindered the vast majority who are concerned about the environment of the lake. Others say the powerboats are changing the face of Windermere and should go.

Whatever the truth, the planning board is determined to put its case forcefully. It recognises that power-boating has taken place on Windermere for many years but says the so-called tradition dates from a time when numbers were low. In 1977, surveys showed that the average number of boats on the lake on a summer Sunday was 417, of which 27 per cent, or 140 boats, were capable of speeds over 10mph. In 1991 the average number had risen to 872 and more than half were capable of speeds over 10mph. John Nash, the Lake District National Park planning officer, says he accepts that there would be loss of trade in certain areas, but any downturn would be overcome. There would be a five-year gap before the limit was introduced and, set against the growth in trade that hotels and other businesses have experienced, the impact of the speed limit would not be noticed.

Source: *The Independent*, 9 May 1994.

Questions

1   Identify the interest groups lobbying on each side of the power-boat debate and comment on the cultural values and political power of each.
2   How does this debate illustrate the interrelationship between the political and socio-cultural spheres?
3   Identify the main opportunities and threats that would result from a power-boat ban on Lake Windermere to leisure and tourism organizations.
4   How might the resolution of this issue affect the general operation of national parks?

Task 10.2 Grey expectations

Whilst global greening is still in its infancy, global greying gathers momentum. Almost everywhere in the world, from Japan to Taiwan, in Singapore, western Europe and the USA, populations are getting older.

In the western European OECD countries, the population of over-65s will grow from a figure of 50 million in 1990 to over 70 million by 2030 – a rise of 40 per cent. With the number of people of working age falling there will be only roughly three workers per retiree compared with five at present. Within these countries, the effects of ageing will be felt most acutely in Germany, with ageing in the UK being more moderate.

Since these predictions can be made with some certainty, we ought to look to the possible consequences: tax and benefit systems may need reviewing. Savings and investment patterns may alter. There will certainly be changes in demand. The market research group Mintel has identified 'third-age consumers' as a significant and distinctive market for leisure, holidays and health care. Another commentator, Ms Frankie Cadwell of a New York advertising firm, Cadwell Davies Partners, expresses surprise that European companies have been much slower to address the needs of this market than their US counterparts. Her firm specializes in selling to the over-50s.

Finally, older populations may be less innovative, more conservative, and have a less adaptive labour force. If this is so, there may be some shift in competitive advantage towards those newly industrializing economies where the average age is lower, such as China, Brazil and India.

Source: author, from news cuttings (1995).

Questions

1 To what extent is it true that population trends can be predicted with certainty?
2 'Economists predict that demographic restructuring could alter patterns of consumption, production, employment, savings, investment and innovation.' Use these headings to predict how a named leisure or tourism organization might be affected by demographic change.
3 Why might ageing lead to a competitive disadvantage, and which countries are likely to be affected by this?

Task 10.3 Generation X – UK: in America, it's a 'lost generation'. How do British twentysomethings see themselves? – Alex Spillius

The American author Douglas Coupland's novel, published 2 years ago, provided the catchphrase Generation X for his country's stricken, middle-class twentysomethings. They couldn't find meaningful work, or didn't want it, and ended up in McJobs – poorly paid roles in the service sector. They were the first generation not able to expect a higher standard of living than their parents and so refused to buy the American dream. The 'baby boomers' had it good, but 'Gen X' were left watching Beavis and Butthead cartoons, smoking dope and listening to grunge and old 70s records.

But what of Generation X-UK? How has it coped with life after God, the nuclear family and jobs for life? There are signs that growing unemployment among graduates and the young, combined with the freelance job culture, are creating disaffection.

A proper survey into the British under-30s' attitudes to work, family and faith has yet to be carried out. But an advertising agency, Collett Dickinson Pearce, interviewed 60 people in the under-30 bracket, whose perceived enervation and non-commitment make them a hard lot to sell to. 'There is a large group who are very pissed off because their expectations rose as their parents told them if they worked hard and did well at school they would get a good job', says Douglas Atkin, the agency's planning director. 'Now they would like jobs in journalism, advertising or the City but their chances are minimal. It's been called boomer envy. One chap said, "They had everything, but they have left us with the bill: AIDS, unemployment and pollution".'

Becky Gill and other students interviewed confessed that the student generation was as politically apathetic as it has been for the past 20 years, with only racism able to motivate significant numbers to protest. The bulk of the under-30 element is just subdued, not subversive.

Paul Clements condemned the indolence of many of his peers. 'I'm 29 and I get depressed seeing people younger than me sitting round doing nothing.

'Why don't they get up off their arse and do something? Anything. There's too many people smoking dope and watching dole TV.' So, what's on Dole TV today? For the really early risers, there's Richard and Judy at the crack of 10 a.m. Only a couple of sluggish errands needed to take you up to Neighbours or Home and Away at half-one, with the former repeated at half-five for keen deconstructionists of modern suburban life in Australia. Not forgetting the idler's favourite quiz show, Countdown, with Fifteen to One also good for half an hour's slack-spined trivia.

Those who choose to be experts in ennui are probably few, but it apparently doesn't take long to learn. As Karl said: 'It's amazing how easy it is to get used to not doing much and not having much, especially if you've never done much'.

Source: *Independent on Sunday*, 12 June 1994 (adapted).

Questions

1 What is Generation X?
2 Why do attitudes of Generation X differ from their parents?
3 What evidence is there to substantiate the theory of Generation X?
4 What are the implications of Generation X for leisure and tourism?

Short questions

1 Distinguish between a manifesto, the queen's speech, a white paper and a law.
2 What effects might the proposals in the queen's speech have on the leisure and tourism sector (see exhibit 10.1, or a later speech)?
3 How might the 1994 Royal Commission on Environmental Pollution affect organizations in the leisure and tourism sector?
4 What changes have occurred to the operating environment of ticket touts?
5 Why is the population of the UK ageing? What are the consequences of this for leisure and tourism organizations?
6 How are changes in lifestyles and attitudes affecting leisure and tourism?

References

Pleasure, leisure and jobs, The Business of Tourism, Cabinet Office, HMSO, 1988.
Broadcasting in the 1990s, HMSO, 1988.
Mason, D., *Expounding the Arts*, Adam Smith Institute, 1987.

Further reading

Adam Smith Institute, *What Price Public Service? The Future of the BBC*, Adam Smith Institute, 1993.
Adams, I., *Leisure and Government*, Business Education Publishers, 1990.
McRae, H., *The World in 2020*, Harper Collins, 1994.
Quest, M., *Horwath Book of Tourism*, Macmillan, 1990.
Seaton, A., *et al.* (eds), *Tourism–The State of The Art*, Wiley, 1994.
Spink, J., *Leisure and the Environment*, Butterworth-Heinemann, 1994.
Urry, J., *The Tourist Gaze*, Sage, 1990.
World Bank, *World Development Report*, Oxford University Press, 1994.

11

The technological environment and opportunities and threats analysis

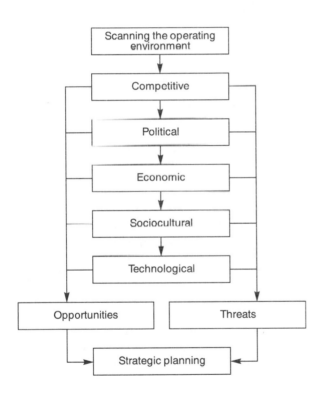

Objectives

First, this chapter concludes PEST analysis by considering the extent and impact of the continuing technological revolution.

Second, this chapter introduces the concept of opportunities and threats analysis. This acts as a

summary of the points made in Chapters 8–11. It also provides a useful tool for organizations to identify the key changes in their operating environment and thus acts as a sound basis for reviewing the appropriateness of the organization's strategy.

By studying this chapter students should be able to:

- define the scope of the technological environment
- identify information sources for analysing the technological environment
- identify technological opportunities and threats to leisure and tourism organizations
- conduct an audit of an organization's operating environment
- conduct an opportunities and threats analysis

The technological environment

Technological change offers two key opportunities for leisure and tourism organizations. First it can lead to cost reductions. The long-run average cost curve (LRAC) is constructed on the assumption that technology remains constant, and thus improved production technology will cause the long-run average cost curve of an organization to fall, as illustrated in Figure 11.1. LRAC1 represents the original long-run average cost curve. The use of improved production

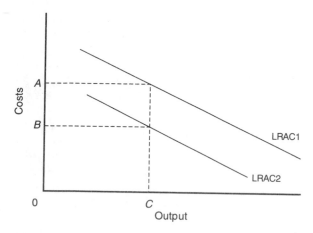

Figure 11.1   Shifting long-run average cost curve (LRAC).

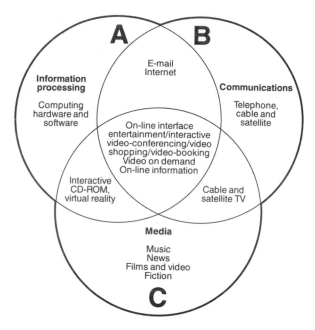

Figure 11.2   Multimedia.

technology enables the curve to shift downwards to LRAC2. Average costs of producing level of output 0C now fall from 0A to 0B.

Second, technology can provide new products and markets. Both of these routes can lead to an improvement in an organization's competitive edge, and can be the basis of price-based or differentiation strategies. However, technological change also poses threats where existing products become obsolete in the face of new developments. Technological change is being delivered mainly at present by the increased processing power of microcomputers, the provision of high-capacity datalinks and the fall in price of hardware and software. Silicon chip developments lead to faster data processing. Fibre optics and digital technology mean that data can be quickly transmitted globally at low cost, and these hardware developments mean that software of ever-increasing sophistication can be developed.

Multimedia is one of the key developments of the 1990s. It is illustrated in Figure 11.2.

Thus at a simple level an organization's computer network on its own can perform word processing, accounting and other functions (circle A). Linked to other computers via datalink services it can access reservation systems and provide E-mail and Internet conferencing (circles A + B). Linked to other media, at the simplest level text, images and video clips can be

incorporated into software programs (circles A + C). At the most sophisticated level virtual reality can be set up. Linking PCs and media sources through datalinks provides access to the whole repertoire of computer applications (circles A + B + C). This includes, for example, video on demand, and video shopping which enables goods to be chosen at home and delivered to your door. Home booking allows access to central reservation and booking systems from home, with the possibility of video clips of resorts and hotels. Developments in voice recognition software, as described in exhibit 11.1, mean that distant databases may be able to be interrogated without the need for home terminals.

Exhibit 11.1   Innovation: now they're talking real phone service: callers will soon be able to chat to computers about anything from booking a flight to buying a suit – George Cole

Ever get the feeling you were talking to a computer? You will be. Talking computers will soon replace recorded messages and human operators in a range of telephone services, such as travel information and home banking. The computer will ask callers what they want to know, retrieve the information from its database and convert it to speech.

Staff of BA at Heathrow are currently testing a system that allows them to ring up and speak to a computer to extract flight information from its database and make bookings. The system, known as Callserver, was developed by Vocalis, a company specializing in speech recognition.

Source: *Independent on Sunday*, 8 May 1994 (adapted).

Technological impacts may be analysed in the following areas:

- hospitality
- tourism
- leisure

Hospitality

Showcases such as Hotech, the exhibition for suppliers of hotel technology, provide a good insight into innovations affecting the hospitality industry. Current developments include the following.

First links into central reservation systems are important so that hotels can capture reservations generated from distant terminals. Most travel agents use one of the central reservation systems such as SABRE or Amadeus to book air travel, car hire and accommodation, and access to these systems represents an important marketing tool. For the future, a system that automatically rebooks accommodation to deal with air delays and missed connections is a possibility.

Second, there has been considerable progress in accounting packages. In management accounting, yield management packages are an important tool enabling hotels to maximize revenue by adjusting rates to best-fit changing market conditions. Yield management packages are able to compare likely demand with actual demand and capacity and suggest rates accordingly. In financial accounting, packages enable financial reporting to take place speedily and efficiently.

Check-in time can be minimized by using credit card readers to automate registration and issue a high-technology key which can even be a credit card itself. High-technology keys reduce the possibility of theft since codes may be changed frequently at minimal cost. It is possible for a reservation system to use its database to provide personalized services such as provision of a particular newspaper. Computerized reservation systems can also reduce check-out time to a minimum.

Other computer-assisted management systems range from energy management systems to conference management systems and computer-intelligent buildings. A computer-intelligent building means that most of the functions of the building are computer-assisted, and so, for example, room cleaning schedules can be computer-generated from information from guests' smart keys, pay rolling can be generated from reading employees' time sheets which themselves are based on electronic monitoring, and a wide range of on-screen services are available in rooms.

Exhibit 11.2 shows how technology is being used to cut costs, enabling some French hotels to pursue an effective price-based strategy.

Exhibit 11.2 Hi-tech hotels are revolutionizing budget accommodation in France – Rob Davidson

You're driving through France and decide to stop for the night. The question is: how do you break your journey without breaking the bank? The answer is the budget hotel where a clean, quiet room for up to three people sharing costs from £15 a night.

How are overheads kept so low? Most cost-trimming is achieved by reducing services to a bare minimum. Hi-tech, manpower-saving devices also help to cut costs. A good example is automatic check-ins, which are placed at entrances for use when reception areas are unattended. *La Réception Automatique* works like a cash machine: you insert a credit card and 'converse' with the facility (in French, English or German) about the room you want, how long you plan to stay and whether you want breakfast. The machine then debits your card and issues a key and room number.

French technology is also applied in the automatic cleaning systems installed in the showers and lavatories of the hotels. Every time the facility is used, a powerful spray of a water–disinfectant mix ensures that it is left spotless for the next user.

The labour-saving devices and basic services mean that budget hotels can be run by just two people plus cleaning staff.

Source: *The Independent*, 9 April 1994 (adapted).

The conference industry illustrates possible opportunities and threats posed by new technology. A recent study found that 36 per cent of hotel room sales was made to conference delegates, and there has been growth in the number of centres with capacities for in excess of 1000 delegates. However, firms such as Xerox are increasingly turning to video-conferencing as a way of reducing travel and hospitality costs, and saving expensive executive time. Some hotels are responding to this challenge and the Hilton National group for example has introduced video-conferencing in its key conference venues.

However, with the growth of multimedia technologies it is possible that conferencing will in future be office- or home-based, utilizing PCs. It should be possible to access video clips of speakers via point-and-click menus and organize discussion groups with video or data links. Similarly, questions can be collected over the conference period and feedback made available on menus. Conferencing would become more flexible and personalized as participants could choose speakers, discussion groups and questions of direct relevance to themselves, and indeed could browse and move between areas with ease. The implications of such a move would be a shift in conference spending away from airlines, hotels, and local hospitality providers towards the providers of datalinks and other hardware and software companies. Exhibit 11.3 describes a possible video-conference of the future.

Exhibit 11.3 *The future is virtually here – David Bowen*

It is 2008 and you are going into a meeting with your bosses. They are in San Francisco and Bavaria; you are in your house in the Scottish Highlands. You sit down in your office, put on a pair of dark glasses and a glove – both linked by wire to the computer on your desk. You find yourself in an electronic 'room', with a table and chairs. You look round to see your American boss – or rather his hologram – sitting next to you. A moment later the German appears, and the meeting starts. Using your glove you can pass electronic documents around the room – a disembodied hand appears in front of you, to mimic your movements. This is a virtual conference.

In the multimedia world, we are told, we will be able to shop, play, learn and even make love while sitting alone in the house. The virtual conference is a three-dimensional (3D) computer graphic, transmitted by telephone. Combined with 3D spectacles it tricks the brain into believing that it is inside an electronically created room.

Computers sufficiently powerful to digitalize have become available. A CD can store the equivalent of two digitalized editions of the *Encyclopaedia Britannica*. So all we need is the 'information superhighway', a telephone line with the capacity to carry all this information. The present copper phone wire can carry only voice and a limited amount of text and data. Replace it with fibreoptic cable and its capacity increases 250 000 times over. The entire contents of Oxford's Bodleian Library could be transmitted in 42 seconds.

Source: *Independent on Sunday*, 26 June 1994 (adapted).

Travel and tourism

Technological changes in transportation are likely to be extensions of existing technologies in the form of larger jumbo jets, and faster trains for travel. Additionally some shortages of air space may be relieved by using information technology to create smaller air tunnels than the existing air corridors.

Booking and reservation systems are likely to become more sophisticated, globalized and more widely available. The main distribution channels currently are Worldspan, SABRE, Amadeus and Galileo and there have been some disputes between the systems providers and the service providers over charges.

The early entry of American Airlines into computerized reservation systems has given it a competitive advantage in its SABRE system which now generates more profits than the airline operations. Multimedia is filtering into computerized reservation systems and SABREVISION now adds pictures and video images of destinations to information about price and availability.

The increasing use of modems to connect home PCs to national and international networks may pose some threats to travel agents. Use of the Windows interface to access databases makes home use straightforward and SABRE is now available via the Compuserve network to home-based PCs. The Windows environment means that it can be used instantly, whereas travel agents had to undergo a half-day training to use the pre-Windows system.

The French Mintel system of networked home PCs claims over 40 per cent of travel reservations. Exhibit 11.4 however suggests that for the UK, home-based bookings have not yet taken off.

Exhibit 11.4   Computers: meagre catch on the travel lines – Mike Hewitt

It is an appealing thought: dial up Compuserve, the computer information service, download your electronic mail, check your Glaxo shares and – what the hell? – while you are about it, why not book a couple of weeks in Alicante, too?

On-line travel services, which have been around in one form or another since the mid-1970s, should be theoretically ideal for finding the best bargains on airline seats and hotel rooms. Their information is updated daily, or even hourly, reflecting availability and the latest discounts.

So are the high-street Thomas Cook and the corner bucket shop about to succumb to technology? In the UK, the most easily accessible on-line travel services are available through Compuserve: American Airlines' EAASY SABRE, the independent OAG (Official Airlines Guides) and TWA's Travelshopper. All three offer 24-hour price and schedule information for hundreds of airlines and thousands of hotels worldwide. In addition, you can hire a car through more than 50 rental companies. In fact, nearly 95 per cent of the people who sign up with EAASY SABRE, OAG and Travelshopper do not use them. Even for those who do, bookings, as opposed just to queries, amount to somewhat less than one trip for each registered user per year.

High-street travel agencies can usually offer better deals. 'On-line services are great tools for finding schedules and fares,' according to one technically aware travel expert. 'But they usually lack the ability to book the absolutely last available seats on a plane. These are the sorts of seats that airlines tend to pass on to travel agencies and discount shops, who then sell them on at reduced rates.'

Basically, you get what you pay for. With a travel agent, you pay for years of specialized training, special deals with airlines and hotels that the ordinary person in the cyberstreet could never hope to clinch, and 8 hours a day on the job. So for the time being the virtual travel agent should be used to complement the high-street variety. A bargain fortnight in Benidorm courtesy of the home computer is probably still a few years away yet.

Source: *The Independent*, 20 May 1994 (adapted).

Leisure

The multimedia revolution offers the prospect of sophisticated home-based leisure and enhancement of attractions away from home.

In the home, video on demand may spell the demise of the video rental store. Digitized movies will be stored in distant databases which can be accessed via a menu and decoding system using cable.

Interactive games which started life on floppy disks are able to exploit the extra speed and memory of CD-ROM technology. Exhibit 11.5 illustrates the development of interactive porn.

Exhibit 11.5   Computer: CD sex for sale

Blatantly heterosexual acts have become one of the big selling points of CD software. One of the first games to address carnal desires was Soft Porn, a text adventure game. Soft Porn was the precursor to the successful Leisure Suit Larry, a series of smutty tales of an ageing swinger and his improbable encounters with a string of young lovelies. In another title, Sex Olympics, Brad Stallion and his Pelvic Thruster must seduce a collection of intergalactic babes before Dr Dildo can get his evil mitts on them.

But it is on the CD-ROM platform that the sexual revolution, software style, has taken place. Things got more serious with the appearance of Virtual Valerie. Val will obey the user's every command, though any sexual activity on her part is of a strictly solitary nature.

Virtual Valerie was produced by Mike Saenz who also told *Mondo 2000* magazine about his idea for a program called Strip Teacher. 'She goes: "Tell me the name of the 13th president of the United States and I'll show you my tits".'

Source: *Guardian*, 24 February 1994 (adapted).

Currently, the ultimate development goal of computer games appears to be virtual reality. Virtual reality, or cyberspace as it is sometimes called, is an extension of the technology of the flight simulator. It enables participants to enter a computer-generated three-dimensional environment and interact with the environment. Headsets, data gloves and data suits are the passport to this cyberworld where participants can travel from scene to scene and interact with cyber people and cyber objects.

Virtual reality is also likely to affect leisure away from home. Sega is developing theme parks in Japan with interactive attractions which will let people shoot and steer their way through adventures. Disney is planning to utilize virtual reality in its heritage theme park in Washington DC so that visitors can experience life as a civil war soldier, or as a slave. The future interpretation of heritage may well rely less on exhibits in glass cases and more on participation and interaction with virtual artefacts and virtual historical figures. Exhibit 11.6 explores the world of virtual theatre.

Exhibit 11.6   Perchance to dream?

The computer firm Sun Microsystems has unveiled a new direction in virtual leisure. Immersion virtual reality is developing apace. A headset projects computer graphics, and headphones complete the effect of immersing you in a computer-generated alternative world. An interactive element can be added by use of a 'data glove' and, in the case of the Sun system, you are equipped literally to walk on to the stage.

The new development creates a virtual replica of the Globe – Shakespeare's original theatre. Virtual actors perform extracts of his plays using recordings of real actors. If you fancy a spell as Hamlet, you can choose to replace any of the actors and take their place on the virtual stage. Might this mean Shakespeare karaoke machines in pubs?

The virtual world is expanding fast. Video games have been slowly extending their frontiers and we are entering an era of virtually anything that takes your imagination. Virtual holidays, virtual skiing, virtual sex, a trip through a virtual art gallery or a journey to a virtual planet. The only limits at the moment are the foggy graphics, and the tendency to fall over if your wear your headset for too long.

Source: the author, from news cuttings, February 1994.

Opportunities and threats analysis

An opportunities and threats analysis examines an organization's operating environment. The operating environment can be audited using the framework established in the previous chapters and this is illustrated in Table 11.1.

Once the key opportunities and threats have been established for an organization, its strategic plan can be updated to show how opportunities can be exploited and threats can be countered. Table 11.2 considers the main opportunities and threats facing BA in 1994.

Review of key terms

- Fibreoptics = high-capacity data transmission lines using optical fibre rather than copper wire.
- CRS = computerized reservation system, such as SABRE or Amadeus.
- Multimedia = combination of media sources (e.g. video), computing and communications.
- Computer-intelligent building = building use monitored and controlled by computer (e.g. security, temperature, staff location, room use).
- Digitalization = transforming images and sound to digital code for ease of storage and transmission.
- Windows = click-and-point menu system using mouse to make choices on computer screen.
- Compuserve = subscription service networking home PCs to distant computers.

Table 11.1 *Opportunities and threats analysis*

Environment	Opportunities	Threats
Competitive		
Threat of entrants		
Power of buyers		
Power of suppliers		
Threat of substitutes		
Competitive rivalry		
PEST		
Political		
Economic		
Sociocultural		
Technological		

Table 11.2 *Opportunities and threats analysis for British Airways 1994*

Environment	Opportunities	Threats
Competitive		
Threat of entrants	Limited slots available at Heathrow	Virgin
		Competition from Paris and Amsterdam as Euro-gateways
Power of buyers	Little competition in domestic markets	
Power of suppliers		BAA monopoly of main UK airports
		Limited competition between aircraft and engine manufacturers
		Cost of use of SABRE and other non-BA CRS
Threat of substitutes		Eurostar routes to Paris and Brussels
		TGV in Europe Video-conferencing
PEST		
Political	EC rules forbidding subsidies to national carriers (e.g. Air France)	
Economic	UK economic recovery	Tax on air travel
	Rapid growth in Pacific Rim economies	
Sociocultural	Move towards multiple holidays each year	Environmental lobby against pollution
		Objections to Terminal 5 at Heathrow
Technological	Yield management systems developing	Overcrowding of air space

- Networked computers = computers linked to other computers.
- Interactive = user response encouraged and allowed.
- Virtual reality = computer-generated three-dimensional environment for user interaction.
- Cyberspace = virtual reality environment.

Data questions

Task 11.1   Inside story: after the media earthquake – David Bowen

Analysts at Salomon Brothers, the US investment bank, predicted an earthquake last summer, saying: 'Usually the contours of business change gradually and even the occasional geological shift is confined to one or two industries. Now, though, tectonic plates are moving before our eyes. Our seismographs tell us interactive multimedia is a Big One that is rearranging, faster than we imagined it could, the borders of the business world we know today.'

They were right. Within 6 months, three of the biggest ever take-over bids had been announced, all triggered by the opportunities and fears raised by multimedia. The cable giant Viacom bid $8.2bn for the last independent Hollywood studio, Paramount.

Sumner Redstone, chairman of Viacom, called his new empire a 'global media powerhouse of unparalleled proportions'. Viacom said it would concentrate on building up its CD-ROM business and would also expand its cable operations. The first vertically integrated multimedia empire – involving a Baby Bell, a cable company and a rich supplier of material – had arrived. Or had it? There was another group, well-established, that was starting to look increasingly like a multimedia empire. Mr Murdoch's News Corporation owned Twentieth Century Fox, Fox Television and more national newspapers than anyone else in the UK and Australia. He also controlled BSkyB, the satellite channel that provided most of the material for the UK's cable companies. Mr Murdoch said

his ambition was to build a 'global highway' – this was the language of multimedia. The shake-out had begun, but how will it end? What will the multimedia industry look like? Who will win, who will lose?

In its narrow sense, multimedia is simply the simultaneous display, on a computer or television screen, of a number of different media such as text, pictures, graphics, voice, music and film. This in itself has uses. Multimedia programs stored on CD-I and CD-ROM disks have brought a new dimension to education – a multimedia encyclopaedia now contains film clips, for example – as well as extra subtlety to computer games. But it is the broader sense that brings up dollar signs in executive eyes. Multimedia display is possible because the different media have been digitized, or turned into a common language consisting of millions of binary digits. This process allows the transmission of vast quantities of data down telephone lines – especially if those lines are 'broadband', made of heavy copper or fibreoptic cable.

Business people and politicians suddenly realized that the multimedia products could be sent down an 'information superhighway'. These could include home shopping, interactive games, videophones, video-on-demand (films piped down the phone lines), tele-schooling. . . . A new industry was in the making.

Companies started to manoeuvre themselves into position. The US telecoms companies believed they could one day be threatened by cable television companies, which already had broadband lines going into homes. At the same time, telecoms and cable groups decided that the value of the material that could be digitized and pumped down the line would inevitably increase. So it would do them no harm, they thought, to own the companies that produced it.

There has also been much publicity about BT's proposed video-on-demand service, by which films would be piped down telephone lines into televisions. But BT stresses it wants to operate the distribution system, including the powerful computers that store the digitized information, but does not want to provide the information itself. It will leave that to the other shareholders in the video-on-demand company – Pearson, London Weekend Television and Kingfisher. Granada, the BBC and a Hollywood studio have also agreed to provide programming for trials.

Multimedia will create a new generation of high-flying companies and high-flying people. The next Bill Gates could be Bill Gates – or somebody else. Whoever invents the better on-line shopping mall, or an interactive game that grips the world, will be worth a million or two. Whoever comes up with the 'killer application' – the product that turns interactive multimedia from an intriguing new service into something everyone has to have – will be counting his fortune in billions.

Source: *Independent on Sunday*, 6 March 1994 (adapted).

Questions

1 Which organizations in the leisure and tourism sector are likely to be victims of the rise of multimedia?
2 How might such organizations adapt to the changes?
3 Which leisure and tourism organizations are likely to gain from the rise of multimedia?
4 Are there any grounds for government control of ownership of multimedia organizations?

Task 11.2 Fast forward to the future: video on demand

Dial a pizza? Half an hour later a spotty boy weaves down your street on an old Honda moped. Dial a video? Perhaps a similar scene springs to mind. A fleet of battered Hondas, panniers full of cassettes.

Not if BT have their way.

From today in BT's pilot area you can have VOD, or video-on-demand. To use the system you need a set-top decoder, a remote control device and of course a telephone line. Choose VOD from the remote control and a menu appears on the screen. You're now on-line to the VOD film database. You can browse through a comprehensive range of video titles, request a synopsis of the movie, a cast list or the running time.

Tap in a few more commands and the video of your choice is downloaded to your decoder. You can choose to watch the film now or later on. The problem of the popular new release always out on rental on the night you want to take it out from the local video store is digitally solved. The trials being conducted at present also allow you to choose a range of TV shows including sports, children's programmes, soaps and comedy.

Steve Main, BT's Director of Visual and Broadcasting Services, explained that the company will charge between £1 and £3 per film to compete head-on with video rental stores, for whom a nationwide VOD system poses a serious threat.

But why BT's sudden interest in films? Competition from cable TV and Mercury means that BT is forced to innovate to keep its market share in a fast-changing environment and if BT fails to capture the emerging VOD market, it will be lost to competitors. So whilst the cable operators are offering telephone services in competition with BT, BT is fighting back by offering entertainment via its telephone lines.

However, VOD technology doesn't stop at the movies. Its scope is enormous and could include home shopping, news services, specialist services, banking and reservation services.

In fact holidays on demand are already possible in the BT pilot programme. Menus allow you to browse through various locations, seeing short video clips of the scenery, hotel facilities and local leisure pursuits. If you like what you see you can make an instant reservation, choosing your dates, your hotels and your airport of departure.

Source: the author, from news cuttings (1994).

Questions

1 What are the constituent parts of VOD technology?
2 What is the likely impact of VOD technology for the leisure and tourism sector?
3 What will determine the success of VOD technology?
4 What other specialized leisure or tourism services could use VOD technology?

Task 11.3 Hornby's not yet at the end of the line – Nigel Cope

Keith Ness, chief executive of Hornby, the train sets and Scalextric maker, was on Friday to be found holed up in his rather drab office in the Kent seaside resort of Margate taking calls on the company's latest set of financial results. It was not an enviable task – they were not exactly spectacular. Profits had ground to a halt at £1.4m on sales that had drifted into the sidings at £28m.

Sales of the core trains and Scalextric ranges have suffered as a result of the recession and the craze for video games. And Fletcher, the speedboat company acquired in 1988 as part of a diversification into the leisure sector, only broke even.

But, given the traumas suffered by the British toy industry in the past 20 years, it is surprising that a company like Hornby is around at all. Few others are. Hornby is one of the last sizeable survivors of an industry where Britain was once an important force. Though it still has about 200 toy companies, most of the larger names have been gobbled up by foreign competition in an increasingly global business.

Matchbox is now part of Hasbro, the American company that is the largest in the world. Corgi was snapped up by Mattel, another US group. Kiddicraft, a once British pre-school toy specialist, was bought by Fisher Price, now merged with Mattel. And ownership of Meccano has crossed the channel to France.

Like all toy companies, Hornby has been squeezed by three trends in the market. The rise of the American multinationals such as Hasbro and Mattel–Fisher Price has made it difficult for smaller companies to compete on marketing budgets. Imports from low-cost producers in the Far East have also taken their toll. As late as 1978, Britain was still a net exporter of toys. Last year imports accounted for nearly half of the country's £1bn toy industry. The final blow was the rise of electronic toys, initially in the early 1980s and then the second wave 10 years later with the phenomenal success of the Sega and Nintendo video games machines.

Founded by Frank Hornby as Meccano in 1901, Hornby has had its fair share of troubles. In the past 10 years Mr Ness has concentrated on making Hornby less reliant on the *Boys' Own* world of fast cars and trains. Back in 1980, it had only its train sets and Scalextric. Now those two ranges account for only 60 per cent of sales as Mr Ness has expanded into fashion toys and dolls. Successful lines includes Gladiators, a range of figures related to the LWT television programme, Clever Cook, and Game Genie, video games software that is played on Sega and Nintendo consoles and gives Hornby a toehold in a lucrative but volatile market. New products are being brought in to shield the core markets from competition. Tyco, an American company, has launched a range of smaller, zippy slot car racing machines, so Scalextric has produced a similar compact range. Other new products such as Cassy, an eight-inch doll launched to tackle the mighty Barbie and Sindy, have been less successful.

While Hornby has done well to survive, it is not completely out of the woods. Hornby's big problem is that its core market is shrinking. 'Hornby railways have virtually no export market and at home they are not the high profile, fast-selling line they used to be,' says Jon Salisbury, editor of *World Toy News*. More than half its sales are in trains and cars, where the audience is young boys. The sector has been ravaged by the Sega and Nintendo craze. Marketing has not been a conspicuous success. A pointer to the future came in January when Hornby took a 10 per cent stake in Original San Francisco Toy Makers, a US company, giving it exclusive UK rights to the range. This and other licensing deals, such as the Gladiators arrangement with LWT which enables it to tap in to the success of the programme, gives access to the potentially lucrative market for fashion toys.

Source: *The Independent*, 28 March 1994.

Questions

1 Compile a list of areas that should be audited when analysing the operating environment of Hornby.
2 Conduct an opportunities and threats analysis on Hornby using the framework devised in question 1.

Task 11.4 First Leisure plays games with Sega – John Shepherd

First Leisure has formed a joint venture with Sega to test the UK market for family high-tech games centres. A trial centre, Sega World, will be housed in the Reading Super Bowl which First Leisure is due to open soon. John Conlan, chief executive, said: 'If successful, we would seek to develop this concept as an ancillary activity elsewhere in bowling.' Sidelines such as American pool have provided a useful fillip for takings at the company's ten-pin bowling centres, which are showing a fall in attendances and pricing pressures. It is also moving into the health and fitness market by buying 75 per cent of ISL, owner of the Berkshire Racquets and Health Club, for an initial £5.3m. Two more bowling centres were opened in Plymouth and Southampton.

Total group profits maintained their uninterrupted record of growth – but only just – at 2.3 per cent to £31.8m. The final dividend has been lifted 6.4 per cent to 4.53p. Resorts operations – fronted by Blackpool and its famous tower, which celebrates its centenary this year – recorded a 5 per cent fall to £11.7m. Blackpool was the main culprit after adverse publicity over beach pollution and the poor summer weather. However, Mr Conlan said: 'Resorts outside Blackpool have done well, and the numbers visiting Blackpool did recover at the end of the season'. The company's most successful division was dancing, which saw attendances at its discos match the peak days in the eighties at 6.2 million. Profits from dancing rose 15 per cent to £14.5m. Mr Conlan added: 'We haven't increased prices in this division. We have traded margin for volume.' As the recession has gone on we have seen a smarter customer, looking for value for money and not afraid to ask for it any more.' The seven bingo clubs acquired last summer contributed £900 000 of profits, and the joint venture in theatres with Cameron Mackintosh doubled its contribution from a low base to £400 000. First Leisure says it will use the Berkshire Health Club, which has full membership of 4700, each paying about £650 a year, as a base to expand into the largely underexploited UK market.

Source: *The Independent*, 3 January 1994 (adapted).

Question

Carry out an opportunities and threats analysis for First Leisure's operations.

Short questions

1 How do fibreoptics and digital technology allow home access to computerized reservation systems?
2 Explain how video-conferencing makes use of multimedia technology.
3 Distinguish between reality and virtual reality and explain the importance of the latter to the leisure industry.
4 What are the elements of an opportunities and threats analysis?
5 What is the purpose of an opportunities and threats analysis?

6   Is home-based reservation an opportunity or a threat?

Further reading

Bowen, D., *Multimedia: Now and Down the Line*, Bowerdean, 1994.

Dyson, R., *Strategic Planning: Models and Analytical Techniques*, Wiley, 1990.

McRae, H., *The World in 2020*, HarperCollins, 1994.

Quest, M., *Horwath Book of Tourism*, Macmillan, 1990.

Rheingold, H., *Virtual Reality*, Summit Books, New York, 1991.

Williams, A. and Hobson, J., Virtual reality and surrogate travel, in, *Tourism–The State of The Art*, Seaton, A. *et al.* (eds), Wiley, 1994.

Part Three

Investing in Leisure and Tourism

12

Investment appraisal in the private sector

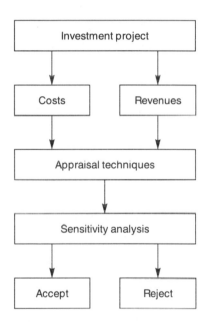

Objectives

With hindsight it is not difficult to analyse the factors that have made some investment projects in the leisure and tourism sector such successes and others such dismal failures. The failures include the Sinclair C5 electric vehicle, the Battersea Power Station leisure project and British Satellite Broadcasting (you do not see many 'squarials' these days). The successes include projects as diverse as films (*Four Weddings and a Funeral*), visitor attractions (Alton Towers), electronic games (the Game Boy) and satellite TV (BSB).

However, at the planning stage, it is much more difficult to forecast the success of investments, largely because of the uncertainty surrounding the future. This chapter seeks to define the meaning of investment, consider how potential investment projects are appraised and stress the shortcomings of quantitative techniques.

By studying this chapter students will be able to:

- define and distinguish between different types of investment
- analyse the factors which affect an investment decision
- utilize techniques for investment appraisal
- understand the uncertainty surrounding investment appraisal
- analyse the effects of investment on the economy
- evaluate government policy with regard to investment

Definition and examples

In general usage people use the term 'investment' to include bank and building society deposits and the purchase of stocks and shares. Economists are more specific in their use of the term. Investment may be defined as expenditure on capital goods and working capital.

Capital goods can be contrasted with consumer goods. The latter are produced because of the direct satisfaction they yield (e.g. food, CDs,

Table 12.1   UK investment 1987–1993 (£m at constant 1990 prices)

Year	Gross domestic fixed capital formation	Increase in stocks and work in progress
1987	92 260	1731
1988	104 726	5532
1989	110 503	3669
1990	106 776	−1118
1991	96 265	−4722
1992	94 714	−1773
1993	95 452	462
1994	99 679	2617

Source: CSO: *Monthly Digest of Statistics.*

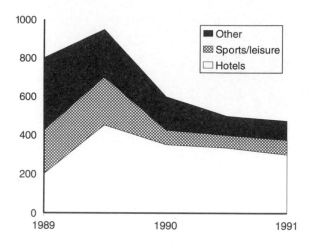

Figure 12.1   Value of new leisure and tourism investment projects commenced in England (£m). Source: various.

clothes), whilst the former are produced because they improve efficiency of production. Fixed capital goods therefore consist of buildings, plant and machinery, and in the leisure and tourism sector examples include hotel buildings, computer reservation and booking systems, aircraft, and golf-ball making machinery. The total expenditure on such items is recorded as 'gross domestic fixed capital formation' in government statistics.

Working capital consists of stocks of raw materials, semi-manufactured goods and manufactured goods which have not yet been sold. Manufacturers monitor stocks of unsold products closely and these tend to be the key signals in a market economy to reduce or increase production. Working capital is an essential part of production, although modern 'just-in-time' production techniques have reduced the need for large stocks of raw materials and components to be held in factories. Expenditure on these items is recorded in government statistics as 'increase in stocks and work in progress'. Table 12.1 illustrates recent data for the UK showing the two major categories of investment.

It can be seen that gross fixed capital formation increased in the period 1987 to 1989, fell to around its 1987 level by 1992, and recovered slightly by 1993.

Figure 12.1 shows the value of new investment projects in the leisure and tourism sector. It shows

a similar picture to the total investment figures, reaching a peak in 1989 and falling in the following period.

Investment can also be divided into gross investment and net investment. Gross investment includes all investment, including that which is for replacement of worn-out machinery, whilst net investment only includes investment that adds to a country's capital stock.

Net investment = gross investment − depreciation

Factors affecting investment

Investment in the private sector is undertaken to increase profitability. Since we assume that the motive of private sector organizations is the maximization of profits, such organizations will seek to invest in those projects which yield the highest return.

Investment projects will incur planning, construction and running costs and yield revenue when in operation. Thus the profitability of an investment project can be analysed by investigating its costs and revenue. Exhibit 12.1 gives a rough idea of the costs and revenue for a hotel development.

Exhibit 12.1   Holiday Inn: Europe

The UK brewery and leisure group Bass plc has announced new investment plans for extending its Holiday Inn hotels into Europe.

Its chosen strategy is to expand mainly by franchising, and to extend its presence in the budget market. The vehicle for this is the Holiday Inn Express concept aimed at price-conscious travellers.

By avoiding costly city-centre sites and concentrating instead on roadside locations, the investment cost to franchisees is expected to range between £28 000 and £30 000 per room and rooms are likely to cost an average of £35 a night.

Both of these figures are substantially less than those associated with standard Holiday Inns.

Source: author.

Cost of investment

The main costs of an investment will be:

- planning costs
- costs of capital goods
- cost of financing investment
- running costs of the investment

Planning costs

The planning costs of an investment include consultancy costs for technical feasibility, market research, competitor scanning, financial appraisal and overall project planning. For large-scale projects, planning costs can be considerable and add to the overall project timetable. For example, BAA's plan to build a new terminal, Terminal 5, at London Heathrow airport had to go before a public inquiry with all the attendant legal costs, and the planning and consultation phase has doubled the timescale for the development, as illustrated in Table 12.2.

Exhibit 12.2 discusses feasibility studies for a new supersonic aircraft to replace Concorde.

Exhibit 12.2   Chocks away for Concorde 2?

British Aerospace, Aérospatiale of France and Deutsche Aerospace are working on plans for Concorde 2. They

Table 12.2   *Terminal 5 timetable*

Year	Projected stage
1992	Local consultations
1992	Submission of planning application
1994	Start of public planning inquiry
1995	End of public planning inquiry
1997	Government decision expected
	Subject to planning approval being granted
1997	Start of construction
2001	Completion of phase 1 construction
2002	Opening of phase 1
2016	Terminal reaches maximum capacity

Source: BAA.

have recently made a request for up to £60m from the government and the EU to finance a continuation into their feasibility studies.

There is however considerable disagreement between the aircraft manufacturers, airline chiefs and industry experts as to the likely feasibility of the project.

The manufacturers would need a production run of over 500 aircraft to break even, but few commentators can foresee a market of more than 100 planes. Even then reaction is guarded. Whilst design teams dream of more seats, and increased range, Ron Muddle, director of planning at BA, has his feet firmly on the ground, noting that running costs per passenger for today's Concorde are several times those for a Boeing 747. He says that only a radical design breakthrough would make the aircraft a commercial proposition.

Hands up those who can remember how many Concorde 1s were ever made?

Source: author, 1994.

Costs of capital goods

The capital costs of an investment are the costs of buildings, plant and machinery. In some cases these are known costs, since there is a market in commonly purchased capital goods such as computer systems, vehicles and standard buildings. For more complex investments capital costs can only be estimated in the planning stage and for large construction projects, estimates of costs are notoriously unreliable. The original estimate for building and equipping the Channel Tunnel was £5bn but by 1993 the figure had been revised to £10bn. Such escalations in costs are typical of large construction projects. In the case of the Channel Tunnel, factors such as price increases in materials, increased wages, unforeseen technical difficulties in boring the tunnel, specification changes to improve safety, and legal disputes over costs between Eurotunnel and the construction company Trans-Manche Link (TML) have all added to the increased costs.

Cost of financing investment

Finance for investment projects may be found internally out of a company's profits, or externally from the capital markets, for example, through banks or share issues.

External funding by loans carries costs in terms of interest rates that have to paid for the duration of a loan. These interest rates may be fixed or variable. External funding by share issue incurs issue costs but the costs of funding (i.e. the dividend payments to shareholders) are then tied into future profits.

It might appear that internally generated funds do not carry any special costs, since a company does not have to pay interest on its own funds. However there is an opportunity cost of using internal funds. That is the cost in terms of other uses to which the funds could have been put. A company could put funds on deposit in the money markets and gain interest on such deposits. Thus even where internal funds are used for investment, a notional interest rate will be used to represent their opportunity cost. In general, higher interest rates will act as a disincentive to investment.

Running costs of the investment

The running costs of an investment will include all the other costs of operating the project. These include labour costs, maintenance costs and raw material costs. New technology which reduces running and production costs can be an important cause of investment.

Revenue from investment

Total revenue from sales resulting from an investment project can be calculated by multiplying the selling price by the quantity sold and thus the main factors affecting the revenue obtained from an investment are:

- price of output
- quantity of output sold
- other factors

Price of output

The price of the output of an investment project will largely depend on demand and the competition in the market under consideration. This is discussed fully in Chapter 6, and in general the less competition, the more power a supplier will have to set price. Where a monopoly or near monopoly exists, price can be producer-determined (but quantity sold will reflect demand). However, potential competitors will move quickly to produce near substitutes where possible, particularly if a premium price is being charged. Where a few producers exist in a market (oligopoly or monopolistic competition), the impact of a new entrant will change the actions of those already in the market and thus lead to unpredictability. In a perfectly competitive market prices will be driven down to reflect the lowest average costs in the industry.

Thus, although a company may have market intelligence about current prices in the market where its investment is to take place, any estimate of prices in future years is likely to be very uncertain. Channel Tunnel prices, for example, have changed considerably between the planning stage and the present. This reflects the changing marketing strategies of competing ferry and airline companies.

Quantity of output sold

Quantity sold will be closely related to price charged. However it will also be related to factors including consumers' income, competitive prices and advertising. Figure 12.2 shows forecasts of passenger demand for airports in the South-east

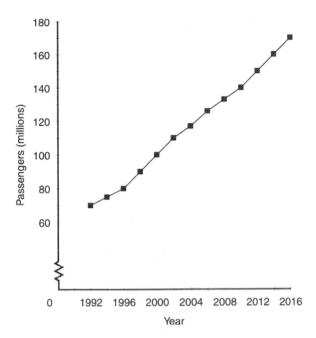

Figure 12.2 Passenger demand forecasts for airports in the South-east. Source: BAA.

of England. These are part of the feasibility study for London Heathrow's Terminal 5. Clearly there are a range of factors, for example environmental pressures, taxes, fuel costs, which might cause the forecasts to be wrong.

Other factors

Government policy may affect the revenue that derives from an investment project in several ways. First, government taxation policy may affect prices (VAT), or spending power (income tax) or profits (corporation tax). Second government legislation may affect the demand for goods, and finally monopolies and mergers legislation may have an impact upon prices that can be charged.

Expectations play a key part in investment decisions. Expectations reflect views about how successful the economy will be in future years. Where investors have a pessimistic view about the future economy they will generally defer investment decisions.

Property development is a prominent feature of much leisure and tourism investment. Whilst rental income is a part of the anticipated revenue from such developments, capital appreciation can also be an important factor. Thus, such developments are often sensitive to expectations about future prices of property.

Above all, the factors surrounding an investment decision are subject to a great deal of uncertainty. Few of the factors have known values. Current interest rates are known, and where an investment obtains funds at fixed rates, this provides a predictable element. However, where funds are obtained at variable interest rates, considerable uncertainty will exist. Similar uncertainty surrounds the final costs of complex capital projects, price of output and demand for the final good or service. These are all subject to changes in the competitive and political, economic, socio-cultural and technological (PEST) environments.

Appraisal techniques

Having identified the factors affecting the profitability of an investment, these can be used in a variety of quantitative methods to aid decision making. Investment appraisal reports may appear very authoritative, neatly summarizing projects in figures. However in view of the uncertainties discussed in the previous section, care should be taken to examine the assumption on which appraisals are made. The main appraisal techniques are:

- payback method
- average rate of return
- net present value
- internal rate of return

Payback method

This method compares investment projects by measuring the length of time it takes to repay the original investment from the revenues earned. It therefore favours projects which have the earliest payback. The key problems with this method

Table 12.3 *Payback method of investment appraisal (£m)*

Year	0	1	2	3	4
Costs	2.4	0.4	0.4	0.4	0.2
Revenue	0	1.0	1.2	1.4	1.4
Cash flow	−2.4	0.6	0.8	1.0	1.2
Cumulative cash flow	−2.4	−1.8	−1.0	0.0	1.2

Table 12.4 *Discounted cash flow method of investment appraisal (£m)*

Year	0	1	2	3	4
Net revenue		2.0	5.0	6.0	6.0
Present discounted value of net revenues		1.82	4.13	4.5	4.1

Note: Discount rate = 10 per cent.

are first that earnings that an investment may make after the payback period are not taken into account, and second revenues are not discounted so earnings within the payback period are given equal weight irrespective of the year they appear in. On the other hand, the sooner the payback, the less a project will be subject to uncertainties, and some companies may see speed of return as a priority over total return. Table 12.3 shows an example of this method and it can be seen that in this example the payback period is 3 years, when the cumulative cash flow reaches zero.

Average rate of return

This method calculates the total earnings from an investment and divides this by the number of years of the project's life. This figure is then expressed as a percentage of the capital costs of the project. For example, if an investment project had a total cost of £100 000 and earned a total of £500 000 over 5 years, the annual earnings would be £10 000, which represents an annual average rate of return of £10 000/£100 000 or 10 per cent on the capital employed. This method also fails to discount future earnings.

Net present value

The net present value method takes into account the fact that future earnings have a lower value than current earnings. For example, £100 today could be invested at a rate of interest of 10 per cent to give £110 in a year's time. Working this backwards, £100 in a year's time is only worth £90.91 today at a rate of interest of 10 per cent.

In other words, it has been discounted at a rate of 10 per cent to find its present discounted value. Discount tables exist to assist such calculations but there is also a formula for calculating present discounted value (PDV):

$$PDV = R_t / (1 + i)^t$$

where R = return, t = year and i = rate of interest or discount rate (expressed as decimal).

Row 2 of Table 12.4 shows the net revenues of a project with an initial capital cost of £16m in years 1–4, and row 3 shows these figures discounted to their present values using a discount rate of 10 per cent.

The net unadjusted revenues sum to £19m and thus the project appears to show a net surplus of £3m. However, the net present value technique compares costs and revenues discounted to their net present values. The total net revenue falls to £14.55m when discounted to present value, and the project shows the following net present value:

Costs at present value	£16.00m
Revenue at present value	£14.55m
Net present value	−£1.45m

This negative figure indicates an unprofitable investment.

Internal rate of return

The internal rate of return method also uses discounted cash flow. It calculates the discount rate that would equate the net present value of future

Table 12.5 *Factors causing changes in investment*

	Investment conditions	
	Good	Poor
Rate of interest	Low	High
Capital costs predictable?	Yes	No
Project duration	Short	Long
Price of output	Predictable	Uncertain
Market for product	Rising	Uncertain
Competition in proposed market	Limited	Competitive
Political stability	Stable	Unstable
Expectations about economy	Optimistic	Pessimistic
Sensitivity of project to shocks	Low	High
Spare capacity	Low	High

earnings of an investment to its initial cost. This rate is called the internal rate of return. An investment will be profitable if its internal rate of return exceeds the rate of interest that has to be paid for borrowing funds for the investment, allowing a margin for risk. A feasibility study into a fixed channel link by Coopers and Lybrand and Setec Economie in 1979 concluded that the internal rate of return on the project would be between 11 and 18 per cent.

When comparing investment projects those with the highest internal rate of return will be selected.

Changes in the level of investment

Changes in the level of investment will be caused by changes in the costs and predicted revenues of investments. These factors are summarized in Table 12.5.

The fall in investment in 1990 shown in Table 12.1 and Figure 12.1 can be attributed to high interest rates making the cost of borrowing funds to invest high, falling consumers' expenditure, and poor expectations about the economy in the medium term. Falling demand leaves machinery

underutilized and thus there is little need for new machinery.

The accelerator principle

Investment activity in economies tends to be volatile, that is subject to considerable fluctuations. One of the explanations of this is the accelerator principle.

When demand for consumer goods and services is relatively stable in an economy, much of the demand for capital goods will take the form of replacing worn-out plant and machinery. However, if demand for final goods rises and there is no spare capacity in an industry, then new machinery will have to be purchased. Thus the demand for capital goods will significantly increase to include new machines as well as replacement machines. Similarly, if the demand for final goods in an economy falls, firms will find they have over-capacity and too many machines. They will reduce the stock of machines to the new lower levels needed by not replacing worn-out machines, so the demand for capital goods will fall. Thus a rise in the demand for final goods will cause an accelerated rise in the demand for capital goods, and a fall in the demand for final goods will cause an accelerated fall in the demand for capital goods. The accelerator theory helps to explain the sudden fall in investment in 1990, in response to a fall in consumer demand.

Risk and sensitivity analysis

Sensitivity analysis is a technique for incorporating risk assessment in investment appraisal. It works by highlighting the key assumptions upon which investment appraisal figures were based. For example, revenue forecasts for an investment might be based upon:

- sales of 100 000 units per year
- market growth of 3 per cent per year
- price of £3 per unit
- exchange rate of £1 = $1.5

Sensitivity analysis would calculate the effects on an investment appraisal of changes in these assumptions. Such analysis would demonstrate the effects of, for example:

- sales of 80 000 units per year
- market growth of 1 per cent per year
- price of £2.50 per unit
- exchange rate of £1 = $1.75

and thus illustrate a project's sensitivity to a variety of scenarios.

Sources of funds

The main sources of funds for private sector investment include:

- retained profits
- new share issues (see Chapter 2)
- loans
- government assistance (see Chapter 13)

Government policy

Government assistance for private investment is discussed more fully in Chapter 13. The policy of the Conservative party is to interfere as little as possible in the free market. However it does offer financial assistance where a project provides employment in areas of high unemployment and where there are wider benefits to the community, as illustrated in exhibit 12.3.

Exhibit 12.3   City Challenge: a neat stroke

City Challenge, the state-funded body responsible for urban renewal projects, has provided £195 000 towards an eight-lane swimming pool that was opened in April at Spitalfields in central London.

The 13-acre site, formerly a fruit and vegetable market, was bought by developers who had planned a large housing and commercial complex but were blown off course by the recession.

The pool represents an interim use for the site which might otherwise remain derelict in a part of London with few local amenities and many social difficulties.

Source: author, 1994.

Review of key terms

- Investment = expenditure on capital goods and working capital.
- Fixed capital = durable capital goods such as buildings and machinery.
- Working capital = finance of work in progress such as raw material stocks, partially finished and unsold goods.
- Net investment = gross investment – depreciation.
- Payback method = appraisal technique to see how quickly an investment repays its costs.
- Average rate of return = appraisal technique where the average annual returns are expressed as a percentage of the original capital costs.
- Net present value = appraisal technique where all future revenues are recalculated to their present value so that a comparison can be made with the project costs.
- Internal rate of return = the rate of return of a project on capital employed, calculated by finding the rate that discounts future earnings to equal the capital costs.
- Accelerator theory = explanation why changes in consumer demand lead to larger changes in demand for investment goods.
- Sensitivity analysis = investigation of sensitivity of an investment project to changes in forecasts.

Data questions

Task 12.1

Shares: flights of fantasy – Quentin Lumsden

One of the intriguing aspects of Euro Disneyland is that it is so difficult to value the shares.

The stockbrokers SG Warburg has done projections, discounting back the stream of future earnings, to a figure from which it concludes the shares are fair value – and a hold – at the current 1650p. One number that stands out is the population of the catchment area for Euro Disneyland – some 400 million people. The projections on which many people have done their sums is that there will be 11 million visitors in the first year, rising gently thereafter. But if revenues grow more strongly than expected, the impact on profits will be dramatic because the costs are largely fixed. If there are 1 million more visitors than expected, or ticket prices in future years are 10 per cent higher than budgeted, or if visitors spend an extra pound more than expected on food and merchandise, then profitability will rise at a meteoric rate.

The reasonable conclusion is that Euro Disneyland has a considerable capacity to provide investors with favourable surprises.

Source: *Independent on Sunday*, 22 March 1992 (adapted).

Will Mickey turn his back on Euro flop?

The tragic tale of Euro Disneyland has dragged on since the Paris-based theme park opened its gates in April 1992. The fairy tale turned horror story is entering a new and crucial chapter. The figures are awesome; the park last year lost £607m. Euro Disney's share prices went into free fall following news of the losses last November and are currently trading around the 400p mark.

Source: *Observer*, 6 March 1994 (adapted).

Questions

1 What is meant by 'discounting back the stream of future earnings'? Why is this done?
2 The first article was written just before the opening of Euro Disneyland. What factors would the writer have taken into account when evaluating Euro Disney's potential profitability? Which of these factors were certainties?
3 What do the two articles demonstrate about investment appraisal?

Task 12.2   Receivers are called in to Broome's sporting estate

Receivers have been called in to Carden Park in Cheshire, the latest venture of John Broome, who founded Alton Towers.

The £22m venture, styled 'Europe's premier resort', is a new sporting estate of more than 1000 acres, 50 miles from Manchester. It offers guests 25 pursuits, including shooting, archery, ballooning, bowls, riding, game fishing and golf.

It was hoped that Carden would stage seven events had Manchester won its bid to host the Olympic Games; instead it had to settle for staging a recent world croquet championship. The estate now includes a luxury hotel with 80 bedrooms, two golf courses, and facilities for conferences, exhibitions, training sessions and seminars.

In 1987, Broome bought Battersea power station from the Central Electricity Generating Board for £1.5m. Work started on a theme park in 1988, but has never been finished. Losses have been estimated at more than £160m and liquidators from Arthur Anderson were put into the one-time operating company, Battersea Leisure Group, last April by the banks.

- Price Waterhouse has been appointed joint administrative receiver to Kettering Leisure Village, a 10-acre Northamptonshire leisure complex, which opened in July 1993 after a £15m investment. The centre employs about 130 people.

Source: *Guardian*, 7 October 1994 (adapted).

Questions

1 Assuming each of these projects was subject to investment appraisal, suggest reasons for their failure.

2 Alton Towers has recently invested in Nemesis, The Runaway Mine Train, The Haunted House, and The New Beast. Suggest why its investments have been more successful.

Task 12.3 City: black hole – Jeremy Warner

There was a depressing familiarity about last week's news that Eurotunnel has lost another round of its battle to keep the lid on the costs of the Channel Tunnel. Unless it can reverse the order on appeal, Eurotunnel is going to have to pay the Channel Tunnel contractors a lot more to complete the project than previously thought – making yet another refinancing of the venture look almost inevitable.

You don't need much experience of the construction industry to know that in all building projects the customer inevitably ends up paying considerably more than anticipated. At the risk of embarrassing Warburg Securities, however, I am going to quote from a City circular issued by the firm as part of the marketing effort for Eurotunnel shares when they were first sold to the public in the Autumn of 1987. 'We believe,' the circular said, 'the balance of probability is that Eurotunnel will be completed both on time – May 1993 – and to budget.' The projected cost of the Channel tunnel was then £4.8bn. After numerous upgradings, that figure had risen to more than £8bn by last November. It's a racing certainty that by the time the tunnel opens (late, naturally) the final tally is not going to be far south of £10bn – or roughly double the original estimate.

So were investors and bankers conned? Sir Alastair Morton, chief executive, and all the others involved in raising finance for Eurotunnel, no doubt were convinced that what they were saying was true. A part of this was to boast how the contracts had been deliberately designed to thwart the contractor's natural tendency to inflate his price. It's all proved so much hogwash and one suspects that deep down everyone must have guessed there wasn't a hope in hell of bringing the project in on budget.

The imperative was to make sure it was built, a noble enough aim in itself, but hardly the first priority of the investor. It's possible the tunnel will still yield an adequate return, but it's looking increasingly less likely.

The inflated cost of the tunnel is only part of the problem. The greater imponderable is revenues once the system is up and running. It's hard to see why Eurotunnel's revenue predictions should be any more believable than its estimate of costs.

Source: *Independent on Sunday*, 5 April 1992.

Questions

1 What would be an 'adequate return' for the channel tunnel project? How would this be calculated?
2 Why are construction costs difficult to predict?
3 What impact does the late opening of the channel tunnel have on profit forecasts?
4 Why is this article sceptical about revenue predictions?

Task 12.4 Port Aventura: trying not to be a black hole

There are black holes and there are black holes. The one is a successful ride at Alton Towers. The other is the financial mess that EuroDisney got itself into. EuroDismal as named by its critics, now renamed Disneyland, Paris, down but not yet out.

The Disney fiasco seems perhaps a strange backdrop against which to launch Port Aventura, Europe's second biggest theme park, near Salou on the Mediterranean coast of Spain, due to open in April 1995.

In fact the Tussauds group, owners of Alton Towers (and owned by Pearson, the *Financial Times*/Penguin books/Thames TV conglomerate), has been negotiating to become the theme park's largest shareholder and operating manager.

'Just because EuroDisney has got problems, it

doesn't mean that major theme parks in Europe are bound to fail,' says Ms Rebecca Winnington-Ingram, a leisure industry analyst with Morgan Stanley. And of course she is right. Perhaps it is the success of Alton Towers in England that has tempted the Tussauds group into this £200m Spanish venture.

There are key differences between Port Aventura and EuroDisney, not least of which is the scale of the projects: Disneyland, Paris attracts 11 million visitors a year, but Port Aventura is forecasting 2.7 million in its first year rising to 5 million. Port Aventura is only open for 156 days a year under summer skies (when more than 15 million summer tourists are within easy reach), where Disneyland, Paris is open all year under much more threatening northerly skies.

Port Aventura has also avoided some of Disneyland, Paris's vast fixed costs by concentrating on the theme park and not investing in the accommodation side. Ray Barret, a Tussauds director, offers the following analysis: 'Euro-Disney got its theme park right and what went wrong was its inability to fill its [six] hotels.' The Mediterranean strip in which Port Aventura operates includes large resorts such as Benidorm and has an abundance of hotels already in existence.

The two parks also have a different gearing for their royalty, management and consultancy charges. The Walt Disney took a massive 31.5 per cent of EuroDisney's operating income from its opening date. Similar charges payable from Port Aventura to Busch Entertainment (the park's designers) and to Tussauds (its managers) start at 12.4 per cent of operating income and are set to fall to 10.4 per cent by 1998.

Source: author, adapted from press cuttings, January 1995.

Questions

1 Why is Port Aventura likely to be more of a successful investment project than Euro-Disney?
2 Identify four key factors that might be used in conducting a sensitivity analysis on this investment and evaluate their possible impact.

Short questions

1 Distinguish between net investment and gross investment.
2 How important is the rate of interest in affecting the decision to invest in a project?
3 Distinguish between the short-term and long-term effects of investment to an economy.
4 Evaluate the payback method of investment appraisal.
5 What is a project's internal rate of return?
6 Distinguish between working capital and fixed capital.
7 Why is sensitivity analysis used?

Further reading

English Tourist Board, *Investment in Tourism*, English Tourist Board, 1991.

Gavin, M. and Swann, P., The economics of the Channel Tunnel, *Economic Review*, **11**(3), 1994.

Kotler, P., *Marketing Places: Attracting Investment Industry and Tourism to Cities, States and Nations*, Free Press, 1993.

Vickerman, R. and Flowerdew, A., The Channel Tunnel: the economic and regional impact, *Business International*, 1990.

13

Investment and the public sector

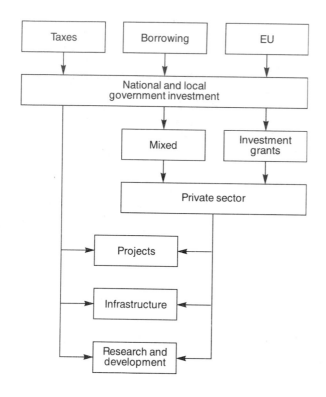

Objectives

The Thatcher revolution caused a fundamental rethink of public investment as the government sought to 'roll back the frontiers of the state'. Opponents of public sector investment pointed to previous symbols of policy failure such as Concorde as representing the worst aspects of public sector investment – consuming ever-increasing sums of taxpayers' money and never achieving viable commercial sales. Thus Mrs Thatcher was adamant that the Channel Tunnel

would be built using private funds or not at all. And so it was.

Yet the Channel Tunnel project also demonstrates the shortcomings of such a policy. The French rail link has been upgraded using public funds, resulting in a fast, efficient journey form Paris to the tunnel at around 185 mph. However, Eurostar trains have to brake sharply to around 60 mph when they enter the British rail link to Waterloo. Lack of private or public funding has meant the track has not been upgraded, and is now unlikely to match the French link before the year 2000.

By studying this chapter students will be able to:

- identify the sources of public sector investment
- identify different types of public sector investment
- describe different methods of public sector investment
- appraise public sector investment projects
- identify public sector incentives for private sector investment
- identify sources of funds for public sector investment

Sources, types, methods and aims of public sector investment

Sources

Public sector investment can be financed from different sources. At the supranational level, the EU is a key source, particularly through the European Regional Development Fund. At the national level, government channels leisure and tourism investment through public corporations, quangos such as the Sports Council and government departments such as the Department for National Heritage. Local government is the other major source of public sector investment.

Types

Public sector investment may also be classified according to type. First public sector investment may be in buildings and land, for example parks, leisure centres and museums. Second public sector investment includes plant and machinery such as playground apparatus, computerized booking systems and canal lock equipment. Third public sector investment may be made in infrastructure.

Infrastructure, or social overhead capital, is the construction needed to support economic development, for example, roads, railways and airports, water and sewerage, power and telecommunications. Public investment on infrastructure has been relatively higher in France than that in the UK and exhibit 13.1 reports on the completion of a cornerstone in French public investment strategy.

Exhibit 13.1 'The train arriving at runway 3 . . .'

Whilst engineering work on the new rail tunnel at London's Heathrow Airport is halted after a landslide, another jewel is set in the crown of the French transport system.

Passengers landing at Charles de Gaulle airport used to be faced by a messy onward journey into France. Now, a TGV high-speed station has been opened. The £300m glass and steel construction links four methods of transport: air, road, *métro* and high-speed rail. The TGV route is able to bypass Paris so that passengers can for example be in Lyons within 2 hours without having to change trains.

Announced by the French government in 1987, the project was co-funded between French Railways (SNCF) and Aéroports de Paris (ADP). Further development of the site is to include banks, restaurants, shops and a Sheraton hotel.

Source: the author, from news cuttings, November 1994.

Infrastructure development is a key part of tourism destination development as it has to precede specific project development such as hotels, leisure sites and restaurants.

Finally public sector investment may be spent on research and development, as illustrated in exhibit 13.2.

Exhibit 13.2   Research: their mission – to create wealth – panels of experts are being formed to advise the government where to spend its money to help British industry – Liz Heron

The UK's first nationwide attempt to direct public spending on science and technology towards research with potential for creating wealth has been launched by the Office of Science and Technology (OST).

Technology Foresight will bring together university scientists with researchers, managers and marketing people from industry to identify key sciences and technologies that British companies could use to get ahead in developing hi-tech products for the world market.

The OST is appointing people to panels in 15 economic sectors that it believes have most potential for exploiting scientific advances. These are: energy; transport; agriculture, natural resources and environment; health and life sciences; leisure and education; food and drink; manufacturing, production and business processes; financial services; defence and aerospace; materials; chemicals; information technology and electronics; communications; construction; retail and distribution.

Source: *The Independent*, 7 April 1994 (adapted).

Methods and aims

The main methods of public sector investment are first via projects which are wholly public sector-financed, second via projects which are jointly financed by the public and private sectors and finally via projects which are private sector investments but which are eligible for public sector investment incentive grants.

The aims of public sector investment include provision of goods and services which have significant public benefits, but which might not be profitable enough to attract private sector investment. Public sector investment may also be focused on projects aimed at the economic development or regeneration of a particular area. Exhibit 13.3 reports on the contribution of mixed public and private sector investment in the arts to the economy of Edinburgh.

Exhibit 13.3   Lights up for Edinburgh's new theatre

Two years ago, Lothian and Edinburgh Enterprise Limited – part of the Scottish Development Board – backed a £21m project to turn a bingo hall into a theatre. It is a mixed investment where £6.6m has come from the private sector and no revenue subsidy will be needed in its operation. The result is a multi-use theatre with the largest stage in the UK.

The theatre represents a major project in Edinburgh's economic revival. It is estimated that 16 000 extra tourists will be attracted to the city, boosting the city's tourism income by £7m to £257m.

Source: the author, from news cuttings, May 1994.

Investment appraisal in the public sector

Cost–benefit analysis

Investment appraisal for private sector projects is relatively straightforward, as described in the previous chapter. If a project yields the required return on capital employed then the investment will go ahead.

The different nature of the public sector makes investment appraisal more complex in this sector.

Some parts of the public sector are run on private sector lines. In these cases an investment is required to earn a specified rate of return on capital employed and thus the investment decision is fairly clear-cut.

However, many public sector investments are made for reasons of wider public benefits and thus private sector methods of appraisal are inappropriate. In such cases cost–benefit analysis provides a more useful method of project appraisal. Cost–benefit analysis is described in detail in Chapter 19; however its essential details

Table 13.1   *Cost–Benefit analysis of canal restoration scheme*

Costs	Benefits
Private costs Construction costs of project, e.g. • Materials • Labour • Professional fees	*Private benefits* Revenue from project, e.g. • Craft licences and charges • Fishing licences • Rentals from renovated buildings
Social costs Inconvenience costs to local residents of construction	*Social benefits* Drownings avoided through improved canal safety New jobs created by project Improved aesthetics of area

are that all the costs and benefits of a project are identified and weighed up, including social as well as private ones.

Table 13.1 shows an example of possible private and social costs and benefits for a canal restoration scheme.

Private sector investment appraisal of such a scheme would calculate the private costs of the project, and the private benefits. These would be discounted to net present value (as explained in Chapter 12) and since the private costs would almost certainly exceed the private benefits, the investment would not proceed.

However, cost–benefit analysis would analyse the wider costs and benefits. Some extra costs such as noise and congestion associated with the construction phase might be identified. Social benefits of the scheme would include lives saved through improved canal safety, greater public well-being caused by improved aesthetics from the project, and the effects on the local economy of new industries and employment attracted to the area because of the project. The total figures would be subjected to discounting to calculate net present value and it might well be the case that total public and private benefits would exceed costs. Thus there may well be an argument for public sector investment in the project.

Other factors affecting public investment

Whilst cost–benefit analysis is used for appraising some major public sector investment projects, its use is far from widespread. Public sector investment decisions are often determined by the priorities of the political party in power at a national or local level. Decisions will also be affected by interest group activity, and the general economic environment. Public expenditure at a local level has come under increasing direct and indirect control from central government since 1979.

Task 13.2 of the data questions at the end of this chapter illustrates how a move to the left in the Labour party on Birmingham council led to a reversal of its public investment policy. 'City boosterism' had been the philosophy behind a massive investment in leisure, sports and arts facilities, designed to bring visitors and jobs to an area suffering form the effects of de-industrialization. The new leadership has returned to a more conventional policy of investment in schools and housing.

Investment incentives for tourism and leisure projects

Areas of the UK which have high areas of unemployment are designated assisted areas, and the government uses incentives to attract firms and jobs to such areas. These include:

- Regional selective assistance. This is a discretionary grant based on the number of jobs that will be created and the capital costs of the project.
- European Regional Development Fund. This provides grants of up to 50 per cent for job-creating projects and projects to develop infrastructure.
- Regional enterprise grants. These encourage the growth of small businesses.

Exhibit 13.4 describes the impact of 'the peace dividend' on the South Devon economy and on steps to encourage inward investment. These include the setting-up of a mixed public and private sector development partnership, the search for funding and the emphasis on leisure and tourism projects.

Exhibit 13.4   An inward investment strategy for South Dorset

The peace dividend is coming to Dorset and it's a bit of a mixed blessing.

The naval base will close in 1996. The Defence Research Agency's Underwater Systems division is relocating 500 staff out of the county in 1995. The Sea Systems Controllerate is relocating to Bristol. Around 50 per cent of the jobs in the Weymouth and Portland areas are defence-related and about 5000 of these are going.

The accountancy firm Coopers and Lybrand published a report in 1992, *An Inward Investment Strategy for South Dorset*. It proposed the setting-up of a South Dorset Economic Partnership (SDEP) to help stimulate economic redevelopment of the area. Several bodies have now joined forces to form the SDEP, including local councils, Dorset Training and Enterprise Council, the Rural Development Commission, local chambers of commerce and local industry.

A £36 000 EU grant has been won to counter the effects of defence cuts. The area has also been designated intermediate assisted-area status, and inward investment will thus be eligible for government subsidy.

Leisure and tourism has been highlighted as a key area which it is hoped can bring new jobs to the area. Weymouth has potential as a resort area. A tourism development action programme has been initiated, but it remains to be seen whether leisure and tourism can provide the quantity and quality of jobs lost in the defence shake-out.

Source: The author, adapted from press cuttings, April 1994.

Table 13.2   *Tourism projects in inner cities*

Project	Area	Former use	Type	Jobs
Holiday Inn	Manchester	Hotel	Private	304
Hull marina	Hull	Docks	Local authority	11
Dry ski slope	Newham	Toxic tip	Private	20
Boat museum	Ellesmere Port	Canal basin	Trust	26
Indoor bowls	Trafford	Steel foundry	Private	58

Notes: Jobs = full- and part-time.
Source: *Tourism and the Inner City* (1990).

Investment incentives are also available for some urban areas and are implemented through the following schemes:

- Enterprise zones. These small designated areas of acute industrial decline have simplified planning rules and 100 per cent allowances against corporation tax for expenditure on buildings.
- Urban development corporations. These have considerable powers to clear and develop derelict sites and encourage private sector investment.
- English Partnerships. This agency has inherited a large portfolio of factories, workshops and offices managed by English Estates.
- City Challenge. This is a Department of the Environment initiative to encourage local authorities to bid for funds for projects to improve inner-city areas.

Finally the Training and Enterprise Councils (TECs) can offer assistance in recruiting and training staff.

Exhibit 13.5 reports on the success of government investment incentives to attract the Sony European games development centre to Liverpool.

Exhibit 13.5   Sony Electronic investment in Merseyside will create 259 jobs

The largest Japanese investment in Merseyside, announced yesterday, will create 259 new jobs when Sony Electronic Publishing opens its European games development centre in Liverpool.

The £35m-plus facility, which will attract £7.2m of public funding, is expected to start production by the middle of 1995. The plant will develop the next generation of video-gaming systems.

The Sony project will receive £1.75m in regional selective assistance. It will also receive £4.3m in derelict land grant from English Partnerships, the new agency set to transform 150 000 vacant and derelict areas into a magnet for social and industrial regeneration.

Source: *Guardian*, 8 November 1994.

The Department of the Environment has actively promoted tourism projects as a means of regenerating inner-city areas and Table 13.2 illustrates some of the projects that have been grant-aided.

Sources of funds

Sources of funds for public investment include:

- operating profits
- taxation
- borrowing
- the national lottery

Operating profits, taxation and borrowing

Operating profits are rare in public sector organizations since, as discussed in Chapter 2, they are run for motives other than profit. Thus

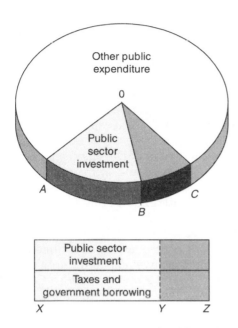

Figure 13.1 Opportunity cost of public sector investment.

public sector investment is mainly financed from taxation receipts and government borrowing. This is a key reason why public sector investment is often under attack, particularly from the Treasury.

First opportunity costs are immediately apparent. Thus the opportunity cost of more public investment is higher taxes, or less government expenditure elsewhere, as illustrated in Figure 13.1.

The circle represents total government spending and no increases in taxes or government borrowing are assumed. An increase in public sector investment from *A0B* to *A0C* can only be accommodated by a fall in other government expenditure of *B0C*. Alternatively, it is assumed below that other government expenditure remains unchanged. In this case an increase in public sector investment from *XY* to *XZ* can only be financed through an increase in taxes or government borrowing of *YZ*.

Second, when the economy is performing badly, investment is often a target of government policy. If government borrowing is running too high, cutting social security payments or pen-

sions has readily identifiable victims. Cutting investment generally results only in some improvement not taking place and therefore its consequences are more blurred.

The national lottery

Whilst public spending is generally being squeezed by the Treasury, leisure and tourism is a key beneficiary of the national lottery. Twenty-eight per cent of the lottery revenue (which is expected to reach £5.5bn annually) goes to five major causes, four of which will benefit leisure and tourism. These are charities, the arts, sports, national heritage and the Millennium Fund.

Projects in the arts hoping to benefit from the national lottery include first, the South Bank arts complex in London. Administrators at the South Bank have recently been reviewing schemes to redesign the complex to make it more coherent, friendly and attractive. The redevelopment costs are likely to be in the region of £66m and it is envisaged that national lottery funds will make a contribution to this. Second, help will be sought for investment funds for the Tate Gallery's proposed new Bankside museum for modern art. The estimated cost of conversion of a disused power station in east London for this project is estimated at £80m. The English National Opera is also seeking funds to renovate the London Coliseum.

The Sports Council has set up a lottery board to distribute its share of funds. Projects of between £5000 and £5m can be considered for a grant of up to 65 per cent. Large projects include a new national stadium and local council sports facilities.

The National Heritage memorial fund has responsibility for channelling funds into areas such as museum collections, historic buildings and monuments, landscapes, libraries and industrial heritage.

The public sector investment debate

Public investment has been subject to considerable debate during the Thatcher revolution and beyond. The Thatcher government took a stance against public investment based on the following arguments:

1   The public sector is not a good interpreter of people's wants and thus often invests in 'white elephants'.
2   The public sector is not good at ensuring efficient use of funds and tends to allow waste.
3   Public sector investment causes an increase in taxation or public borrowing.
4   Public sector investment 'crowds out' private sector investment.

The Thatcher government therefore removed a large slice of investment from the public sector through its privatization programme. It then concentrated its efforts on creating an 'enterprise economy' which it hoped would stimulate private sector investment by reducing income and corporation tax and making the labour market more flexible.

The arguments favouring public sector investment are:

1   There is insufficient incentive for the private sector to invest in public goods (see Chapter 7).
2   The public sector underinvests in goods which have mainly social benefits.

Thus, where the market is used as the main determinant of investment, infrastructure projects with important public and merit angles will tend to be overlooked, despite the fact that the future capacity of the economy may depend on them. This has led to calls to distinguish between capital spending and current spending in PSBR figures, since the former will involve future benefits.

Review of key terms

- Infrastructure = construction needed to support economic development.
- Cost–benefit analysis = full analysis of public and private costs and benefits of project.
- Net present value = discounting money paid at a future date to its present value.
- 'City boosterism' = investment in projects to regenerate city centres in economic decline.
- Assisted areas = areas of country eligible for government investment grants.
- Regional selective assistance = grant to attract job-creating projects.
- European Regional Development Fund = EU fund for projects and infrastructure to bring jobs to designated areas.
- Regional enterprise grants = grants to promote small businesses in assisted areas.
- Enterprise zones = designated areas of acute industrial decline having simplified planning rules and incentives expenditure on buildings.
- TECs = Training and Enterprise Councils.

Data questions

Task 13.1   Canals and the superhighway

No – its not that the UK's network of canals is about to take the loads off the roads. Its just a brilliant piece of lateral thinking that is all part of British Waterway's (BW) search for additional revenue. The result – a creative fusion of the old and the new. Starting in Scotland, optical fibre cables are being laid along canal networks to meet the growing demand for data communications.

BW itself reflects an odd mixture of the old and new. At its centre is a network of partially derelict canals and navigable rivers, most of which are some 200 years old. But its chief executive, Mr Brian Dice, brought with him modern management techniques honed over 25 years of working in the private sector at Cadbury Schweppes.

Private sector? But surely BW was itself privatized in the 1980s along with, amongst others, BT, BA and BAA. Apparently not. BW is still responsible to the Department of the Environment and privatization was ruled out because of its continuing need for public subsidy.

But BW has not been immune to the harsh winds of economic reality and the Treasury has cut its annual funding over the past 10 years by around 25 per cent to an annual figure of £50m.

Brian Dice has sought to mitigate these cuts. 'I made it a priority that we stop whingeing and concentrate our efforts elsewhere, on the European Regional Development Fund, on central government's City Challenge and derelict land grant schemes and on local authorities and development corporations. The redevelopment of Sheffield canal basin, for example, uses all those sources. We are also keeping leisure fees, for the 1 million boaters and anglers on our canals, marginally ahead of inflation. Freight traffic, principally on the navigable waterways of northern England, also enhances our revenues, although no one is going to put computers on a barge. We have to exploit the honeypot sites and have more income under our own control. The transformation of Gloucester Docks, which now houses the National Waterways Museum, shows what can be done with local authority and private sector involvement. We are seeking similar partners for other undeveloped sites,' he explains.

However, the Treasury prefers BW to sell off surplus sites for private sector development, rather than participate in joint ventures which might involve exposure to financial risk.

The canal network was overlooked for years, and despite recent renovations such as the Kennet–Avon canal in Wiltshire, has a huge and urgent backlog of expensive repairs to lock gates, leaking channels and aqueducts. Although it still carries some freight, its main future lies more as a source of recreation for boaters, anglers, walkers, cyclists and nature-lovers. Nor should its contribution to the country's industrial heritage be overlooked.

But whilst people may agree on the importance of conservation and preservation in the current climate of environmental concern, the question as to how it is to be paid for remains unsolved.

Source: the author, from press cuttings, February 1995.

Questions

1 What are the sources of investment funds for BW?
2 What sources of funds would be available to a privatized BW?
3 Compare the methods of determining the amount of investment in canals under private sector and public sector ownership.
4 Consider how the canal networks might appear by the year 2010, under private and public sector ownership.

Task 13.2 Rattled of Symphony Hall: Birmingham's bid for new greatness included balletic endeavour, Olympic attempts and brave new temples of culture. Then the city council changed its tune – Nick Cohen

When Simon Rattle raised his baton on 15 April 1991 to lead the City of Birmingham Symphony Orchestra into the first chords of Stravinsky's *Firebird*, the idea that a funding crisis could bring the most acclaimed conductor in the country close to resigning would have seemed preposterous.

At the opening night of the Birmingham Symphony Hall the evidence of the city's bold, almost reckless commitment to economic regeneration through the spending of millions on culture, tourism and service industries could not have been more obvious to the 2200 guests. The symphony hall, everyone agreed, was one of the finest in the world. Labour-controlled Birmingham City Council had, with the support of local Conservatives, uncomplainingly paid the bulk of the £30m cost. No expense had been spared.

Next door, in Centenary Square, a £150m convention centre, which was confidently expected to attract business tourists from around the world, was all but complete. Behind the centre a new 13 000-seat indoor athletics stadium which, city planners assured the voters, would help make Birmingham the UK sporting capital, was ready to receive athletes.

The policy of growth through prestige developments was outlined in a council development plan published shortly after the hall opened. 'To a large degree the prosperity of the whole city will depend on the city centre,' it said. 'Entertainment, culture, leisure and recreation have an increasingly valuable role. Indeed, [they] represent the very essence of a large metropolitan international centre.' In the seventies, the essence of Birmingham was making things people wanted to buy. But the recession of the early eighties wiped out 110 000 jobs in a city of 1 million people. In desperation at first, then with an increasingly evangelical conviction, Birmingham's councillors turned to American models of urban regeneration pioneered in the rust-belt cities of Baltimore and Detroit. Civic boosterism is the jargon label – the belief that eye-catching developments in the city centre could replace the lost manufacturing jobs by attracting high-spending tourists, conventioning businessmen and sports fans.

There were early warning signs that the policy was not working. Two Olympic bids failed in the eighties and a Super Prix car race collapsed. But it seemed almost bad taste at the time to mention these setbacks as the right-wing Labour council and their allies in business and the council bureaucracy exuberantly proclaimed that Birmingham 'was ready to compete with Barcelona and Lyon's'.

Birmingham's boosterism in the eighties has been followed by a profound shift in the city away from prestige projects to a kind of left-wing, back-to-basics policy. Last year, Theresa Stewart, a 63-year-old grandmother and veteran left-winger, beat the right-wing candidates for the Labour leadership on a policy of stopping the search for prestige. Ever since, there has been a changed atmosphere in the city. Education, housing, social services were the priority, not tourists, theatre-goers and conventions. 'For 10 years I was told the council was developing municipal socialism,' she said after winning office. 'It's been more like municipal stupidity.' Ed Smith, the orchestra's general manager, recognizes the shift in emphasis. 'Not a day goes by without money worries,' he said. Other attractions are also in trouble.

Councillor Stewart has said she would 'not spend £10 on another Olympic bid'.

Stand outside the gleaming concert hall and strike out in any direction and in 15 minutes you will hit Birmingham's inner city – a ring of misery running clockwise from Handsworth through New Town, Aston, Small Heath and Sparkbrook to Ladywood. The statistics give a prosaic idea of the poverty. In the nine inner-Birmingham wards, 31 per cent of adults are out of work. Almost four out of 10 of the city's population receive state benefits. In the New Town district, to take just one example, the number of single-parent families is three times the national average and two out of three residents do not have a single O-level or GCSE. If the symphony hall, convention centre and the rest were really to be the source of regeneration, then these are the people who should have benefited from the trickle-down effect. They have not. Most of the jobs created were menial, part-time and low-paid. The council recognized the problem and devised a training programme to prepare the unemployed for full-time work in the convention centre. The result was pitiable. Just 19 inner-city residents got jobs. More significantly, money was diverted from the core services the poor depend on to fund the building boom. An analysis by the University of Central England (formerly Birmingham Polytechnic) estimated that £123m was taken from Birmingham City Council's housing budget and that spending on school buildings fell by 60 per cent while the lavish city centre developments were being built. Most notoriously of all, the council took more and more from the budget for education, leaving Birmingham with some of the worst schools in the country. In 1991 Birmingham was spending £46m less than the amount recommended by central government. Birmingham city centre may look marvellous, but it is a gleaming heart surrounded by a decaying body. Councillor Stewart cannot knock down the convention centre, much as she may like to, and the symphony hall and indoor arena will remain. But it is clear that from now on the council's priorities will be housing and education. An extra £43m will be pumped into schools this year and the money will have to come from somewhere.

Source: *The Independent*, 9 March 1994 (adapted).

Questions

1 What was the economic rationale behind 'city boosterism'?
2 What factors would you take into account in conducting a cost–benefit analysis on investment in 'city boosterism'?
3 What factors caused a change in Birmingham's investment strategy?
4 What were the opportunity costs of 'city boosterism' in Birmingham?

Task 13.3 New line signals profit

Prime Minister of Spain, Felipe Gonzales, faced considerable political criticism when the decision to build the Madrid–Seville high-speed train (AVE) was announced. It seemed to defy economic sense. Why not instead build a link between Madrid and Barcelona? After all, Barcelona is roughly double in importance and size compared with Seville, and it is next to the French border. In short, a key international route had been ignored.

Cynics suggested that Gonzales was favouring his home town in defiance of any rational arguments. The government claimed that the Seville link was crucial to the development of the poorer south of Spain and an important part of a strategy to ensure balanced national growth.

The facts speak for themselves: the AVE is set to become one of the few parts of the Spanish railway system to make a profit. In 1994, its second year of operation, passenger growth is likely to exceed 24 per cent to around 4 million and operating costs should be covered. Income is expected to be in excess of Pta22bn by 1998 and the Pta45bn investment in rolling stock will

have been paid off. The construction costs of the project of Pta450bn have been paid by the Ministry of Transport.

AVE facts

Between Madrid and Seville ...	Before AVE	After AVE
Railway travel time	5 h 55 min	2 h 40 min
Rail passengers	20%	44%
Car passengers	51%	39%
Air passengers	18%	7%

In the wake of the success of the AVE, the Ministry of Transport has authorized the construction of the Madrid–French frontier link which should be completed by the year 2003.

Source: author, adapted from press cuttings, March 1994.

Questions

1 What political factors affected the AVE investment decision?
2 What factors would be considered in a cost–benefit analysis of the AVE Madrid–Seville link?
3 What are the arguments for and against leaving this type of investment to the private sector?

Short questions

1 Under what circumstances would investment grants be available for the construction of a theme park?
2 What is cost–benefit analysis and why is it sometimes difficult to calculate?
3 Compare the sources of funds for public investment projects with sources available in the private sector.
4 What specific leisure and tourism projects might benefit from the national lottery?

5   Compare the factors determining an investment decision in the public sector with those
in the private sector.

Further reading

Polytechnic of Central London, Leisureworks and
DRV Research, *Tourism and the Inner City. An*
Evaluation of the Impact of Grant Assisted Tour-
ism Projects, HMSO, 1990.

Wanhill, S., Development and investment policy
in tourism, in Witt, S. and Moutinho, L. (eds),
Tourism Marketing and Management Handbook,
Prentice Hall, 1989.

World Bank, *World Development Report*, Oxford
University Press, 1994.

Part Four

Leisure and Tourism Impacts on the National Economy

14

Leisure and tourism: income, employment and inflation

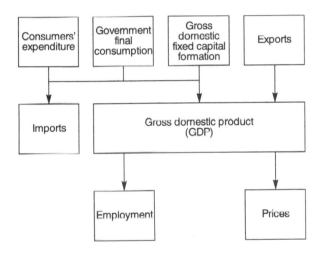

Objectives

Chapter 9 looked at the effects of the economic environment on leisure and tourism organizations. The aim of this chapter is to examine the other side of this question, and ask how the leisure and tourism sector contributes to the general level of economic activity. In particular it will examine the contribution of leisure and tourism to national output, national income and national expenditure, to the level of employment and consider the question of inflation. The issue of economic growth will be covered in Chapter 15, and international impact of leisure and tourism will be addressed in Chapter 16.

By studying this chapter students should be able to:

- distinguish between microeconomics and macroeconomics
- measure the total level of economic activity in an economy
- distinguish between changes in real and money GNP
- measure the contribution of leisure and tourism to GNP
- understand the contribution of leisure and tourism to employment
- utilize simple economic models of the macro-economy
- understand and apply the multiplier principle
- measure inflation in the leisure and tourism sector
- interpret government policy in this area

GNP and the level of leisure and tourism activity

Macroeconomics

Chapters 2–7 dealt mainly with microeconomic issues. These were issues concerning the actions of individuals (demand) and firms (supply) and their interaction to determine prices in specific markets (e.g. the market for television sets, the market for air travel).

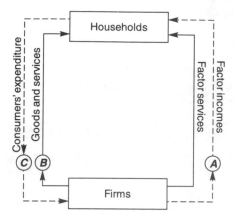

Figure 14.1   The circular flow of income.

Chapters 14–16 look mainly at macroeconomic issues. These are issues that affect the whole economy. Macroeconomics deals with aggregates. Thus it adds together the spending of individuals to calculate consumers' expenditure, or aggregate demand. It adds together the output of individual organizations to measure national output or product. Similarly, the general price level and rate of inflation are investigated rather than prices in individual markets.

A simple macroeconomic model

Figure 14.1 illustrates a simple model of the national economy.

The economy is divided into two sectors, households and firms. Households own factors of production whilst firms utilize factors of production to produce goods and services. It is assumed in this initial model that all the output of firms is sold, and all income is spent. Additionally, there is no government activity, no savings or investment, and no international trade.

There are two flows in this system. First, 'real' flows are designated by unbroken lines. These represent the flow of factors of production (land, labour and capital) from households to firms, and the flow of goods and services, made from these factors of production, from firms to households. Second, 'money' flows are designated by broken

lines. These represent factor rewards and payments for goods and services. For example, if a member of a household works for a firm it supplies the factor of labour and receives the reward of wages in payment. This payment can then be used to purchase goods and services from firms.

In this simple model of the economy firms buy factors of production to make goods and services, and households sell factors of production to buy goods and services. The model can be used to illustrate the concept of national income. National income is a measure of the total level of economic activity which takes place in an economy over a year. In Figure 14.1, if the total flow of money at point A was measured over a year, this would represent the level of national income. The same picture can be viewed from different angles. The total value of goods and services passing point B over a year would represent national output or national product, and the total amount of expenditure passing point C over a year would represent national expenditure. This gives an important accounting identity:

National income = national product = national expenditure

GNP and its measurement

The key rule in deciding how an item should be treated for national income calculation is whether it represents income earned by, or output (or expenditure on that output) produced by, UK factors of production. The three methods of measuring GDP are described in outline below.

Income method

In this method incomes are added up. Stock appreciation (the increase in the value of firms' stocks due to inflation over the year) is deducted since no increase in output has actually occurred because of this. A residual error figure is included since there will be discrepancies between each of the methods due to statistical collection errors:

Incomes from employment
+ Incomes from profits
+ Incomes from rents, etc.
– Stock appreciation
– Residual error
= *Gross domestic product*

Expenditure method

Here total spending on final output under different headings is measured. Some goods will be semifinished or finished but not yet sold, so these are added as 'increase in stocks and works in progress'. Exported goods have been produced in the UK but not bought here, so their value is added. Imports have been bought in the UK but not produced here, so their value is deducted. Finally, taxes artificially inflate prices and subsidies undervalue the underlying production costs, so these are deducted and added respectively to move from market prices to factor costs. Once again a residual error is included.

Consumers' expenditure
+ Government final consumption
+ Gross domestic fixed capital formation
+ Value of increase in stocks and works in progress
+ Exports of goods and services
– Imports of goods and services
– Residual error
= *Gross domestic product* (*at market prices*)
– Expenditure taxes
+ Subsidies
= *Gross domestic product* (*at factor cost*)

Output method

Outputs of different sectors of the economy are valued, taking care to avoid double-counting. This occurs where the output of one industry is the input to another. Double-counting can be avoided by measuring the value of final, rather than intermediate output.

+ Value of outputs from different sectors of economy
= *Gross domestic product*

From GDP to national income

Gross domestic product values the flow of goods and services produced in the UK. Some income arises from investments and possessions owned abroad, and thus an adjustment for net property income from abroad is made to GDP to calculate GNP. Finally, some investment spending occurs to replace worn-out machinery. Net national product (NNP) or national income deducts this amount (capital depreciation). These final calculations are summarized below:

Gross domestic product
+ Net property income from abroad
= *Gross national product*
– Capital consumption
= *Net national product (national income)*

Real and money national income

When national income figures are compared over two different time periods, the effects of inflation can be misleading. Money national income or national income at current prices includes the effects of inflation. Real national income or national income at constant prices has had the effects of inflation removed.

Leisure and tourism contribution to GNP

Table 14.1 gives an indication of the importance of the leisure and tourism sector to the UK economy. From the data it can be seen that nearly 17 per cent of household spending in 1992 was on leisure items. Spending on holidays and home computers has risen significantly in real terms between 1986 and 1992. Spending on DIY items has fallen, reflecting uncertainty and a reduction in moves in the housing market.

Care needs to be exercised in interpreting the contribution of leisure to national income using Table 14.1 alone. The exhibit records UK household expenditure, but as the earlier section on GNP calculation explained, exports of leisure goods and services need to be added to this figure and imports deducted. Imported services are

Table 14.1 *Household expenditure on selected leisure items at 1992 prices (£ per week and percentages)*

Category	1986	1991	1992
Alcoholic drink consumed away from home	8.40	7.85	7.79
Meals consumed out	6.19	6.24	6.10
Books, newspapers, magazines, etc.	3.86	3.80	3.84
TV, video and audio: purchases	4.14	4.77	5.20
TV, video and audio: rentals and licence fee	2.81	2.31	2.39
Home computers	0.23	0.54	0.61
Materials for home repairs etc.	4.33	4.07	3.96
Holidays	7.61	10.21	11.21
Hobbies	0.09	0.13	0.07
Cinema admissions	0.14	0.19	0.19
Theatre, concert, etc. admissions	0.41	0.53	0.55
Participant sports: subscriptions and admissions	1.01	1.10	1.50
Spectator sports: admissions	0.16	0.19	0.24
Sports goods (excluding clothes)	0.52	0.45	0.52
Other entertainment	0.70	0.84	0.88
Total weekly expenditure on above	40.61	43.24	45.04
Expenditure as percentage of total household expenditure	16.1	16.1	16.6

Source: CSO: *Social Trends.*

clearly an important part of holiday expenditure. Similarly, some leisure activity does not involve an activity which is bought and sold in the market. Neither informal sports games nor DIY labour are measured in GNP statistics because of this, although both result in services enjoyed or value added.

Leisure and tourism employment

The demand for labour is a derived demand. Labour is demanded when a good or service is demanded. Employment in the leisure and tourism sector is thus directly related to expenditure on goods and services provided by the sector. Figure 14.2 shows the possible outcomes of leisure and tourism spending.

Some expenditure will be on imported goods or services and will therefore create employment overseas. UK leisure and tourism goods and services will be supplied as a result of domestic expenditure and exports. The resulting derived demand for labour will also depend upon the price of labour relative to other factors of production and the possible technical mix of factors of production able to provide the goods or services. For example, if the price of labour rises, producers will attempt to use more machinery (capital) where this is technically possible.

Sector employment

Table 14.2 shows recent employment trends in leisure and tourism service industries.

Table 14.3 shows the total number employed and unemployed during the same period.

The general employment picture shown in Table 14.3 is one of rising employment (and falling unemployment) in response to the boom in the economy in the late 1980s, with employment prospects worsening again towards 1992 as a result of the recession and a fall in consumers' expenditure. The total employment in leisure and tourism services recorded in Table 14.2 mirrors this national trend, but within the data, numbers employed in libraries, museums, galleries, sports and other recreational services have increased

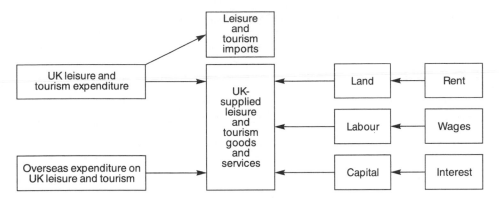

Figure 14.2 Demand for labour in leisure and tourism sector.

Table 14.2 *Employment in leisure and tourism service industries (UK; in thousands)*

	1988	1989	1990	1991	1992	1993
Hotels and other tourist accommodation	281	301	323	326	310	306
Restaurants, cafés, etc.	265	290	306	296	306	298
Public houses and bars	289	326	337	317	335	323
Night clubs and licensed clubs	141	141	143	146	139	137
Libraries, museums, galleries, sports and other recreational services	374	373	395	402	408	407
Total	1350	1431	1504	1486	1497	1471

Source: British Tourist Authority: *Digest of Tourist Statistics.*

Table 14.3 *UK employed and unemployed (millions)*

	1988	1989	1990	1991	1992	1993	1994	1995
Employees in employment	22.2	22.7	22.9	22.3	21.8	21.6	21.5	
Unemployed	2.4	1.8	1.6	2.3	2.8	2.9	2.6	

Source: CSO: *Monthly Digest of Statistics.*

despite the recession of the early 1990s. The figures also show that unemployment has been a persistent feature of the UK economy in recent years, with unemployment not dipping below 1.6 million.

It is more difficult to extract employment in leisure manufacturing from published data, as many of the industrial classifications used by the Department of Employment include leisure and non-leisure items.

Table 14.4 shows the employment totals for manufacturing industries as a whole and for printing and publishing, sports goods, and alcoholic, soft drink and tobacco manufacture.

Table 14.4   *Employees in selected manufacturing employment in the UK (in thousands)*

	1988	1989	1990	1991	1992	1993	1994	1995
Alcoholic, soft drink and tobacco manufacture	97	90	86	86	82	76		
Sports goods	8.1	8.2	8.5	8.0	7.8	7.0		
Printing and publishing	338	347	345	333	332	328		
Total manufacturing industries	5089	5080	4994	4599	4396	4190		

Source: CSO: *Monthly Digest of Statistics.*

Table 14.5   *Total labour costs per hour for selected industries in 1994 (£)*

Industry	£
Retail trade and repair	6.87
Hotels and restaurants	5.35
Insurance and pension funding	14.12
Computer and related activities	16.55

Source: Department of Employment: *Employment Gazette.*

Whereas employment in the services sector has grown in importance, manufacturing employment in the UK has shown a long-term decline. This is caused by two factors. First, technological progress enables productivity increases in manufacturing and thus the ratio of labour input to output declines. Second, manufacturing has been subject to intense competition from overseas where low labour costs in particular result in increased import penetration in UK markets. This is known as deindustrialization.

Wages

Wages in any particular labour market will be determined by the demand and supply of labour. The supply of labour to some parts of the leisure and tourism (for example, hotels and catering) sector is largely unskilled and this exerts a downward pressure on wages. This is illustrated in Table 14.5 which shows the total wage costs per hour of selected industries. The costs shown include all employer costs (training and national insurance, for example) and thus are roughly 20 per cent higher than wages received.

Leisure and tourism multipliers

The analysis of data in the previous sections has looked at tourism and leisure contributions to national income and the economy at a single point in time. This is termed as 'static' analysis. However, consideration of Figure 14.1 shows that tourism and leisure expenditure, like any other form of expenditure, also has 'dynamic' effects due to the circular flow of income and expenditure in the economy. The initial effects of expenditure will generate income but there will be further effects as that income generates expenditure and so on.

Figure 14.3 illustrates the circular flow of income and expenditure derived from Figure 14.1. Assume now that there is an investment into this closed system of £100 000 on a new leisure complex. Firms will hire factors of production to the value of £100 000 and therefore national income, measured at point *A*, will rise by £100 000. However, the effects of the investment do not stop there. The workers who earned money from building the complex will spend their money in shops and bars, etc. Thus the incomes of shop and bar owners will rise. They in turn will spend their incomes. In other words, a circular flow of income and expenditure will take place. The investment expenditure sets in motion a dynamic process, and the total extra income passing point

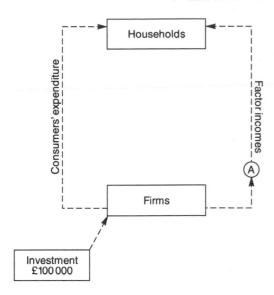

Figure 14.3 Investment and the circular flow of income.

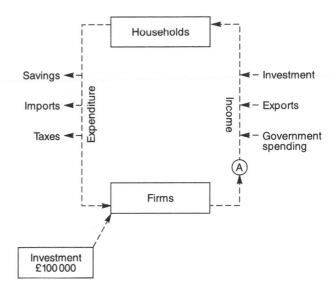

Figure 14.4 Circular flow with injections and leakages.

A will exceed the initial £100 000. This is known as the multiplier effect.

In the closed system illustrated by Figure 14.3, the effect would be perpetual and infinite, with the extra expenditure circulating round and round the system. In the real world however there are points at which money can leave and enter the system. This is illustrated in Figure 14.4.

The key leakages or withdrawals from the economy are savings, imports and taxes. Savings represents funds retained by households and firms. Imports result in expenditure flowing overseas, and taxes represent money taken out of the circular flow of income by the government in the form of income tax, VAT and corporation tax, for example.

On the other hand there are also injections or flows into the circular flow of income. These are investment exports resulting in money from overseas entering the circular flow, and government spending including for example pensions and unemployment benefit. Clearly there are often strong relationships between specific leakages and injections. To keep the model simple, injections and leakages are located neatly around the system but in reality they occur in many different places.

The existence of leakages means that money is flowing out of the economy during each cycle. So, in the example of the £100 000 investment in a leisure complex, perhaps £10 000 might be saved by workers, £5000 spent on imported goods, and £10 000 taken in taxation. Thus the initial effect on national income measured at point A in Figure 14.4 is £100 000. Out of this, £25 000 will be lost in leakages from the economy, leaving £75 000 to recirculate, adding another £75 000 to national income at point A. This process then continues, but with each cycle becoming smaller. It should be seen that the size of the multiplier effect will depend upon the amount of the original injection under examination and the leakages from the economy.

The Keynesian multiplier

The Keynesian multiplier can now be formally analysed. The multiplier (k) shows the amount by which a change in expenditure (ΔEXP) in an economy leads to a change in national income (ΔY):

$$\Delta EXP \times k = \Delta Y$$

Table 14.6   *Multiplier rounds*

Round	ΔS	ΔT	ΔM	ΔEXP	ΔY
1				100 000	100 000
2	10 000	10 000	5 000	75 000	75 000
3	7 500	7 500	3 750	56 250	56 250
4	5 625	5 625	2 812.50	42 187.50	42 187.50
5	4 218.75	4 218.75	2 109.36	31 640.63	31 640.63
6	3 164.06	3 164.06	1 582.03	23 730.47	23 730.47
7	2 373.05	2 373.05	1 186.52	17 797.85	17 797.85
8	1 779.76	1 779.76	889.89	13 348.39	13 348.39
$9 - n$	. . .	. . .	. . .	. . .	. . .
Total				400 000	400 000

Note: Rounds $9 - n$ represent the remaining multiplier rounds.
S = Savings; T = taxes; M = imports; EXP = expenditure; Y = income; Δ = change in.

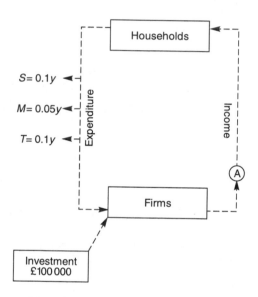

Figure 14.5   The multiplier round. S = Savings;
M = imports; T = taxes; Y = income.

Thus if an increase in investment on a leisure complex of £100 000 led to a final increase in national income of £400 000, then the multiplier would have a value of 4.

The multiplier can be illustrated by reference to Table 14.6 and Figure 14.5.

Investment in the leisure complex of £100 000 is made and national income at point A is raised by £100 000. In round 2, leakages consist of £10 000 in savings, £10 000 in taxes and £5000 in imports, leaving £75 000 in domestic expenditure to recirculate round the circular flow. An extra £75 000 is therefore added to national income at point A. In round 3 leakages consist of £7500 in savings, £7500 in taxes and £3750 in imports, leaving £56 250 in domestic expenditure. This process continues, and the leakages reduce the value of extra domestic expenditure and national income at every round. In fact, the extra amounts of national income tend towards zero. If the additions to national income in column 6, for years $1 - n$ (where n = the year in which the effect has dwindled to near zero) were added up, they would sum to £400 000, thus giving a value for the multiplier of 4.

There is also a formula for calculating the multiplier:

$$k = 1/MPL$$

where MPL = the marginal propensity to leak (the proportion of extra income that leaks out of the economy).

$$MPL = MPS + MPM + MPT$$

where MPS = marginal propensity to save (the proportion of extra income saved), MPM =

Table 14.7 *Multiplier and expenditure impacts*

Value of multiplier	Leakages from the economy	Impact of expenditure on income
High	Low	High
Low	High	Low

marginal propensity to spend on imports (the proportion of extra income spent on imports) and MPT = marginal propensity to be taxed (the proportion of extra income taken in taxes.

In the above example, MPS = 0.1Y, MPM = 0.05Y and MPT = 0.1Y, where Y = income. Therefore:

$$k = 1/(0.1 + 0.05 + 0.1)$$
$$k = 1/0.25$$
$$k = 4$$

Tourism multipliers

Considerable research has been done into the impact of tourism and leisure expenditure using multiplier techniques. The aim is to assess impact on incomes, output and employment at national, regional and local levels. This is clearly an important issue for governments in assessing the contribution of such developments to economic activity. The main multipliers developed for impact analysis are:

- the output multiplier
- the income multiplier
- the employment multiplier
- the government revenue multiplier

Taking the case of the tourism income multiplier (TIM), values vary according to leakages, as summarized in Table 14.7, and actual results include Canada (TIM = 2.5), UK (TIM = 1.8), Iceland (TIM = 0.6) and Edinburgh (TIM = 0.4).

Exhibit 14.1 discusses tourism multipliers in Scotland.

Exhibit 14.1   Small is beautiful

The Scottish Office has been studying the relationship between size of tourism establishments and effects on local income and spending. Its findings are that smaller organizations are more beneficial to local economies because the centralized buying activities of large organizations take spending out of the local area.

The Scottish Tourism Multiplier Study on Edinburgh made the following findings. In 1990, it is estimated that domestic and overseas tourists spent £276m in Edinburgh. For every £1000 spent by UK-resident tourists in Edinburgh, approximately £346 in income is generated locally and £127 in income is generated in the rest of Scotland. It takes about £27 000 of spending by domestic tourists to create one new job in the city.

Source: Scottish Office.

Leisure and tourism inflation

Inflation can be defined as a rise in the general level of prices or a fall in the purchasing power of money. It is measured by the retail price index (RPI). If one country has a faster rate of inflation than that of other countries, it can cause a decline in international competitiveness. This is likely to affect firms producing leisure products for the export market, and countries which rely on tourism. It is less likely to affect firms in leisure services since customers rarely have the option to seek lower prices overseas for these.

Constructing a tourism destination price index

It is possible to construct a tourism destination price index (TDPI) using a similar methodology to that used to construct the general RPI. Table 14.8 gives an example of such an index. The steps are as follows (with rows and columns referring to Table 14.8):

- First it is necessary to define the population for whom the index is intended. This might be a specific index for golfers or skiers.
- Next an expenditure survey must be conducted to establish the spending patterns of

Table 14.8 *Tourism price index, example (pesetas)*

Item	Weight (W)	1992			1993		1994	
		Price (P)	P × W		Price (P)	P × W	Price (P)	P × W
Babycham (25 cl)	0.4	200	80		220	88	250	100
Beer (0.5 l)	4.0	190	760		195	780	200	800
Three-course meal	11.6	800	9 280		880	10 208	950	11 020
. . .	. . .	. . .	. . .		. . .	. . .	. . .	. . .
. . .	. . .	. . .	. . .		. . .	. . .	. . .	. . .
Total			50 107			52 612		56 119
Index multiple				0.0019957291				
Index			100			105		112

Notes: Item = row 1, column 1; the dots in rows 6 and 7 denote the rest of the basket of goods.

the target population, ensuring that a representative sample of the target population is surveyed.

- From this two important findings should emerge – first a 'basket of goods' (and services) that lists the items bought by tourists can be compiled (column 1), and second the relative importance of each item can be gauged from the expenditure survey and each item given a weighting accordingly. For example, if an expenditure survey in Magaluf, Majorca showed 10 times more beer to be consumed than Babycham, then beer would be assigned a weighting 10 times more than that for Babycham (column 2). Thus if beer and Babycham both rose in price by 20 per cent, the effect of Babycham on the TDPI would be less than the beer effect.
- A survey of the prices of the basket of goods is then conducted (column 3).
- Expenditure on each item is determined by multiplying its price by its weighting (column 4).
- The total expenditure on the basket of goods is recorded (row 8).
- This amount is then converted to a index number with base 100, by using a multiplier (row 9), and this becomes the base year reading. (For example, if the expenditure total is £50, a multiplier of 2 is needed to convert the result to 100.)

Table 14.9 *Tourism price index (exchange rate-adjusted)*

	1992	1993	1994
Total (Pts)	50 107	52 612	56 119
£1 = ? Pesetas	180	191	197
Total (£s)	278.37	275.46	248.87
Index multiple		0.359234	
Index	100	98.95	89.40

- The basket of goods is priced at regular intervals (columns 5 and 7), with expenditure totals (row 8) being converted to an index number (row 10) using the multiplier established in the base year (row 9).

The index resulting from this exercise (Table 14.8) gives a picture of tourism inflation in the local currency. It is possible to adjust the index to reflect exchange rate conditions in different countries. Thus, whilst Table 14.8 measures tourism inflation for a Spanish visitor to a Spanish destination, Table 14.9 shows how the index can be adapted for a British visitor.

Table 14.9 uses the expenditure data from row 8 of Table 14.8. This is then converted to an equivalent in the currency under consideration

Table 14.10 *The Costa Livin': holiday living index 1994*

Destination	Three-course meal	Bottle of house wine	Bottle of mineral water	Week's car hire (group 1)
Algarve	£ 8.55	£3.90	£0.50	£103.25
Balearic Islands	£ 9.20	£3.90	£0.60	£136.60
Canary Islands	£10.75	£4.40	£0.50	£131.70
Cyprus	£ 8.00	£3.30	£0.90	£173.30
Florida	£10.90	£5.45	£1.30	£ 96.75
Greek Islands	£ 5.85	£3.20	£0.30	£198.40
Italy	£ 7.55	£2.45	£0.30	£204.00
Mainland Spain	£ 6.85	£2.90	£0.60	£145.00
Malta	£ 8.15	£2.55	£0.35	£ 85.00
Tunisia	£ 7.50	£3.50	£0.50	£190.00
Turkey	£ 6.60	£3.30	£0.65	£195.00

Source: *Guardian*, 16 July 1994/Thomas Cook.

Table 14.11 *UK retail price indices (January 1987 = 100)*

	July 1994	July 1995	July 1996
All items	144		
Travel and leisure	146		
Audiovisual goods	75		
Tapes and discs	113		
Toys, photographic and sport goods	121		
Books and newspapers	159		
Gardening products	141		
Television licences and rentals	118		
Entertainment and other recreation	193		

Source: Department of Employment: *Employment Gazette*.

(sterling in this example). A new index multiple is calculated to convert the raw expenditure figure to an index number with base 100. Comparison of the two tables shows the importance of considering exchange rate fluctuations when comparing prices between tourist destinations.

It must be remembered that any tourism price index represents an average picture, and individuals will be affected differently according to their particular expenditure patterns. Care must also be exercised in the collecting of data. There must be consistency of sources, otherwise the index will be distorted by changes in prices which result for example by moving from a local store to a supermarket.

Table 14.10 shows the relative sterling prices of commonly consumed goods and services for some major tourism destinations.

Table 14.11 shows some of the components of the RPI for the UK. It can be seen that inflation in the travel and leisure sector as a whole has been similar to that of the general level of inflation. However, within the sector audiovisual equipment prices have actually fallen whilst entertainment and other recreation prices have shown steep rises.

Government policy

Income and employment

Governments throughout the world see leisure and tourism as a source of employment, particularly where structural changes in the economy have led to job losses, as exhibit 14.2 shows.

Exhibit 14.2   Banana blues

The banana has long been a staple part of the economy of many Caribbean Islands, providing local jobs and foreign currency. But in Grenada prices have been fluctuating in response to two major threats. Competition from Latin America and the ending of tariff-free sales to the UK are threatening local banana production and farmers are looking for new sources of income.

It seems that tourism is to fill the gap, and the Windward Islands have been focusing their efforts on attracting more foreign tourists. Paul Slinger, chairman of the Grenada Tourism Board, explains the challenge. 'Last year there were 1700 school-leavers looking for jobs. Next year there will be 2200'.

Tourism to Granada rose by 10 per cent last year to 66 400 and so it looks increasingly likely that those school-leavers will find their jobs in hotels, bars and shops rather than on the land.

Source: the author, from news cuttings, January 1994.

Government policies to promote employment may include the following:

Demand management

Where there is unemployment throughout the economy, some economists advocate government stimulation of aggregate demand so as to induce more production and thus employment. Aggregate demand may be stimulated through tax cuts, increased government spending and interest rate cuts. The major drawback to such a policy is its tendency to encourage inflation.

Export-led policies

Overseas expenditure on leisure and tourism products can contribute to employment. Government policy here includes expenditure on the BTA which promotes the UK overseas and thus overseas demand for UK leisure and tourism services.

A low exchange rate also assists exports of services and leisure goods.

Wages and conditions of employment

The Conservative government has a policy of 'flexible labour markets'. The Conservative government view is that high wages, complex labour laws and unionization act as a disincentive to employers to create jobs. To this end wages councils which enforce minimum wages have been abolished, and the UK is opting out of EU labour laws, including paternity leave for fathers. A succession of laws curbing trade union activity was passed in the 1980s.

Project assistance

The government also considers direct assistance with projects on an individual basis, particularly where a project can be shown to bring employment to areas of high unemployment. There was for example considerable competition between France and the UK over inducements offered to lure EuroDisney to each country. The EU also has a regional fund which can be a source of financial assistance.

Inflation

Governments of countries with comparatively high rates of inflation may utilize counter-inflationary policy. However it is important first to diagnose the causes of inflation.

Causes of inflation

The causes of inflation can be divided into the categories of cost-push, demand-pull, monetary, taxation and expectations.

Cost-push inflation occurs when increased production costs are passed on as price rises. These can include first wage increases which outstrip productivity increases. Second increased raw material prices can be important. If raw materials are imported, a fall in the exchange rate can increase their local currency price.

Demand-pull inflation tends to occur when an economy is growing too fast. It arises because the aggregate demand in the economy exceeds the aggregate supply in the economy and therefore prices are bid up. Labour for example may become scarce, putting an upward pressure on wages.

Too rapid an increase in the money supply of an economy can cause an increase on consumer credit which can stimulate demand-pull inflation and accommodate cost-push inflation.

Increases in indirect taxes such as VAT will have an effect on prices, whilst if people expect inflation to rise, they will often seek to protect their living standards by higher wage demands. These of course will then cause the very inflation that people are seeking to avoid.

Counterinflationary policy

Government counterinflationary policy will affect the economic environment of leisure and tourism organizations.

Cost-push inflation may be tackled by a high exchange rate policy. Whilst this may be good for tackling inflation, it makes firms' exports less competitive.

Wage rises may be tackled by government-imposed incomes policy to curb pay increases. This may cause a deterioration in industrial relations.

Deflationary policy may be used to tackle demand-pull inflation. This may entail increasing interest rates to curb consumer borrowing, or increased taxes to reduce consumer spending. Either way, whilst inflation may be tackled, firms will suffer a general contraction in demand.

High interest rates are sometimes also used to curb overexpansion of the money supply by reducing the demand for borrowing.

Review of key terms

- Macroeconomics = the study of the national economy.
- National income = a measure of the total level of economic activity which takes place in an economy over a year.
- GDP = gross domestic product.
- GNP = gross national product.
- NNP = net national product (national income).
- Money national income = national income calculated at current prices.
- Real national income = national income calculated at constant prices (inflationary element removed).
- Tourism income multiplier (TIM) = exaggerated effect of a change in tourism expenditure on an area's income.
- TDPI = tourism destination price index.
- Basket of goods = typical items bought by a defined group.
- Cost-push inflation = inflation caused by changes in input prices.
- Demand-pull inflation = inflation caused by excess of aggregate demand over aggregate supply.
- Demand management = government policy to influence total demand in an economy.

Data questions

Task 14.1

Table 14.12 shows retail price indices for selected countries.

Questions

1 If entrance to Disneyland cost $16 in 1980, and its price has kept pace with inflation, what would the admission cost in 1992?
2 Why might the retail price index for a country not be a good guide to tourism prices?
3 What other information would you seek before deciding on which countries might be good or bad value to visit?

Table 14.12   *Retail price index (1980 = 100)*

	1980	1983	1986	1988	1990	1992
USA	100	121	133	144	159	170
China	100	107	131	172	203	NA
Japan	100	110	115	116	122	129
Gambia	100	130	294	406	493	587
Israel	100	1174	33 330	46 447	65 418	87 144
Bahamas	100	123	243	155	171	194

Notes: NA = not available.
Source: various.

Task 14.2   Local reflections on the Channel Tunnel

The Channel Tunnel is dug, equipped and running. How does local opinion see its effects?

John Ovenden, Labour leader, and Allison Wainman, Liberal Democrat leader on Kent County Council, made a joint statement reflecting on possible impacts, on the official tunnel opening.

'For Kent, the tunnel is a mixed blessing. There is no doubt that many people in Kent have paid and will continue to pay a high price in terms of the environmental effect of the project.

'Equally, traditional cross-channel operators, who provide many jobs for Kent people, face a real challenge, although there is every sign that they are responding positively.

'However, we are determined to maximize the benefits for Kent of the tunnel. By opening up transport corridors at the heart of Europe, it represents an opportunity too good to be missed at a time when the county is well-placed to take advantage. For too long, parts of the county have been in the economic doldrums.'

It is certainly true that Kent has had its fair share of economic misery in recent years. Agricultural employment in the county, renowned for hop growing and orchards, has suffered a steady long-term decline in the face of mechanization. It is easy to forget that Kent once had a coal industry which closed in the face of cheap imports in the 1980s. Defence cuts and the peace dividend have been responsible for the decline of Chatham whose prosperity has rested on its naval dockyards. Such is the level of unemployment in north and east Kent that they have gained assisted-area status. Thanet is eligible for assistance from the EU on account of its 17 per cent unemployment rate.

Consultants estimate that nearly 2000 jobs will have been created by the Channel Tunnel by 1996. However, it is also estimated that about 15 000 people are employed in jobs related to port activities in Kent and that a net loss of 3000 of these jobs will result from the impact of the tunnel on ferry services by 1996.

More difficult to estimate is the employment effects of the tunnel on the tourism industry. The county is second only to London as a destination for overseas visitors, who spent £132m in 1992. It is likely that the tunnel will boost this figure.

Source: the author, from news cuttings, 6 May 1994.

Questions

1 What general employment conditions are described in the article for Kent?
2 Describe the employment effects of the channel tunnel using the following headings:
   (a) Direct (employment provided by the project itself)

Table 14.13   *Consumers' expenditure at 1990 market prices (£m)*

	1987	1988	1989	1990	1991	1992	1993	1994
Radio, television and other durable goods	3574	4234	4602	4795	4803	5314	5740	
Television and video hire charges, licence fees and repairs	3093	3198	3261	3204	3122	2989	3036	
Sports goods, toys games and camping equipment	2673	2815	3086	3426	3241	3393	3609	
Betting and gaming	3092	3120	3152	3110	2930	2934	3029	
Newspapers and magazines	3271	3219	3222	3287	3093	3103	3155	

Source: CSO: *Annual Abstract of Statistics.*

(b) Displacement (employment lost because of the project's effects)
(c) Indirect (employment gained or lost by the project's effects)
3 What are the likely mulitplier effects on Kent of:
(a) the construction phase of the tunnel?
(b) the operation phase of the tunnel?

Task 14.3

Table 14.13 shows consumers' expenditure on selected leisure items.

Questions

1 What is the significance of the term 'at 1990 market prices'?
2 How would these figures need to be adapted if they were used to help compile GNP?
3 To what extent are such figures on expenditure a guide to changes in the level of employment in each of the above areas?

Task 14.4 The law of supply and demand behind reports of D-Day rip-offs

D-Day, the mainstay of Normandy tourism, is very big business this year [1994], its 50th anniversary. It will feature 45 000 veterans, up to 2 million extra summer visitors, a bit of price inflation and a supply–demand ratio that only local entrepreneurs and foreign tour operators could love.

The extra visitors will spend Fr650m (£78m) – this is in addition to the Fr2.6bn tourists spend yearly in the region. In turn, local government is investing Fr200m in new facilities.

Naturally, there's no lack of 'instant businesses' set up to cash in on what is considered the last big commemoration of Operation Overlord. Visitors will be able to quaff Burgundies labelled 44–94 Liberté, fly over the beaches in a Douglas-Dakota DC3 or charge over the dunes in US Army Jeeps of the era. More than 1000 history buffs, mainly Britons, will join Holts' Battlefield Tours of Kent for the 4-day tour over June 6. Another 2000 Americans have signed up for Grand Circle of Boston's tours such as 'Freedom's Finest Hour' – 18 days from England to France to Germany for up to $3395.

With only 50 000 hotel rooms, a price spiral was possible, but in practice it only meant that early birds got the worm. The exceptions – such as the Hotel Mercure, 5 miles from Omaha Beach, whose prices jump by 45 per cent during the first week of June – have been savaged by the press. And while hoteliers point accusing fingers at tour operators, claiming that they are reselling rooms for two and three times the purchase price, the operators, in turn, protest that they build in only the 18–20 per cent margin usual in such tours.

'We know cases exist of tour operators re-selling for far higher, and it is true there have been abuses by hotel owners,' says Jean-Claude Demais, director of the Normandy Regional Tourism Board. 'It's the law of supply and demand.'

Source: *Guardian*, 9 April 1994 (adapted).

Questions

Discuss the following with reference to the D-Day anniversary commemorations:

1 contribution to GNP
2 contribution to inflation
3 contribution to employment
4 significance of tourism multipliers

Short questions

1 Distinguish between changes in money and real GNP.
2 What are the main leakages and injections into the circular flow of income?
3 What is meant by the tourism income multiplier and what determines its size?
4 Outline the main steps involved in constructing a tourism price index.
5 What recent government polices have (a) encouraged; (b) discouraged employment in the leisure and tourism sector?

Further reading

Brent Ritchie, J. and Hawkins, D., *World Travel and Tourism Review*, C.A.B. International, 1993.

Fletcher, J. and Archer, B., The development and application of multiplier analysis, in Cooper, C. (ed.), *Progress in Tourism, Recreation, and Hospitality Management*, vol. 3, Belhaven, 1990.

Harrison, D. (ed.), *Tourism and the Less Developed Countries*, Belhaven, 1992.

HMSO, *Tourism and the Inner City*, HMSO, 1990.

National Economic Development Office, *Working for Pleasure: Tourism and Leisure Tomorrow*, NEDO, 1990.

Pompl, W. and Lavery, P. (eds), *Tourism in Europe*, C.A.B. International, 1993.

Williams, A. and Shaw, G. (eds), *Tourism and Economic Development*, Belhaven, 1991.

15

Leisure and tourism and economic growth

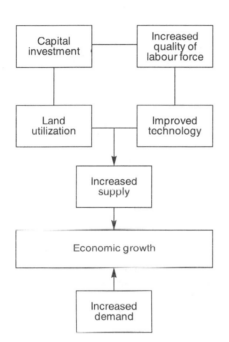

examined. Case studies of China and Kenya will be used to illustrate the role of leisure and tourism in such development. There is clearly much further scope for tourism development in less developed countries which had only about a quarter share of world tourism receipts in 1990.

Issues surrounding the costs of economic growth and development will be examined in Chapters 18 and 19.

By studying this chapter students should be able to:

- define and explain economic growth
- review critically the concept of economic growth
- understand the determinants of economic growth
- evaluate appropriate growth strategies for developed and developing countries
- evaluate the contribution of the leisure and tourism sector to growth

Objectives

The objective of this chapter is to examine how leisure and tourism can contribute to the long-term growth of economies. First general aspects of economic growth will be discussed. Second case studies will demonstrate how leisure and tourism have contributed to economic growth in developed countries such as France, Japan and Spain.

Third, the special problems of growth and development in less developed countries will be

Meaning and measurement of economic growth

Meaning and measurement

Economic growth is defined as the increase in real output per capita of a country. There are thus three elements involved in its measurement. First the change in output of an economy needs to be measured. The most commonly used measure of output is GNP. However, as explained

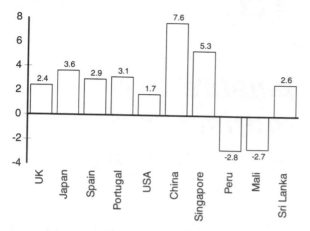

Figure 15.1 Growth rates for selected countries (average annual growth in gross national product per capita 1980–1992).

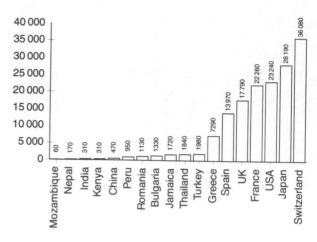

Figure 15.2 Dollar gross national product per capita for selected countries (1992).

in Chapter 14, money GNP, or GNP at current prices, can overestimate changes in a country's output. This is because they include increases due to higher prices as well as higher output. Therefore real GNP figures are used to calculate growth. Second, the GNP figures need to be adapted to take account of increases in population. Dividing real GNP by the population gives real GNP per capita. Figure 15.1 illustrates some comparative data for international growth rates.

It can be seen that the economy of China has exhibited remarkable growth of over 7 per cent per annum, due largely to its economic reforms which have allowed foreign investment and private enterprise. However it is control of population growth (1.4 per cent per annum) that has enabled high per capita economic growth. On the other hand, relatively high population growth in Peru (2.7 per cent per annum) has meant that per capita economic growth has been negative.

Problems of measurement

Figure 15.2 records per capita GNP data for various countries and demonstrates the huge international inequalities that are apparent.

However, there are several problems involved in the measurement of GNP and thus economic

growth. First there are the problems associated with collecting national income data, as discussed in Chapter 14. Data collection is a particular problem in countries which do not have a highly developed statistical branch of government. Less developed countries also have a bigger subsistence sector where goods and services are produced for self-consumption and therefore do not enter the market or appear on national income statistics. Second, in making international comparisons, country information measured in local currency is generally converted to dollar units. Thus some apparent changes in growth may in fact stem from currency movements against the dollar. Third, over a period of time the labour force may work fewer hours in a week. GNP figures do not reflect this and they may therefore underestimate some aspects of economic improvement. Fourth, GNP per capita figures are an average. They may disguise the fact that there are large differences in incomes of the population, or that some sectors of the community may actually be becoming poorer. Finally, economic activity which contributes to GNP has some unwanted side-effects in the form of pollution. GNP information takes no account of these, a matter which is discussed more fully in Chapters 18 and 19.

Rationale for growth

The rationale for the pursuit of growth is that people become better-off in an economic sense. There are more goods and services produced to meet people's material wants. This may result in some combination of more employment, more public services, less taxes, more leisure time or more consumption. How the benefits of growth are actually distributed depends on the workings of the economic system and government policy.

In less developed countries the results of economic growth are generally much more profound, bringing social and environmental changes with material prosperity. Distribution of benefits is often less even. 'Those with land to sell, housing to rent, hotels to run, and labour, goods and services to sell favour it. The landless poor are generally less impressed'.

The causes of economic growth

Economic growth is promoted by an increase in the quality or quantity of inputs into the economy. It can therefore be examined under the headings of land, labour, capital and technology.

Land

Different countries have not only differing amounts of land but also different types of land. Resources may include mineral and agricultural ones, and in the leisure and tourism sector, climate, scenery, coasts and countryside are important resources. It is by the exploitation of such resources that countries can use their comparative advantage against other possible tourist destinations. The success of the French tourism industry is largely dependent on the country's natural endowments which allow skiing and beach and countryside leisure developments. Similarly, specific land resources can be identified as attractions for other destinations, including:

- Nepal: Everest
- Caribbean: Coral Reef, climate
- USA: Grand Canyon, Niagara Falls, Death Valley
- Kenya: game parks
- The Gambia: beaches and climate

Labour

The labour force can be analysed in terms of its quantity and quality. The importance of the quantity of the labour force depends largely upon its relationship with other factors of production, land and capital. Where labour is a scarce factor of production, growth may be achieved by increasing the supply of labour, for example by encouraging immigration. However in many economies labour is in overabundant supply. This means that the productivity of labour is low. This is particularly true in less developed countries in the agricultural sector where land is overcrowded. On the other hand the low wages that result from an abundant labour force can in some cases be a source of economic growth. Wages in China, for example, are very low by international standards, and this has partially accounted for the inflow of foreign investment and the growth of China's industrial sector. The production of leisure goods such as audio equipment and toys is an important part of this industrial growth.

It is the quality of the labour force that is important in increasing productivity and improvements in quality stem from education and training programmes. Education and training can take place in both the public and private sector. In the UK, the government funds most general education and much vocational education, whilst industry often invests in specific training.

Exhibit 15.1, an extract from a Confederation of British Industry (CBI) report, identifies some key UK training deficiencies:

Exhibit 15.1 Towards a skills revolution

The UK still cannot match the skills of key international competitors. On average British children:

● are 2 years behind the Japanese in terms of basic mathematical competences
● have fewer and lower level educational qualifications than is the case for most of our major European competitors, as highlighted in the following table:

Table E15.1 *Highest qualifications of school-leavers (per cent)*

	UK	France	Germany
University entrance level	15	35	30
Intermediate level (1 A-level and below)	40	55	60
Low-level school-leaver (below GCSE grade C)	35		
No qualification	10	10	10

The UK has one of the lowest rates of participation in post-compulsory education and training of all the OECD countries.

Ambitious targets are being set by other countries:

● South Korea is aiming by the end of the century for 80 per cent of its young people to reach university entrance standard.
● France has set a similar target of 75 per cent.
● The current figure for the UK is only 30 per cent.

Source: CBI (1989), adapted.

The government has responded to the criticisms of UK education and training raised in exhibit 15.1. It has set up a system of vocational qualifications (national vocational qualifications or NVQs and general national vocational qualifications or GNVQs) to complement A-level provision and established education and training targets for the year 2000 which include:

● 50 per cent of school-leavers to attain NVQ level III, GNVQ advanced level or 2 A-levels
● 50 per cent of the employed workforce to attain NVQ level III, GNVQ advanced level or 2 A-levels
● 30 per cent of school-leavers to enter higher education

For leisure and tourism education and training, this has meant:

● the rationalization of training qualifications under NVQs. These are available, for example, in sport and recreation (coaching adults) or (facility operations) and travel services (guiding services)
● the introduction of GNVQs in leisure and tourism
● the expansion of degree and HND programmes in leisure and tourism

Finally it is different cultural aspects of countries' populations that is an important motivation for tourism.

Capital

Capital, in the form of plant and machinery, results from investment and distinction must be made between gross investment and net investment. Net investment refers just to investment which increases a nation's capital stock and therefore does not include replacement investment.

Net investment = gross investment – depreciation

Investment in new plant, machines and other capital enables labour productivity and GNP to rise. This can be an important source of economic growth for developing countries as labour moves from a relatively unmechanized agricultural sector to a mechanized industrial sector. Figure 15.3 records data for changes in investment and economic growth for selected countries. Since this chapter is showing that there are a range of contributors to economic growth, it is clearly not possible to make direct correlations between rates of investment and rates of growth. However it can be noted that Japan, Singapore and Korea have recorded relatively high levels of investment and growth, in contrast to Australia, Denmark and Finland.

The quality of investment is also an important

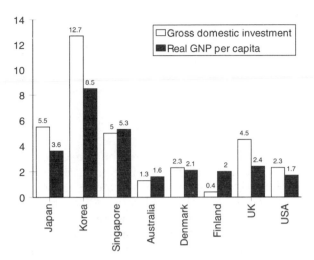

Figure 15.3 Investment and growth in selected countries (percentage annual average growth 1980–1992).

stereos, CDs, PCs and the electronic games market. Exhibit 15.2 illustrates the importance of such technological development for leisure electronics firms.

Exhibit 15.2 Battle for video domination

Yesterday Sega snatched from rivals a 5-year-old Yorkshire company at the forefront of games software development. With the acquisition of Cross Products came Snasm software, which is claimed to be the most advanced development tool for video game systems. It allows programmers to concentrate on making computer games ever more creative and adventurous.

'Without it we would be stuck in the Dark Ages of games programming,' said one Cross Products customer.

Source: *Guardian*, 17 August 1994 (adapted).

issue. Investment in inappropriate machinery will have little effect on productivity and growth.

Investment in infrastructure is important to develop industry in the leisure and tourism sector. This includes airports, ports and motorways, which allow access.

A nation's cultural heritage includes investments made in previous generations and preserved for enjoyment today. For example, a third dimension to France's tourism attraction is its rich and well-preserved historical built environment. Other examples of cultural heritage capital include:

- China: the Great Wall, the Forbidden City
- Rome: the Sistine Chapel, the Coliseum
- Egypt: the Pyramids
- Peru: Macchu Picchu

Technology

Improved technology can increase growth by reducing production costs and creating new products for the market. The leisure products industry has particularly benefited from new product technology with camcorders, personal

Promoting growth

Growth-promotion policies tend to split into those that require government intervention and those that rely on liberalizing the free market.

Intervention

Interventionists believe the government should play a key role in funding appropriate education and training, and investing in infrastructure. They also note that the volatility of interest rates and exchange rates in the free market inhibits growth and so argue that government should manage the economy to provide a stable environment.

Government intervention can also promote balanced growth where aggregate demand expands at a similar rate to aggregate supply, thereby avoiding the problems of inflation or unemployment associated with unbalanced growth.

Free market

The free market approach blames government intervention for lower growth. It is claimed that

Table 15.1 *International tourist arrivals to Spain (millions)*

1955	1960	1965	1970	1975	1980	1985	1990	1991
2.5	6.1	14.3	24.1	30.1	38.0	43.2	52.0	53.5

Source: various.

government spending programmes 'crowd out' funds, leaving less available and at higher interest rates for the private sector. Similarly, it is claimed that high taxes act as a disincentive for firms to invest. Supporters of market liberalization argue that profit is the best incentive for investment and that the price mechanism will ensure that investment and other resources are attracted to high-growth areas of the economy. Such policies are often referred to as 'supply side' policies.

BA is used as an example to illustrate the improved economic performance that can be obtained when an organization is privatized and freed from government control.

Leisure and tourism development in developed countries

The following case studies illustrate the role of different factors in the economic growth of Spain, France and Japan.

Leisure and tourism development in Spain

Leisure and tourism development has clearly made an important contribution to raising Spain's GNP per capita to levels approaching its EU partners.

Table 15.1 shows the rapid growth of international tourist arrivals to Spain since World War II.

The rapid growth of Spain's tourism industry can be attributed to a number of causes. First its natural resources – particularly of coastline, beaches and climate. However many countries enjoy similar natural features but have not enjoyed such growth. It is Spain's proximity to the fast-growing economies of western Europe that provided the demand, with tourists from the UK, Germany and France being the most numerous. Accessibility in terms of air transport and motorway developments has also played a part. The success of tourism in Spain has itself stimulated investment whilst earlier investment was often subsidized by overseas aid. For example, German investment in Gran Canaria was encouraged by the German government as a result of the 1968 Strauss Act which granted tax concessions for investments in underdeveloped countries. To these factors must be added the low wage costs which have enabled Spain to compete successfully with France and the active encouragement of government.

There is a government ministry with direct responsibility for tourism, the Ministry of Transport, Tourism and Communications, and tourism has been represented at ministerial level in Spain since 1951. It has provided direct investment (for example in the *paradores* – the chain of state-run hotels often using renovated buildings of historical interest), as well as subsidies and infrastructure improvements (for example to develop ski resorts). The government also funds the Institute of Tourism of Spain which promotes Spain abroad. Since joining the EU in 1986, Spain has benefited from European Regional Development Fund grants for infrastructure, particularly for providing better road access in the northern coastal region.

Tourism expenditure contributes more than 10 per cent to Spain's GDP and contributes to 11 per cent of total employment. Spain's projected balance of tourism payments for 1993 was US$17 772m.

Table 15.2 *International arrivals and tourism balance of payments for France*

	1991	1992E	1993F
Tourist arrivals (thousands)	55 731	59 800	63 400
Tourism balance of payments (US$m)	8 692	10 770	12 500

Notes: E = estimate, F = forecast.
Source: *World Travel and Tourism Review*, CAB International, Oxford (Ritchie, J.R.B. and Hawkins, D., eds).

The main problems that have arisen from Spain's reliance on tourism are first its dependence on economic prosperity in countries such as the UK, Germany and France. Recessions in those countries in the early 1980s and early 1990s caused tourism expenditure to fall in Spain. Second, tourism employment tends to be low-skilled and seasonal, and finally the dash for tourism growth in the 1960s and 1970s caused environmental degradation which threatens the continued prosperity of some of the earlier resort developments.

Leisure and tourism development in France

Leisure and tourism is central to French economic prosperity. France is the world's most popular international tourist destination and it runs a healthy surplus on its tourism balance of payments, as illustrated by Table 15.2.

As well as being the premier international destination, France is the premier destination for its own residents, with around 70 per cent of bed-nights being taken by French nationals. One reason for this is that, in contrast to Japanese workers, French workers receive a minimum of 5 weeks' paid leave and this represents considerable potential domestic demand.

As well as tourism services, France exports leisure goods – particularly skiing and camping equipment, and has domestic air and ferry capacity in the form of Air France and Brittany Ferries. The latter was set up specifically to promote tourism to Brittany so as to promote that region's economic development.

The demand for tourist facilities stimulates considerable private investment in hotels and other provision, but there is also a history of state encouragement. In terms of infrastructure, for example, France has a well-developed system of roads and railways. Recent investment in the high speed train (TGV) has resulted in links between Paris and Lyons, Lille, Nantes and Bordeaux.

The Maison de France, mainly financed from public funds, was set up in 1987 to promote French tourism products. It is estimated that every franc spent by the Maison de France generates FF100 in tourism receipts and its main activities include information, advertising, sales promotion and public relations.

There have been two major government-assisted regional development schemes based on tourism. First the Languedoc-Roussillon project. This was supported by more than FF6bn of state funding and commenced in 1963. It stimulated private investment and increased tourist visits to the area from 500 000 in 1964 to over 3.5 million by the late 1980s and it has been estimated that 30 000 new jobs were created in the region between 1965 and 1980. The second government initiative was the Aquitaine scheme which planned a big increase in tourism capacity on the Atlantic coast south of La Rochelle.

Leisure and tourism development in Japan

Japan's postwar economic development was largely driven by the export of manufactured goods. These included a comprehensive range of leisure goods. Indeed, it was the quality and innovative nature of much of these products that made them so successful. The product list includes recreational cars and motor cycles, jet-skis, audio and video equipment, sports equipment and musical instruments.

Following the wave of manufacturing investment there has been a movement towards investment in leisure projects. This has been encouraged by the government with the passing of the Comprehensive Resort Region Provision Act in 1987 which provides tax relief and infrastructure support for resort construction projects. One of the aims of this is to create more balance in Japan's growth. Japanese economic growth has relied heavily on exports and these are subject to external factors such as overseas recessions and exchange rate movements. Investment in domestic leisure provision stimulates domestic demand and provides development in rural areas. Projects have included golf courses, ski facilities, marinas and amusement parks along with hotel and infrastructure development.

Ironically, Japanese workers have generally elected not to take the benefits of economic growth in increased leisure time. Their working year is around 200 hours more than in comparable industrialized countries.

Japan's persistent surplus on the current account of its balance of payments (US$131bn in 1993) accounts for two other important features in its leisure and tourism activities. First Japan runs the world's biggest tourism account deficit, with tourism expenditure overseas exceeding tourism receipts by US$20 548 in 1991. Second Japan is very active in overseas investment. Some of this has involved aid to developing countries (for example, loans for resort infrastructure in Thailand). The majority is in the form of private investment. It is estimated for example that Japanese companies own 150 golf courses overseas.

In contrast to many developing countries, Japan is able to build on its strong economic base. High GNP enables high savings which can finance more investment which further contributes to GNP.

Economic growth in developing countries

Stages of development

The World Bank divides economies into the following categories:

- low-income economies (e.g. Mali, India, Nepal)
- lower middle-income economies (e.g. Peru, Turkey, Jamaica)
- upper middle-income countries (e.g. Brazil, Greece, Poland)
- high-income oil-exporters (e.g. Kuwait)
- industrial market economies (e.g. UK, USA, France)

The main basis for placing countries in these categories is GNP per capita and the low- and middle-income countries represent various stages of economic development and growth. There are a number of explanations for the low incomes of countries and several strategies for promoting economic growth. For some of these countries, promotion of the leisure and tourism sector will be an appropriate strategy.

Characteristics

The low standards of living enjoyed by less developed countries (LDCs) are characterized not just by low per capita GNP but by a range of other indicators. These include high levels of mortality, and low levels of literacy, medical care and food consumption. The economic circumstances of LDCs vary widely but barriers to economic growth in LDCs may include:

- high population growth (leading to overpopulation of land and low productivity)
- low incomes, leading to low savings, leading to low investment, leading to low incomes (low rate of capital formation)
- undeveloped financial sector to recirculate savings
- low levels of training and education
- few resources
- dependence on raw material exports
- employment centred on the agricultural sector of economy
- traditional (non-entrepreneurial) culture
- foreign currency shortages
- poor terms of trade (exports cheap, imports expensive)
- international debt

Table 15.3 *Development indicators for China and India*

Country	GDP per capita ($)		Life prospect at birth (years)		Under-5 mortality per 1000		Adult literacy rate (%)		School enrolment rate (%)	
Year	1965	1991	1960	1990	1960	1989	1970	1990	1970	1987
India	90	330	47	58	282	145	34	48	48	66
China	85	370	43	69	203	43	NA	73	66	83

Notes: GDP = gross domestic product; NA = not available.
Source: various.

Development strategies

Strategies to promote faster economic growth in LDCs generally involve investment in the agricultural, manufacturing or service sectors of the economy in order to improve labour productivity. This then raises the two key considerations for development. First, given the low rates of GNP per head, where will investment funds be obtained from? Second, what specific projects are most appropriate?

The main sources of investment funds are:

- domestic savings (but these are often low because of low incomes)
- government investment funded through taxes or borrowing
- private foreign investment
- overseas aid

The main strategies for development include:

- import substitution (producing goods that are currently imported)
- export-led growth (producing goods and services where a local cost or other advantage can be established)–leisure and tourism can be important elements in this strategy
- population control
- education and training projects
- infrastructure projects

These strategies may take place under a planning environment which can be either market- or government-led.

However the history of development projects includes a number of projects that have been inappropriate for the circumstances of the particular developing country. This particularly applies to technologies which require expert foreign management and costly imports, and projects which are labour-saving in countries with high unemployment.

The following case studies show the contribution of the leisure and tourism sector to economic development in China and Kenya, illustrating different development strategies.

Leisure and tourism development in China

The characteristics of the Chinese economy are atypical of many developing countries, yet its population of over 1 billion and rapid rate of development will ensure its growing importance over the next few decades. It is atypical first because of its communist government and second because, despite its low per capita GNP and large agricultural sector, it has relatively high literacy, low mortality rates, and its economic growth has recently been spectacular, averaging 7.6 per cent between 1980 and 1992 and exceeding 10 per cent in 1994. Its population growth is slowing rapidly with a one-child policy. Some of these features are illustrated in Table 15.3, which compares China with India.

China is a good example of how leisure goods and tourism services are being mobilized as part of a general development strategy. Table 15.4

Table 15.4 *China's tourism receipts and expenditure (US$m)*

	1985	1990	1991
Tourism receipts	979	2212	2845
Tourism expenditure	314	470	417

Source: *World Travel and Tourism Review*, CAB International, Oxford (Ritchie, J.R.B. and Hawkins, D., eds).

shows the growth in tourism receipts over the past few years.

Tourism is expanding first because of China's open-door policy, which has replaced a long period of mistrust of foreigners and barriers to tourism. Second, China is rich in cultural capital, and third, its low-wage economy makes tourism relatively cheap.

However, investment in infrastructure and accommodation is crucial to tourism development and to counter the low level of investment associated with its low per capita GNP, China has encouraged private foreign investment in the form of joint ventures. This has been important in the accommodation sector for the development of hotels. In Beijing, for example, the Hotel Beijing-Toronto was financed with Canadian capital, is run by Japanese management and profits are shared with China.

China's growth is fuelled primarily by its growth in exports. Here China exploits its international advantage in wage costs. Exports cover a range of goods and include audio equipment, toys and sports goods from the leisure sector. Exhibit 15.3 shows China's success in the toy market.

Exhibit 15.3 Mr Blobby bounces in from Peking: fair shows the decline of British toys – Michael Fathers

Even the plastic Union Jack to wave when the Queen drives by is made in China. Cheap foreign competition from the Far East wiped out local manufacturers in the seventies and eighties. Garry Conrad, chairman of the British Toy Importers and Distribution Association, said labour costs were the main reason for the British toy industry's collapse. British manufacturers were simply unable to compete with factories abroad.

Just under half Britain's £980m toy imports come from the Far East, according to figures released at Harrogate. Imports from China (including Mr Blobby) account for some 20 per cent of this total, a statistic representing the value of Chinese goods rather than their volume. It also masks the fact that many toys assembled elsewhere have Chinese-made components.

Warren Cornelius, head of WH Cornelius, Britain's main and perhaps oldest supplier of so-called pocket-money toys, said that out of 1700 toy lines he has for sale, 70 per cent are made in China. 'The Union Jacks I buy in China for 75p a dozen would cost four times as much if they were made in Britain'.

Source: *Independent on Sunday*, 16 January 1994 (adapted).

The movement of labour from China's agricultural sector to the manufacturing and service sector has enabled labour productivity to increase.

Leisure and tourism development in Kenya

In Africa, tourism development has been particularly important in the Kenyan economy. Kenya's tourism industry is based around beach and safari holidays and its international tourists come mainly from Germany, the UK, Switzerland and Italy. By 1988, tourism was the most important source of foreign currency, accounting for 37 per cent of export earnings, compared to 26 per cent for coffee and 20 per cent for tea.

Tourism represents a route to diversification of the economy away from its dependence on commodities such as coffee and tea, which are subject to considerable price fluctuations on international markets.

It has been noted in Chapter 14 that leakages from tourism expenditure can be high and diminish the benefit to the destination country's economy. For example, expenditure from UK tourists to Kenya travelling with operators such as Kuoni and Hayes and Jarvis is subject to initial leakages to the UK travel agent and the tour operator. Thereafter it depends on the ownership of facilities such as transport and hotels. In terms of transportation, Kenya has its own scheduled airline (Kenya Airways) and charter operator (Kenya Flamingo Airways), but both of these have to compete with UK operators. There is a natural preference by many tourists to use domestic airlines, and foreign operators often have less convenient slots at airports such as Heathrow.

The Kenyan government, anxious to develop tourism, tackled the problem of scarcity of investment capital by encouraging private foreign investment and joint ownership in hotels and 60 per cent of major hotels have an element of foreign ownership with investment from firms such as Kuoni, Hayes and Jarvis, BA and Lonrho.

Private foreign investment is a mixed blessing for host economies. As well as providing capital, it can also be a source of expertise, but it results in higher levels of leakages and thus makes the tourism income multiplier lower. Perhaps because of this, government policy now favours 'Kenyanization'. This change of direction is in contrast to that in Tanzania. Here initial hostility to private foreign investment ensured a higher tourism income multiplier, but a lower level of investment and provision. Since 1990 the Tanzanian government has attempted to attract more private foreign investment to stimulate economic growth.

Review of key terms

- Economic growth = the increase in real output per capita.
- Per capita = per person.
- Net investment = gross investment – depreciation.
- Productivity = output per employee.
- NVQs = national vocational qualifications.
- GNVQs = general national vocational qualifications.
- LDC = less developed country.
- Import substitution = producing goods that are currently imported.
- Infrastructure = social capital such as roads and railways.
- Joint venture = overseas and domestic investment partnership.

Data questions

Task 15.1 World travel and tourism council report on Brazil

Brazil offers an unenviable mixture of contrasts for tourists.

On the one hand, the Rio Carnival when, as the Journey Latin America (JLA) brochure describes, 'Brazilians let go – over-eating, over-drinking, overdressing, overundressing: overindulgence in just about everything'. 1994 bookings for carnival week are well up on last year according to tour operators.

Brazil boasts equatorial rainforest, most of the length of the Amazon river, and the Iguassu Falls, said to be more spectacular than Niagara and more panoramic than Victoria.

On the other hand Brazil is equally famous for its death squads, for its violence and for its street children.

A JLA spokesperson illustrates the contrasts, saying, 'We brief our groups when they arrive in Brazil and tell them to be careful, and not to wear lots of jewellery or carry video cameras. Outside Rio, it is much more relaxed and there are stunning areas of jungle popular with wildlife watchers. There is not really a problem with making arrangements, but the *mañana* syndrome is still there – the feeling that everything will happen, in time.'

A recently published World Travel and Tourism Council (WTTC) report suggests that Brazil's enormous untapped tourism potential could create wealth, jobs and a way out of the poverty the country suffers through lack of economic development.

The report catalogues some of Brazil's current economic difficulties such as hyperinflation, unemployment and international debt, but concludes that tourism could provide the country's biggest source of employment.

Currently, Brazil is largely undeveloped as a package destination and a successful tourism-development strategy, says the WTTC report, will depend on the injection of massive investment funds by the government.

Some parts of the tourist infrastructure are partially in place. Hotel room rates, for example, are competitive with those of other destinations in the Caribbean. Sanitation, roads and airports however all need considerable investment to provide extra capacity and the level of standards expected by international tourists. The WTTC report points out that investment in these areas will benefit tourist and locals alike.

Above all, the WTTC suggests an urgent need for a national travel and tourism policy in Brazil. This should contain, it states, partnership ventures between the public and private sectors, a plan to remove the bureaucratic barriers to entry which deters foreign visitors, and an effective strategy to market the country internationally.

Source: the author, from WTTC report, January 1994.

Questions

1 How should investment in tourism in Brazil be tackled to ensure a maximum impact on local unemployment?
2 What infrastructure investment needs to take place to develop tourism and where is such investment likely to stem from?
3 What current economic problems facing Brazil inhibit growth?
4 What arguments are there for and against government investment in tourism?
5 How does 'mañana syndrome' relate to growth?

Task 15.2   No flights, no booze, no hotels – and guess who's in charge? – Frank Barrett

Britain's hard-pressed package holiday industry received an unexpected fillip last week. A Mediterranean country, untouched by the rough hand of the tower-block hotel developer and unspoilt by the sight of sunburnt beer bellies bulging over the top of Union Jack shorts, announced that it is keen to open its doors to tour operators.

The news seemed too good to be true. Not only can this country offer one of the richest collections of classical antiquities outside Greece and Rome, it has unlimited supplies of sun and sand.

As with the holiday-brochure small print, there are catches. The man laying down the welcome mat for British holiday firms is Colonel Muammar Gaddafi, ruler of that international pariah Libya. In a televised speech last week, Col Gaddafi outlined solutions to its economic and political problems: one way, he said, was to invite foreign firms to invest in mass tourism.

'Tourism produces a very big income. Libya had a ban on tourism. However, Libya is very, very rich in tourist attractions.' Britain's travel companies, famous for their ability to run wild at the glimpse of even the smallest commercial opportunity, were resisting the temptation to pop the champagne corks.

'Because of the UN sanctions there are no flights into Libya; there are no hotels; and the country is dry, no alcohol is allowed. Apart from all that, I can't see any problems in developing tourism,' observed one tour operator dryly.

Libya's hopes for economic salvation through tourism are shared by other unlikely destinations. Ten years ago Cuba was hard to get into: now it enjoys pride of place in Thomson's Winter Sun programme. Iran, Syria, Bhutan, Cambodia, Laos and Vietnam are similarly keen to attract tourists. Justin Fleming, managing director of Panorama Holidays, which specializes in package holidays to Libya's neighbour, Tunisia, has no designs on Libya. 'The country I'm looking at right now is Vietnam. The country has enormous potential, terrific potential: there are superb beaches. All we have to do is change people's perceptions of the place.'

Source: *Independent on Sunday*, 16 May 1993 (adapted).

Questions

1 What are the obstacles to hotel development and tourism in the countries named in the above article?

2   What are the attractions for hotel development and tourism in these countries?
3   What are the main economic indicators for the Libyan economy? How could hotel development and tourism improve these?
4   How could hotel and tourism development be promoted in Libya?

Task 15.3 Economics: investment vital to sustain revival – Robert Chote

British manufacturers have long devoted fewer resources to equipping their employees with plant and machinery than their competitors in France, Germany, the USA and Japan. This culture of underinvestment now threatens to cripple economic recovery.

The amount companies invest in capital equipment helps determine how rapidly the economy can grow before its gears begin to grind. A lack of investment leaves industry with too little capacity to meet rising demand from consumers at home and abroad. If industry falls behind, exports stall, imports surge and inflation accelerates as frustrated consumers bid up prices.

The Trade and Industry Select Committee highlighted the threat of underinvestment in a report on the competitiveness of British manufacturing last week. But it is important to remember that investment is vital throughout the economy.

Tuesday's quarterly industrial trends survey from the CBI did not show any signs of an imminent surge in capital spending to rectify the problem. Only 30 per cent of manufacturers said they intended to increase investment in the coming year, while 26 per cent expected to cut it back. More than half the manufacturers questioned said they were deterred from investing by uncertainty about demand. Slightly fewer said they were discouraged by inadequate rates of return. The select committee sensibly proposed tax changes to encourage retention and reinvestment of profits. But the pessimism of the CBI survey notwithstanding, there are good reasons to expect that another sharp rise is about to occur.

Companies have plenty of funds with which to invest, and utilization of existing capacity now exceeds its long-term trend. Growing sales revenues, lower taxes and smaller interest payments have all helped the corporate sector reverse the enormous deficit it ran in 1989 and 1990 after companies overinvested in the boom. Profits are growing rapidly, with plenty being retained despite the high dividend payments. Given this scenario, it would not be surprising to see investment rise by 5 per cent this year and more still in 1995.

One response to this problem would be for the government to pick a sector it thought had potential and invest in it itself. The Clinton administration took this route on Thursday, granting up to US$700m (£490m) for the development and manufacture of flat-screen technology such as that used in laptop computers. The plan is to create an industry virtually from scratch – the USA has only 3 per cent of the market. But the omens are not good. Western governments have been notoriously inefficient in 'picking winners', be they companies or industries. The British government would be ill-advised to follow suit. Far better to address the general barriers to investment identified by the select committee and to provide funding to individuals to buy themselves flexible technical education and training. The benefits will be slow coming, but more durable once they appear.

Source: *Independent on Sunday*, 1 May 1994 (adapted).

Questions

1   What are the positive and negative signs of investment activity in the UK economy?
2   How can investment in the UK be promoted and does it guarantee faster economic growth?
3   Identify a major leisure or tourism investment which the government could undertake. Evaluate the pros and cons of such a strategy for growth.

Short questions

1   What is real GNP per capita?
2   What are the key determinants of economic growth?
3   What is balanced growth?
4   What factors led to the importance of leisure and tourism in the economies of France and Spain?
5   What are the advantages and problems of joint ventures for the Chinese economy?
6   Why is China successful in exporting toys?
7   Compare private foreign investment with government investment in a hotel as alternative development strategies.

Further reading

Confederation of British Industry, *Towards a Skills Revolution*, CBI, 1989.

De Kadt, E. (ed.), *Tourism – Passport to Development?*, Oxford University Press, 1979.

Harrison, D. (ed.), *Tourism and the Less Developed Countries*, Belhaven, 1992.

Lea, J., *Tourism and Development in the Third World*, Routledge, 1988.

National Economic Development Council, *Developing Managers for Tourism*, NEDO, 1991.

Williams, A. and Shaw, G. (eds), *Tourism and Economic Development*, Belhaven, 1991.

World Bank, *World Development Report*, Oxford University Press, 1994.

Part Five

International Aspects of Leisure and Tourism

16

Leisure and tourism: the balance of payments and exchange rates

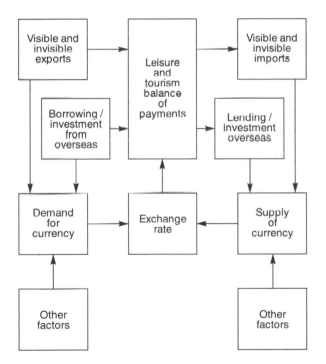

Objectives

As well as measuring the contribution of the leisure and tourism sector to the level of national income we can consider its contribution at the international level to a country's balance of payments. The balance of payments records export earnings and import expenditure.

Exchange rates are an important part of the picture. The exchange rate of a country's currency is inextricably linked with the balance of payments. Changes in a country's balance of payments may cause changes in the demand and supply for its currency and thus movements in its exchange rate. These currency movements may subsequently cause changes in the patterns of exports and imports which can cause feedback to the balance of payments.

The balance of payments is also one of the key macroeconomic variables which government policy-makers monitor closely. If the balance of payments should move into an unsustainable deficit, government policy would be changed to address the problem, causing repercussions throughout the rest of the economy.

After studying this chapter students will be able to:

- understand the balance of payments accounts
- analyse the contribution of the leisure and tourism sector to net export earnings
- describe and explain comparative data for balance of payments accounts
- understand the significance of exchange rates to leisure and tourism organizations

Table 16.1   *UK balance of payments (£m)*

Current account	1993	1994	1995
Visible trade	−13 680	−10 527	
Invisible trade	2 799	10 359	
Current balance	−10 881	−168	
Transactions in UK assets and liabilities			
Transactions in assets	−162 797	−30 016	
Transactions in liabilities	174 939	24 271	
Net transactions	12 142	−5 745	
Balancing item	−1 261	5 913	

Source: CSO: *Monthly Digest of Statistics.*

- distinguish between spot and forward rates of exchange
- analyse exchange rate movements
- understand government and EC policy in trade and international payments

Trade and trading blocs

The EU continues to liberalize trade within community countries. The Single European Act, which came into effect in 1992, defines the single market as 'an area without internal frontiers in which the free movement of goods, persons, services and capital is ensured in accordance with the provisions of this Treaty'.

Some of the specific outcomes of this act which impinge on the leisure and tourism sector include the dismantling of EU internal border checks (some exceptions remain), and more competition in air and shipping services.

The move towards a single European currency is considered later in this chapter.

The balance of payments

The balance of payments is an account which shows a country's financial transactions with the rest of the world. It records inflows and outflows of currency. It is divided into three parts – the current account, net transactions in UK assets and liabilities, and the balancing item. The main difference between these parts is that the current account measures the value of goods and services traded, whilst the net transactions in UK assets and liabilities measures flows of capital, for example loans, and investments. The balancing item is an error term which arises from compiling the data from a diverse range of surveys. Table 16.1 shows recent balance of payments data.

The balance of payments account always balances in an accounting sense. Every expenditure of foreign currency must be offset be a receipt, otherwise the expenditure could not take place. For poorer countries (as with poorer people), this means that expenditure (on imports) cannot exceed earnings (from exports) because they simply run out of (foreign) currency.

However for countries with a developed financial sector, current import expenditure may exceed current export income. This can be financed, perhaps by borrowings, or perhaps by selling assets. In such a case, although the account would balance in an accounting sense, it would show structural imbalance. This is because such a position could not be sustainable over a long period. Sources of borrowing would dry up and there is only a finite stock of assets to be sold. The implications of such a structural deficit are discussed below in the section on government policy.

In the balance of payments account for 1993,

shown in Table 16.1, it can be seen that the three parts of the balance of payments sum to zero:

$$-10\,881 + 12\,142 - 1261 = 0$$

The current account

The current account records payments for trade in goods and services and is thus divided into two parts – visible and invisible trade.

Visibles

Visibles represents exports and imports in goods and is divided into the following sections:

- food, beverages and tobacco
- basic materials
- fuels
- semimanufactures
- manufacture
- others

The leisure sector is represented in this part of the account, for example, by trade in alcoholic beverages, electrical goods and sports equipment and sports wear. Figure 16.1 shows the balance of trade in sports footwear, whilst Table 16.2 shows the UK total visible trade balance over recent years.

The information for sports footwear demonstrates similar characteristics to that for UK visible trade as a whole. First it exhibits a deficit, with imports exceeding imports. This has been caused by uncompetitive UK exchange rates (although this is less evident since sterling's exit from the ERM in 1992), and cheap overseas production costs – particularly labour costs. Countries such as South Korea, Indonesia and the Philippines, for example, account for more than 50 per cent of the value of imports for trainers.

Second the information shows the deficit peaking in 1989–1990. This demonstrates the relationship between growth in the economy as a whole and the balance of payments. During the late 1980s the UK experienced a period of rapid growth followed by a sharp recession. For the

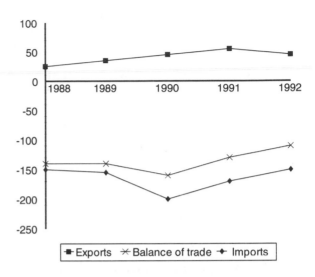

Figure 16.1 Value of foreign trade in sports footwear (£m). Source: Adapted from CSO; *The Pink Book 1994.*

UK there is a strong link between economic growth and import demand.

Invisibles

Invisibles records the trade in services or intangibles under the following headings:

- government
- sea transport
- civil aviation
- travel
- financial and other services
- interest, profits and dividends
- private transfers

The key items of relevance to the leisure and tourism sector are civil aviation and travel. Also significant are interest, profit and dividends, which records payments relating to overseas business investments. For example, profits returned to the French-owned Brittany Ferries from its activities in the UK would represent an invisible trading debit under this section. Table 16.3 records data for overseas travel and tourism earnings and expenditure. This covers goods and

Table 16.2   *UK visible trade balance (£m)*

	1987	1988	1989	1990	1991	1992	1993	1994	1995
Visible trade	−11 582	−21 480	−24 683	−18 809	−10 284	−13 104	−13 394	−10 527	

Source: CSO: *Monthly Digest of Statistics.*

Table 16.3   *Overseas tourism: UK earnings and expenditure at current prices (£m)*

Item	1987	1988	1989	1990	1991	1992	1993	1994	1995
Credits (visitors to UK)	6 260	6 184	6 945	7 748	7 386	7 891	9 090		
Debits (UK visits abroad)	7 280	8 216	9 357	9 886	9 951	11 243	12 781		
Net UK earnings	−1 020	−2 032	−2 412	−2 138	−2 565	−3 352	−3 691		

Source: CSO: *Monthly Digest of Statistics.*

Table 16.4   *Net UK earnings from civil aviation and total services at current prices (£m)*

Activity	1987	1988	1989	1990	1991	1992	1993	1994	1995
Civil aviation	−616	−911	−528	−295	−384	−547	−451	NA	
Invisible balance	6599	4863	2171	541	2632	2867	2799	10 359	

Notes: NA = Not available.
Source: CSO: *UK Balance of Payments.*

services provided to UK residents during trips of less than 1 year in overseas countries (and vice versa) but excludes transport. The data are based upon international passenger surveys.

The value of tourism earnings depends not just upon the number of visitors but also their average expenditure. Resort officials are increasingly concentrating on the latter, as exhibit 16.1 shows.

Exhibit 16.1   Backpacker ban backfires

Roberto Avogrado is the Mayor of Alassio, a resort on the Italian Riviera. He has a strong puritanical streak and has made a seemingly odd request for a town which depends on tourism. He has called on railway managers to provide fewer weekend trains to the resort.

His target? The *sacopelisti* (sleeping baggers) who make their way to the resort and sleep on the small public beach. Signor Avogrado fears that the bohe-

mian visitors upset not only the residents of the resort, but also are in danger of discouraging well-heeled tourists on whom local trade depends.

Avogrado has appeared on a popular TV show, Right to Reply, saying that local police would ask visitors to the resort to produce the equivalent of £22 to prove they are not beach bums. Those who failed this test would be expelled from the town.

The result? Outraged backpackers have converged on Alassio in their hundreds in protest.

Source: the author, from news cuttings, June 1994.

Table 16.4 shows invisible trade for civil aviation and total UK invisibles.

It can be seen from Tables 16.3 and 16.4 that invisibles as a whole contribute to net earnings of foreign currency for the UK, albeit on a downward trend. Civil aviation shows a small, variable deficit, and tourism shows a net outflow of

Table 16.5 *International tourism balance of payments (US$m)*

Country	1991	1992	1993	1994	1995
USA	6 133	5 814	3 144		
France	8 962	10 770	12 500		
Spain	14 474	16 511	17 772		
UK	−4 205	−5 171	NA		
Germany	−20 703	NA	NA		
Japan	−20 548	NA	NA		
Turkey	2 062	3 400	5 350		
China	2 482	NA	NA		
Greece	1 555	NA	NA		
Bahamas	1015	NA	NA		
India	957	NA	NA		

Notes: Exhibits for 1992 are provisional and for 1993 are forecasts. NA = not available.
Source: *World Travel and Tourism Review*, CAB International, Oxford (Ritchie, J.R.B. and Hawkins, D., eds).

foreign currency for the UK, a trend which is growing, as noted in exhibit 16.2.

Exhibit 16.2 Tourism deficit: CBI seeks action

The appetite of UK tourists for holidays abroad has steadily outpaced that of their foreign counterparts, leading to a tourism trade deficit of £4bn, compared to zero only nine years ago.

The Confederation of British Industry has viewed this development with alarm and is to set up a campaign group to pressurise the government into a programme of action for tourism development.

Early indications suggest that the campaign will urge

- a cut in VAT on hotel bills
- promotion of Britain as a tourist destination to the fast-growing economies of the Pacific Rim and Latin America
- promotion of short breaks within the UK

Source: CBI, May 1994.

Tourism is a net earner to the balance of payments of some countries and Table 16.5 shows some of the main net tourism surplus and deficit countries.

France and Spain boast large tourism surpluses, and tourism surpluses are rising rapidly for Turkey (1985 = $1108m), and China (1985 = $665m). On the other hand, Germany and Japan both have significant deficits in their tourism payments accounts, and, as shown earlier, the UK has a steadily deteriorating deficit. Exhibit 16.3 shows how important tourism is to countries with general balance of payments problems.

Exhibit 16.3 Value of Czech tourism disputed

The Prince of Wales, co-president of the Prague Heritage Fund, cautioned against tourism development at a conference at Hradcany Castle in the Czech Republic.

Prince Charles lamented the destruction of architectural monuments that had taken place under communism, adding, 'Our culture, once lost, can never be retrieved'. Lord Rothschild, who was also on the discussion panel, suggested that cars should be banned from historic districts of Prague and urged the Czech authorities not to allow 'mass tourism' to spoil the city.

A note of economic realism was immediately struck by the Czech Trade and Industry Minister, Vladimir Dlouhy, who put up a robust case for tourism. 'Do not demonize mass tourism,' he said. 'We have lost many export markets, and tourism helps our balance of payments.'

Source: the author, from news cuttings, June 1994.

Net transactions in assets and liabilities

Whilst the current account of the balance of payments records the export and import of goods and services, this part of the account deals mainly with movements of capital. It is divided into transactions in external assets and transactions in external liabilities. Such capital movements can be considered under the headings of investment, lending and borrowing, and official reserves activity.

Investment

This can be further subdivided into direct investment and portfolio investment. Direct investment is the direct purchase of firms or land or buildings abroad. Portfolio investment is the purchase of securities or shares abroad. Such activity leads to an outflow of funds, but a potential future inflow of profits or dividends under invisibles in the current account. Conversely, disinvestment or overseas inward investment causes an inflow of capital.

The transaction featured in exhibit 16.4 would lead to an outflow under the net transactions in assets and liabilities heading of the UK balance of payments and a corresponding inflow in the French balance of payments.

Exhibit 16.4 Forte wins £230m battle for Meridien hotel group

Forte yesterday won control of the four-star Meridien hotel chain, as Air France, its majority owner, announced that it would sell its 57.3 per cent Meridien stake to the British group.

Forte, owner of 853 hotels worldwide, will take control of the 58 hotels in the Meridien chain for a cash payment of·FF1.09bn.

Source: *Guardian*, 15 September 1994 (adapted).

Lending and borrowing

This records international loans. A loan to an overseas company will lead to an outflow of capital but future inflows of interest payments in the invisible part of the current account.

Official reserves activity

Government use of official reserves of foreign currencies is recorded here. An increase in reserves leads to a corresponding outflow of capital from the balance of payments account.

The balance of leisure and tourism payments

The complex effects of leisure and tourism activities on a country's balance of payments are illustrated in Table 16.6 by an example of international currency flows associated with Disneyland Paris

Table 16.6 illustrates many of the issues surrounding leisure and tourism contributions to foreign currency earnings on the balance of payments. Potential earnings can be diminished in several ways. First, consider the element of overseas ownership. The greater the share of overseas ownership, the more profits are exported in the form of dividends to overseas shareholders. Second the role of overseas banks is significant. A high initial loan from foreign banks results in significant capital and interest repayments flowing overseas. Third, the degree of import content of goods sold must be considered. Tourists buying Disney *Dumbo* video tapes are making more of a contribution to the US balance of payments than the French one. Fourth some projects employ a high proportion of foreign nationals who repatriate some of their earnings. Finally the construction of a project may entail the use of overseas contractors and importation of equipment.

Trends and comparisons

UK balance of payments

Table 16.7 shows recent changes in the totals and components of the UK balance of payments.

The current balance recorded a record deficit in 1989 of nearly £23bn, largely reflecting the boom in the UK economy of the late 1980s. Even during the recession the current balance remained in deficit, falling to £8bn in 1991. It remains in deficit, albeit at a more manageable level. The implications of this for UK leisure and tourism organizations, and the economy as a whole, are discussed in the next section.

Government policy

In the short term a balance of payments deficit on current account is not necessarily a problem. It can be offset by borrowing from overseas, or overseas direct or portfolio investment into the UK. There are, however, limits to borrowing and the selling of UK assets abroad, and so an acute long-term current account deficit will require

Table 16.6 *The balance of Disneyland Paris payments for France*

	Exports/credits	Imports/debits
Current account		
Visible trade	Exports of Disneyland Paris merchandise	Purchase of overseas equipment
		Merchandise imported from USA and Far East for sale
		Imported foods for catering
Invisible trade	Admission charges paid by overseas residents	Royalties and management fees paid to US parent company
	Souvenirs bought by overseas residents	Dividends paid to overseas shareholders
	Meals bought by overseas residents	Interest paid on loans to overseas banks
		Overseas marketing
		Private transfers by overseas workers employed
Transactions in assets and liabilities		
Investment in France by overseas residents	Direct investment from the US parent company of 49% of Disneyland Paris	Sales of Disneyland Paris shares by overseas residents to French residents
	Purchase of Disneyland Paris shares by overseas residents	
Investment overseas by French residents		
Banking transactions	Borrowings from overseas banks	Capital repayments to overseas banks

government intervention. This may take the form of:

- devaluation or currency depreciation
- deflation
- protectionism

Each of these will affect leisure and tourism organizations.

Devaluation or currency depreciation

This is a policy of allowing a country's currency to fall in value or depreciate under a system of floating exchange rates, or moving to a lower rate under a fixed exchange rate system. The aim is to stimulate exports by making their foreign currency price cheaper and to curb imports by increasing their sterling price. An example of the effects of devaluation is shown later in Table 16.8.

Success of the policy will depend upon demand elasticities. For example, devaluation will only increase total foreign currency earnings from exports if demand is elastic, so that the fall in the foreign currency price per unit is compensated for by a larger proportionate rise in demand.

Deflation

A deflationary policy involves the government reducing spending power in the economy. The

Table 16.7 *The UK balance of payments (£m)*

Year	Current account			Net transactions in UK assets and liabilities	Balancing item
	Visible trade	Invisible trade	Current balance		
1987	−11 582	6 599	−4 983	7 026	−2 043
1988	−21 480	4 863	−16 617	10 352	6 265
1989	−24 683	2 171	−22 512	19 415	3 097
1990	−18 809	541	−18 262	10 960	7 308
1991	−10 284	2 632	−7 652	6 728	924
1992	−13 406	2 867	−10 539	7 098	3 441
1993	−13 680	2 799	−10 881	12 142	−1 261
1994	−10 527	10 359	−168	−5 745	5 913
1995					

Source: CSO: *UK Balance of Payments.*

rationale is that, since imports form a significant proportion of consumer expenditure, a reduction in spending power will in turn reduce imports. Figure 16.2 shows the relationship between imports and the overall level of consumer spending in an economy.

Deflation is achieved through increasing interest rates or increasing taxes. If deflationary policy reduced consumer expenditure from 0A to 0B, then import spending would fall from 0C to 0D.

The effects of deflationary policies of the early 1990s on the imports of sports footwear can be noted from Figure 16.1, where it can be seen that imports fell considerably.

Protectionism

This entails direct controls on imported goods, including taxes on imports (tariffs) and limits on import volumes and values. The threat of retaliation and the rules of international treaties such as the EU and GATT (the General Agreement on Tariffs and Trade, which exists to reduce protectionism) make protectionism a difficult option.

Exchange rates

Significance of exchange rates

The exchange rate is the price of one currency expressed in terms of another currency. Exchange rates are important to leisure and tourism organizatons for a number of reasons. Firms selling or manufacturing goods in the UK may import either the finished good or the raw materials to make the finished good. For example, ski equipment is mainly imported and a fall in the

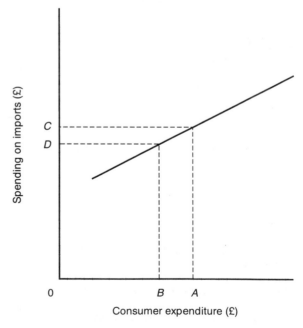

Figure 16.2 The effects fo deflationary policy on export spending.

Table 16.8 *The effects of currency movements on prices*

		Local currency price	Purchase price: £1 = 10FF	Purchase price: £1 = 8FF
Visible import	Rossignol skis	1000FF	£100	£125
Invisible import	Apartment for week in Val d'Isère	2000FF	£200	£250
Visible export	Litre of Scotch whiskey (before tax)	£5	50FF	40FF
Invisible export	Night at Heathrow hotel	£50	500FF	400FF

value of sterling against the currency of the exporting country will mean a rise in the sterling cost of equipment. The purchase of tourism facilities abroad is classed as an invisible import and so a fall in the value of sterling will increase the sterling price of such facilities.

A fall in the value of sterling will however reduce the foreign currency price of UK visible exports such as Scotch whiskey and invisible exports, including inbound tourism.

Table 16.8 shows the effects of a fall in the value of sterling from £1 = 10FF to £1 = 8FF. Notice that the UK price of imports rises whilst the foreign currency price of exports falls.

The conclusion from Table 16.8 is that organizatons selling imported goods and services may favour a higher exchange rate, whereas those exporting goods and services may favour a lower one. Exhibit 16.5 links a fall in the value of the peseta to tourism growth in regional Spain.

Exhibit 16.5 Recovery in tourism and exports in Catalonia

Catalonia – on Spain's Mediterannean coast – boasts the city of Barcelona and the beaches of the Costa Brava, but still fell victim to negative economic growth of 1.8 per cent in 1993.

Economic factors are now improving. The peseta is 20 per cent lower against the Deutschmark than 2 years ago and short-term interest rates have fallen from 15 to 9 per cent.

Both exports and tourism are sensitive to the exchange rate and are showing signs of recovery.

Exports rose by 22 per cent in 1993. Catalonia's hotels enjoyed occupancy rates approaching 90 per cent over Easter and the number of summer visitors for the region is expected to grow by 12–15 per cent this year.

Source: the author, from news cuttings, May 1994.

Above all, stability of the exchange rate is crucial for organizations whose operations involve significant foreign currency transactions. It was very difficult for firms to engage in transatlantic business in the early 1980s for example when the exchange rate fluctuated between £1 = $2.40 and £1 = $1.10.

Determination of floating exchange rates

A floating exchange rate is one which is determined in the market without government intervention. This has been the case for the UK since 1972, with the exception of the period October 1990 to September 1992, when sterling was part of the exchange rate mechanism (ERM) of the European monetary system (EMS). The exchange rate is determined, like most prices, by the forces of demand and supply. On the foreign exchange markets sterling is demanded by holders of foreign currency wishing to buy sterling and sterling is supplied by holders of sterling wishing to buy foreign currency. Using the Deutschmark (DM) to stand for all foreign currencies, we can identify the main determinants of the demand for and supply of sterling as follows:

Demand for sterling (supply of DM)

- demand for UK visible exports
- demand for UK invisible exports

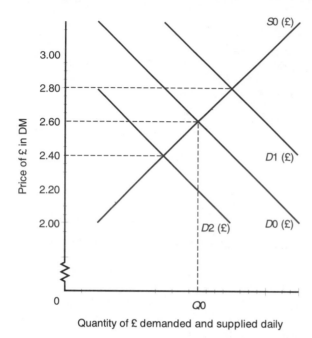

Figure 16.3 The price of sterling in Deutschmarks. See text for details.

- demand for funds for direct and portfolio investment in the UK
- demand for funds for overseas deposits in sterling bank accounts
- speculation
- government intervention

Supply of sterling (demand for DM)

- demand for German visible exports
- demand for German invisible exports
- demand for funds for direct and portfolio investment in Germany
- deposits for funds for deposits in DM bank accounts
- speculation
- government intervention

Figure 16.3 shows typical demand and supply curves for sterling against the DM.

The demand for pounds is represented by the demand curve $D0$, and $S0$ shows the supply of pounds. The equilibrium exchange rate is at £1 =

DM2.60, where the number of pounds being offered on the foreign exchange market is equal to the number of pounds demanded ($0Q0$). Should any of the determinants of the demand or supply of sterling change, the demand and/ or supply curves will shift position and a new equilibrium price will be achieved.

The price of sterling will rise if the demand curve for sterling shifts to the right. In Figure 16.3 a shift of the demand curve from $D0$ to $D1$ causes the exchange rate to rise to DM2.80. This could be caused for example by a significant increase in the value of UK exports, or a rise in UK interest rates causing foreign currency holders to switch their deposits into sterling accounts to earn higher interest rates. A leftward shift of the supply curve for sterling would have a similar effect on the exchange rate.

The price of sterling will fall if the demand curve for sterling shifts to the left. In Figure 16.3 a shift of the demand curve from $D0$ to $D2$ causes the exchange rate to fall to DM2.40. This could be caused for example by a significant fall in the value of UK exports, or a fall in UK interest rates causing foreign currency holders to switch their deposits out of sterling accounts to earn higher interest rates abroad. A rightward shift of the supply curve for sterling would have a similar effect on the exchange rate.

Determination of fixed exchange rates

In October 1990 the UK entered the ERM of the EMS. This was a system designed to maintain a fixed rate of exchange between currencies of EU member states to assist intracommunity trade. The UK joined at a rate of £1 = DM2.95. To allow some flexibility in the system, most currencies were allowed to fluctuate within a band of ±3 per cent, although sterling was allowed to operate within a wide band of ±6 per cent. Figure 16.4 shows the main features of the system.

Notice that a trading ceiling is drawn at £1 = DM3.13, which is 6 per cent above the central rate of £1 = DM2.95, and similarly a floor is drawn at £1 = DM2.77. The factors which affect demand and supply are the same as those

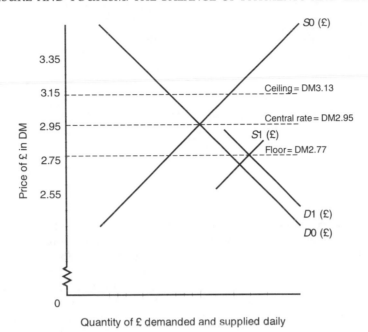

Figure 16.4 The exchange rate under the exchange rate mechanism.

identified in the previous section and within the ± 6 per cent band the exchange rate is determined as if in a free market.

However, should trading conditions move the rate of exchange outside of its permitted band, the government is committed to take steps to return the exchange rate within the band. This process was illustrated dramatically on Black Wednesday (16 September 1992), as exhibit 16.6 recalls.

Exhibit 16.6   £ leaves ERM

Speculators led by George Soros, sensing the pound was under pressure, sold pounds on the foreign exchange markets and the supply curve shifted towards S1, taking sterling beneath its ERM floor. The Bank of England was thus forced to intervene in the market to restore the exchange rate. It raised interest rates from 10 to 15 per cent to stimulate demand for sterling and spent £7bn in purchasing sterling, shifting the demand curve towards D1.

However at the end of the day selling of sterling still exceeded government-inspired buying and the pound closed at DM2.75 at the end of the day – 2 pfennigs below its permitted floor. The government

was forced to suspend sterling's membership of the ERM the same evening.

One of the difficulties of membership of the ERM was that interest rates were the main policy instrument available to the government to maintain the exchange rate and sudden changes in interest rates were detrimental to the economic environment in which firms operate (see Chapter 9) and the level of investment (see Chapter 12).

Trends

Table 16.9 traces recent changes in key exchange rates against sterling.

It is possible to discern relative stability for sterling in the EC exchange, markets brought about by ERM membership, between 1990 and 1992. Thereafter movements in sterling are more pronounced, with particularly large falls registering against the French franc and the Deutschmark.

Forecasting exchange rates is notoriously difficult, as these two quotations from *The Times* demonstrate:

Table 16.9 *Selected exchange rates against sterling*

	1989	1990	1991	1992	1993	1994	1995
US dollar	1.64	1.79	1.77	1.77	1.5	1.53	
Deutschmark	3.08	2.88	2.93	2.75	2.48	2.48	
French franc	10.45	9.69	9.95	9.32	8.51	8.49	
Peseta	194	181	183	180	191	205	
Drachma	265	282	321	335	344	371	
Italian lire	2247	2133	2187	2163	2360	2467	

Source: CSO: *Financial Statistics.*

Sterling continued to strengthen against the mark yesterday, gaining another pfennig, but the rise came mostly from the German currency's weakness against the dollar (14 January 1994).

the pound is also becoming increasingly vulnerable to perceptions, overseas, that Britain is heading for severe problems on its current account (6 April 1994).

Spot and forward foreign exchange markets

The spot market is the immediate market in foreign currency and represents the current market rate. Payment is made today and the transaction takes place today at today's rate. There is a margin making dealers' selling prices slightly more than buying prices.

However some organizations seek protection from exchange rate fluctuations, particularly if they need to quote for contract prices involving a large foreign currency consideration. The forward market exists to satisfy demand for a guaranteed future exchange rate. Payment is made today but the transaction is made in the future (e.g. 3 months) at a rate agreed today.

Government policy

The government faces a dilemma in its exchange rate policy as in many other policy areas. A lower exchange rate for sterling makes export prices competitive and discourages imports, whilst a high exchange rate, by cutting import prices,

helps to combat inflation. Between the late 1980s and 1992, policy was to encourage a high rate of exchange to counter inflation, but after 1992, post-ERM, the exchange rate was allowed to fall, improving the UK international competitiveness.

Policy instruments to affect the exchange rate consist of interest rates and direct buying and selling by the Bank of England. Raising interest rates will generally increase the demand for sterling as currency is moved from overseas banks to UK banks to benefit from higher interest rates.

EU policy regarding exchange rates remains that of eventual European Monetary Union (EMU) – a single European currency. The ratification of the Maastricht Treaty established a European Monetary Institute (EMI) responsible for coordinating monetary union. However monetary union depends upon convergence of the economies of member states in the key areas of inflation, interest rates, budget deficits and balance of payments. Current divergence between economies and continued difficulties in the ERM mean that monetary union from 1999 may be feasible only for certain member states.

Review of key terms

- Balance of payments = record of one country's financial transactions with the rest of the world.
- Exchange rate = price of one currency in terms of another.
- Current account = value of trade in goods and services.

- Net transactions in UK assets and liabilities = record of international movements of capital.
- Balancing item = error term.
- Visible trade = trade in goods.
- Invisible trade = trade in services.
- Devaluation or currency depreciation = movement to a lower exchange rate.
- Deflationary policy = government policy to reduce economic activity.
- Protectionism = policy to control imports
- GATT = General Agreement on Tariffs and Trade (tariff-reducing treaty).
- Floating exchange rate = one which is determined in the market without government intervention.
- ERM = Exchange Rate Mechanism.
- EMS = European Monetary System.
- Fixed exchange rate = constant rate of exchange maintained by market intervention.
- Spot market = the immediate market in foreign currency.
- Forward market = futures market for currency.
- EMI = European Monetary Institute.

Data questions

Task 16.1

Table 16.10 shows inward and outward tourism receipts. The 1986–1993 figures have been collected by the CSO and the 1994 and 1995 figures are BTA forecasts made in 1993.

Questions

1 Comment on the changes shown in the data.
2 Calculate the net tourism surplus/deficit for 1994 and 1995.
3 How are forecasts made?
4 What are the benefits and problems of forecasts?
5 What policies could be used to counter the UK's balance of tourism trade deficit?

Table 16.10 *Overseas tourism spending in UK/British tourism spending overseas at current prices (£m)*

Year	Overseas tourism spending in UK	British tourism spending overseas
1986	5 553	6 083
1987	6 260	7 280
1988	6 184	8 216
1989	6 945	9 357
1990	7 748	9 886
1991	7 386	9 951
1992	7 891	11 243
1993	9 090	12 781
1994	9 800F	13 400F
1995	10 460F	14 200F

Notes: F = forecast.
Source: CSO/BTA/ETB.

Task 16.2 Bank of Greece fights off speculation against drachma

Speculators turned their attention last week to the drachma, selling the currency hard in an attempt to turn a quick profit. A concerted policy in defence of the currency gained widespread support. 'We must defend the drachma as we would defend our borders,' was the rallying cry of Miltiadis Evert, leader of the conservative New Democracy opposition party.

The Bank of Greece used classic currency defence measures to stabilize the rate of exchange. It spent almost £1bn worth of Deutschmarks in support of the currency and interest rates on the overnight deposit rate was allowed to rocket. By the close of trading last week it had settled at 150 per cent after briefly hitting 500 per cent

Source: the author, from press cuttings, 22 May 1994.

Questions

1 Illustrate the attack and defence of the drachma using a supply and demand graph.
2 How do the two measures used by the Greek central bank work?

3   Is devaluation of the drachma good or bad for Greece's balance of tourism payments?
4   What are the main factors which determine the rate of exchange for the drachma?

Task 16.3   Greek tourism: past, present and future

Greece, like many other tourism destinations, has suffered two poor seasons. The culprit is not hard to find. The recession which has gripped Europe and the USA with rising unemployment and high interest rates cut deeply into consumer spending and non-essentials such as holidays were inevitably hit hardest.

The forecast for this year is promising and the Greek government and travel trade agree that over 10 million tourists will visit the country this summer. Tourism's significance to the Greek economy is illustrated by some key statistics. The population of Greece is 10 million. According to official figures, last year's 9.4 million tourists boosted Greece's balance of payments by $3.5bn – a useful contribution to a country which ran a total current balance of payments deficit of around $6bn.

But further probing of the data gives cause for concern. Per capita spending by tourists is one of the lowest for any tourist destination. The shortness of the season is also seen as a problem, running from May to mid-September.

Many of the hotels in Greece are in the two- or three-star category, family-run and over 25 years old. This puts them in a poor bargaining position with the European tour operators who insist on low costs. They also find themselves in competition with up to a million unlicensed beds. The householders who let out these extra beds pay no taxes and can offer low prices for tourists. Market conditions, then, keep accommodation prices depressed.

A favoured strategy to raise per capita spending and boost tourism foreign exchange is to take the tourism product upmarket. The construction of seven new casinos is the centrepiece of the new thinking. The government is providing incentives for new hotel construction and modernization, with funds also available for the development of golf courses, conference centres and marinas.

Source: the author, from news cuttings, June 1994.

Questions

1   Detail the factors affecting the level of tourism receipts in Greece.
2   Which of these factors have helped growth in tourism receipts and which have hindered such growth?
3   What policies can encourage an increase in per capita tourist spending, and what are the dangers of such policies?

Short questions

1   Illustrate which parts of the balance of payments account are affected by the activities of a named organization in the leisure and tourism sector.
2   Under what circumstances would a fall in the value of the drachma (a) increase and (b) decrease earnings of sterling for Greece?
3   How might persistent current account deficits affect organizations in the leisure and tourism sector?
4   Explain how a fall in the value of sterling would affect three different organizations in the leisure and tourism sector.
5   Explain what factors have caused fluctuations in the sterling exchange rate over the past year.

Further reading

Central Statistical Office, *UK Balance of Payments*, HMSO, London, yearly.
Baretje, R., Tourism's external account and the balance of payments, *Annals of Tourism Research*, 1982; **9**(1).
Smith, C., *UK Trade and Sterling*, Heinemann, 1992.
Williams, A. and Shaw, G., *Tourism and Economic Development*, Belhaven, 1991.

17

Multinational enterprises

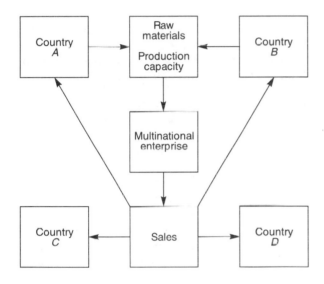

Objectives

A significant trend in the 1980s and 1990s is the globalization of the economic environment. This means that goods and services are increasingly being produced and sold across national economic boundaries. This chapter investigates the rise of the multinational enterprise (MNE) and analyses the motives for multinational operations as well as the effects of MNEs on consumers, parent countries and host countries. It also considers the relationship between MNEs and governments in parent and host economies. The significance of MNEs cannot be underestimated since it has been estimated that the 200 largest MNEs have a combined sales equal to about one-third of the world's GDP.

By studying this chapter students should be able to:

- explain the meaning of an MNE
- understand the motives for extending operations overseas
- analyse the effects of MNEs
- evaluate government policy relating to MNEs

Meaning and extent of multinational enterprise

An MNE is one which has production or service capacity located in more than one country. The MNE has a headquarters in a parent country and extends its operations into one or more host countries. The headquarter countries for many of the key MNEs in travel and tourism are the USA, the UK, France, Germany, Japan and Hong Kong.

The main ways in which multinational operations are extended are by investment in new or 'greenfield' capacity, by taking an equity stake in a foreign company (i.e. buying up shares) or by operating a franchise or alliance with a foreign company.

Forte is a good example of an MNE intent on globalizing its operations, as illustrated in exhibit 17.1.

Exhibit 17.1 Life begins at Forte

Travel and tourism is the world's largest industry. And there is no doubting the global ambition of Forte, the hotel and catering combine, to become an international luxury hotel chain rivalling Hilton, Hyatt and Sheraton.

Forte is only just beginning a strong cyclical recovery, led by its luxury London hotels such as the Grosvenor House, the Hyde Park Hotel and Browns. And the £230m takeover of the French Meridien chain gives it 54 hotels in 34 countries, including 10 in Southeast Asia, including Tokyo and Singapore, where Forte had none. When the ink dries on the documents this December, Forte will be represented in 54 countries, compared with only 24 now.

Source: *Observer*, 2 October 1994 (adapted).

Motives for going multinational

The general motive for companies going multinational is profit maximization. In this respect investment overseas can be viewed in a similar way to any investment. The criterion for profit maximization for an investment is that the rate of return should be better than other possible uses for the capital that is to be employed. The rate of return will be related to the cost of, and the revenue derived from, the investment. Thus motives for overseas investment will include cost reductions or increased sales resulting from production or service provision overseas.

Companies involved in manufacturing leisure as well as other goods now have much weaker ties with any particular region or national economy. The increase in international trade has made the market place more competitive and companies much more aware of the need for achieving price leadership or adding value to their products in order to achieve market share and profitability. Thus firms are more ready to transfer production to another location should circumstances favour this.

Service sector companies that wish to extend their services to overseas markets generally have little option other than to invest in capacity overseas.

Specific motives for multinational expansion can include the following:

- lower labour costs
- lower other costs
- exploiting 'national diamonds'
- marketing advantages

- scale economies, integration and competition
- extension of product life cycles
- tariff avoidance
- incentives in host economies

Labour costs

In order to achieve price leadership, firms are constantly attempting to lower their costs below those of their rivals. One of the key factor costs that can be reduced by globalization is labour costs. Countries such as China, Malaysia, Singapore and Thailand are popular destinations for production plants for MNEs because of their cheap labour rates. As well as cheap rates, labour and health and safety legislation is much less onerous on organizations in these countries. Union power is also very limited. Thus in the audio products industry, Motorola, a Swiss company, has an assembly plant in China for some of its car stereo range which it sells in the UK. Similarly, the Japanese Sony company has products assembled in Malaysia. It is not uncommon for UK publishers to have books printed in Singapore and Hong Kong.

A similar trend towards investment in tourism destinations can be observed with countries such as Turkey offering lower wage rates than those found in Spain and France.

Other costs

MNEs have access to international capital markets, so local interest rates are rarely a consideration. Land costs and planning regulations, though, can be an important factor, particularly in 'greenfield' developments. The rate of exchange between the parent and the host economy will also be significant.

'National diamonds'

Porter (1990) investigated the source of different countries' competitive advantage in the production of goods and services. He suggested an important factor which he calls the 'national diamond' effect. Why should the Japanese for example be so competitive in the production of cars when they have few local raw materials and relatively high wages? Porter's answer is that intense competition and demanding consumers in the home market are key factors which cause firms to improve technology, quality and marketing. In other words, the product is polished and reworked into a national diamond. This then enables such companies to compete successfully in overseas markets where local products are comparatively uncompetitive since they have not been similarly honed.

Marketing advantages

Some companies have an internationally renowned corporate image which can be exploited by extending operations overseas. Examples here include Holiday Inn (hotels), McDonalds (fast food) and Disney (entertainment). The name is important for two reasons. First it guarantees a standard. This may encourage use, for example, by tourists in foreign destinations who may want their hotel room to represent 'a slice of home', or who are sceptical about using unknown hotels. Second, foreign branded names, particularly US ones, are popular status symbols in some less developed countries. The queues around McDonalds in Beijing and Moscow are testimony to this.

Scale economies, integration and competition

Multinational expansion may be a way of extending profits through vertical integration. For example, tour operators and airlines invest in accommodation overseas to extend their profits.

Similarly, a strong incentive for horizontal integration may be the reduction in competition that occurs from buying foreign competitors. There are also considerable economies of scale to be achieved through transnational ownership. Economies of scale are discussed more fully in Chapter 5, and include bulk purchasing, advertising economies and utilization of specialist inputs from different geographical areas.

Extension of product life cycles

Product life cycle refers to the different stages in the marketing of a product. Products which have reached the mature end of their product life cycle in their initial market and are thus suffering a decline in sales may be revived by launching them in overseas markets – particularly in less developed economies.

Tariff avoidance

Where the exports of a country are affected by tariffs, companies affected may elect to set up production within the tariff area. This is perhaps one of the reasons why the UK has attracted so much investment from Japanese MNEs in the past decade. Such companies can thereby market freely into the EC without tariff barriers.

Incentives in host economies

Investment and running cost can often be reduced by operating overseas and taking advantage of government incentive packages.

Multinational enterprises in leisure and tourism

Air travel

There is a growing tendency for global strategies in major airline companies. The two main directions to this strategy are horizontal globalization and diversification.

Horizontal globalization involves extending service networks worldwide. The motives for this include the general benefits of horizontal integration as discussed in Chapter 5, but increased market share is clearly a key motive. Figure 17.1 shows BA's turnover in world markets for 1993.

As can be seen, BA's turnover is highest in Europe, but there is significant potential growth in passengers in the Americas, Southern and Pacific regions. Hence BA's global strategy has involved investment in foreign airlines to provide global representation and extend BA's

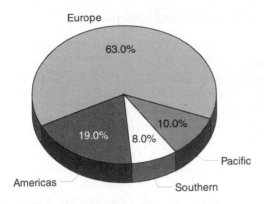

Figure 17.1 BA turnover by area in 1993 – percentage of total.

passenger base. An added advantage is that linked airlines practise code sharing. Under code sharing, connecting flights of an airline group can share a common flight number. So a passenger flying from the UK to Perth, Australia will see the flight as one BA flight number rather than a BA flight and a Qantas transfer.

Exhibit 17.2 records BA's international investments from its 1993 *Annual Report and Accounts,* illustrating the company's global strategy.

Exhibit 17.2   Directors' report: investments

USAir: On 21 January 1993, British Airways announced that it had agreed terms for a new alliance between British Airways and USAir Group inc. The first stage of the transaction has been completed with the investment of £198m in new convertible preferred stock of USAir and the signing of a flight code sharing agreement.

Qantas: On 10th March 1993, British Airways completed the agreement to acquire 25 per cent of Qantas Airways limited for £304m.

TAT: On 1 January 1993, British Airways acquired for £15m a 49.9 per cent share of the equity of TAT European Airlines S.A., the largest independent French airline.

Source: BA: *Annual Report and Accounts 1992–1993.*

Figure 17.2 shows some of the major airline partnerships.

There is also an incentive for airlines to diversify into complementary activities. The logic behind this is that the airlines have customers who are likely to require related travel services – primarily car hire and accommodation. Thus it is not uncommon for airlines to have alliances with or equity stake in or ownership of car hire companies and hotel operators.

Shipping

Ferry and cruise operations tend to be multinational in their operations. Many UK, US and Scandinavian cruise companies operate in the

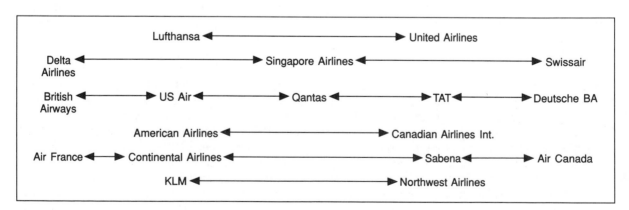

Figure 17.2 World airline partnerships.

Table 17.1 *Lonrho plc: principal overseas companies including associates (hotels)*

	Country of incorporation	Direct interest in ordinary share capital (%)	Beneficial interest (%)	Principal activities
Heinrich's Syndicate Ltd.	Zambia	90	90	Proprietors of the Edinburgh and Lusaka Hotels
Hotel Cardoso S.A.R.L.	Mozambique	50	50	Proprietors of the Hotel Cardoso
Hotel Investments (Ghana) Ltd.	Ghana	55	65	Proprietors of the Labadi Beach Hotel
Lonrho Inc.	USA	100	100	Proprietors of hotels in the USA and investment holding
Merville Ltd.	Mauritius	100	31	Proprietors of the Merville Beach Hotel
Mount Kenya Safari Club Ltd.	Kenya	68	68	Hotel proprietors
OI Pejeta Ranching Ltd.	Kenya	83	83	Proprietors of a ranch and game reserve
Princess Properties	Bermuda	100	100	Proprietors of hotels in the Bahamas, Bermuda and Mexico. Casino operators in the Bahamas
The Ark Ltd.	Kenya	60	60	Hotel proprietors
The Norfolk Ltd.	Kenya	100	81	Proprietors of the Norfolk Hotel

Source: Lonrho plc: *Annual Accounts and Report, 1993.*

Caribbean. Typically such ships are registered not in the country of their parent firm but in countries which offer flags of convenience, such as Panama and the Bahamas. In doing this, shipping companies can benefit from less stringent shipping regulations and lower taxes. The crewing of such ships is often provided from low-wage countries to cut costs, whilst the officers tend to be recruited from parent countries. Purchases of ship's stores and refittings can be done in ports which offer lowest costs.

Hotels

Major MNEs in the accommodation sector include Club Med. (France), Forte (UK), and Sheraton and Westin (USA). Lonrho plc owns international hotels as well as manufacturing companies. Lonrho's hotel interests are outlined in Table 17.1.

Scottish and Newcastle plc has interests in hotels including Golf Course Hotels Ltd., and the Netherlands-based Center Parcs NV, which operates holiday centres internationally. Bass plc owns the Holiday Inn Worldwide group. MNE hotels are able to exploit their international brand names and can often take advantage of cheap land prices at an early stage of the development of a tourist destination.

Leisure goods

BTR plc is a UK industrial conglomerate company which owns the Dunlop, Slazenger, Carlton and Maxfli sporting goods brands. It has recently commissioned a new factory in the Philippines to supply tennis balls to the North American and Far East markets. It is therefore able to combine cheap sourcing of goods from less developed countries with high-priced branded sales in developed countries' markets. Pro-Kennex, the world's largest manufacturer of rackets, also sources much of its products from low-wage economies and has been manufacturing in Taiwan since the 1960s. Wilson Sporting Goods, a leading supplier of golf and rackets to the UK market, is owned by the Amer Group, a Finnish company.

Leisure services

Wembley plc is known mainly for its ownership of Wembley stadium, but it also has multinational interests which exploit its stadium management skills. It won the contract to manage the Hong Kong stadium which opened in March 1994. The contract is operated through Wembley International (Hong Kong) Ltd. for the period to March 2004 with a further 5-year option. It also engages in international consultancy. Recent activities include design projects for Le Grand Stade, near Paris, for a new national stadium for the 1998 World Cup, and a stadium for the 1998 Commonwealth Games in Kuala Lumpur, Malaysia.

Effects of multinationals on host economies

The effects of MNEs on host economies are mixed. The main benefits can include:

- extra investment and related effects
- technology and skills transfer

However some of the problems that can arise from MNE activities include:

- leakages from the economy
- prices and bargaining power

- exporting of externalities
- threat to local competition
- power to pull out
- enclaves and dual development
- resource grabbing

Benefits of multinationals to host country

Extra investment

The key benefit to host economies is the introduction of new investment. Such investment will represent investment which is extra to that which a host economy is able to generate itself and is important because capital tends to be scarce in developing countries and such capital shortages can retard economic development. The effects of such investment will be the primary effects (resulting from construction of facilities, etc.) and the secondary effects (resulting from running of the facilities). As discussed in Chapter 14, the investment will give rise to extra income and growth in the economy and the associated benefits in terms of employment and foreign currency earnings.

Technology and skills transfer

It may be that the use of skilled labour and advanced technology introduced to an area by MNEs transfers to the local economy by way of demonstration effects. This depends partly upon the training and level of skilled employment offered by the MNE.

Problems of multinationals for host country

Leakages from the economy

MNE investment in an economy will generally generate more leakages than investment funded locally. This is because MNEs will remit profits to the parent company, often employ more foreign staff and sometimes use more imported inputs.

Prices and bargaining power

MNEs who represent monopoly or near-monopoly purchasers of a local input (for example, hotel rooms) will be able to negotiate low prices with suppliers and thus reduce the impact of foreign expenditure in a local host area.

Exporting of externalities

It is sometimes alleged that the reaction of MNEs to environmental pressures and legislation in parent countries is to set up overseas in order to avoid extra compliance costs. In this view, externalities of production are simply exported, often to less developed countries which are sometimes keen to accept such externalities in order to retain international competitiveness.

Threat to local competition

The low-cost, high-technology and high-quality goods and services associated with MNEs may make it difficult for new local firms to enter the industry. This is illustrated in Figure 17.3.

LRAC represents a typical long-run average cost curve associated with the production of a particular product. It is downward-sloping, reflecting the considerable economies of scale that are derived from large-scale production. Because of its size and international buying power, an MNE is likely to enjoy low average costs of 0C at a large global level of output 0B. New domestic firms trying to enter the market will face higher average costs of 0D associated with their small size 0A, and thus find it difficult to compete.

Power to pull out

MNEs, like other private sector organizations, seek to maximize profits. They are therefore constantly monitoring the environment to exploit changes in international costs or demand patterns. They thus have no particular loyalty to an area and can pull out, taking with them foreign expenditure (in the case of tour operators) or employment (in the case of manufacturers).

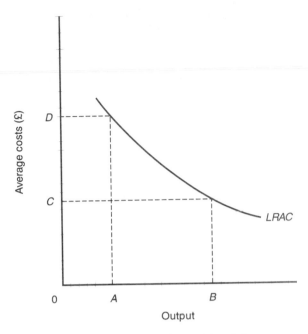

Figure 17.3 Costs for MNEs and local firms. LRAC = Long-run average cost curve.

Enclaves and dual development

One possible result of MNE investment is that a development will be exclusively for foreigners and exclude local people. For example, the Coral Resort owned by a Japanese company on the island of Cebu in the Philippines is guarded by armed security personnel and the beach area is only accessible to Coral Resort guests. Exclusive developments such as these are termed enclaves.

Resource grabbing

Local resource prices in developing countries (particularly land) are often low in international terms, and developing countries are generally short of capital and foreign exchange. MNEs tend to have ready access to capital and thus are granted planning permission. One result of this is that MNEs may purchase large areas of land relatively cheaply. This resource is then lost to local exploitation which might be appropriate at a future stage of a country's development. At a

Japanese golf course development in the Philippines it was calculated that 150 hectares of land were bought for 150 million yen, a fraction of land prices in Japan, and that the development would yield 600 million yen of income by recruiting just 300 members out of an eventual target of 1600 members.

Government policy and multinationals

Governments view the activities of MNEs with mixed feelings, on the one hand attempting to encourage them and the increased income, employment and foreign exchange earnings they can bring, but on the other hand conscious of less attractive characteristics.

Government assistance for multinationals

Because of the potential benefits to a host economy, governments often offer incentive packages to MNEs to attract their projects. For example, Initial estimates for Disneyland Paris suggested that the project would create 18 000 jobs in the construction phase and 12 000 jobs in the operating phase as well as earning US$700m in foreign currency each year. Because of this there was considerable competition between the governments of France, the UK and Spain to provide the most attractive incentive package to attract Disneyland Paris and enable their national economies to benefit from its effects. In the event the French government provided a comprehensive infrastructure package including new roads and rail connections. It assisted Disneyland Paris with land purchase, provided a loan at preferential interest rates and gave planning permission for future linked developments.

Government resistance to multinationals

Competitive threat

In some cases governments may think that MNE expansion in their country may pose a danger to domestic companies and thus may attempt to limit MNE expansion, as exhibit 17.3 illustrates.

Exhibit 17.3 Britain tries to break US stalemate over Virgin–Delta deal

The UK transport secretary John MacGregor has announced that he is willing to approve the Virgin–Delta code-sharing partnership which would enable the companies to market an integrated service.

Yesterday, however, Mr Pena, his US equivalent, was unable to give Mr MacGregor any commitments over the deal, because he is still receiving representations from other US carriers which have been lobbying hard to block it.

Source: *Guardian*, 2 August 1994 (adapted).

Power and accountability

Another government concern regarding MNEs is that of their power and accountability. Some MNEs have turnovers that exceed the GNPs of smaller economies, and this can make some governments feel impotent in terms of policy. Similarly, MNEs, through their substantial resources, can exert considerable powers lobbying governments to protect and promote their interests. In some cases the nature of a MNE's product or service can be threatening to governments. This is particularly so in media services. News Corporation has worldwide ownership of newspaper titles as well as world satellite television interests. News Corporation is thus able to exert a considerable influence on public opinion.

Transfer pricing and tax losses

Because MNEs conduct business across national frontiers, they can often rearrange their accounts to minimize their tax position. This is known as transfer pricing. Transfer pricing takes advantage of different rates of corporation tax in different countries. Assume there are two countries. Country A has corporation tax of 40 per cent and country B has corporation tax of 20 per cent. It will clearly pay an MNE that operates across countries A and B to ensure that most of its profits are earned in country B and thus pay a smaller amount of tax. It does this by adjusting the internal prices of goods traded within the company.

For example, if it imports raw materials for its manufacturing plant in country A from its plant in country B, it can charge itself an artificially high price for these materials. In doing so it will make high profits in country B but pay the lower rate of 20 per cent corporation tax on them. The results of this will mean that profits on finished goods sold in country A will have been lowered due to the high import charges, thus payments of high corporation tax (40 per cent) in country A are minimized. This means that more profits are retained across the MNE's international operations and that country A loses tax revenue.

Review of key terms

- Globalization = organization of a firm's production and sales on a worldwide basis.
- Multinational enterprise (MNE) = one which has production or service capacity located in more than one country.
- Parent country – base country of MNE.
- Host country – country in which MNE is operating.
- Greenfield development = new investment on a new site.
- National diamond = product or service for which a country has built a world reputation.
- Product life cycle = stages in marketing of product from growth to maturity and decline.
- Tariff barriers = taxes on goods imported into a geographic area (e.g. the EU).
- Code sharing = packaging of interconnecting flights of linked airlines into one flight code.
- Demonstration effect = method by which skills and technology are transferred to a host economy by participation of local labour.
- Enclave = local MNE development which is isolated from the main host economy.
- Resource grabbing = MNE utilizing of host country's resources which prevents later domestic utilization.
- Transfer pricing = adjusting the prices of goods traded internally within MNEs to minimize tax.

Data questions

Task 17.1   Holiday Inn Worldwide

Holiday Inn Worldwide has more than 1770 hotels and 338 000 guest rooms, making it the single largest hotel brand in the world. Throughout 1993, 159 hotels were added and joint venture agreements signed in Mexico, Indonesia and India, with development agreements in Germany and South Africa.

Approximately 90 per cent of Holiday Inn hotels are owned by franchisees. Hotel owners select the Holiday Inn name because they want the global marketing power of the strongest brand name in the hotel industry. They want the most advanced hotel reservation system to deliver the maximum number of room nights. Over the past year, a global sales force has been established to market hotel rooms to multinational corporations, travel agents and tour operators. Holiday Inn is the industry leader in provision of regular on-site training to staff. Holiday Inn Worldwide believes that its brand strength, enhanced by the investment in the systems described above, will enable it to increase significantly over the next five years the number of hotels flying the Holiday Inn flag.

Source: *Annual Report of Bass plc* (1993).

Questions

1 Why did Bass plc acquire Holiday Inn Worldwide?
2 Why does Holiday Inn Worldwide use franchising rather than direct ownership to expand its international operations?
3 What are the benefits to Holiday Inn Worldwide of multinational expansion?
4 What are the main benefits and problems to the Indian government of the Holiday Inn joint venture agreement?

Task 17.2   Dixons will revamp loss-making US arm – Heather Connon

Dixons Group, the electrical retailer, yesterday admitted that it had to make significant changes at Silo, its US operation, where it ran up £58.6m in losses and restructuring provisions in the year to 1 May.

John Clare, group managing director, said that it was unlikely that Silo could be returned to profit in its current format. 'In most of our markets we are number three, so we are always under pressure from the competition.' The stores were too small and poorly located, which meant 'we are working with one hand tied behind our backs'.

It has already closed 45 stores, mainly in the Midwest, and another 11 are earmarked for closure this year, leaving it with 185. That required a £36.2m provision, and Dixons warned that further provisions could be required this year, depending on the strategy it adopted.

The actual business lost £22.4m, up from £16.9m last time, despite static like-for-like sales, as it tried to woo customers with lower prices. California, which accounts for a fifth of selling space, suffered particularly badly. Two new formats were now being tested which, if successful, could be expanded to other areas. But Mr Clare warned that any changes would be made slowly, one region at a time.

The first pilot, which started trading at the weekend, is in Rochester, New York. Dixons has increased the size of three Silo stores, rebranding them as YES – Your Electronics Store. These specialize in brown goods – particularly computers and other home office equipment – but do not stock any white goods such as fridges. The second is in Chicago, where four stores have been expanded and started trading a few weeks ago. The results of the pilot studies, however, will not be clear for some months.

Silo is the latest in a series of disastrous forays into the USA by British retailers. Marks & Spencer, Laura Ashley, Sock Shop and Ratners are among those that have suffered from expansion there. Dixons paid £210m for Silo in 1987, and it made £16.8m profit on £398.3m of sales the following year. Since then, however, profits have fallen consistently despite rising sales. Mr Clare admitted that Dixons had allowed the management to continue its traditional strategy of increasing sales, even if it was at the expense of profits.

The Silo losses meant that Dixons' profit before tax fell from £50.1m to £33.5m despite a strong performance on the British high street. The results were worse than the market had expected and Dixons shares closed down 15p at 190p.

Source: *The Independent*, 8 July 1993 (adapted).

Questions

1   Why did Dixons buy US retailer Silo?
2   Why has the Silo arm of Dixons been unsuccessful?
3   What problems might Marks & Spencer, Laura Ashley, Sock Shop and Ratners face in extending their operations overseas?
4   What has happened to the Dixon/Silo link post-case? Why?

Task 17.3   Shares: buy American pie: eight big US stocks should thrive on global prospects – Quentin Lumsden

Shares in big, often branded, high-quality US multinational growth companies as Coca-Cola, McDonalds, Gillette and Microsoft, have recently been trading close to all-time peaks.

The most important reason for buying these shares is that they are in transition from being US companies to global enterprises, and they have the whole world to target for sales growth.

One of the most dramatic developments in that world market is the emergence of millions of consumers with significant discretionary spending power and a taste for the material trappings of US culture – fridges, soft drinks, computer software, films and television programmes.

The flavour of what is happening is reflected in two recent cover stories in the US business magazine *Fortune*. One highlighted the explosive growth of middle classes around the world; the other conjured up a picture of a global market for teenagers, with shared tastes and styles from London to Tokyo.

Many of these companies have relatively mature operations in the USA and are increasingly looking overseas for their future growth. Further benefit comes from an undervalued dollar, which makes US business highly competitive in world terms and means that their overseas earnings translate into large numbers of dollars.

Last, but not least, is the way these great corporations have teamed to operate on foreign soil where, like McDonalds in Russia or Toys 'R' Us in Japan, they have plenty of tricks to teach the natives. Eight US companies would give UK investors quality exposure to these trends. The shares are Microsoft, McDonalds, Coca-Cola, Mattel, Whirlpool, Compaq, Toys 'R' Us and Walt Disney. Not the least of the attractions of these companies is that they have huge experience in defending their brands against fierce competition.

Source: *Independent on Sunday*, 12 June 1994 (adapted).

Questions

1 What is the stimulus for the above firms to expand their overseas operations?
2 What is meant by the expression that MNEs 'have plenty of tricks to teach the natives'?
3 Should foreign governments welcome investment by the above firms in their countries?
4 Explain the success of McDonalds' global strategy compared with the problems of Dixons' global strategy examined in the previous case.

Task 17.4 Auntie battles for the skies – Neil Thapar

Two of the most venerable members of the UK establishment are joining forces to take on the world's giants in the booming satellite television industry. They are the BBC, with a 60-year tradition in public service, and Pearson, the banking-to-publishing conglomerate.

Last week, the duo set the seal on an ambitious global alliance aimed at developing satellite television in key markets around the world. That task will begin with the launch of two channels in Europe later this year, and could be the blueprint for similar ventures in other parts of the world, including North America and the Middle and Far East.

The move is the latest in the massive carve-up of the world's burgeoning satellite television market by a handful of media tycoons, including Rupert Murdoch, who runs News Corporation, and Ted Turner, the American who controls the CNN news channel. The British face an uphill task in winning their share at the table, because they are joining the party much later than their rivals. For example, western Europe is already being bombarded by a mix of pop music, news, sport and special-interest stations that range from Red Hot Dutch, the porn broadcaster, to the Parliamentary Channel for political junkies.

In the past 6 months, the BBC and Pearson have been engaged in intense talks to hammer out a broad strategy for exploiting the booming demand for satellite TV. The BBC already has a huge following through its World Service radio station. BBC World Service Television, launched 3 years ago, has built up a loyal audience running into 10s of millions across Asia, Africa and Europe. Further expansion is expected later this year with the start of a new service in the Middle East and Japan.

But, hampered by limited cash resources – it is not allowed to use its licence fee for satellite TV because of its charter – the BBC has been forced to seek partners with deeper pockets. Enter Pearson, which has ambitions to become a big international media group. Last year, Pearson hoped to buy a £100m stake in Star Television, the rapidly growing Asian satellite station. It was outgunned by Mr Murdoch, who paid Li Ka-shing, the Hong Kong billionaire who founded Star, £350m in return for a 63 per cent interest.

But together, the BBC and Pearson could soon be in a position to mount a serious challenge to the global media Goliath already hovering over the world's skies. 'We are already number one in world radio; we are determined to be number one in TV,' John Birt, BBC's director-general, said. Above all, the venture will draw on the BBC's network of more than 250 correspondents worldwide to provide news and features tailored for a European audience.

However, the new venture is entering an increasingly crowded market. According to a recent survey by *Satellite TV Finance*, an industry newsletter, more than 90 satellite channels are already available to European homes and the total is rising inexorably.

Experts believe that to succeed it will have to offer something audiences across the Channel cannot obtain from existing suppliers.

'The unique selling feature of these two channels could be the BBC brand name which is generally associated with high-quality programmes,' said Dan Allen, media consultant at the accountants Coopers & Lybrand. 'Confidential studies show that the viewers recognize only two brands in the media industry – Disney and the BBC. That could be very important in attracting a large audience in Europe.'

By all measures, the European market for satellite is growing rapidly. According to Zenith, which buys airtime on behalf of advertisers, the total number of homes with access to satellite television has risen from 37 million in 1992 to almost 50 million, and is forecast to increase to 71 million by 2000. The two are also considering similar ventures in North America, Africa and the Far East.

The Asian market, centred around China and the Indian subcontinent, with a total population of about 2 billion – half the world's total – is likely to be high on its list. In the past 3 years, Star TV has built up an audience of 45 million in Asia – mostly Chinese and Indian viewers. But last year, the BBC's existing television service was taken off Star's 'northern beam' – one of its two transmission beams – on Mr Murdoch's orders as a result of political pressure from the Chinese government. Alarmed by the impact of uncensored current affairs and western culture on public opinion, Peking had threatened to ban the ownership of satellite receivers in China.

Satellite television has also sparked political controversy in India through concerns that the Indian culture could come under siege from western broadcasters, over whom the government has little control. Many Indians are also worried that western soaps, suggestive music videos and other foreign programmes could destabilize a deeply traditional society that is, as yet, unprepared for an massive onslaught of consumerism and alien moral values.

However most experts believe that the encroachment of satellite TV is unstoppable, even in closed societies. Chris Jenkins at management consultants PA Consulting said: 'There are so many ways western programming can get in that attempts to stop it will probably not succeed.'

Source: *Independent on Sunday*, 15 May 1994 (adapted).

Questions

1 Who are the major players in the global provision of satellite TV?
2 What is the motive of the BBC for global expansion?
3 Identify and explain the main barriers to the BBC/Pearson plans.
4 Identify and explain what factors may enable successful global expansion for BBC/ Pearson.
5 What are the main benefits and problems for receiver countries of MNE satellite TV provision?

Short questions

1 What MNEs exist in the leisure goods, leisure services and tourism sectors of the economy? What makes these companies MNEs?
2 Why and how are airlines 'going global'?

3 Using a a named overseas project of an MNE, evaluate:
   (a) the benefits of the project to the host country
   (b) the problems of the project to the host country
   (c) the benefits of the project to the MNE
4 What is meant by transfer pricing?
5 Why do MNEs invest from and to the UK?

Reference

Porter, M., *The Competitive Advantage of Nations*, Macmillan, 1990.

Further reading

Bull, A., *An Evaluation of Direct Foreign Investment in the Australian Tourism Industry*, Proceedings of the Frontiers of Australian Tourism Conference, Canberra, 1988.

Crum, R. and Davies, S., *Multinationals*, Heinemann, 1991.

Davies, S. and Lund, M., MNEs: some issues and facts, *Economic Review*, March 1989.

Doganis, R., *Flying Off Course: The Economics of International Airlines*, Allen and Unwin, 1985.

Dunning, J., *Transnational Corporations and the Growth of Services: Some Conceptual and Theoretical Issues*, UN Center on Transnational Corporations, 1990.

Jones, G. (ed.), *British Multinationals: Origins, Management and Performance*, Gower House, 1986.

Littlejohn, D., Towards an economic analysis of trans/multinational hotel companies, *International Journal of Hospitality Management*. 1985; 4.

Part Six

Leisure and Tourism and Environmental Issues

18

Environmental impacts of leisure and tourism

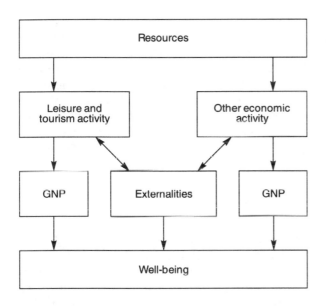

Objectives

Chapters 14–16 examined the contribution of leisure and tourism to countries' national economies. Traditionally, economic analysis has measured impacts in terms of readily measurable variables such as employment, balance of payments and GNP. The objective of this chapter however is to examine the issues raised by environmental economics.

Environmental economics involves a wider view of the impact of economic development and growth, taking into account well-being rather than just measuring how much richer people

become in monetary terms. Issues such as global warming, acid rain and resource depletion have been highlighted as threats to economic growth and even to the future of our species, and critiques and techniques developed by environmental economists can be readily used in the leisure and tourism sector.

First, questions can be raised about the validity of focusing measures of success solely on the uncritical use of GNP data. Second, environmental accounting techniques seek to include a wide rage of considerations when considering the cost and benefits of particular projects. These include effects on the natural and built environment, as well as raw material and waste product issues.

When subjected to environmental scrutiny, the leisure and tourism sector can display examples of previously unaccounted overall benefits as well as costs. Additionally, as well as being the perpetrator of negative environmental effects, the sector is sometimes the victim of environmental pollution caused elsewhere.

After studying this chapter students will be able to:

- distinguish between growth in GNP and growth in well-being
- distinguish between renewable and non-renewable resources (sources) and analyse the use of such resources
- understand the significance of waste disposal capacity (sinks) to the economy
- analyse the effects of the existence of open-access resources on resource use

- identify the existence of externalities and their contribution to well-being

Economic growth and well-being

Chapter 15 considered the contribution of the leisure and tourism sector to economic growth. Economic growth was measured by examining changes in real GNP per capita. Environmental economists point out that such figures may give a misleading impression about improvements in economic well-being for the following reasons:

- The environmental costs of producing goods and services which appear in GNP are not always accounted for.
- The distribution of the benefits of economic growth is not always even.
- GNP figures may include 'defensive' expenditure.
- The destruction of the natural environment is not shown.

Exhibit 18.1 demonstrates some of these concepts in relation to the development of an airport.

Exhibit 18.1 Development and well-being

The building and the running of an airport will add to GNP in terms of expenditure on building materials, fixtures and fittings, roads and access, staffing and consumables. However local residents will suffer from increased noise and atmospheric pollution as well as traffic congestion – none of these costs will appear in GNP data.

Whilst some local residents may benefit in terms of job opportunities, gainers and losers are often different people. The main gainers from the development are the shareholders of the airport company, airlines and tour operators, employees, and travellers themselves. Local residents are likely to form only a small fraction of these categories and so the benefits of such growth will be unevenly shared. GNP per capita figures only show average effects of growth.

Because of the extra noise, some residents will buy double glazing, more petrol will be used because of traffic congestion, and roofing contractors will gain more work because of vortex effects of aircraft (the tendency of aircraft engine thrust to cause intense patches of air currents which remove roof tiles). This is defensive expenditure. It is expenditure made to try to combat some of the ill-effects of the development. It does not leave anyone better off than before the development, but it contributes to GNP data, exaggerating the apparent benefits of the development.

Finally the development will involve loss of the natural environment. This represents the loss of an amenity to some people in terms of views or tranquillity or open space, but again this loss fails to register in GNP data.

The discussion in exhibit 18.1 shows the need for caution in equating growth in GNP with growth in well-being. Indeed, some economists have argued that when a wider view of economic growth is taken, the costs may exceed the benefits. Such analysis has caused the questioning of policies which lead to fastest economic growth without regard to the wider consequences and some environmental economists have called for a halt or limit to economic growth.

Externalities

The notion of externalities has already been briefly discussed in Chapter 7. Externalities are those costs or benefits arising from production or consumption of goods and services which are not reflected in market prices. Because of this there is little incentive for firms to curb external costs, since they do not have to pay for them. Externalities can be divided into the following categories:

- Production on production. This is where one firm's external costs interfere with the operation of another firm, e.g. noise form discos and clubs which creates a noise nuisance to hotel residents.
- Production on consumption. This is where industrial externalities affect individuals' consumption of a good or service, e.g. aircraft noise affects people trying to listen to music; increase in crime levels in resorts; visual

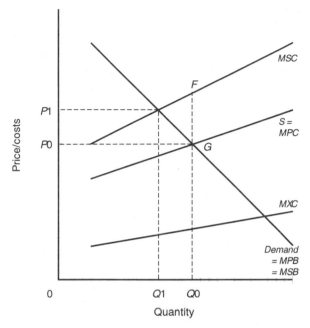

Figure 18.1 External costs, private costs and optimium output. See text for details.

pollution of hotels, caravans and car parks affects enjoyment of landscape.

- Consumption on production. This occurs when for example external costs of consuming a good or service interfere with a firm's production process, e.g. traffic jams caused by a leisure park cause transport delays to local firms.
- Consumption on consumption. This is where the external effects of an individual's consumption of a good or service affect the well-being of another consumer, e.g. holiday-makers destroying coral reef, congestion around a football stadium causing inconvenience to other people.

Figure 18.1 shows how firms tend to over-produce goods and services which are subject to externalities.

Demand curve *D* shows the marginal private benefit of consuming the good and, assuming there are no external benefits, it also represents the marginal social benefit. It shows how much

consumers are willing to pay for extra units of output. Supply curve *S* shows the marginal private costs of production, i.e. costs per extra unit of output.

Producers will wish to expand their output to $0Q0$ since the price they receive from extra units of production will exceed the costs of extra units of production up to that point. Beyond that point the extra costs of producing each good will exceed the price received for it. Thus $0Q0$ represents the optimal market level of production.

Curve *MXC* represents marginal external costs, perhaps because of noise or other pollution effects. Adding *MXC* to *MPC* generates the marginal social cost curve *MSC*. Notice that now we include external costs, i.e. previously unpriced environmental resources, the level of output $0Q0$ is no longer optimal, since marginal social costs exceed marginal social benefits by the amount *FG*. A reduction in output to $0Q1$ where *MSC* = *MSB* would need to take place to provide the optimal social level of production.

The case of sewage discharges into the sea illustrates this point. Whilst there is little marginal private cost to the water companies for pumping sewage into the sea, it represents a loss of well-being to people who want to use the sea. There is a considerable marginal external cost which takes the form of cleaning costs to surf equipment, medical costs to treat infections and loss of earnings caused by sickness. These are readily quantifiable costs to which must be added the general unpleasantness of contact with sewage. Exhibit 18.2 considers some of the externalities posed by tourism development in Greece.

Exhibit 18.2 Tourism curse visited on this blessed Aegean isle

The Greek island of Amorgos is rugged, barren and beautiful.

But things are changing fast since locals can now make more money through tourism in 2 months than they could otherwise make in a year.

The tourism boom is taking its environmental toll. There are growing problems with water, sewage and rubbish, although officials are reluctant to acknowledge them.

'If we're careful we'll be all right. Our only real problem is plastic water bottles,' says Mr Vekris, a local mayor. 'You know the quality of our lives has really improved with tourism'.

And indeed it has. It has meant washing machines and colour televisions for local inhabitants, but these are luxuries that will ultimately be at the expense of Amorgos.

Source: *Guardian*, 6 September 1994 (adapted).

It demonstrates the fine balance that has to be achieved in tourism development, with over-development causing degradation of the place itself, which can threaten future demand and prosperity.

Another consequence that may stem from such development is that price inflation and property prices may rise, making it increasingly difficult for those not participating in the development, and thus benefiting from rising wages and profits, to remain in the area. This effect is termed economic dualism and occurs where a traditional and a growing sector of the economy exist side by side. The growing sector may increasingly threaten the traditional sector and participants in the traditional sector may only be able to access limited parts of the growing sector.

It is also possible to identify less obvious, distant, external costs of tourism and leisure developments. For large-scale resort developments, for example, consideration can be given to the sources of raw materials for building and the subsequent effect of quarrying for stone or forest depletion for timber.

Use of resources

Environmental economics distinguishes between two types of resources. Non-renewable resources are those which have a fixed supply. Once they have been used up there will be none left for future generations. Renewable resources are those which are capable of being replenished.

Non-renewable resources

Landscapes, views, open spaces and tranquillity represent non-renewable resources in the leisure and tourism sector. They are used up by general economic development as well as by leisure and tourism development itself. An important consideration concerning the use of non-renewable resources is the rate of depletion and hence the level of resources bequeathed to future generations.

The urgency of this problem can be illustrated as follows: Economic development uses up such resources. It also generates increases in incomes and leisure time and thus the demand for such resources. Thus we have the prospect of dwindling natural resources having to provide for increasing demands and thus degeneration occurring at a quickening pace.

Renewable resources

An important renewable resource for large-scale tourism development in some parts of the world is water. Large-scale development requires considerable resources of fresh water. It is here that the technique of impact assessment is important. Forecasts need to be made of water use against water renewal, although in some circumstances the latter may be supplemented by water diversion schemes. If water is obtained from underground aquifers, these will eventually run dry or be subjected to salt or other pollution if the rate of extraction exceeds the rate of replenishment.

This problem is compounded by the free access problem, where it is not in anyone's interests to preserve water if everyone is drawing it from the same source.

Resources such as footpaths and public parks also have a renewable resource element to them. If the rate of wear of footpaths for example exceeds the rate of regeneration of protective vegetation, degradation will occur, as illustrated in exhibit 18.3.

Exhibit 18.3 Calls for brake on mountain biking – Nicholas Schoon

The government is pondering whether restrictions on mountain bikes may be necessary because their growing popularity is damaging some of the nation's best scenery.

This week a report to be published by the Council for the Protection of Rural England will highlight mountain biking as one of the ways in which unrestricted countryside leisure and tourism are increasingly harming the environment. The cyclists often use footpaths, although the law says they should be restricted to bridle ways and byways. The broad, high-grip tyres they use are stripping out vegetation and leaving deep, muddy furrows.

Walkers and ramblers complain that they are irritated and frightened by mountain bikes that pass them at speed. Some regard the bicycles as an inappropriate, unnatural leisure pursuit in cherished landscapes such as the 11 national parks of England and Wales.

Source: *Independent*, 9 May 1994 (adapted).

One of the reasons for such overuse and degradation is that the use of footpaths and public parks is free to the user. In markets where prices prevail, price is an important factor in rationing the demand for scarce resources. Consumers economize on use so as to conserve their limited money income. Where price is zero, there is no incentive to economize. The use of unmetered water illustrates this point. For example, many people leave the tap on when they are cleaning their teeth, using a couple of pints of water where only half a cupful is needed since there is no incentive to economize on use. Figure 18.2 shows the economics behind this.

Curve D represents the demand curve for the use of a footpath. As price falls, demand rises. At price P2 demand would be Q2. If zero price is charged, demand rises to 0Q0. For some paths this may result in usage which exceeds the limits where the resource can regenerate itself. If 0Q1 represents the point of use beyond which regeneration cannot take place, then Q1Q0 represents use which causes degeneration of the resource at zero price.

The macroeconomy and waste

Figure 18.3 recalls the simple circular flow of income model used earlier to underpin introductory macroeconomic analysis.

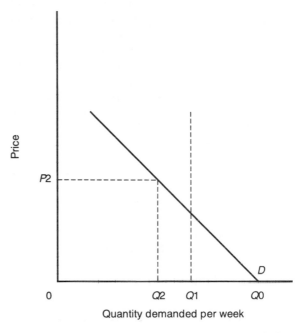

Figure 18.2 Effects of zero price on demand. See text for details.

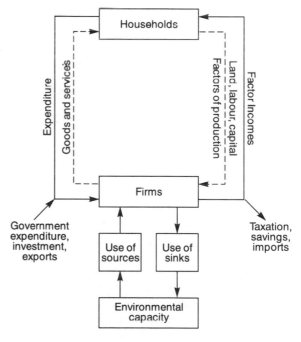

Figure 18.3 The circular flow of income and environmental capacity.

Factors of production are purchased by firms from households and combined to produce goods and services which are then sold to households. Household expenditure is financed from the income derived from selling factors of production to firms. Additionally there are leakages from the system in the form of taxes, savings and imports, as well as injections into the system of government spending, investment and exports.

However, in its simple form, the model fails to illustrate some key points about the relationship of the economy to the environment. In particular it fails to show the production of waste materials (use of sinks) and the using-up of resources (use of sources). In fact the production of waste materials is partially covered by the model and partially not. Exhibit 18.4 illustrates this point.

Exhibit 18.4   Surfing in the sewers

'I've just come back from a surf. The water quality wasn't too bad today because the wind was blowing offshore and the tide was going out. When the wind blows on to the shore and when the tide is high you still get the occasional pad or condom floating by.'

The surfers are far from happy. And it's not hard to see why. A quick walk on to the headland and you notice the air begins to smell rich, sweet and vile. A brown slick drifts out to sea off the point. Tucked away beneath the cliffs is its source – the same old sewage outflow pipe, pumping out output all day long.

Source: *Guardian*, 5 August 1994 (adapted).

The article is about Newquay in Cornwall, UK, whose population of 100 000 is swollen by up to a million summer visitors. A key product of the tourism industry is sewage. This waste is collected and partially treated by South West Water, and this activity is picked up by traditional economics in the simple circular flow diagram as the use of factors of production to perform a service. However the raw sewage that is discharged directly into the sea represents the use of a waste sink and the simple circular flow model does not reflect this.

The circular flow model can show an increase in economic growth caused by tourism – increased expenditure, generating increased incomes which in turn allow increased expenditure – without highlighting a significant threat to such growth in terms of pollution effects. The use of the waste sink is free to South West Water and thus there is little incentive for it to amend its behaviour. There is, though, clearly a limit to the capacity of the sea to assimilate this waste. Where this assimilative capacity is exceeded, degradation of the sea occurs.

Environmental economics seeks to make the link between economic production – in this case tourism – on the one hand, and the production of and the ability of the ecosystem to absorb waste on the other. It further seeks to amend economic models to incorporate this relationship so that such economic development can take place without causing feedback which would threaten economic development, or cause an unacceptable level of pollution.

Thus Figure 18.3 adds an environmental dimension to the simple circular flow model to highlight that production uses sources and sinks and that the environment has a limited capacity to meet these demands.

Open access and overuse

There is a particular problem posed by open access to resources. The sea is an example of an open-access resource. It does not have a clear owner and therefore it is difficult to exert property rights over it – for example, preventing waste dumping. Because of this there is little incentive to reduce outflows into the sea.

The problem becomes more difficult with seas such as the Mediterranean. The Mediterranean coastline is shared by a number of countries. If one country should decide to reduce outflows of sewage into the sea, it will still suffer the ill-effects of the outflows from other countries who might even think that there is now more capacity for their sewage.

Exhibit 18.5 goes beneath the sea to record the destruction of an open-access resource.

Exhibit 18.5   Reefs under threat

It took thousands of years to create the majestic coral reefs that lie under the earth's oceans. These vast limestone structures have been laid over the centuries by reef-building corals. They are home to a huge diversity of plants and over 200 species of fish.

The Great Barrier Reef, off the coast of Australia, extends for some 2000 kilometres and is a magnet for scuba divers. The Belize Barrier Reef stretches for some 250 kilometres off the coast of Belize in central America.

But the reefs are under threat from industry, from agriculture and from tourism. Industrial fishing techniques using dynamite can blow up the fragile polyps that create the reefs. Rain forest clearance smothers the Belize Reef as thickly polluted run-off flows out of the rivers into the oceans.

Meanwhile, the tourism trade is set to kill one of its golden gooses. Whilst some boat operators practise good conservation methods and coach and cajole their clients to respect the coral, the growing size of the tourist tide threatens reef preservation. Boatloads of inexperienced snorkellers and divers regularly inflict unintentional damage, by touching sensitive polyps or smashing coral branches with a kick of a flipper.

But not all the damage is accidental. Some boat operators let their anchors drop on the reefs – the damage is evident by the clouds of debris thrown up. And some tourists seem unable to resist taking home just one small momento ('that won't make any difference'). For those who don't make the dive themselves there are plenty of willing hands – and souvenir shops in reef resorts are often full of rare shells and coral curios.

Source: *the author*, from press cuttings, January 1995.

Environmental effects of other sectors on the leisure and tourism sector

The general environmental concerns of global warming, ozone depletion, acid rain and atmospheric pollution each have impacts on the leisure and tourism sector.

The early 1990s for example witnessed successive years of poor snow conditions in European ski resorts. Global warming would clearly have an impact on the height of snow cover, thus putting low-level resorts out of business and shortening the length of the ski season. Exhibit 18.6 demonstrates alarming possible effects of global warming.

Exhibit 18.6   'Paradise' islands unite against sea-level threat: alarm over global warming – Geoffrey Lean

Fakaofu Atoll, the main island of the watery territory of Tokelau, has just one of the world's 400 million automobiles and it is making a lonely contribution to the island's impending extinction.

Tokelau, a group of islands administered by New Zealand – just 12 square kilometres of land in more than 250 000 square kilometres of Pacific Ocean – is expected, literally, to be wiped off the map by pollution. So are six other scattered strings of atolls, including similar dependencies and independent nations, among them the 1196-island state of the Maldives in the Indian Ocean.

As carbon dioxide emitted by fuel burned in the world's cars, homes and industries heats up the climate, many scientists believe that the seas will rise and eventually drown such low-lying islands.

Though small may be beautiful, however, it is also vulnerable. These islands' water supplies are usually limited and are increasingly being depleted by the tourism on which at least half their economies depend. Tourism increases pollution – only one-tenth of the sewage produced by the 20 million people who visit the Caribbean each year receives any kind of treatment. Increasingly dirty seas and oil spills imperil economies.

But the greatest threat of all comes from global warming. The highest point on the main island of Kiribas, in the Pacific Ocean, is 2 foot above sea level; and scientists' best estimate is that the seas will rise higher than this over the next century.

Source: *Independent on Sunday*, 13 March 1994 (adapted).

Carbon dioxide emissions, the main source of which is fossil-fuel burning, are the main contributor to global warming. Some commentators have predicted an increase in the average surface temperature of the earth of between 2 and 5°C over the next hundred years if carbon dioxide emissions double over the same period.

However not only are the physics and the chemistry of this calculation fraught with uncertainty, but so are the economics. It is difficult to predict the rate of economic growth and the subsequent demand for fossil-fuel burning for energy provision. Also there is a time lag between the emission of greenhouse gases and the effect on global warming.

Ozone depletion may also affect the leisure and tourism sector. The ozone layer is a layer of gas around the earth which protects it from ultraviolet radiation from the sun. Recent thinning of the ozone layer has been attributed to use of CFCs – chlorofluourocarbons – which have been used in the manufacture of spray cans and refrigerators. The main harmful effects of ozone depletion are to increase the danger of skin cancer after exposure to the sun. Clearly this may affect the demand for holidays based around sunbathing.

Acid rain is the term given to acidic deposits caused mainly by the emission of sulphur dioxide into the atmosphere by industry. Its main effects in the leisure and tourism sector include:

- corrosion of buildings (particularly the stonework found on cathedrals)
- damage to trees (making forest areas less attractive to tourism)
- pollution of rivers and lakes

The external effects of specific industrial developments can also have an impact on the leisure and tourism sector, as exhibit 18.7 illustrates.

Exhibit 18.7   Like lambs to the slaughter? – Jan Morris

When I came home from abroad recently to the village of Llanystumdwy in Gwynedd, I found a sort of maelstrom swirling around the place. And what had aroused the whirlwind was the district council's proposal to build an abattoir – to be attended, it seems, by various agricultural processing plants in what Eurospeak calls an 'agro-park'.

Our particular part of Gwynedd is a delightful but not a spectacular landscape and deserves its old classification as an area of Outstanding Natural Beauty. It also appears that the ordinary-looking patch of countryside where 12 acres for the agro-park are already being cleared is not only part of a Heritage Coast but also Some of the Best Farming Land in Gwynedd.

Then I learnt to my astonishment that the river into which the abattoir's effluent would flow is the Fourth Most Important Sea-Trout River in Great Britain. The effect on fishing and tourism, the pollution of local beaches – I cannot enumerate all the aspects of the issue towards which the indefatigable activists opposed to the abattoir, apparently in a few short weeks, had applied their minds.

Source: *Independent*, 16 April 1994.

Positive environmental effects of leisure and tourism

Although much of the environmental debate focuses on the detrimental effects of economic development, there are also benefits which can be noted. The inflow of foreign tourists to London for example sustains a breadth of theatres that could not be supported by the indigenous population. The existence of tourism in remote rural areas can make the difference between local shops remaining profitable, and therefore open, or not. Similarly the income and interest derived from tourists help to preserve heritage sites, contributing to restoration and upkeep. National parks and forest provide not only facilities for tourism but also preserve habitats for flora and fauna.

Review of key terms

- Environmental economics = analysis of human well-being as well as the flow of money in the economy.
- Defensive GNP expenditure = expenditure that takes place to defend or protect one party from the external effects of the activities of another (e.g. double glazing as a defence from noise pollution).
- Externalities = those costs or benefits arising from production or consumption of goods and services which are not reflected in market prices.

- Non-renewable resources = those which have a fixed supply.
- Renewable resources = those which are capable of being replenished.
- Waste sink = part of the environment where waste products are deposited.
- Assimilative capacity = ability of sink to absorb waste.

Data questions

Task 18.1 Cashing in on a hole in the sky: David Nicholson-Lord argues that green economics should replace Adam Smith

The adage that every cloud has a silver lining is even truer now that the sun is shining. This month saw the start of an alliance between Boots and the Cancer Research Campaign to promote 'sensible sun behaviour'. The benefits for the Cancer Research Campaign are obvious: extra money for research. But what's in it for Boots?

Here's a clue. There are five 'play safe in the sun' guidelines and at least three involve buying something: sunhats, sunglasses, suncream. Who sells sunglasses? Why, Boots does – in fact it is offering customers discounts if they trade in their old ones. Boots also sells suncream. The lucrative sun-protection market is worth £110m and Boots has about 47 per cent of it.

The hidden factor in all this is the gap in the ozone layer opening up 20 miles above our heads and letting in carcinogenic radiation. Skin cancer rates in the UK are double those of 20 years ago, and although lazing on foreign beaches is still largely to blame, the ozone factor is catching up fast. In the USA alone, accelerating ozone loss could cause an extra 200 000 skin-cancer deaths over the next 50 years. Profit margins on suncreams are about 50 per cent and the market is growing at around 4 per cent a year. Suncreams with a high protection factor make up 70 per cent of it. From a purely business perspective, holes in the ozone layer are exceptionally good news.

There is another, more serious angle to this. When the Treasury does its sums, that portion of the £110m sun-protection market arising from worries about ultravilet radiation will be added to GNP and will count as economic growth. Thanks to the hole in the ozone layer and the skin cancer epidemic, we will all be that little bit richer. As a way of measuring progress, this is clearly a nonsense, since the quality of our lives will undoubtedly be poorer.

Fortunately, some economists are developing a better way of assessing growth. Later this year the New Economics Foundation, a group of 'green' economists, will produce the UK's first index of sustainable welfare, a form of alternative GNP measuring progress since the fifties, not only in income but in areas such as health, education, diet and environmental quality. These developments signify that the environmental movement is evolving a coherent critique of conventional economic theory which includes a response to the accelerating pace of planetary degradation – global warming in particular.

The global free market emerges as one of the villains. To a generation nourished on the idea that unlimited free trade is a good thing, this may be hard to accept. It rests on the assumptions that, first, cash relationships are invading and destroying areas of community life in which they have no place; and second, far from being a benevolent 'invisible hand' – Adam Smith's phrase – the market is blind to the environmental and social destruction it causes. Hence the global cash economy is a game that only the rich and powerful can win.

Which brings us back to Boots and the GNP. In the postwar era, GNP has been transmuted from being a purely statistical tool into a national political goal. Unscrambling it promises to be an exercise both cathartic and revelatory. An index of sustainable economic welfare developed in the USA, for example, shows that while the sum total of economic activity, measuring both 'good' and 'bad' expenditure, has continued to increase, improvements in welfare levelled off in the late sixties and since 1979 have declined.

In other words, we have lots more suncream, sunglasses and sunhats – but we can't really enjoy the sunshine any more.

Source: *The Independent*: 31 May 1993 (adapted).

Questions

1 'Thanks to the hole in the ozone layer . . . we will all be that little bit richer.'
   (a) Explain what is meant by this.
   (b) Explain why 'this is clearly a nonsense'.
2 'The environmental movement is evolving a coherent critique of conventional economic theory.' Explain the meaning of this statement.
3 Explain what economic 'goods' and 'bads' derive from leisure and tourism economic activities.
4 Should green economics replace Adam Smith?

Task 18.2   Tourist overcrowding spoils enjoyment of historic venue: Chester approaches saturation point – David Nicholson-Lord

So many tourists are crowding into Chester, one of Britain's oldest and most beautiful cities, that they are spoiling it for each other, according to the first 'environmental capacity' study by a local authority.

The study, to be published next month, highlights the dilemma faced by many historic towns where visitor numbers are nearing saturation point. It examines pedestrian densities in the city using a test of psychological 'comfort' developed by an American academic.

According to the English Historic Towns Forum, centres such as Cambridge, York and Canterbury are struggling to cope with pollution, congestion and growing tensions between residents and visitors. Some towns are now trying to discourage visitors. The Chester study examined walking speeds, traffic flows and pedestrian numbers and found widespread evidence of tension caused by the 'competing demands for the limited street space in the heart of the city'. In much of the historic centre, pedestrian comfort was 'below acceptable levels', it said. 'In the most critical locations, [the] tension is strained beyond capacity.' The crowding was 'detracting from any pleasure of being in this historically rich environment'.

Chester, a city of 119 000, has an estimated 2–3 million visitors a year, most of whom crowd into a narrow centre inside the Roman walls. A spokesman for the city said pedestrian pressures were sometimes 'uncomfortable', adding: 'We are looking at what development Chester can sustain without further erosion of the fabric and the historic centre.' Pedestrianisation and new bus routes are being considered.

In a new guide for historic towns, the forum, and the English Tourist Board, urge them to adopt 'visitor management plans'. Stephen Mills, head of development at the board, said many places felt they had too many visitors 'but you can't stop people coming – therefore you need to manage them in order to survive'.

In Cambridge, however, the council has refused to promote the town. One theme suggested – but not adopted – was the 'Great Cambridge stay away day', with the slogan: 'Cambridge is full – we don't want you.'

York, according to the forum, has reached a ceiling on visitors.

Bourton-on-the-Water, the most visited village in the Cotswolds, also 'suffers intensely from congestion and other problems'. In Bath, residents had turned hosepipes on open-top tourist buses.

Source: *The Independent*, 31 May 1994.

Questions

1 What are externalities?
2 Classify the leisure and tourism-related externalities into:

(a)   production on production
(b)   production on consumption
(c)   consumption on consumption
(d)   consumption on production
3   What are the economic causes of 'crowding [that is] detracting from any pleasure of being in this historically rich environment [of Chester]'.

Task 18.3   Book review: 'A postcard home' by Robert Minhinnick – Jan Morris

There are many people in Wales who think the Welsh Tourist Board fulfils its functions deplorably, on the one hand representing Wales and the Welsh in a tired parade of clichés, on the other blindly hastening the country towards a national degradation of heritage centres, theme parks and horrible marinas.

Among them is the poet Robert Minhinnick, and this small book is a gentle polemic which is of far more than local import, and might well be addressed to tourist authorities anywhere. It is a cogent and persuasive plea for a redirection of the tourist industry, away from mere monetary exhibitionism towards a truly instructive and creative role in society.

Minhinnick is not ideologically opposed to tourism, though he rightly scoffs at official statistics that vastly overstate its importance to Welsh well-being. A large proportion of the people who earn their living by it are incomers from England, the Welsh themselves all too often being flaccid puppets in the business. He wants it, though, to be publicly dedicated not to the exploitation, but the conservation of Wales – its landscape, its language and its culture.

This means, as it must everywhere in the world, abandoning the heedless encouragement of mass tourism. The greater the influx of tourists, the cruder their quality (and Wales stands next door to the crudest reservoir of tourists in Europe) and the more corroding their influence upon the host country. Everyone admits that the inexorable migrations of holidaymakers distort the identities of vulnerable small countries; yet still tourist authorities everywhere, and not least Mr Redwood's quango in Cardiff, boast of the increasing number of tourists they attract each year.

Minhinnick is urging a change of heart among tourist authorities. He wants the Welsh Tourist Board, in particular, to produce a Charter for Tourism unequivocally committing itself to supporting the environment and the language of Wales.

Minhinnick is not altogether despondent anyway. He even allows himself to think that tourism, like coal-mining, may not be a permanent industry after all. I wish I could believe him. When I walk along the sand at Morfa Bychan on the Gwynedd coast, though, below the church where the beloved poet Dafydd y Garreg Wen lies, looking across to Harlech and the grey-blue Rhinog mountains – when I walk this lovely strand on a summer morning to see the chalets and caravans proliferating ever further along the sand dunes, and yesterday's crisp packets blowing along the foreshore, I remember wistfully an expert recommendation recently made to the Government of Tasmania that went much farther than Minhinnick's proposal; namely that Tasmania's best bet was to declare itself a tourist-free zone.

Source: *The Independent*, 22 January 1994.

Questions

1   What would be the impact on the Welsh economy and the Welsh environment of declaring Wales a tourist-free zone?
2   Is Minhinnick right to scoff at official statistics 'that vastly overstate [tourism's] importance to Welsh well-being'.
3   Compare the externalities of tourism to those of coal-mining.

Short questions

1   What additions and what subtractions would environmental economists like to see with regard to GNP figures?
2   Distinguish between the four types of externalities.
3   What unpriced externalities arise from the:
    (a)   location of a football stadium?
    (b)   building of the channel tunnel?
    (c)   development of a lakeside campsite?
4   Under what circumstances are renewable resources exhaustible?
5   What environmental problems arise from open-access resources?

Further reading

Jenner, P. and Smith, C., *The Tourism Industry and the Environment*, Economist Intelligence Unit, 1992.

Pearce, D.W., Markandya, A. and Barbier, E.B., *Blueprint for a Green Economy*, Earthscan, 1989.

Turner, R.K., Pearce, D. and Bateman, I., *Environmental Economics*, Harvester Wheatsheaf, 1994.

World Travel and Tourism Environmental Review Committee, *Travel and Tourism: Environment and Development*, WTTERC, 1992.

19

Sustainability and 'green' leisure and tourism

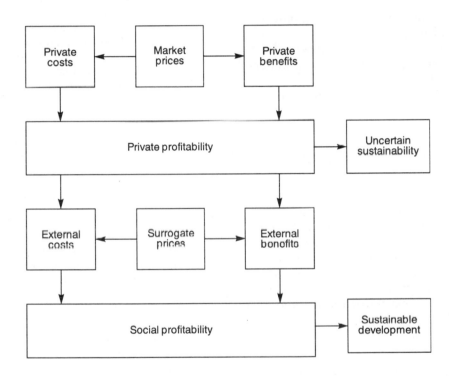

Objectives

Chapter 18 examined the environmental impacts of the leisure and tourism sector. It considered ways in which the market failed to signal long-term problems of resource depletion, waste production and disposal, and other unpriced externalities. It highlighted the distinction between what was most profitable for firms and what was most profitable for society as a whole. It chroni-cled a wealth of evidence of undesirable results if the market was left to dictate future developments without any regard for wider environmental considerations.

This chapter examines strategies for utilizing environmental economic analysis to enable development of the leisure and tourism sector to take place with due regard to possible side-effects. The aim of such analysis is to prevent the side-effects of development causing socially unacceptable damage to the environment or indeed to stifle the very developments themselves.

By studying this chapter students will be able to:

- understand the limitations of the price mechanism in allocating resources in respect of environmental considerations
- explain the meaning of sustainable development
- utilize the concept of cost–benefit analysis to determine the value of a project to society as a whole
- evaluate a variety of methods to impute value to unpriced externalities
- evaluate different policy instruments for encouraging sustainability and environmental consideration
- understand the range of influences on environmental policy

The price mechanism and the environment

The market economy does in fact have an inbuilt tendency to conserve resources. In the model where competing firms seek to maximize their profits, since profit is defined as total revenue minus total costs, there is a constant pressure to economize on resources and hence minimize costs. Exhibit 19.1 is a transcript of a report on the Radio 4 Today Programme which shows this principle in action.

Exhibit 19.1 Costs of green business a lie

Sue MacGregor:	Now, a book published this week appears to knock on its head the old adage that it costs business the earth to protect the environment: the authors of the book say the opposite is often the case. Roger Harabin reports on a news story that seems almost too good to be true.
First woman:	This is your room, sir.
Roger Harabin:	Hotels gobble power, and power pollutes.
First woman:	You've got the television over here; over here we've got a mini-bar, fully stocked . . .
Roger Harabin:	But one hotel group has switched on to a little-used form of power generation that's cleaner than others. At the Russell Hotel in central London the secret is in the basement. Here under the plush reception rooms is the hotel's very own generating station. In a normal power station the heat from making electricity goes to waste, but the Forte group has installed a system called combined heat and power which pipes the hot water to warm the bedrooms. The manager, Ben Sington, says the savings are enormous.
Ben Sington:	When they told me that they were going to give me a machine in this useless piece of space, and give me £6000 worth of savings a year I couldn't believe it, and it's true, it has given me that.

Source: The Today Programme, Radio 4, 12 September 1994 (adapted).

However the current market price of resources is not always an accurate measure of its true cost. This is particularly the case for unpriced open-access resources such as the sea. Chapter 18 explored the fact that, whilst the costs of sewage pumping into the sea were minimal for water companies, considerable pollution costs are incurred by other users of the sea. Similarly the loss of landscape and views caused by tourism destination development is not apparent in the profit and loss accounts of the organizations involved. Equally the price mechanism does not give due regard to the future. Overexploitation of non-renewable resources such as coastline, countryside, rivers and mountains may leave future generations materially worse off than the current population. These considerations mean that the market often leads to overproduction and overdevelopment of projects where there are considerable unpriced externalities.

Meaning of sustainable development

There is considerable debate about the precise definition of sustainable development. It should also be noted that several levels of sustainability may be considered. At the widest level, sustainability of world economic development embraces those planet-threatening issues of global warming, resource depletion and ozone loss. Sustainability can also be considered at a national economy level, at a regional level, at a tourism destination level and at an individual leisure or tourism project level.

The 1987 *Brundtland Report* for the World Commission on Environment and Development defined sustainability as 'development that meets the needs of the present without compromising the ability of future generations to meet their own needs'. It therefore laid considerable emphasis on what is termed 'intergenerational equity'.

Key elements in this approach to sustainable development are first, the rate of use of renewable and non-renewable resources and maintenance of natural capital. Implicit here is that renewable resources should not be used beyond their regenerative capacities. Additionally, where non-renewable resources are used up, future generations should be compensated by the provision of substitute capital in some form so that, at the minimum, a constant stock of capital is maintained across generations.

The second key element in the *Brundtland Report* is consideration of the effects of development on waste sinks.

Sustainability has also been defined as growth which is not threatened by feedback, for example, pollution, resource depletion or social unrest. This can be related to tourism destination development. In this case sustainability would be that level of development which did not exceed the carrying capacity of the destination and thus cause serious or irreversible changes to the destination. It is development that can sustain itself in the long run.

It is also possible to consider environmental costs and benefits when considering specific projects. This approach considers the total social and private costs against the total private and social benefits of a project with a view to summarizing its total social value, taking into consideration environmental impacts as well as market profitability.

The key principles of sustainability can be summarized as:

- consideration of externalities
- consideration of depletion of non-renewable resources
- tailoring use of renewable resources to their regenerative capacity
- tailoring of economic activity to the carrying capacity of the environment

Since the operation of the free market in its present form does not guarantee the inclusion of the above principles in resource allocation, it follows that the implementation of sustainable development will involve modifications of free market activity. These implementation issues are considered in the remainder of this chapter.

Cost–benefit analysis

Individuals are constantly, if unconsciously, performing private cost–benefit analyses when making purchasing decisions. They compare the costs to themselves of purchasing an item (its price) with the benefits of purchase (the satisfaction they receive). Similarly, firms compare the costs of producing an extra good or service with the benefits (revenue) received from doing so. Cost–benefit analysis makes similar comparisons except that it includes the wider costs and benefits to society as well as those accruing privately to firms and individuals.

For a project or development to be socially acceptable the sum of the benefits to society (including external and private benefits) must exceed the sum of the cost to society (including external and private costs). This may be written as

$$\Sigma B > \Sigma C$$

where Σ means 'the sum of', B = to the benefits to society and C = the costs to society.

A problem arises from using this equation in its raw form. When we measure costs and benefits, some happen immediately, and some happen at some future date. People would prefer to have money today than in the future. This is because £100 today is worth more than a promise of £100 in 10 years since it can earn interest in the intervening period. Therefore future values must be adjusted to give present values. This is known as discounting and the rate used to discount is generally related to the long-term interest rate. The formula for finding a present value is:

$$\frac{B_t}{(1+r)^t}$$

where B_t = the benefit in year t and r = the discount rate.

Thus incorporating discounting techniques to the formula for social acceptability for projects gives:

$$\frac{B_t}{(1+r)^t} > \frac{C_t}{(1+r)^t}$$

where C_t is the benefit in year t.

There is considerable debate amongst environmental economists about the use of discount rates since, if environmental damage resulting from a project results in the distant future, then its effects are minimized in cost–benefit analysis by discounting. It is felt by some that this attributes too little significance to, for example, the potential damage caused by storing nuclear waste.

Pricing the environment

It is relatively straightforward for firms to perform private cost–benefit analysis and determine a profit-maximizing level of output. The costs of inputs are readily available and selling prices can be gauged from scanning the competition, from historical data and, ultimately, are determined in the market. There are thus some firm figures which inform production levels.

However when we move into the arena of external costs and benefits we encounter the problem of missing markets and thus find pricing difficult. We can easily calculate the costs of aircraft use in terms of fuel, staffing and depreciation, but how do we measure the cost of aircraft noise? We clearly need to address this problem if we are to use cost–benefit analysis to determine a level of economic development which maximizes total private and social profitability.

Several methods have been developed by environmental economists to impute value for unpriced goods or services and these are now explained.

Willingness to pay (WTP) method

Here survey techniques are used to find out how much households are willing to pay for the preservation of an environmental asset – for example, a piece of woodland threatened by a road development. The survey can include people who are currently visiting the asset and those who do not visit it but care about it. The total valuation of the asset can then be found by multiplying the average WTP by the number of people who enjoy the asset.

The main difficulty of using the WTP method is whether respondents reply to the hypothetical WTP question in the same way as they would if faced with actual payment.

Hedonistic pricing method (HPM)

Hedonistic pricing values environmental resources by considering their effect on the prices of goods or services that have readily observable market prices. House prices are a convenient yardstick for this exercise.

House prices are affected by a number of factors – condition, number of rooms, central heating, garden size and nearness to transport and shops. They are also affected by environmental factors, for example prices will be depressed by the presence of aircraft noise and increased by the presence of a park. HPM involves the collection of data recording price, and the presence or absence of all the salient determinants of price. Once a price can be established to reflect the non-environmental factors (number of rooms, etc.) then the effects of the environmental factor under analysis (e.g. aircraft noise) can be attributed to variations in the price of houses with otherwise similar characteristics. An imputed cost can then be attributed for aircraft noise nuisance.

Difficulties involved with HPM mainly centre around the large number of differences that occur between houses, and the changes in other factors such as interest rates during data collection.

Travel cost method (TCM)

The assumption behind this method of environmental asset valuation is that there is a relationship between the travel costs that a visitor has incurred to visit a tourism or recreational site and their valuation of that site. The attraction of this method is that travel costs for visitors by car are readily measurable as they consist mainly of petrol costs. A survey records the distance visitors travelled to the site, and technical details about their car. From this, travel costs are calculated. This is then compared to the number of visits the individual makes per year to the site.

Figure 19.1 illustrates a typical scatter diagram which might result from plotting travel costs against number of visits, after adjusting for other factors such as income differences. A typically shaped demand curve D0 relates the price of visiting the site (measured by travel costs) to the demand (the number of visits per year). A total value of the site for recreational use can be obtained from this information.

There are however problems which arise in using TCM. First travelling involves use of time which represents an additional cost for many people. Second, some people may arrive on bicycle or on foot and thus register no travel cost, even though their actual valuation of the site may be positive. Third, people may combine visiting the site with other activities on the same journey and it is difficult to unscramble the contribution of travel costs to each.

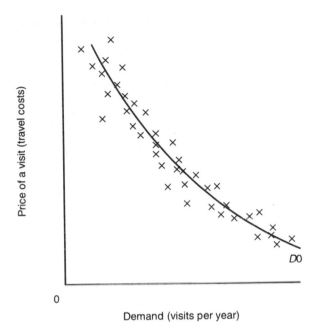

Figure 19.1 Use of travel cost method to construct a demand curve for a tourism/recreational site.

Dose–response method

This valuation method depends upon the availability of data linking the effects of pollution to a response in, for example, human health, or crop production. The effects of sewage pollution in the sea could be measured in terms of medical resources needed to remedy pollution-induced sickness, and loss of earnings.

Replacement cost technique

This might offer a way of measuring some of the environmental effects of acid rain. For example, the cost of restoration of buildings damaged by such pollution could be measured and thus the cost of acid-rain pollution measured.

Mitigation behaviour method

Some pollution effects result in households undertaking defensive expenditure which can be measured in the market. The existence of aircraft noise pollution, for example, may lead households to fit double glazing to mitigate its effects. This defensive expenditure can be summed to find costs incurred from the pollution.

Privatization of free-access resources

Since free-access resources are often overused (for example the sea as a waste sink), privatization of such resources is sometimes advocated. In such a case use of the resources (e.g. sewage disposal) would have to be bought and thus a price would be charged for a hitherto free service. The price would fluctuate, like all market prices, to reflect the demand and supply of the service.

Controlling environmental damage

The first step towards controlling environmental damage and promoting sustainability is understanding the environmental impacts of economic activity, as described in Chapter 18. The next step is the measurement of external costs and benefits in monetary terms, as described in the previous section. This then raises the question of how such information can be used to provide a socially optimum use of resources in the economy (one that considers wider environmental effects than that produced from actions based solely on free market prices).

There are several possible solutions ranging from ownership, to direct regulation and market-based incentives.

Ownership

There is little incentive for an organization in the private sector to consider cost–benefit analysis when appraising a project. It will, instead, attempt to satisfy its shareholders by seeking to maximize profits. However, in principle a public sector organization has an incentive to consider social costs and benefits, since external costs will fall upon the electorate. The actual way in which public sector organizations approach external-

ities will in practice depend upon the demands of the government.

Voluntary sector organizations may have aims and objectives which encompass consideration of the full social costs and benefits. Exhibit 19.2, describing National Trust conservation work, illustrates this.

Exhibit 19.2   Issues

As a major conservation charity, the Trust does its utmost to practise what it preaches: it therefore aims to minimise adverse effects of its activities on the environment. Surveys of sewage and farm-waste discharges were largely completed in 1993, and innovative ways of treating waste and of minimising it in the first place are being brought in.

The Trust also committed itself to reducing its energy consumption and to producing full Environmental Impact Assessments for all proposals exploiting renewable energy.

Source: The National Trust; *The Year in Brief 1993–4*.

Direct regulation

Direct regulation methods, sometimes known as command and control (CAC), involve the government setting environmental standards. These might take the form of water quality standards or planning regulations. They can be divided into preventive controls and retrospective controls. By and large the preventive controls are more effective.

Planning permission is a preventive control seeking to stop developments that do not meet planning guidelines. Planning guidelines are devised to ensure that developments consider wider environmental issues and impacts. Enforcement is relatively straightforward since building may not commence without the necessary permission. This type of control is criticized for its bureaucratic nature and the extra costs that are generated.

Retrospective controls include the setting of environmental control targets, after the externality-producing project has been commissioned. These include limits to aircraft and other noise, and water quality levels. Litter laws and penalties also fall under this category. Critics argue that such control methods themselves use considerable resources in monitoring and policing the limits, and that non-compliance rates can be high. Figure 19.2 in the next section compares their effectiveness with green taxes.

Market-based incentives

The idea behind market-based incentives is to incorporate externalities into existing market prices so as to cause producers to adapt their behaviour accordingly. It follows the polluter pays principle (PPP) adopted by the OECD in 1972 as its key economic instrument for environmental policy.

The key to PPP is the adjustment of market prices so that firms pay the full and true costs of externalities or environmental degradation. Thus, instead of the environment being separate and external to the free market, the two are integrated, and market prices signal not just private costs and benefits but full social costs and benefits.

The main ways of implementing the PPP include deposit-refund schemes, marketable permits, product charges and emission charges.

Deposit-refund schemes

This is a scheme for encouraging recycling, as in bottle deposits, or in minimizing dumping, as in supermarket trolley schemes. If you dump your trolley you lose your deposit.

Marketable permits

Permits are issued allowing a given level of pollution. For example, the total number of noise units for aircraft could be stipulated for a particular airport. These permits are then tradable. Supporters of this system stress its flexibility. Some aircraft operators can reduce noise pollution more cheaply than others. They can do so and sell permits to those who find it expensive to reduce noise pollution. Thus the total amount of pollution is limited, but how it is achieved is likely to involve flexibility and lowest costs.

Product charges

This involves charges on goods or services which cause externalities in production, use or disposal. One of the economic justifications for taxes on alcohol is to reduce consumption and thus minimize externalities in use (being drunk and disorderly). It is interesting to speculate whether scenes such as those described in exhibit 19.3 are less common in countries such as Norway and Sweden where there are much higher alcohol taxes.

Exhibit 19.3   Emergency: Britons having fun – Sandra Barwick

It was New Year's Eve, but the mood was not exactly festive in the accident and emergency department of St Thomas's Hospital. 'We don't normally have vomit bowls laid out at reception,' sighed the assistant director, Susan White, 'but those are what we are going to need.' The first casualty arrived, at 11.25, prone on his trolley, visible only in patches: large hairy legs, a pair of immobile trainers, some vomit-speckled hair. 'He's had a combination of beer, champagne and something else,' said the ambulanceman, deadpan. 'We think he's Spanish.' A faint cry of 'Waaaa-aaaa' came from the trolley as it was wheeled away.

At midnight, the chimes of Big Ben came over the television. In they came, one after the other, bound to their trolleys. Almost all were men in their late teens or early 20s, in dirty jeans over which they had vomited. Outside the minor surgeries department a line of men sat or lay: punchmarks embedded on their cheeks, bottles broken on their heads, noses broken, lips cut. One had been bitten, one had had a cigarette stubbed out on his eye.

'Happy New Year,' the ambulancemen said with ironic detachment to their prone charges.

Source: *The Independent*, 2 January 1993 (adapted).

Emission charges

These are taxes on the emission of air, noise, water and solid waste pollution. Figure 19.2 compares the operation of an environmental tax with a direct environmental control.

D represents the demand curve and marginal private benefit for a product. S represents the

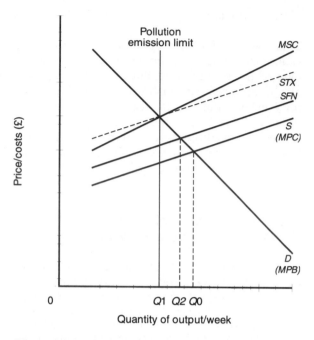

Figure 19.2 Comparison of taxation and direct environmental control. See text for details.

supply curve and marginal private costs of production. Profit-maximizing firms will continue to produce where the price paid for extra sales (indicated by the demand curve) is greater than the extra costs of production (marginal private cost). They will thus produce a level of output of 0Q0.

However, in this example, production causes pollution, and external costs. Adding these to marginal private costs generates the marginal social cost curve MSC. The socially optimum level of output is now found at 0Q1 since production should be increased at all points where marginal private benefit (MPB; indicated by how much consumers are willing to pay for extra units of the good) exceeds marginal social cost.

The imposition of a pollution tax is designed to make the firm internalize the previously external costs of pollution and integrate environmental considerations. A pollution tax which raised the marginal private costs curve (S or MPC) to STX would cause the firm's private profit-maximizing level of output to coincide with the social profit-maximizing level of output at 0Q1.

A similar result could be achieved by imposing a pollution emission limit at 0Q1. A system of fines would be needed to enforce such pollution limits. The system of monitoring of standards and imposition of fines is not totally effective, though. If, considering the likelihood and level of fine, the firm's MPC were only increased to SFN, then the firm would produce a level of output of 0Q2 – thus the system of direct control would be less effective than the system of taxation. It would also incur administrative costs.

In reality, although administrative costs are lower than for direct controls, there are several problems in setting an environmental tax. These include imputing monetary value to pollution costs, long-term pollution costs and the relating of pollution levels to output levels.

A further criticism of environmental taxes and environmental charging is their regressive nature, in that their effects will hit the poor proportionately more than the rich. In theory this problem might be addressed by compensating the poor by income tax adjustments.

Green Consumers

Leisure and tourism consumers themselves have power to change the environmental effects of goods and services by purchasing those which are environmentally friendly. In order to do this they first need raised consciousness about the environmental effects of their purchases. Special-interest groups such as Friends of the Earth are an important source of consumer education in this respect.

Second consumers need more information supplied with goods and services about their environmental effects. Such 'ecolabelling' has gained ground in areas such as detergents but has yet to be widely adopted in key leisure and tourism products.

The power of the individual is also spreading from the high street to the stock exchange as ethical investors ask questions about environmental impacts when considering share purchases.

Policy shapers

Government environmental policy and thus its deployment of direct controls and market-based incentives is informed by a wide range of sources. The government itself will have a general political agenda which it wishes to pursue. Its own government departments, particularly the Department of Heritage, the Department of Transport and the Department of the Environment, are an important source of ideas. Publicly funded quangos such as the Sports Council, English Heritage and the Countryside Commission add to the picture. The leisure and tourism industry itself will lobby government either via individual firms or through trade associations such as the British Hospitality Association. Finally there is a range of voluntary associations and interest groups which generally focus on a particular issue. Examples include Tourism Concern, the Council for the Protection of Rural England and the Ramblers Association.

Firms' environmental policies

Increasingly, individual firms are appointing environmental managers, compiling environmental policies and conducting environmental audits and action plans. There are several motives for this. First, anticipation of government controls may save money in the long run or even preclude their need. Second environmental action leads to savings on input costs. Finally an improved market image may result.

Leadership in this area has come from the CBI and the World Travel and Tourism Council (WTTC), both of which have published guidelines. The key WTTC guidelines are listed in exhibit 19.4.

Exhibit 19.4 World Travel and Tourism Council environmental guidelines

Environmental improvement programs should be systematic and comprehensive. They should aim to:

- identify and continue to reduce environmental impact, paying particular attention to new projects
- pay due regard to environmental concerns in design, planning, construction and implementation
- be sensitive to conservation of environmentally protected or threatened areas, species and scenic aesthetics, achieving landscape enhancement where possible
- practice energy conservation
- reduce and recycle waste
- practice fresh-water management and control sewage disposal
- control and diminish air emissions and pollutants
- monitor, control, and reduce noise levels
- control and reduce environmentally unfriendly products, such as asbestos, CFCs, pesticides and toxic, corrosive, infectious, explosive or flammable materials
- respect and support historic or religious objects and sites
- exercise due regard for the interests of local populations, including their history, traditions and culture and future development
- consider environmental issues as a key factor in the overall development of travel and tourism destinations

Source: World Travel and Tourism Environmental Research Centre, 1994.

Organizations such as BA produce a regular environmental report setting and monitoring targets for:

- noise
- emissions
- waste
- congestion
- tourism and conservation

Finally, environmental impact assessment (EIA) has become an EU requirement for some projects.

Review of key terms

- Sustainable development = development which can endure over the long run.

- Intergenerational equity = ensuring future generations do not inherit less capital than the current one.
- Natural capital = raw materials and the natural environment.
- Regenerative capacity = limit to harvesting of renewable resource whilst maintaining stock level.
- Cost–benefit analysis = comparison of full social costs and benefits of a project.
- Discounting = adjusting future monetary values to present monetary values.
- Willingness to pay (WTP) method = discovery of what people would be prepared to pay for a currently unpriced resource.
- Hedonistic pricing method (HPM) = imputing a price for an environmental externality by determining its effect on other prices.
- Travel cost method (TCM) = imputing the value of a site by measuring the cost of travel to it.
- Dose–response method = measuring effects of pollution in monetary terms.
- Replacement cost technique = measuring costs of pollution by calculating restoration costs.
- Mitigation behaviour method = measuring costs of pollution by counting defensive expenditure.
- Command and control (CAC) = direct regulations, e.g. water quality regulations.
- Market-based incentives = adjusting prices to reflect external costs.
- Polluter pays principle (PPP) = polluter pays the full cost of pollution effects.

Data questions

Task 19.1   A real adventure (and so cheap): 'sustainable tourism' gives little back to the Third World – Rupert Gordon-Walker

We wait on a path in the Hinku Valley as another weather-battered group creaks towards us from Mera, one of Nepal's 20 000 ft (about 6000 m) trekking mountains. Their strained, peeling faces contrast with their porters' clear complexions and bored expressions. One scabby Lancastrian in hi-tech gear gasps through wind-cracked lips, 'It's amazing. But now I'm shattered; I'm emotionally and physically drained.' Another mumbles that he will be back to 'conquer it next time', while 20 over-burdened, under-clad porters rush past, anxious that nothing should interrupt their journey home to the comfort of a wood fire. It is just as well they hurried away, as they might not have cared for the parting words of one of our number. 'They have to learn,' he said. 'They can't keep chopping down trees.' His remarks epitomised one of the chief ambiguities in what has come to be known as 'sustainable tourism' – tourism that, according to its proponents, should do minimal harm to the environment and tries to put something back.

The campaign for 'sustainable tourism' is a branch that sprouted from the 1987 report of the UN-sponsored World Commission on Environment and Development. The report, *Our Common Future*, extends the most recent hand-hold for those who feel, with Ruskin, fear and loathing for the 'plague wind' of industrialization.

Organisations like Tourism Concern, founded in 1988, are in the vanguard of a movement that derides so-called 'eco-tourism' – tourism to wilderness areas – as a marketing gimmick used by travel companies. 'Sustainable tourism', which aspires to put something back into under-developed countries, appears to be having little effect.

While World Tourist Organisation figures show a 17 per cent shift towards the Third World as the holiday-maker's preferred destination between 1980 and 1989, this increase has not had the predicted effect. If you ignore unquantifiable 'trickle-down' benefits, the Third World's share of receipts from tourism has actually fallen by 4 per cent.

This paradox is explained by a feature of such tourism that is depressingly evident to anyone who has endured the affronted whine of the professional on sabbatical when 'overcharged' for a taxi trip to the Giza pyramids that costs less than his Tube fare to work. You cannot help suspecting that the campaign for 'sustainable tourism' is little more than a rationalised desire to keep the Third World a cheap place to visit.

It is an inescapable fact that the notion of 'sustainable tourism' is riddled with internal conflicts. Its adherents tend to assume that the interests of the local communities coincide with their own desire to preserve such regions, whereas the local communities might actually prefer their national government's development schemes. It also tends to forget that by trying to preserve the colourful backwardness that supports their image of primitive arcadia, it may also be maintaining hideous levels of poverty and deep social injustices. In other words, 'sustainable tourism' may fail to make either an economic or a moral contribution to the regions it says it wants to help.

In a paper commissioned by the World Wide Fund for Nature called *Beyond the Green Horizon* (1992), Tourism Concern pleads for what we all yearn for when faced with wear and tear on our favourite landscape: the preservation of the status quo through restraint and positive conservation policies. It also insists that local people must determine whether their own backyard should receive visitors at all, and then reap the economic benefits if they do.

The alternative to preservation does not have to be sex tours to Manila, but nor should it be the creation of parks for Western interest groups that designate indigenous communities as 'guardians of nature and local customs'.

Self-indulgence is not the least of the faults of the self-righteous. In Banos, Ecuador, a 25-year-old Australian globe-trekker consults his *Lonely Planet* guide book. He eats muesli in a bed-and-breakfast run by a young ex-advertising couple from London, while New Age music hums from the CD player. He turns to a man who has recommended a cheap local guide for a jungle trip. 'It says he kills animals.' 'He has to, there aren't any cafés out there.' 'I don't care. I'm not impressed.'

Source: *The Independent*, 13 August 1993.

Questions

1 What definition of sustainable tourism is given in the article? How does it compare to the *Brundtland* definition of sustainability? Does the Nepal trek fulfil the conditions for sustainable tourism?

2 Is the chopping down of trees by local sherpas sustainable? If not, why does it occur?

3 'You cannot help suspecting that the campaign for "sustainable tourism" is little more than a rationalised desire to keep the Third World a cheap place to visit.' Is this a just criticism or misunderstanding of sustainable tourism?

4 What problems of valuation of the natural environment might arise if cost–benefit analysis were used to judge between 'preserving colourful backwardness' of a tourism destination or providing industrial development?

Task 19.2   Environment: under deafening skies

Residents of the tiny village of Longford barely flinch any more. Living within a few hundred yards of one of Heathrow's two runways, they have become accustomed to the deafening roar of transatlantic jumbos as they heave themselves into the skies. Lunchtime conversation under umbrellas outside the White Horse stops involuntarily every few minutes to allow the ear-splitting din to die down. The plane passes, chatter resumes . . . for a moment.

'You get used to it,' the locals shrug philosophically. Many work or have worked at the airport. They have learned to rely for their sanity on the hours of relative peace when Heathrow switches its operations to the south runway. Until then, those at home tend to spend most of the time locked behind double glazing.

It might seem bad now, but with a dramatic increase in the number of passengers forecast by the aviation industry and consequent expansion plans, environmentalists are fearful of what lies ahead. At Heathrow, already the world's busiest international airport, the BAA has lodged a formal planning application for a massive fifth terminal costing £900m, which will double the airport's annual capacity to nearly 80 million passengers.

Clusters of opposition groups have mushroomed around the country's main airports to fight the expansion plans. The argument they have to counter is the creation of much-needed jobs and the economic shot-in-the-arm which the aviation industry claims they would bring.

Rita Pearce, who has lived in Longford for 23 years and worked for Pan-American at Heathrow for 16, now believes enough is enough. The pollution has already taken its toll on her family's health, she says – she has had pleurisy five times in 2 years and her two daughters have developed asthma – and she believes increased air traffic and the introduction of night flights from October will make life there unbearable. 'It's going to be absolute hell,' she said.

If planning permission for the fifth terminal is granted, in addition to the main terminal building with up to three satellites, there are plans for three giant car parks, with access provided by a new spur road from the M25 spanning the Colne Valley Park, described by Friends of the Earth as a unique river valley in the capital, important for wildlife and recreation. The plans also assume the M25 will be widened to 14 lanes in the Staines area to the south-west. The sewage works, meanwhile, occupying the site of the proposed T5, would have to be shifted on to green belt land to the north-west of the airport.

Families in the area don't believe reassurances that T5 will not require a third runway. A report last week suggested that BA had drawn up plans for a new Heathrow runway to the south of the existing two.

Source: *Guardian*, 23 July 1993 (adapted).

Questions

1 Draw up a list of private and social costs and benefits of the development of T5.

2 In what ways could you attempt to measure the monetary value of the costs and benefits?
3 Under what economic circumstances should the T5 development go ahead?

Task 19.3   Leisure explosion threatens rural calm: council warns of pressures on land – Nicholas Schoon

A noisy, suburban, floodlit countryside of golf courses, holiday villages and roads full of traffic is the dismal prospect for the next century, the Council for the Protection of Rural England warned yesterday.

The CPRE foresees a countryside riven by conflicts between rival groups wanting to use it for different purposes – rambling, horse riding, holiday cabins and caravan sites, theme parks, mountain biking, war games and noisy sports such as power boating. Groups as diverse as huntsmen and New Age travellers add to the complexity and confusion.

The need for farmers to find alternatives to agriculture due to dwindling subsidies is accelerating the change. So is the attitude of local and national government to tourism and leisure – which are now recognized as major growth industries worthy of promotion because of the jobs they create.

The CPRE believes that organisations such as the English Tourist Board, the Sports Council and the Government's Department of National Heritage must change their thinking. The report urges a 'radical restructuring' of the English Tourist Board, altering its remit to include on the board representatives with a more long-term, 'culturally sensitive' outlook. It finds that the Government and its leisure and tourism quangos 'have all shown some awareness, but they don't seem up to the task of dealing with these increasing conflicts in the long term.' They believed they could 'have their cake and eat it' – continuing to favour exploitation of rural areas without facing up to the gradual devaluation of the essence of the countryside which resulted, he said.

Table 19.1 *Leisure and tourism costs and benefits*

Benefits	Costs
Satisfaction of wants	Distortion of local prices
Employment	Satisfaction of some wants at the expense of others
Foreign exchange earnings	Imports
Technology transfer	Congestion
Improved health	Aesthetic degradation
Better understanding of things	Pollution
Regeneration in depressed areas	Resource depletion
Engine for economic growth	Erosion
Source of profit	Loss of natural environment
	Loss of local control of resources

The report says that new planning regulations are required which will allow local councils to crack down on currently unrestricted leisure uses and developments in the countryside.

Attending the conference yesterday was Peter Moore, managing director of Center Parcs, which owns holiday villages in Britain and on the Continent. The company recently won planning permission to build a 400-acre complex of chalets and a domed leisure centre for 3500 visitors in a designated Area of Outstanding Natural Beauty near Longleat, Wiltshire. The development was singled out in the report because all visitors will have to come by car. Mr Moore rejected the criticism, pointing out that cars are banned within the holiday village itself.

Source: *The Independent*, 13 May 1994.

Questions

1 What are the private costs and benefits of the Center Parcs development at Longleat?
2 What are the external costs and benefits of the development?

3 What existing mechanisms are there to control environmental damage by such developments?
4 What additional mechanisms might be used?

Task 19.4   WTTC environmental guidelines

Refer to WTTC guidelines listed in exhibit 19.4.

Questions

1 What incentives and disincentives are there for firms to adopt these guidelines?
2 Use the guidelines to evaluate critically the environmental friendliness of a named organization in the leisure and tourism sector.

Task 19.5

Table 19.1 illustrates some of the possible economic benefits and costs of leisure and tourism. Critically review the comprehensiveness of the table and use it as a basis to analyse the effects of two leisure or tourism developments.

Short questions

1 List the various parties that would wish to influence a named leisure or tourism development and identify their viewpoints.
2 Explain the various ways in which the cost of aircraft noise could be imputed.
3 What is the approximate present value of £100 due in a year's time, if the discount rate is 10 per cent?
4 What are the essential elements of sustainable development?
5 What are the five key stages in cost–benefit analysis?

Further reading

British Airways, *Annual Environmental Report*, British Airways, yearly.

Commission of the European Communities, *Taking Account of the Environment in Tourism Development*, Office for Official Publications of the EC, 1994.

Feber, S. (ed.) *Beyond The Green Horizon: Principles for Sustainable Tourism*, WWWF UK, 1992.

Inskeep, E., *Tourism Planning: An Integrated and Sustainable Development Approach*, Van Nostrand Reinhold, USA, 1991.

Jenner, P. and Smith, C. *The Tourism Industry and the Environment*, Economist Intelligence Unit, 1992.

Pearce, D.W., Markandya, A., and Barbier, E.B. *Blueprint for a Green Economy*, Earthscan, 1989.

Turner, R.K., Pearce, D. and Bateman, I. *Environmental Economics*, Harvester Wheatsheaf, 1994.

World Commission on Environments and Development, *Our Common Future*, OUP, 1987.

World Travel and Tourism Environmental Review Committee, *Travel and Tourism: Environment and Development*, 1992.

Part Seven

Integrated Case Studies

20

Integrated case studies

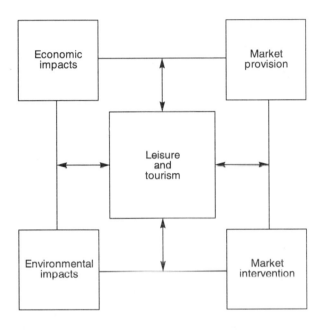

Objectives

The objectives of the case studies in this chapter are to analyse economic features and developments in the leisure and tourism sector which cut across chapter headings. This is shown in Figure 20.1.

Case 1 (Raleigh) develops themes from:

- Chapter 2 – types of enterprise
- Chapter 3 – demand
- Chapter 6 – strategic options
- Chapter 8 – the competitive environment
- Chapters 9–11 – PEST and opportunities and threats analysis

Case 2 (the economics of the drinks industry) develops themes from:

- Chapter 7 – social costs, and methods of market intervention
- Chapter 10 – tax revenue
- Chapter 16 – foreign exchange earnings
- Chapter 18 – cost benefit analysis
- Chapter 19 – pricing externalities and controlling environmental damage

Case 3 (Forte) develops themes from:

- Chapter 2 – share prices and dividends
- Chapter 5 – integration
- Chapter 6 – pricing strategy
- Chapter 8 – the competitive environment
- Chapter 9 – the economic environment
- Chapter 11 – opportunities and threats analysis

Case 4 (the Louvre and the Bankside museum) develops themes from:

- Chapter 7 – externalities and market intervention
- Chapter 9 – government economic policy
- Chapters 12/13 – public and private sector investment
- Chapter 16 – tourism balance of payments

Case 5 (tourism development in India) develops themes from:

- Chapter 12 – private sector investment
- Chapter 14 – economic impacts of tourism
- Chapter 15 – tourism and economic development
- Chapter 16 – tourism balance of payments
- Chapter 17 – multinational enterprises

	Case 1	Case 2	Case 3	Case 4	Case 5	Case 6	Case 7
CH1							
CH2	X		X				X
CH3	X						X
CH4						X	X
CH5			X				
CH6	X		X				
CH7		X		X			X
CH8	X		X			X	
CH9	X		X	X		X	
CH10	X	X				X	
CH11	X		X				
CH12				X	X	X	
CH13				X		X	
CH14					X	X	
CH15					X	X	
CH16		X		X	X	X	
CH17					X		
CH18		X				X	X
CH19		X					X

Figure 20.1 Matrix of chapter subjects in case studies.

Case 6 (tourism and leisure in Austria) develops themes from:

- Chapter 4 – demand elasticities
- Chapters 8–10 – external environmental analysis
- Chapters 12/13 – investment in leisure and tourism
- Chapters 14/16 – economic Impacts
- Chapter 18 – environmental impacts

Case 7 (the Thames landscape strategy) develops themes from:

- Chapter 2 – organizations and aims
- Chapters 3/4 – markets and demand
- Chapter 7 – market intervention
- Chapters 18/19 – environmental impacts and green development

Case 1

Raleigh hears the wheels of the pack – Nigel Cope

Raleigh's premises north of Nottingham are a powerful reminder of the long history of Britain's biggest bicycle maker. Raleigh has been making bicycles here for more than 100 years. On top of an old brick office building are the signs of some of the great names of cycling absorbed by Raleigh over the years, names like BSA, Rudge and Carlton. That Raleigh is still dominant in a market shrunk by the popularity of the car and cheaper imports makes it one of Britain's great corporate survivors. Other companies are older, of course. But there are few that have managed both to survive and thrive. 'We are trying to be right up there in terms of competitiveness and productivity,' says Howard Knight, the company's softly spoken managing director.

There are grounds for his optimism. At a meeting for the company's top dealers in Nottingham in January, Mr Knight told his audience that in spite of the recession the company had turned in a 'strong and significant profit'. The latest accounts filed at Companies House show that Raleigh Industries, which is now part of the privately owned Derby International, made a profit of just over £3m on sales of £76m for the year ended 1991. Raleigh guards its privacy jealously. The company does not seek attention in the financial press and instead cultivates its dealers and the cycling magazines. But Raleigh's position as market leader is beyond question. Industry estimates suggest that the company accounts for about 34 per cent of the UK's £311m bicycle market, well ahead of its nearest rival, Townsend.

Owned by Casket, a publicly quoted company, Townsend has 20 per cent. It is followed by Moore Large, an importer, with 10 per cent and Peugeot with 5–7 per cent. 'Raleigh is the Ford of the cycle business,' Casket's chief executive, Joe Smith, says. 'But we believe we can take market share above and beneath them.' Critics say Raleigh cannot innovate and that all the new ideas come either from the Far East or the US, where the BMX bike was developed. Some, like John Moore, managing director of Moore Large, say Raleigh has been shielded from the full force of foreign competition by high European import duties.

Raleigh was founded in Nottingham in 1887 by Frank Bowden, a lawyer who only became interested in cycling when his doctor advised him to take it up for health reasons. It pedalled along quite happily for more than half a century. This was the pre-car era and before importers had begun to penetrate the market. Meanwhile, Raleigh still had the pick of colonial markets. But the halcyon days didn't last. Although the company employed 8000 people at its Nottingham site until as late as the 1950s, it slipped a gear in the early 1960s when the post-war boom in cycling ran out of puff. UK sales sank from 3.5 million a year in 1955 to 1.6 million 10 years later.

In what was billed as a merger but was really a takeover, Raleigh fell into the arms of TI, the manufacturing conglomerate. The TI regime lasted 25 years and was not an unbounded success for either party. The business was being poorly run, and the market collapsed. Imports from the Far East turned into a flood by the mid-1980s. The early 1980s boom in BMX bikes began to tail off. Raleigh made substantial losses and became an embarrassment to TI, whose balance sheet was gushing red ink. In 1987 a relieved TI sold all its bicycle interests to Derby International, a group of American industrialists and financiers, for £18m.

Under Derby, a full-scale rationalisation programme wrenched the business back on course. Half of the 65-acre site was sold off for housing. Staff numbers were cut. Raleigh now operates with 1200 core staff, rising to 1800 in the busier seasons. New technology has been brought in, something of a novelty in a business where many bicycles are still assembled largely by hand. Laser welding equipment was introduced into the main mass-market factory in February. Other robotic equipment has helped to speed up production on a shop floor that now produces about 800 000 bikes a year. Mr Knight says £14m has been invested in the factory over the past six years. More emphasis was placed on marketing and the promotional push has thrown its weight behind the brand. While other manufacturers, such as Casket, have preferred to retain individual brands such as Claud Butler and British Eagle in their portfolios, Raleigh has simply bought Carlton and BSA and absorbed them into the Raleigh brand. Some in the industry say Raleigh is not the force it was. 'I don't think they make the most of their assets,' Mr Moore says. 'Raleigh could sell more bikes if it had bikes made in the Far East and badged them under names like BSA and Hercules.' Mr Moore believes it is a mistake to sell a £150 bike under the same name as a £600 dream machine. 'If you bought a Gucci bag, you wouldn't expect to get it for £2.50.' He is also critical of the duties that protect European manufacturers. 'I think that unless Raleigh changes its strategy, it will be under increasing pressure.'

Competition is growing. Last year Moore Large took on 100 extra staff to finish bikes part-assembled in the Far East. The company is making 5000 bikes a week in Derby. Raleigh might say it has seen all this before, of course. But it will have to keep pedalling hard to stay ahead of the chasing pack.

Source: *The Independent*, 7 March 1994.

Questions

1 What type of organization is Raleigh?
2 Analyse the changes that have occurred in the demand for bicycles in the past 20 years.
3 Why are the concepts of income and cross-price elasticities of demand useful for Raleigh?
4 Analyse Raleigh's competitive environment.
5 Conduct a current PEST analysis on Raleigh.
6 What opportunities and threats exist in Raleigh's external environment?
7 Evaluate Raleigh's strategy as described in this case.

Case 2

Guinness and friends toast benefits of Euro-booze: the industry fears a mission to curb EC drinkers – Leonard Doyle

The benefits of booze are being toasted by the European drinks industry, which is fearful of the sobering effect Scandinavia could have on the European Community. Sweden, Finland and Norway, which all have vigilant temperance movements and strict anti-drinking policies, are due to join the EC by 1995 and may seek to curb the number of Euro-drinkers. Public opinion in these countries is already concerned that the EC's open-borders policy will flood Scandinavia with cheap liquor. Furthermore, the Maastricht Treaty will give EC health ministers new powers to curb advertising for alcohol if they feel it could improve health in the Community.

To head off such moves, the drinks industry has produced and distributed widely a four-volume, boxed and bound report, *Alcoholic Beverages and European Society*. The report celebrates the heady sums generated by drink and drinkers but ignores the heavy price Europe pays for its lager louts, wine imbibers and Scotch drinkers. The EC spends almost £2bn a year subsidising alcohol production and exports – some 2000 times more than it spends on alcohol-prevention and education programmes – and the drinks industry naturally wants to see that pattern maintained. But under Maastricht, health ministers will have the power to coordinate EC health policy, while the Scandinavians are already voicing concerns about alcohol consumption.

The huge EC subsidies to the drinks trade take the form of millions of pounds in payments to low-quality wine producers to distil their produce, often undrinkable, into ethanol. Other hefty payments go to Scottish whisky producers in the form of export subsidies and to the makers of Irish cream liqueurs – these count as 'dairy produce' and are entitled to help with exports outside the EC.

The drinks industry report was coordinated by Guinness Plc and underwritten by, among others, Carlsberg, Moët Hennessy, Martini & Rossi, Pernod Ricard, Seagram, Whitbread and Becks. It points out that the alcoholic-drinks industry is worth £95bn a year to the Community – an unsurprising figure given that some 225 million people, or 85 per cent of EC adults, are regular tipplers. Per capita, Europeans consume 42 litres of wine per year, 81 litres of beer and 5.6 litres of spirits. Britons are drunk under the table by the citizens of France, Germany, Spain and Belgium. The industry produces a £4bn trade surplus and it raises £36bn in taxes, an amount the report points out is almost equal to the entire EC budget.

What the report ignores are the massive subsidies given to alcohol producers. They take the form of payments in excess of £1bn a year to mostly French and Italian producers of unpalatable wines. Another £75m is spent subsidising exports outside the EC of Scotch whisky made from grain already subsidised for export. Some £4m is given back to beer, wine and spirits producers who sweeten their products with sugar for the same sorts of reasons, while another £7.5m is spent subsidising the exports of various Irish dairy-cream liqueurs. The EC spends only £750 000 throughout the Community on education, prevention and treatment of alcohol abuse. While the subsidies to alcohol producers are handled from Brussels, the alcohol prevention programmes are coordinated from a small office in Luxembourg. The industry report, which is littered with statistics demonstrating the benefits of Europe's ancient drinking culture, is almost silent on the havoc that heavy drinkers and alcoholics wreak on society through motor accidents, domestic violence, broken homes and lost productivity.

Economists in Britain and elsewhere calculate that alcohol abuse can cost society between 2 and 3 per cent of gross national product when account is taken of social costs to industry, health-service costs, road accidents and extra police work. The report says, however, that 'it is not possible to identify the extent of irresponsible use and sensible use of alcoholic drinks'. It concludes: 'There is no scientific evidence showing that a policy of reducing excessive alcohol consumption by decreasing average consumption works.' A forthcoming report by the World Health Organisation challenges this view and says the best way to prevent heavy drinking in society is by reducing the overall levels of consumption. 'As you increase the price of alcohol the number of heavy drinkers goes down. We think it's obvious,' a WHO official commented yesterday.

Source: *The Independent*, 11 August 1993.

Questions

1 Examine the economic case for intervention in the drinks industry.

2 Consider the most appropriate form of intervention.

Case 3

Suite dreams: Rocco Forte has finally emerged from the shadow of his father, with the city giving the nod to his plans for streamlining Britain's biggest hotel and catering group to fit his own vision – Nicholas Faith

There was a distinct air of *schadenfreude* at 166 Holborn last week. The clouds over the headquarters of Forte, the biggest hotel group in Britain, had miraculously cleared, thanks not so much to any act of Rocco Forte, the group's executive chairman, as to the feet of clay now revealed by two of his main rivals – the Savoy and Queens Moat. The Savoy reported its first-ever loss 10 days ago, while Queens Moat is in breach of its banking covenants.

In comparison, Forte looks relatively sound, giving Rocco confidence that he has successfully stepped into his father's shoes, and has survived the attacks of the past few years, some of which – like the fact that he has not inherited his father's talent as a deal maker – were fairly well founded. Last week's results marked a further decisive step in reshaping the group in line with his ideas, which in many ways are a marked contrast to those of his father, Charles. The son is prepared to run Forte less autocratically and is itching to streamline the magpie collection of assets he inherited into a far more focused company, concentrating on groups of branded hotels and chains of roadside restaurants.

Without the bad news from the rest of the sector, last week's figures would have looked pretty terrible. Pre-tax profits before exceptional items were virtually unchanged at £72m and the dividend was reduced, albeit by less than the market had feared. Even more important, the cash flow is clearly insufficient to match the group's ambitions without considerable further sales: allowing for the dividend, and interest payments of £129m, Forte had to draw heavily on the net

£297m from disposals, most obviously from Gardner Merchant, to meet the £196m needed to refurbish and improve Forte's hotel portfolio. Yet the market obviously believes Forte looks sound next to many of its competitors, and marked the shares up by 13p in response. As recession hits Germany, Forte's concentration in Britain suddenly looked fortuitous. The outlook in London, where the group is heavily involved, is more promising than for years past. As Frank Croston of Pannell Kerr Forster, the hotel consultant, said at a recent hotel conference: 'The yield per room has declined by nearly a quarter between 1989 and 1992, and profits per room by a third. But despite some increase in supply there will be a steady recovery, helped by devaluation, and yield could be above the 1989 figures by 1995.' Even in the British provinces, Forte's marketing efforts are bearing fruit. Like the group's sophisticated corporate advertising campaign, these were characteristic not so much of Rocco himself, but of the team that helped him to define and tackle objectives.

Rocco had a difficult act to follow. Lord Forte was responsible for building the biggest catering-cum-hotel business in Europe from the small chain of ice-cream parlours/sandwich bars built up by his father. It was in the 20 years after the Second World War that Lord Forte revealed a formidable talent for spotting business opportunities and homing in on them. His appetite was omnivorous. Around Piccadilly alone he bought the Criterion (and Lillywhite's department store) and the Café Royal – for a mere £170 000. In Paris he bought three leading hotels (including the Lancaster) for a derisory price from a well-heeled widow, the Frederick group in London at a price which worked out at £2600 a bedroom (a hundredth of the figure reached a couple of years ago) and in the early 1970s he snapped up 32 more hotels from a cash-strapped J Lyons for £27.5m – only £7m of which was in cash. These successes far outweighed the bad deals, such as his return to his roots as a purveyor of ice-cream (remember Mr Whippy?).

But in the end the spread was too great to be manageable. It included such odd lots as nine piers, airport cafés, 15 motorway service areas –

and the chain of genteel high-street cafés, the Kardomah group. He even bought a publisher, Sidgwick & Jackson, and a magazine, the weekly *Time & Tide*. Although Charlie Forte was a stock market favourite during a couple of decades when 'no one in the City ever got fired for buying Forte', he had trouble soon after his company went public in the early 1960s, particularly over a profits 'pause' in 1965–66. But his worst difficulties came after what had appeared his biggest coup, the 1968 merger with Trust Houses, then far and away the most respectable – and biggest – British chain, with 200 hotels, mostly in country towns, but including such well-known names as Brown's and the Hyde Park. Trust Houses was headed by Lord Crowther, the urbane former editor of *The Economist* and epitome of the Establishment figure, and the two soon became bitter enemies – at one point Forte found himself fighting not only Crowther but also Allied Breweries, which was moving in with a bid.

The bid failed, and Crowther died unexpectedly a couple of years later. One of Lord Forte's five daughters, Olga, who married an Italian marquis, is now a director of the family firm, but the father's hopes were concentrated on the only son, Rocco. He was given the appropriate training, sent to Downside, the smart Catholic public school, then Oxford, and through accountancy training, before entering the family firm in 1973. Ten years later, at 38, he was appointed chief executive. As heir apparent, he faced a daunting task: to emerge from his father's shadow, and to tidy up his mixed inheritance. He has gone a lot further in both directions than the City has given him credit for. No one took Rocco's post as chief executive seriously at first. Rocco did not help his own case when his first independent deal turned sour. In April 1988 he paid £280m for the Kennedy Brookes hotel and restaurant group, and almost immediately the forecast profits of £10m turned out to be the result of property deals. Four years later he attracted adverse publicity by havering over the sale of the successful Gardner Merchant contract catering company.

But more recently his reputation has improved and his strategic vision of the future shape of the group has become much clearer. Gardner

Merchant has at last been sold for a respectable £402m, with Forte retaining a 20 per cent stake in the company. He has increased the group's previously minimal presence in Continental Europe with a number of deals, including the purchase of 40 French motorway cafés from Accor for between £65 and £70m. He has entered two partnership deals, which show not only the general respect felt for Forte's management skills but also reveal the group's cash shortage, which prevents outright purchases.

Forte has established a network of 100 motorway motels-cum-restaurants in Spain, in partnership with Repsol, the Spanish oil giant. And it has won the contract to manage 18 hotels in Italy for another oil company, Agip. This is not the end. 'Within five years,' says Rocco Forte, 'we hope to have much bigger roadside catering and hotel chains in Continental Europe, as well as a bigger hotel portfolio. But the opportunities for purchase may well be greater in a year's time' – when, perhaps, Forte's finances may be healthier than they are now.

Although Rocco Forte airily dismisses talk of cash shortage, the group is obviously unable to exploit the opportunities presented by the recession, because of its gearing, which remains high despite the sale of Gardner Merchant. In Britain, for instance, Forte is unable to take full advantage of its strong position in roadside catering, with its leading brands of Little Chef and the associated Travelodge hotels. Abroad, it is having to rely on management contracts for hotels which cannot bring in more than £2m to £3m profit even when successful (as they have been in the Middle East). The group's hotel problems have been compared with those of an airline. Airline seats and hotel rooms are highly perishable products. In the US Travelodge had a good reputation for offering better-than-average motel accommodation. In this country Travelodges had grown as part of the Little Chef roadside restaurant chain. They were separated and strict discipline was imposed. To keep to the price and profit guidelines, there can be no 'amenity creep', no additional touches such as telephones in the rooms. But cash shortage is preventing expansion in what is the fastest-growing sector of the

hotel market. Cash shortage is also preventing the establishment of a real presence in another expanding sector, the resort hotels, with their range of sporting activities, even though many country house hotels are on sale at bargain prices as a result of the recession.

Travelodge is one of the three 'brands' in the Forte portfolio; the others are Post House and Crest. All offer a guaranteed price and standardised accommodation in precisely defined categories, where 'the customer knows what he or she is going to pay before arriving, with no unpleasant surprises or extras'. By contrast, the three 'collections', Heritage, Grand and Exclusive, are supposed to 'offer individual service'. Post House was an inherited brand name, but, says Neep, 'it had rather lost its way, with four-star add-ons to its original chain of three-star hotels'. The brand (or chain) of 55 hotels is now aimed squarely at the middle-management market, in competition with but much cheaper than Novotel, while the Forte Crest name covers 'high-quality modern business hotels'. Heritage is largely the old Trust House's inheritance, the coaching inns and hostelries in county towns. (The name Trust House was dropped.) One up are the Grand Hotels such as the Randolph in Oxford or the Waldorf in Aldwych, London. Here, as with Travelodges, the cash squeeze slows down modernisation, for these mainly old buildings can absorb immense amounts of cash. The Waldorf, the first hotel Lord Forte ever bought, was recently refurbished under the direction of Rocco's sister, Olga Polizzi, at a cost of £15m and today, although the tea-dances it runs are back in fashion, the lavish restaurant facilities face daunting competition. Forte himself believes that the refurbishment programme for these older hotels can be completed within two or three years for a total of £150m, though this will absorb much of the group's cash flow until then. But perhaps the most significant category was the 'collection' of 'Exclusive Hotels of the World'. There are 17 of them, each of which, the company claims, is a brand name in its own right. The Exclusives, such as the Hyde Park in London and the Plaza Athénée in Paris, were chosen 'as a combination of location, the rate they could charge, and their reputation', and are allowed considerable independence.

The whole group – from Exclusives at the top to humble Travelodges – has a sophisticated reservation system, now being installed airline-fashion in travel agents. It can, for instance, ensure individual managers don't take on business at any price when the computer reckons there is a good chance that the rooms will be filled with full-price customers. The branding has worked surprisingly well. Even a hotel as apparently well-known as the Cavendish in the heart of Saint James's has enjoyed a remarkable increase in bookings since it was marketed as a Crest.

Source: *Independent on Sunday*, 18 April 1993.

Questions

1 What factors affect Forte's share prices and dividend?
2 Explain the merger/acquisitions activity evident in the case.
3 'The group's hotel problems have been compared with those of an airline'. Explain the meaning and implications of this statement.
4 Conduct an opportunities and threats analysis on Forte at the date of the case.

Case 4

A tale of two cities

The Louvre in Paris goes from strength to strength. Five years ago the controversial Louvre pyramid was opened, and attendances have risen from 3 million to 5 million per year. At the end of 1993, the new Richelieu wing was opened, causing admissions to soar by 50 per cent. However, despite the whir of the turnstiles, ticket sales only cover around 20 per cent of the total running costs of the Louvre.

Meanwhile, back home, the fate of the proposed Bankside museum of modern art has hung in the balance. Like the Louvre, there is no possibility that the project can run at a profit. Like the Louvre, the project depends on government subsidy. But the climate is not good. Government borrowing is forecast for £40bn for this year. The government has had to raise VAT on fuels – how, the Treasury argues, can expenditure on an art museum be justified? There is no prospect of a return on the investment in the short run or the long run.

But that is precisely the point of government investment. The returns are largely in the form of externalities from intangibles such as aesthetics and cultural maintenance, to foreign currency earnings from tourists.

The tourism infrastructure needs a whole range of improvements to attract a steady stream of visitors. This must include not just improvements in transport and accommodation but also innovation and novelty in those features that attract tourists in the first place and decorate the operators' brochures.

The statistics speak for themselves: during the 1980s, whilst France's foreign tourism earnings (adjusted for inflation) rose by 9 per cent, Britain's rose by a lowly 5.7 per cent. Britain's balance of tourism payments slumped from a £688m surplus in 1979 to a £3.4m deficit in 1992. France's rose from £2bn to £5bn.

Source: the author, from news cuttings, January 1994.

Questions

1 What economic reasons are there to support the creation of a Bankside museum of modern art?
2 If there are compelling reasons, why has the private sector not built one?
3 What economic objections might the Treasury have to funding such a museum from public funds?
4 What solutions are there to the UK's deteriorating balance of tourism payments?
5 Is a museum such as the Louvre a leisure or a tourism asset?

Case 5

India plans to attract more tourists

Tourism is India's third largest earner of foreign exchange. The country's potential for tourism is vast with a wide range of destinations, and so, with the recent reduction of political unrest and a liberalization of the economy, tourist arrivals have been increasing. Statistics published by the Ministry of Tourism and Civil Aviation show an increase in tourist arrivals from 1.5 million to 1.76 million over the past year, with foreign exchange earnings rising by 14 per cent to US$1.47bn. However India still hardly figures in league tables of international tourism destinations.

Now the government has launched an ambitious tourist development programme to increase foreign visitors to 5 million over the next 3 years. Developments in infrastructure will be crucial in achieving these targets.

Liberalization of domestic air transport has resulted in improved availability and choice for flights within the country, and Bombay airport has coped with a large increase of international as well as domestic air traffic. However, Tourism Ministry officials have pointed to accommodation as a potential barrier to tourism expansion. An official commented that, whilst there was sufficient capacity in five-star hotels and basic 'backpacker' accommodation at either end of the amenities scale, there was limited choice in middle-range rooms.

It is anticipated that foreign hotel chains will help to fill this gap now that investment rules have been liberalized to encourage joint ventures. Recently a spate of plans has been announced. The Australian Southern Pacific hotel group is planning a chain of three-star travel lodges throughout the main cities of India. Budget accommodation is to be offered at Buddhist pilgrim destinations by a consortium of Kamats (owners of restaurants in southern India), and the Japanese Dai Ici and Pearl Hotels. Accor of France is linking with the Oberoi group to develop a chain of motels. Detic management, an Irish company,

is leading a group of investors to build a £185m luxury hotel in Bombay. Finally, the Indian Taj Group is planning a series of Club Med. resorts in partnership with a French company.

Source: the author, from press cuttings, May 1994.

Questions

1   What are the main benefits of MNE investment in India for:
    (a)   the economy of India?
    (b)   MNEs?
2   What are the main problems of MNE investment in India for:
    (a)   the economy of India?
    (b)   MNEs?

Case 6

Come and see the new member (please)

Austria's joining of the EC planned for 1995 is to be marked by a Sch3–4m marketing campaign throughout Europe, with the theme of 'Come and see the new member'.

There is more than a hint of desperation in this. Arrivals and overnight stays fell in Austria between 1991 and 1993 such that foreign currency earnings from tourism were reduced from Sch161bn to Sch156bn.

Tourism plays a crucial part in the economic and social life of Austria. Tourism accounts for some 8 per cent of GDP. Those employed directly and indirectly in the industry – from hotels to gift shops and restaurants – amount to around 400 000, or around 13 per cent of the total workforce. Tourists from Germany top the visitor league, accounting for 67 per cent of overnight stays. Dutch tourists account for about 8.7 per cent, with 3.8 per cent coming from the UK.

Austria's tourism industry has reached its position of prominence through a long period of investment and training. Government policy continues to encourage the sector and recent moves have concentrated on upgrading the tourist experience. For example, the number of three-, four- and five-star hotels has risen from around 300 000 in 1981 to over 400 000 in 1993. This has been almost exactly mirrored by a shrinkage of one- and two-star hotels over the same period: the number fell from nearly 400 000 to under 300 000. Programmes of special-interest tourism have been expanded in the areas of music, fishing, golf, tennis, water sports and health and an emphasis on family holidays has been apparent in marketing literature.

Nineteen ninety-four and beyond offer the prospects of Europe recovering from the recession which was seen as a key factor in Austria's recent tourism blip. There were also some unfavourable currency readjustments in EC member states, particularly devaluations in the UK and Italy.

The effects of the collapse of communism in eastern Europe are not yet fully understood. On the one hand there is more potential tourism demand, but on the other hand cities such as Prague and Budapest may bring unwelcome competition.

There are other problems facing Austrian tourism. Some destinations face overcrowding – particularly winter ski resorts. There is a strong environmental lobby campaigning to limit the expansion of ski facilities. Labour costs are rising, particularly after the introduction of the 5-day working week in 1992.

But Michael Raffling, head of the hotels and restaurants section of the Austrian Chamber of Commerce, is optimist about Austria's tourism future. 'Guests are becoming more and more environment-conscious,' he says, 'and we are well-placed to meet that demand.'

Source: the author, from news cuttings, April 1994.

Questions

1 Analyse the impacts of leisure and tourism on Austria.
2 Analyse the economic factors upon which the future success of Austria's tourism depends.
3 'Austria's tourism industry has reached its position of prominence through a long period of investment and training.' Analyse the possible motives, sources and economic effects of such investment.
4 Analyse the effects of devaluations in the UK and Italy on Austria's tourism industry.

Case 7

Future for Thames lies in past – Helen Nowicka

A strategy to preserve the character of an 11-mile stretch of the Thames fringed by listed buildings, parkland and historic villages has been drawn up. *The Thames Landscape Strategy*, to be published tomorrow, outlines proposals for managing the river between Hampton and Kew, and sets out goals to be pursued during the next century. They include conservation projects, guidance for building schemes, restoring historic views, and creating new rights of way.

The document is the first to cover any part of the river in such detail. It will be launched by John Gummer, the Environment Secretary, with the support of the Countryside Commission, English Heritage, English Nature, the National Rivers Authority and the Royal Fine Art Commission.

Crucially, the publication has also been adopted by the boroughs of Hounslow, Elmbridge, Richmond and Kingston – the local authorities for this stretch of the Thames. Each will incorporate the strategy into planning regulations, ensuring that the height of future construction will not intrude upon views of the Thames. The boroughs will also work together to evaluate the visual impact any new building will have beyond individual planning authority boundaries.

The author of the strategy, landscape architect Kim Wilkie, said it filled a planning void. He is certain that broad support from statutory bodies and local community groups will ensure they are translated into action. The first effects could be seen within months. In Kingston, 40 per cent of the waterfront is to be redeveloped in the next few years; the report suggests how that can be done sympathetically.

Key proposals include: Reintroduction of ferry links at strategic points, such as between Isleworth and Kew; Sensitive river bank maintenance to provide habitats for wildlife; Advising landowners on traditional farming methods which will not damage native flora and fauna; The conservation of historic boatyards, discouraging their replacement by large-scale non-river related developments; Preserving the distinct character of towns and villages along the waterfront by preventing developments which would blur their boundaries; Improving access to nature conservation areas; Stricter control over speed boats in the interests of other river users, wildlife, and bank erosion, and the creation of a committee uniting representatives of the various backers to monitor progress, and the appointment of a project officer.

Most proposals will be inexpensive to implement, or have been linked to existing budgets. However, grants and sponsorship will be provided for larger projects by national and local agencies.

The strategy developed from research by Mr Wilkie in 1991 into historic vistas along this stretch of the Thames. Some views are the result of formal garden planning, such as tree-lined avenues at Hampton Court, which lead the eye to distant landmarks. Others, like King Henry VIII's mound in Richmond Park, are natural phenomena used for communication – it is said that from this hill the king watched for a signal from the Tower of London 10 miles away that Anne Boleyn had been beheaded, so he could ride off to marry Jane Seymour.

Plans to restore vistas which have disappeared, and improve others in danger of being lost are also included. One project involves clearing sycamore scrub which largely obscures an 18th century obelisk in Richmond's Old Deer Park, part of a group aligned by George III's astronomers to calculate the time and to study planetary movements. Others include the improvement of views of Syon Park, Kew Gardens and on the river itself, by clearing away undergrowth and felling some trees.

Despite the consensus supporting the strategy, Mr Wilkie is aware that proposals to encourage tourism by promoting parks, villas, museums and palaces could prove contentious, as could plans to enhance views which involve even limited tree felling. But he defends both by returning to the plan's long-term aims. 'You can have people visiting the Thames and not have it turning into a theme park. Inevitably, when a tree comes down people are opposed, and it is the familiar view they want to keep, they don't remember what it was like ten years ago. It's very important that schemes which involve tree felling are fully explained to people who will be affected. When you say it's to help nature conservation, they see there is a need. We are one stage in the evolutionary process. If we don't contribute to it but simply say "conserve", we will build up pressure for radical change, like in the Sixties. That would sweep away much that is good, and that is what we must prevent.'

Source: *The Independent*, 13 June 1994.

Questions

1 What are the main free market determinants of land use?
2 Why is there a need for *The Thames Landscape Strategy*?
3 What methods are proposed in this strategy for market intervention?
4 Should the free market be allowed to determine land use, and if it does not, how is land use determined?
5 What are the economic costs and benefits of introducing a ferry service from Isleworth to Kew?
6 Discuss the environmental economics issues that surround this article.

Index